Early Modern Cultural Studies

Jean Howard and Ivo Kamps, Series Editors

PUBLISHED BY PALGRAVE MACMILLAN

Idols of the Marketplace: Idolatry and Commodity Fetishism in English Literature, 1580–1680
by David Hawkes

Shakespeare among the Animals: Nature and Society in the Drama of Early Modern England
by Bruce Boehrer

Maps and Memory in Early Modern England: A Sense of Place
by Rhonda Lemke Sanford

Debating Gender in Early Modern England, 1500–1700
edited by Cristina Malcolmson and Mihoko Suzuki

Manhood and the Duel: Masculinity in Early Modern Drama and Culture
by Jennifer A. Low

Burning Women: Widows, Witches, and Early Modern European Travelers in India
by Pompa Banerjee

Shakespeare and the Question of Culture: Early Modern Literature and the Cultural Turn
by Douglas Bruster

England's Internal Colonies: Class, Capital, and the Literature of Early Modern English Colonialism
by Mark Netzloff

Turning Turk: English Theater and the Multicultural Mediterranean
by Daniel Vitkus

Money and the Age of Shakespeare: Essays in New Economic Criticism
edited by Linda Woodbridge

Prose Fiction and Early Modern Sexualities in England, 1570–1640
edited by Constance C. Relihan and Goran V. Stanivukovic

Arts of Calculation: Numerical Thought in Early Modern Europe
edited by David Glimp and Michelle Warren

The Culture of the Horse: Status, Discipline, and Identity in the Early Modern World
edited by Karen Raber and Treva J. Tucker

The Figure of the Crowd in Early Modern London: The City and its Double
by Ian Munro

Citizen Shakespeare: Freemen and Aliens in the Language of the Plays
by John Michael Archer

Constructions of Female Homoeroticism in Early Modern Drama
by Denise Walen

Localizing Caroline Drama: Politics and Economics of the Early Modern English Stage, 1625–1642
Edited by Adam Zucker & Alan B. Farmer

Re-Mapping the Mediterranean World in Early Modern English Writings
edited by Goran V. Stanivukovic

Islam and Early Modern English Literature: The Politics of Romance from Spenser to Milton
by Benedict S. Robinson

Women Writers and Public Debate in 17th Century Britain
by Catharine Gray

Global Traffic: Discourses and Practices of Trade in English Literature and Culture from 1550 to 1700
edited by Barbara Sebek and Stephen Deng

Remembering the Early Modern Voyage: English Narratives in the Age of European Expansion
by Mary C. Fuller

Memory, Print, and Gender in England, 1653–1759
by Harold Weber

Violence, Politics, and Gender in Early Modern England
edited by Joseph P. Ward

Early Modern Ecostudies: From the Florentine Codex to Shakespeare
edited by Ivo Kamps, Karen L. Raber, and Thomas Hallock

Women's Work in Early Modern English Literature and Culture
by Michelle M. Dowd

Race and Rhetoric in the Renaissance: Barbarian Errors
by Ian Smith

Masculinity and the Metropolis of Vice, 1550–1650
edited by Amanda Bailey and Roze Hentschell

Coinage and State Formation in Early Modern English Literature
by Stephen Deng

COINAGE AND STATE FORMATION IN EARLY MODERN ENGLISH LITERATURE

Stephen Deng

palgrave
macmillan

COINAGE AND STATE FORMATION IN EARLY MODERN ENGLISH LITERATURE
Copyright © Stephen Deng, 2011
Softcover reprint of the hardcover 1st edition 2011 978-0-230-11023-6

Permissions
Some material in Chapter V was previously published in Stephen Deng, "'Healing Angels and Golden Blood': Money and Mystical Kingship in *Macbeth*." In *Macbeth: New Critical Essays*, ed. Nick Moschovakis. New York: Routledge, 2008.

Some material in Chapter VI was previously published in: Stephen Deng, "'So Pale, So Lame, So Lean, So Ruinous': The Circulation of Foreign Coins in Early Modern England." In *A Companion to the Global Renaissance*. Edited by Jyotsna G. Singh. West Sussex: Blackwell Publishing Ltd, 2009.

All rights reserved.

First published in 2011 by
PALGRAVE MACMILLAN®
in the United States—a division of St. Martin's Press LLC,
175 Fifth Avenue, New York, NY 10010.

Where this book is distributed in the UK, Europe and the rest of the world, this is by Palgrave Macmillan, a division of Macmillan Publishers Limited, registered in England, company number 785998, of Houndmills, Basingstoke, Hampshire RG21 6XS.

Palgrave Macmillan is the global academic imprint of the above companies and has companies and representatives throughout the world.

Palgrave® and Macmillan® are registered trademarks in the United States, the United Kingdom, Europe and other countries.

ISBN 978-1-349-29261-5   ISBN 978-0-230-11824-9 (eBook)
DOI 10.1057/9780230118249

Library of Congress Cataloging-in-Publication Data

Deng, Stephen, 1970–
  Coinage and state formation in early modern English literature / Stephen Deng.
    p. cm.—(Early modern cultural studies)

  1. English literature—Early modern, 1500–1700—History and criticism. 2. Money in literature. 3. Coinage in literature. 4. State, The, in literature. 5. Money—Political aspects—Great Britain—History—16th century. 6. Money—Political aspects—Great Britain—History—17th century. 7. Politics and literature—Great Britain—History—16th century. 8. Politics and literature—Great Britain—History—17th century. I. Title.

PR428.M66D46 2011
820.9′3553—dc22   2010035167

A catalogue record of the book is available from the British Library.

Design by Newgen Imaging Systems (P) Ltd., Chennai, India.

First edition: March 2011

To Richard Helgerson, who continues to inspire

Contents

List of Figures	ix
List of Abbreviations and Note on the Text	xi
Series Editors' Foreword	xiii
Acknowledgments	xv
Introduction: Rough Economies—The Politics and Poetics of Coinage	1
Chapter I Dimensions of State Formation	23
Chapter II More's *Utopia* and the Logic of Debasement: Reason, Custom, and Natural Laws of Coinage	59
Chapter III The Great Debasement and Its Aftermath	87
Chapter IV Coining Crimes and Moral Regulation in *Measure for Measure*	103
Chapter V "Mysteries of State": The Political Theology of Coinage in *Macbeth*	135
Chapter VI Foreign Coins and Domestic Exclusion in Thomas Dekker's *The Shoemaker's Holiday*	161
Conclusion: The Changing Matter of Money	187
Notes	197
Works Cited	243
Index	259

Figures

Note: Due to copyright restrictions, the figures listed below are accessible only at www.stephendeng.com

3.1 Debased Henry VIII Shilling/Testoon
4.1 Counterfeit Portague
4.2 Clipped Coins
4.3 Cracked Crown
5.1 Jacobean Angel
5.2 Jacobean Rose Ryal
6.1 Clipped French Crown

Abbreviations and Note on the Text

APC	Acts of the Privy Council of England. 32 vols. Edited by J. R. Dasent, London: HM Stationery Office, 1890–1907.
CPR, Eliz.	Calendar of the Patent Rolls, Elizabeth I. 8 vols. London: HM Stationery Office, 1939–86.
CPR, P&M	Calendar of the Patent Rolls, Philip and Mary. 4 vols. London: HM Stationery Office, 1936–9.
CSP, Dom.	Calendar of State Papers, Domestic Series, of the Reigns of Edward VI, Mary, Elizabeth (and James I) 1547–1625. Edited by Robert Lemon. Nendeln, Liechtenstein: Kraus Reprint, 1967.
CSP, For.	Calendar of State Papers, Foreign Series, of the Reign of Mary, 1553–1558. Edited by William B. Turnbull. London, 1861.
CSP, Ven.	Calendar of State Papers—Venetian. 37 vols. London, 1864–.
Kent	Calendar of Assize Records: Kent Indictments, Elizabeth I. Edited by J. S. Cockburn. London: HM Stationery Office, 1979.
L&P	Letters and Papers, Foreign and Domestic, of the Reign of Henry VIII. Vol. 20. Part 2. London: Public Record Office, 1862–1910.
Salisbury	Calendar of the Manuscripts of the Most Hon. The Marquess of Salisbury. 24 vols. Edited by Richard Arthur Roberts and Giuseppe Montague Spencer. London: HM Stationery Office, 1883–1976.
Surrey	Calendar of Assize Records: Surrey Indictments, Elizabeth I. Edited by J.S. Cockburn. London: HM Stationery Office, 1980
TED	Tudor Economic Documents. 3 vols. Edited by R.H. Tawney and Eileen Power. London: Longmans, 1924.

TRP   Tudor Royal Proclamations. 3 vols. Edited by Paul L. Hughes and James F. Larkin. New Haven: Yale UP, 1964–69.

Note on the Text

In all quotations, I have emended where appropriate "i" and "ie" to "y" and vice versa, "j" to "i" and vice versa, "vv" to "w," "v" to "u" and vice versa.

Series Editors' Foreword

In the twenty-first century, literary criticism, literary theory, historiography, and cultural studies have become intimately interwoven, and the formerly distinct fields of literature, society, history, and culture no longer seem so discrete. The Palgrave Early Modern Cultural Studies Series encourages scholarship that crosses boundaries between disciplines, time periods, nations, and theoretical orientations. The series assumes that the early modern period was marked by incipient processes of transculturation brought about through exploration, trade, colonization, and the migration of texts and people. These phenomena set in motion the processes of globalization that remain in force today. The purpose of this series is to publish innovative scholarship that is attentive to the complexity of this early modern world and bold in the methods it employs for studying it.

As series editors, we welcome, for example, books that explore early modern texts and artifacts that bear the traces of transculturation and globalization and that explore Europe's relationship to the cultures of the Americas, of Europe, and of the Islamic world and native representations of those encounters. We are equally interested in books that provide new ways to understand the complex urban culture that produced the early modern public theater or that illuminate the material world of early modern Europe and the regimes of gender, religion, and politics that informed it. Elite culture or the practices of everyday life, the politics of state or of the domestic realm, the material book or the history of the emotions—all are of interest if pursued with an eye to novel ways of making sense of the strangeness and complexity of the early modern world.

Jean Howard and Ivo Kamps
Series Editors

Acknowledgments

This book would not have been possible without the help of so many wonderful mentors, colleagues, friends, and family members. Like many first books, *Coinage and State Formation* has its basis in a dissertation, so I must first thank my dissertation committee at The University of California, Santa Barbara: Patricia Fumerton, whose infectious intellectual energy kept me excited about the project; Alan Liu, whose sheer brilliance helped open my eyes to the profounder implications of the subject; Mark Rose, who constantly pushed me toward more nuanced arguments; and—last but certainly not least—my committee chair Richard Helgerson, who is sorely missed and represents for me the epitome of everything a scholar should be.

I am also grateful to my colleagues at Michigan State University, who have made the pre-tenure process quite bearable. My early modern colleagues Jyotsna Singh and Sandra Logan have been extremely supportive, offering wonderful advice for the book project and for scholarly matters in general. Steve Arch and Barbara Sebek (of Colorado State University) took on the unenviable task of reading the entire manuscript; they graciously provided careful, detailed responses for revisions. Lloyd Pratt was kind enough to help me polish my book proposal, and Andrew Kranzman's diligent research aided in checking the accuracy of the book. I am entirely responsible, however, for any remaining inaccuracies.

Beyond MSU, I would like to thank the anonymous reader for Palgrave, whose recommendations for revision were spot on. Jean Howard, Ivo Kamps, Brigitte Shull, Lee Norton, Joanna Roberts, Erin Ivy, and the staff at Newgen Imaging Systems made each stage of the publication process relatively painless. Earlier feedback from Gil Harris, Matthew Dimmock, and Nick Moschovakis helped me to shape particular essays that became the basis for some of the chapters in this volume. In the process of working on different parts of this project, I also received generous comments from various participants in Shakespeare Association of America seminars, including Dan Vitkus, Ben Robinson, Amanda Bailey, David Baker, Hilary Eklund, and Elizabeth Williamson. I am grateful also to the Coins and Medals Department of the British Museum, and the staff at the British Library and the British National Archives, who helped obtain requisite research materials, as well as to Seth Freeman at Baldwin's Auctions for use of the cover image.

Thanks finally to my family for their patience and encouragement, especially to my wonderful wife, Ling-I, whose unwavering support helped me through graduate school and the early years of professorship, and my beautiful son, Geoffrey, whose smile provides all the motivation I need to succeed.

Introduction

Rough Economies—The Politics and Poetics of Coinage

> *There are many things to be said on coined money; as on the unjust and ridiculous augmentation of specie, which suddenly loses considerable sums to a state on the melting down again; on the re-stamping, with an augmentation of ideal value, which augmentation invites all your neighbors and all your enemies to recoin your money and gain at your expense; in short, on twenty other equally ruinous expedients.*
>
> —*Voltaire*, Philosophical Dictionary[1]

This book is founded on three main premises: (1) the state's monopoly on coin production was an important component of early modern English state formation; (2) allusions to coins and the language of coinage, which are ubiquitous in English literature of that period, represent sites of productive engagement with these tokens of state; and (3) while money in the period still assumed primarily a material form (the coin), monetary conceptions vacillated between intrinsic and extrinsic value theories, between the value embodied in a coin's material and that ascribed by the state's stamp. Both the material and representational circulations of coinage thus offer fertile and mostly unexplored loci of investigation into relations between subject and state at the "everyday" level.[2] I argue that the manifold interactions between literary representations and the materiality of coinage—in light of shifting theories of value and the political uses and meanings of coins—complicate conceptions of state formation with respect to economy in early modern England. In particular, while purely economic perspectives often present the ideal of a consolidated state providing a ready supply of good money to lubricate the wheels of commerce, from the perspective of the intersection between literary, political, and economic domains, the interrelations between state formation and economy exhibit a far rougher dynamic.

The conditions of production and circulation of coinage elucidate its significance as a component of state formation. Since the origin of coinage in Lydia in the seventh century B.C.E., the production of money typically remained a prerogative of state authorities, and agents of the early modern English state likewise attempted to maintain monopoly control over its coinage. In fact, the establishment of coinage control went hand in hand with formation of state *as* a source of authority. For example, the physical characteristics of coins, including stamped portraits of monarchs and other iconography of state as well as mottoes that were often propagandistic in nature, served a political function beyond the assumed purpose of facilitating economic exchange. While Marxian critics have focused on money as a latent force operating within "invisible" realms of power, Shakespeare's Timon of Athens reminds us that in the early modern period it was also a "visible god" (4.3.391).[3] In addition to bearing financial value, coins emanated state authority and so were sometimes perceived as representatives or even agents of the state. While most commoners had very little direct contact with monarchy, coinage was one of the few such elements of governance through which the monarch "touched them obliquely."[4] Coins with monarchs' portraits embodied personae of state authority that permitted a more general "face to face" interaction than did other state representatives such as justices of the peace, with whom subjects would interact only for a specific legal matter. Promiscuous by their nature, coins circulated across the multitude of transactions within England or assumed a temporary place in the various purses of English subjects.[5]

But in addition to traversing space, coins also circulated within language and representation, not necessarily subject to the state's stamp of authority. As Sandra K. Fischer has demonstrated, allusions to particular coins and coinage metaphors appear widely throughout the drama of the period,[6] and they similarly frequent non-dramatic poetry, fictional and non-fictional prose. Because of coins' association with the state, the manipulation of various meanings and implications of coinage within these texts could—and, as I demonstrate throughout this book, often did—serve as a form of political critique. Once the state released a coin into general circulation, its use and abuse as economic object would be monitored, however effectively, as would the production of counterfeits. Nevertheless, because of their materiality, especially their malleability, coins were sometimes altered or used in ways not intended by the state. In the next section, I give an example of exploitation of this malleability in a rebellion against Mary I. Moreover, once released, the coin as *representation* could be transformed in a variety of ways. As Jonathan Parry and Maurice Bloch note, "what money means is not only situationally defined but also constantly re-negotiated."[7] Even if writers did not forge, clip, or adulterate actual coins (though some, for example, Christopher Marlowe, did), they could manipulate metaphors and the conceptual framework of coinage. Indeed, the various material abuses of coins both by the subject and state—for example, debasement—enriched the manipulable framework. The possible discrepancy between intrinsic and extrinsic values (the worth of the gold or silver versus the legal value ascribed by the stamp)—especially representational engagements with this discrepancy—created problems for the state's attempts to provide a reputable supply of liquidity for a flourishing economy. The state's success or failure in doing so had a direct impact on its formative process.

In the remainder of this introduction I first illustrate the stakes for the political work of coinage by examining historical anecdotes of coins used as tokens of emergent colonialism (by Sir Walter Raleigh and Christopher Columbus) and of treasonous rebellion (in a plot against Mary I). I then critique common critical representations of idealized money in the relation between state and economy by pointing out the various problems of material money, such as counterfeiting, clipping, debasement, and divergence from the commodity sphere. I demonstrate how these problems relate to conceptions of monetary value that fluctuate between intrinsic and extrinsic value theories, which also inform literary representations of the period. The final section of the introduction outlines the chapters of the book. Each chapter examines the circulation of coinage in its material and symbolic forms and, more importantly, considers the various interrelations between these forms. Throughout the book, I posit that coins and their (especially literary) representations were inextricably bound with several key factors for English state formation within the period, each of which demonstrates a more intricate dynamic between state and economy than has previously been recognized.

I

In order to illustrate the stakes of the political work of coinage, let me begin with two examples of coins employed within the context of emergent colonialism in the early modern period. The first comes from Christopher Columbus's log-book, in which he describes to Isabella and Ferdinand how on December 18, 1492 he showed a ruler of Tortuga and his counselors a gold coin with the portraits of the Spanish king and queen:

> I sent for some beads of mine on which, as a token, I have a gold *excelente* on which Your Highnesses are sculptured, and I showed it to him; and again, as yesterday, I told him how Your Highnesses commanded and ruled over all the best part of the world, and that there were no other princes as great.

The second example comes from "The Discovery of Guiana," in which Sir Walter Raleigh describes a peculiar transaction he makes with the local inhabitants. "I gave among them," he writes, "many more peeces of gold, then I received, of the new money of 20 shillings with her Majestys picture to weare, with promise that they would become her servants thenceforth."[8] Each of these examples comes from a site of exploration, a potential location of commerce for European interests. Moreover, the consummate technology of commerce—namely, money—serves to bridge the gulf between the local economies of Europe and the New World.

But the "money" exhibited by Raleigh and Columbus has no numeric referent within the sites of exploration. The local inhabitants have no comprehension of the coins' worth in relation to useful commodities, other than a general sense of how the gold of which they are composed may be used for local purposes. What is significant for the inhabitants is instead the image on the coin, the visual component that differentiates it from a mere block of gold. Raleigh, in essence, trades gold for gold, but with the important difference that the metal he gives the people of Guiana bears the image of Elizabeth. Rather than "spend" the money by trading it among themselves for useful commodities, he asks the inhabitants to wear the coins around their necks as tokens signifying their allegiance to the English queen, as a pledge to "become her servants thenceforth." Although Raleigh "gave among them many more peeces of gold, then [he] received," he nevertheless recognized that the inhabitants' act of wearing these coins had a political value transcending the economic value of the gold. From Raleigh's perspective (which, as I discuss further below, is not necessarily coincident with the natives'), the coin's image clearly bears a surplus symbolic value serving a distinct political purpose beyond economic exchange.

This marginal example points to an often overlooked but central component of coinage. Coins constitute a critical point of contact between state and subject—in this case as something akin to an ideological state apparatus for the *interpellation* of subjects in Althusserian terms. Indeed, the willingness of English subjects to accept the stamp of legitimacy on coins, the state's guarantee that each coin contains an inherent value based on the quantity of precious metal, might be construed as acknowledgment of their position *as* subject to the terms the state has set forth for exchange. The use of an English coin for a personal transaction could in effect amount to a declaration of loyalty to the English state. Like the subject Moses responding to God's utterance of his name in Althusser's example, the subject consumer responds to the state's "utterance" of coinage.[9] Columbus testifies that he uses his coin as a "token" attached to beads, presumably to be worn around his neck to show his own allegiance to the Spanish king and queen.

Although he offers other gifts to the Tortugans, he retains his beads, most likely because they bear a significant personal value that should not be traded away as a mere commodity. The coin with beads has become what Igor Kopytoff calls a "singularized" object, diverted from its commodity path—the use as currency—into a non-commoditized, more *personal* sphere of value.[10] Whereas Raleigh transformed common currency, Elizabeth's freshly minted gold coins, into several objects, each singularized to bear personal value for all of their individual recipients, Columbus's *excelente* had already become singularized for his own use.

This symbolic act of wearing a coin around one's neck has a peculiar resemblance to the African fetishes just coming into European consciousness during the early modern period. In the first edition of *Purchas His Pilgrimage* (1613), Samuel Purchas describes the "strawen Rings, called *Fetissos*, or *Gods*," that "many [Guineans] weare...next their body, as preservatives from those dangers, which else their angry God might inflict upon them." In the 1614 edition he calls these practices "superstitious fancies" that the people believe prevent such ailments as "vomiting," "falling," "bleeding," or lack of sleep. At the same time in England, King James performed a ritual that according to legend had been initiated by Edward the Confessor: the ceremony of "touching" for scrofula or the "king's evil." A year before Purchas's first edition was printed, James Maxwell praised the "Excellencie of our Soveraigne King IAMES His HAND, that giveth both health & wealth, instanced in his Curing of the Kings evill by touching the same, in hanging an Angell of Gold about the neck of the diseased, and in giving the poorer sort money towards the charges of their iournie."[11] Maxwell is careful here to separate the two forms of charity that pass through James's hand: the health provided by his curative touch and the wealth offered in the form of a gold coin called an angel. But according to a popular belief of the time that stemmed from a long tradition of employing coins for therapeutic purposes, these forms were not so distinct. Many maintained the "superstitious fancy" that the gold coin itself was a curative or protective amulet similar to the fetishes of Guinea.[12] James's ability to turn a gold coin into a healing token exemplifies what Kopytoff calls power "assert[ing] itself symbolically precisely by insisting on its right to singularize an object, or a set or class of objects." Moreover, once the coins assumed the monarch's charisma in the popular imagination, they were construed as autonomous restorative agents and exchanged as seemingly oxymoronic "sacred commodities."[13] The sanctification of coins through their association with the king seems aberrant to our modern sense of money as measure in commodification, but we might consider how the modern state can, by its authorized stamp, magically transform paper into a valuable object linked to no underlying valuable commodity such as gold.

Hanging a gold coin around one's neck is not what Karl Marx had in mind in his discussion of the "money fetish," though he drew his concept from such popular beliefs. As the socially sanctioned universal equivalent for commodities, money is essential to Marx's analyses of commodity fetishism, exchange, and capital accumulation. By tracing the process of commodity valuation, from its labor-based "use" value to its market-based "exchange" value, Marx hopes to disclose and thereby dispense with the great "mystery of money." He borrows the concept of the *fetish* from the "misty realm of religion" to describe how the products of labor appear to become "endowed with a life of their own" and enter into relations with people and with each other. These relations tend to set aside one particular commodity for use as a measure of all other commodities: the money-form, the universal equivalent that governs relations between products while concealing relations between people, which it actually embodies. While appearing to measure itself, therefore, money instead contains the true measure of value, social labor-time going into the production of all commodities to which money has become an equivalent. Thus, by the end of Book I, Chapter 2 of *Capital*, Marx has revealed the "mystery of money": though it appears to have an autonomous existence in its relations with both people and commodities, even assuming "a material shape which is independent of their control and their conscious individual action," money is, in fact, "the incarnation of all human labour." The "riddle of the money fetish," Marx writes, "is therefore the riddle of the commodity fetish, now become visible and dazzling to our eyes."[14]

Readers of Marx often forget this "visible" quality of money in order to emphasize invisible power relations. For example, Richard Halpern contrasts early modern progresses, entertainments, propaganda, and "overt force or threats of force" with the Marxian notion of capital, the most primitive and liquid form of which is money. Although Halpern argues that capital "replaces the visible or patent form of sovereign political power with an invisible and resolutely *latent* form of economic domination," capital in the form of money clearly bears both invisible *and* visible power, as Shakespeare's Timon acknowledges in his epithet "visible god." The examples from Columbus and Raleigh suggest that it is primarily the visual component in the coin's association with the monarch that endows it with extraordinary symbolic value. And although coinage is a principal component in the flow of capital, it was also, as Walter Benjamin notes, the first propagandistic product of mechanical reproduction.[15] Money is an instrument of both state and economy, and critics should not occlude the former category in the pursuit of understanding the latter.

Moreover, as material objects invested with significance, coins have the capacity to function outside of the commodity cycle. For example, the popular superstition that coins could have magical healing powers shows that "the secret of money" is not limited to the commodity sphere. Kopytoff describes as part of the "cultural biography of things" this potential for objects to move in and out of the commodity phase across their life cycles. He proposes "a culturally informed economic biography of an object," which "would look at it as a culturally constructed entity, endowed with culturally specific meanings, and classified and reclassified into culturally constituted categories." Ann Rosalind Jones and Peter Stallybrass analyze early modern dress along the lines of Kopytoff's prescription, and yet they surprisingly contrast clothes, which they describe as "material that was richly absorbent of symbolic meaning and in which memories and social relations were literally embodied," with what they call the "'neutral' currency of money." As my examples from Raleigh and Columbus suggest, "neutral" money, because of its material form, especially its visual association with monarch and state, maintained a similar capacity to embody memories and social relations. Parry and Bloch believe it is "impossible to predict [money's] symbolic meanings" from its economic functions alone because "the meanings with which money is invested are quite as much a product of the cultural matrix into which it is incorporated as of the economic functions it performs."[16] Commoditization might be seen as merely one process within this cultural biography. Even objects that had been intended for commoditization may be diverted to some other use, for example, Columbus wearing the *excelente* attached to his beads or the use of angels in the ceremony of "the royal touch." The latter produces cultural significance beyond the realm of commerce, whether the coins are perceived as mementos of an extraordinary event, as protective amulets (like the fetishes of Guinea), or as relics assuming power through their metonymic association with the monarch.

However, the examples from Columbus and Raleigh demonstrate only one side of the power relation between state and subjects: that is, how state agents might exploit the materiality of money in order to control subjects. But in addition to having the capacity to interpellate subjects, coins could also be used in ways not intended by the state. Consider another example that illustrates a more subtle form of expression by the state and by subjects exploiting the material form of money. In 1556 Queen Mary issued a proclamation encouraging any subject who discovered a counterfeit coin to "immediately deface or cause to be defaced, and break or cause to be broken in pieces" every such counterfeit coin before turning it over to a local justice of the peace.[17] Destroying the coin would guarantee that it could not pass current to the country's detriment, that the coin would not be mistaken for the real thing. Yet such destruction also connotes the symbolic dismemberment and erasure of all traitors attempting to usurp the queen's authority. Moreover, it encourages subjects to uphold the law by invoking the consequent punishment. As a treasonous offense, counterfeiting or altering the queen's coin could be punished by hanging, drawing, and quartering. The queen, therefore, asks her subjects to quarter the offending coins prior to the state quartering the offending coiners.

In the same year as the proclamation, brothers Francis and Edmund Verney along with one Henry Peckham were involved in a plot to murder Mary. As a sign of allegiance and "for greater trust Peckham in Edmund's presence and with his consent broke a gold coin called 'a dymye soveran' in two and delivered one part to Francis for an undoubted sign of their common consent." The broken coin resembled a legal indenture—a document split in two with a piece given to each party—that contractually bound them to fulfill an agreement. But it also resembled the ancient *symbolon*, a token such as a coin that bore witness to a transaction, providing a sign of trust in its authenticity. With "this undoubted sign" in the broken coin, the court found that Edmund and Francis Verney had "traitorously imagined and encompassed the death of the queen and the overthrow of her realm," and the conspirators were convicted of high treason and ordered to be hanged at Tyburn.[18]

The broken coin provided material evidence of the conspiracy, not only in its support of spoken testimony about the circumstances surrounding the performative act of breaking the coin, but also in its very symbolic violence. Peckham appropriately uses a "dymye soveran," a coin that already signals a divided ruler, the separation of the body politic from Mary's body natural.[19] And although based on an established contractual practice, breaking the coin also entailed the destruction and defacing of Mary's portrait and thus the representational rupture of her authority. Roy Strong points out that throughout Elizabeth's reign, rebels attempted to "dispose of the Queen by stabbing, burning, or otherwise destroying her image."[20] The court interprets the symbolic act against the coin as a clear sign of conspiracy against the queen. In this example, the coin as material object granted subjects a point of agency from which to "utter" their own version of their relation to the state, an utterance the court clearly understood. While for Queen Mary the counterfeit coin signified traitorous bodies, for the conspirators the genuine coin embodied the state cast in the image of the ruler, especially the head that needs to be separated before restoring proper authority.

Like the Raleigh and Columbus examples, this case suggests that early modern money maintained a key political dimension besides the economic inequalities it tended to promote due to its purchasing power. A gold coin was used for its material properties to bind conspirators in a plot against the queen, at the same time the queen provoked violence against false coins. However, the conspiracy example suggests that "face to face" interactions between state and subject in the circulation of money were not typically those of pure dominance—the propagandistic employment of money as an ideological state apparatus interpellating subjects—but of hegemonic negotiation. Recall Michel de Certeau's discussion of how New World inhabitants "*made of* the rituals, representations, and laws imposed on them something quite different from what their conquerors had in mind."[21] Money's materiality, its malleability, permitted negotiability. Moreover, the material form of money was especially fraught during the early modern period, when a developing commercial economy depended on a stable form of currency, but coinage proved anything but stable. As I discuss in the next section, the lack of uniformity in circulating coinage, which resulted in oscillation between intrinsic and extrinsic value theories, created problems for valuing the state's stamp, and thus for the efficacy of the state itself as a stable source of authority.

II

Craig Muldrew's recent study of credit relations within the early modern period has raised doubts about the English economy's dependence on circulating coin.[22] Personal credit and the system of reputation upon which it relied were indeed critical components of the early modern economy. However, at least in England no technology yet existed whereby banks could create money by issuing quantities of credit tied only to a certain percentage of precious metal reserves. That is, all forms of credit in early modern England depended on beliefs that the precious metal implicit in a loan circulated *somewhere* out there and could be returned by a designated date. Not until the late seventeenth century do we see the circulation of negotiable bank-notes issued by London goldsmiths to individuals depositing precious metals. The first bank-note from 1633 promises only the given deposited amount to the initial depositor upon return of the note. By 1670, the words "or bearer" were added to such notes, which could then circulate as currency like coins.[23] Goldsmiths, assuming that many such notes would continue to circulate without all debts being claimed at once, could rely on a certain reserve amount to meet any such contingent claims and make loans against precious metal they did not actually possess. Hence, we would eventually see creation of money through reserve deposits, our modern basic form of banking. But since all such money in early modern England depended on a presumed one-to-one correspondence with precious metals, credit in the period served primarily as a supplementary medium of exchange. Glyn Davies concludes that for more than two thousand years after the invention of coinage, coins "in the main constituted money and also provided a simple and therefore universally understood and accepted base and reference point for all other financial accounting devices and exchanging media."[24]

However, not all early modern coins were alike. Whereas modern coins are all valued at designated amounts as long as they were genuinely produced by a legitimate mint and enough of the metal still remains,[25] early modern coins would often be clipped, shaved, or debased and so have varying intrinsic values. By taking precious metal from a coin, one could have the value of the coin—assuming the person could still pass it at face value—as well as the value of any precious metal extracted from it. Only by weighing and assaying the purity of each coin could one verify the intrinsic value. Despite varying quality, though, many coins still circulated as currency without being closely examined for each transaction. The assumption was that the coin's recipient could likewise pass it as current and even, perhaps, also extract some precious metal before doing so. Although treasonous, such alterations were quite common nonetheless.[26] Because heterogeneous coins continued to pass at the same nominal value, a case could be made that average everyday consumers had accepted an extrinsic value theory of money: value designated by the monarch's stamp and not by the quantity of precious metal. At some point, however, the coin becomes so damaged, either through purposeful alteration or general wear and tear, that the intended recipient of the coin questions its value. At this point, the intrinsic value theory enters into the prospective transaction and disrupts the normal flow of the circulating medium. The general public must continue to believe that the coins are good enough to be accepted by other parties, or else the whole currency system breaks down.

Oscillation between intrinsic and extrinsic value theories becomes especially pronounced when the general coinage quality excessively deteriorates, a frequent occurrence in the medieval period and one not uncommon in the early modern. In fact, according to the oft-cited "Gresham's Law"—named after the Elizabethan financier Thomas Gresham, although the theory predated him—the general tendency of coinage would be to deteriorate because "bad" money drives out "good." That is, a consumer who receives a good quality coin is likely to hoard it for its precious metal content rather than spend it. The consumer would instead spend coins of relatively bad quality. Therefore, good money tends to get culled out of circulation because of its relatively high intrinsic value until only bad coins remain. If consumers refuse to accept such coins because of their low intrinsic value, an insufficient supply of money remains to support commercial activities. The state must then perform a general recoinage and either fund the endeavor by itself (which very few states were inclined to do) or find someone else to do so by announcing a devaluation of the currency. The latter is what Elizabeth did to restore the coinage after the "great debasement" by her father, Henry VIII, as I discuss further in Chapter III.

Such effects from coinage quality underscore the main problem with typical Marxian assumptions about state control over money supply. For example, Frankfurt school associate Alfred Sohn-Rethel writes,

> A coin has it stamped upon its body that it is to serve as a means of exchange and not as an object of use. Its weight and metallic purity are guaranteed by the issuing authority so that, if by the wear and tear of circulation it has lost in weight, full replacement is provided. Its physical matter has visibly become a mere carrier of its social function.

Sohn-Rethel describes a state that provides the coins necessary for a smoothly functioning economy. He assumes a near-perfect machine of commerce in the relation between state and economy; monetary flow from the state serves as a productive lubricant for the copious activities of trade and exchange. Moreover, whenever the instruments of state cannot meet the needs of economic activity, primarily because they have become too worn to serve as an appropriate measure of value, the state immediately and efficiently replaces them with adequate instruments. Any coin, therefore, "conforms to the postulates of the exchange abstraction and is supposed, among other things, to consist of an immutable substance, a substance over which time has no power, and which stands in antithetic contrast to any matter found in nature."[27] The state's willingness to replace worn coins whenever necessary leads Sohn-Rethel to the conclusion that the very substance of coins has become transformed into something almost supernatural because of its permanence.

Sohn-Rethel's account of this "immutable substance" prompted Slavoj Žižek to explore transcendent qualities of the coin, which exemplifies his conception of the "sublime object of ideology." Žižek notes the apparent cognitive dissonance from users of coins knowing that "money, like all other material objects, suffers the effects of use, that its material body changes through time," and yet insisting on nonetheless "*treat[ing]* coins as if they consist 'of an immutable substance...over which time has no power.'" He considers this a "problem unsolved by Marx, that of the *material* character of money: not of the empirical, material stuff money is made of, but of the *sublime* material, of that other 'indestructible and immutable' body which persists beyond the corruption of the body physical."[28]

The problem with Žižek's assessment, at least regarding money in the early modern period, is that the "sublime" material, which continues to pass at the same value despite diminishing material quality, maintained a precarious existence and was not, therefore, "immutable." It is true that for most transactions under most circumstances a coin would pass at face value because the recipient would believe that the same coin could be used for future purchases. But at any point the coin could lose its transcendent materiality and be once again perceived according to its everyday earthly existence. Far from the state restoring coins every time they became worn, at times subjects refused to accept certain coins whose nominal value had diverged significantly from their intrinsic worth. At other times, subjects felt the need to produce their own money because the state was failing in its duty to provide an appropriate medium, especially in smaller denominations. And even when the state performed recoinages, its representatives debated over what standard should be used. Persistent coinage problems in early modern England suggest that this "empirical, material stuff" was more often the rule than the exception.

To be fair, Marx, who according to Žižek failed to solve the problem of money's materiality, did indeed address this question of empirical versus sublime materiality. In *A Contribution to the Critique of Political Economy*, Marx acknowledges that a

> coin, which comes into contact with all sorts of hands, bags, purses, pouches, tills, chests and boxes, wears away, leaves a particle of gold here and another there, thus losing increasingly more of its intrinsic content as a result of abrasion sustained in the course of its worldly career. While in use it is getting used up.[29]

Moreover, Marx recognizes problems caused by counterfeiting and debasement, two terms he uses interchangeably to denote alteration by either state or subject. He notes that the "disparity between its nominal content and its real content," as a result of the wear and tear of daily circulation, "has been taken advantage of both by governments and individual adventurers who debased the coinage in a variety of ways" (ibid., 109). Indeed, he concludes, "The entire history of the Monetary System from the early Middle Ages until well into the eighteenth century is a history of such bilateral and antagonistic counterfeiting..." (ibid., 109–10). The more a coin circulates over time, subject to normal erosion as well as various alterations, "the greater becomes the divergence between its existence as a coin and its existence as a piece of gold or silver." As a result of this divergence all that "remains is *magni nominis umbra*, the body of the coin is now merely a shadow" or what he subsequently calls a "pseudo-existence" (ibid., 109). Marx acknowledges, therefore, that the empirical material of coinage experienced a consistent process of deterioration as a result of circulation.

However, at this point in his discussion, Marx, like Žižek, articulates the sublime or "ideal" quality of money's materiality. Despite the coin's wear and tear, he notes, "in each individual purchase or sale it still passes for the original quantity of gold," the coin "becomes increasingly *ideal* as a result of practice" (ibid., 109; emphasis mine). This "idealization" of money also transforms the standard of price so that "the same monetary titles continued to stand for a steadily diminishing metal content" (ibid., 110–11). While the empirical material gradually diminishes, the sublime material that allows the coin to be perceived as equivalent to its original form persists. As a result of the discrepancy between its value in circulation and the value of its gold content, "the process of circulation converts all gold coins to some extent into mere tokens or symbols representing their substance" (ibid., 111). But since "a thing cannot be its own symbol," gold gradually assumes a "symbolic existence" in the form of other tokens such as "silver or copper counters" whose value is "not determined by the value of silver or copper in relation to that of gold, but is arbitrarily established by law" (ibid., 111–12).

By this point, the symbolic or token existence of money depends entirely on the state's stamp, which designates the face value of the coin. That is, extrinsic value has displaced intrinsic value. Moreover, since the metal of these counters also erodes, they likewise assume a "merely imaginary, or shadow existence," being then replaced by some other form of "symbolic money, such as iron or lead" (ibid., 113). This process of substitution inducing symbolic existence continues until "relatively worthless things, such as *paper*, can function as symbols of gold coins" and, therefore, the "names of coins become...detached from the substance of money and exist apart from it in the shape of worthless scraps of paper" (ibid., 113, 114). Marx summarizes the entire process: "gold money in circulation is sublimated into its own symbol, first in the shape of worn gold coin, then in the shape of subsidiary metal coin, and finally in the shape of worthless counters, scraps of paper, mere *tokens of value*." The gradual shift from gold to paper money reveals the symbolic nature of money. Gold was eventually "worn to a symbol because it continued to circulate," and it was only because gold had assumed this symbolic or token quality that other forms could replace it as circulating currency (ibid., 114).

The process Marx describes, the shift to purely symbolic money, did indeed transpire, but it took several centuries and was not complete during Marx's own lifetime. In fact, the culmination of this process in which "scraps of paper" become "mere *tokens of value*" describes modern fiat money, currency that is not convertible to gold or any other precious metal. Despite brief appearances of fiat money in U.S. history—including "bills of credit" issued by the state that could be used to pay taxes, and the "greenbacks" issued during the Civil War—a permanent system of fiat money was not established until Richard Nixon took the country off the gold standard in the 1970s. European countries also left the gold standard permanently only during the twentieth century. Although the paper currency utilized in Marx's day seemed to have a mere shadow or symbolic existence, it nevertheless derived its value from gold, which (in theory at least) could be redeemed upon presentation of the currency. Paper money was a symbol for gold, but this symbolic relation also meant ready convertibility of the symbol into that which it represented.

Moreover, the eventual shift to fiat money also meant that monetary value had become entirely extrinsic, based only on the state's stamp; the material became irrelevant. Modern paper money has value only because the state says it does, and a dollar is convertible only to another dollar. A case could be made that while still on the gold standard, Europe and the United States permitted the intrinsic value theory of money to persist. That is, the monetary instrument remained connected to the value of gold because it could theoretically redeem gold. Only when economies left the gold standard did intrinsic value theory become meaningless; paper could then redeem only more paper. Therefore, under the gold standard intrinsic and extrinsic value theories continued to coexist, though conceptions were shifting toward the extrinsic value theory since consumers recognized the value from circulating paper money and generally did not think to redeem gold from paper.

For this reason, Michel Foucault's argument about money in *The Order of Things*, in which he similarly describes a complete shift from intrinsic to extrinsic value theories, is also historically inaccurate. Foucault contends—within the context of his theory of governing epistemes that permit the possibility of knowledge across various disciplines—that this shift occurred between the sixteenth and seventeenth centuries. Prior to the sixteenth century, Foucault writes, "money was a fair measure because it signified nothing more than its power to standardize wealth on the basis of its own material reality as wealth."[30] But because of the various problems associated with coinage, there emerged a divergence between the signified wealth and its "material reality," a divergence that prompted calls for reform during the sixteenth century when there

> was an attempt to bring monetary signs back to their exactitude as measures: the nominal values stamped on the coins had to be in conformity with the quantity of metal chosen as a standard and incorporated into each coin; money would then signify nothing more than its measuring value.

Foucault cites Elizabeth's coinage reform of the 1560s, after decades of damage to the coin brought about by her father's "great debasement," as one such attempt at reconciliation (ibid., 170).

However, with the rise of mercantilism during the seventeenth century, according to Foucault, the conception of monetary value changed. He quotes Scipion de Grammont's *Le Denier royal, traité curieux de l'or et de l'argent* (1620) as a reflection of this transformation in thought: "'Money does not draw its value from the material of which it is composed, but rather from its form, which is the image or mark of the Prince'" (ibid, 175–76). While during the Renaissance, the two functions of coinage as measure and device for substitution were based on

> its intrinsic *character* (the fact that it was precious), the seventeenth century turns the analysis upside down: it is the exchanging function that serves as a foundation for the other two characters (its ability to measure and its capacity to receive a price thus appearing as *qualities* deriving from that *function*). (ibid, 174)

Continuing, Foucault notes, "Gold is precious because it is money—not the converse. The relation so strictly laid down in the sixteenth century is forthwith reversed: money (and even the metal of which it is made) receives its value from its pure function as sign." As a result of this change, value becomes a system of relations between objects, and "the metal merely enables this value to be represented, as a name represents an image or an idea, yet does not constitute it." Again quoting Grammont, "'Gold is merely the sign and the instrument commonly used to convey the value of things in practice; but the true estimation of that value has its source in human judgement and in that faculty termed the estimative'" (ibid., 176).

However, Foucault's shift is not as clearcut as he describes it. For example, Copernicus, writing in the early sixteenth century, was already articulating a conception of extrinsic value theory:

> Now this standard of value in economic transactions is in my opinion to be found in the value of money. Although this value may have as its basis the value of the money as a precious metal, it is necessary to distinguish the value of money as money from the value of money as metal. Money in fact may be valued at a higher value than that of its metallic content and the opposite may also be true.[31]

This separation between the "value of money" and the "value of money as metal" implies the insufficiency of intrinsic value theories and the need for considering how value derives from external factors. Moreover, the intrinsic value theory remained prominent in the seventeenth century despite Foucault's argument for an epistemic shift. For example, the personal motto of William Camden, inscribed in the seventeenth-century portrait of Marcus Gheeraerts, was "pondere, non numero," "by weight, not by tale."[32] "By weight" means valuing according to the intrinsic value of coins, which should be weighed and tested to guarantee the accuracy of the stamp. "By tale," however, means valuing according to the nominal value designated on the coin. Camden appears to have resisted the newfangled theories of value from contemporary authors such as

Grammont. Moreover, persistent problems of coinage throughout the seventeenth century, culminating in a massive recoinage in the 1690s, suggest that some continued to uphold intrinsic value theories. Indeed, John Locke's recoinage plan, in which he argued that consumers trade the metal content of coins and not their nominal valuation, constituted a restatement of the intrinsic value theory even though most other commentators supported extrinsic value theories.[33] As I discuss further in my conclusion, Locke's plan won out despite the vehemence of the extrinsic value arguments, a victory that attests to the persistence of belief in intrinsic value theories, challenging arguments by Marx and Foucault for a complete historic shift.

III

Each of my chapters expands upon the premises I outline in the previous sections: two operative theories of value and visual and material properties of coins that are politically significant. In light of these premises, interactions between literary representations and the materiality of coinage inform the complex dynamic between economy and state formation in early modern England. After developing my approach to the state in terms of sociological and recent historical work on the concept of "social power," I identify in Chapter I five dimensions of state formation that provide the framework for the chapters: centralized institutional developments; the limits and extent of state and monarchical authority according to custom, reason, and natural law; the development of a legal framework, statute law, for expanding state prerogatives into areas such as moral regulation; the political theology of state, evident especially in the charisma of kingship; and the territorial boundaries of state authority, including their impact on hierarchical intra-state relations. The final section of the first chapter then describes institutional developments related to coinage, from its origins in Lydia, to its designation as a royal prerogative, to its dissemination throughout Europe, to its adoption, standardization, and centralization within England. I examine the significance of various mint locations, especially the movement toward a central mint at the Tower of London, and describe the institutional structure of minting privileges in the early modern period.

The final section of Chapter I, therefore, lays the groundwork for the material *production* of coinage while the rest of the chapters consider also its material and representational *circulation*. Chapter II, "More's *Utopia* and the Logic of Debasement: Reason, Custom and Natural Laws of Coinage," presents a limit case for examining the extent of state authority with respect to natural law and/or ancient standards in light of a fantasy of arbitrary monetary value in Thomas More's *Utopia*. A key debate about money involved the question of whether its value was governed by natural or customary law. To the extent that monetary value was merely arbitrary, the state might justify altering its value in times of need through enhancement (changing the ascribed value of a particular coin) or debasement (changing the quantity of precious metal in each coin). But in the fourteenth century, Nicole Oresme had invoked the authority of natural law, reason, and custom in order to proscribe debasement, which became less common in continental Europe as a result. Coin production thereafter became tied to the rule of law, ancient standards, and the limits of state authority.

However, with the circulation of accounts from the New World and their evocation of a past Golden Age described by Ovid and others, scholars began to question how "natural" and "rational" these standards of value indeed were. More's *Utopia* offered one such challenge to these assumptions by presenting a case for the arbitrary nature of monetary value. Although he alludes to stateless societies in Golden Age literature and accounts of the New World, More depicts a strong, rational state attuned to both custom and natural law that nevertheless places, at least publicly, little or no value on gold and silver. In effect it presents a thought experiment with real world implications: how strong would a state be that had no competition for resources because of public indifference or even hostility to "precious" metals? Utopia is a state that relies, primarily for the purposes of military defense, on the fiscal resources offered by the abundant gold and silver within the commonwealth even as it implicitly promotes the belief that these metals are immoral. Therefore, upholding the moral commonwealth of Utopia depends not only on immoral money but also on the very *immorality* of money.

And yet when such debasement was actually implemented in the mid-sixteenth century, the results were disastrous for the state, as I describe in Chapter III. In the 1540s representatives of Henry VIII, who faced persistent financial difficulties, decided to alter his coinage in what became known as the "great debasement." In doing so, Henry and his agents ignored the Statute of Purveyors, established under Edward III, which stipulated that any coinage transformations must be discussed in parliament before being executed. Moreover, this measure was implemented despite the influential legal argument made against the practice by Oresme. In effect, the state was seduced by the fantasy of fiscal abundance as described in *Utopia*, but More's text also highlights the very problems Henry encountered with debasement. While Henry's state could transform the coinage, it could not change cultural attitudes toward the metals, which limit the state's prerogative on coinage and constitute, according to More, an essential component of the state's monetary technology. Therefore, while *Utopia* attempts to refute the intrinsic value theory of money, it nevertheless reveals, by the island's stark contrast to sixteenth-century England, the inability of the state to control the *demand* side of the money equation, a component that continued to rely on intrinsic value theories, despite the state's monopoly on *supply*. As a result, even rulers who espoused absolutist ideas, such as James I, insisted on upholding coinage standards once they recalled the failed experiment under Henry VIII.

The fourth chapter, "Coining Crimes and Moral Regulation in *Measure for Measure*," considers the state's engagement with the reverse side of debasement: "coining" crimes, which included counterfeiting, clipping, and all illegal alterations of the coin. The discourse against "coining" emerged primarily from state initiative rather than from religious doctrine. The crime (unlike other crimes such as usury) is not condemned expressly by biblical prohibitions, thus state authorities had to articulate its immorality by association, especially by employing the recurrent metaphor of God coining his image in humans and the Aristotelian metaphor of offspring as the product of men stamping their image in the material of women. Both metaphors carried implications of bastardy: respectively, of humans usurping God's stamp in producing an illicit child, and of men coining their images in forbidden material. The God's stamp metaphor also contained an implicit denunciation of coin alteration, since God's creatures should recall and preserve the value of the stamp in the coin He has given them. Such coining metaphors, I argue, partially explain coin imagery in *Measure for Measure*, a play concerned with the state's ability to regulate morality. For example, Angelo employs a coin metaphor in his explanation of why illicit procreation is immoral.

However, the subsequent actions of its agents call into question the state's own offenses against the coin, especially debasement. In addition to connotations of bastardy, coinage had historical associations with *justice*, another key concern of the play. At the beginning Angelo is compared to a coin receiving the duke's stamp (commission) to enforce old laws of Vienna that had gone into disuse. Although Angelo proves false, Duke Vincentio cannot avoid the fact that it was his own legitimate stamp that permitted his judicial subordinate to perpetrate the crimes. The state's hypocrisy induced a competing and even mimicking strategy of producing metaphoric associations between debasement and other immoral acts. Historically, monarchs who debased their coinage (starting with Philip IV of France who *had* received the title) were threatened with the epithet "Le Faux Monnayeur" [counterfeiter] to remind them of their hypocrisy in committing crimes for which they had been prosecuting their subjects. In *Measure for Measure*, the underlying currency that permits state officials to measure equivalence between crimes proves deficient and, therefore, arbitrary. Moreover, the duke's comic foil Lucio, despite his own deficiencies, offers a constant interrogation of the ruler's character and refuses to allow the duke to have monopolistic control over the economy of poetic exchange that equates coining with other acts of immorality.

The fifth chapter, "'Mysteries of State': The Political Theology of Coinage in *Macbeth*," examines the theological dimension of the state's political use of money, especially in the way the charisma of kingship extends into the realm of coinage. *Macbeth* contains an allusion to the use of a gold coin in the ritualistic healing of scrofula or the "king's evil." Historically, the coin came to be considered essential to the ceremony under the Tudors, and subjects who removed it were reported to have suffered relapses. This putative power was based on a tradition that saw mystical powers in coins, whose combination of precious metal, royal effigy, and "magical" inscription made them suitable for healing purposes. As a result, the coin served to promote state power by helping to produce the ideology of mystical kingship. Moreover, it fostered the idea that the king's stamp and the personal loyalty it inspired somehow transcended the material value of the coin.

However, the strategies and motivations of the mystical and financial economies in which the coins circulated were often at odds. In *Macbeth*, the financial economy is represented by a system of tribute and reward between Duncan and Macbeth as well as by the material "sinews of war" that Macbeth attempts to use to maintain power, especially by hiring mercenaries and establishing a system of paid spies. The mystical economy is emblematized by Macbeth's vision of Duncan's body, whose "golden blood" invokes the trope of money as blood flowing through the immortal body politic. Macbeth's subsequent insecurities about his position reveal that money is not a *sufficient* mechanism for power despite its function as "sinews of war" and its effective ideological deployment in what Max Weber calls the "routinization of charisma." Historically, for James, the healing coin connected more strongly to what he described as the "mystery of State" than to miraculous powers of kingship per se. If James did not believe that the ceremony or coin actually cured individual patients, he believed at least that the latter's material and symbolic circulation contributed to the political strength of his state.

The sixth chapter, "Foreign Coins and Domestic Exclusion in Thomas Dekker's *The Shoemaker's Holiday*," investigates the territorial boundaries of state authority by considering the circulation of foreign coins within England. On the surface, critique of foreign coins—as in John Donne's elegy "The Bracelet" and Thomas Dekker's *Shoemaker's Holiday*—appears to be a merely xenophobic expression of English nationalism celebrating the English state's own ability to produce reputable coinage. However, foreign coins, especially the internationally respected "prestige coins," tended to be higher-valued coins circulating mostly among aristocrats and wealthy merchants. Even the frequently disparaged French crown was worth approximately a week's wages for unskilled laborers in 1600—or two weeks' wages for Dekker's shoemakers—and, therefore, would be considered "aristocratic" in contrast to hardworking domestic pennies. Therefore, not all English subjects would experience foreign coins in the same way. Perceptions of their corrupting influence could signal class tensions as much as national or state pride.

I argue that the discrepancy in coin use within *Shoemaker's Holiday*—aristocrats and merchants who employ (especially foreign) gold versus laborers who employ silver—indicates political realignments depicted at the end. Although the play begins with tension between aristocrats and merchants—represented in the conflict between Lincoln and Oatley—by the end of the play a coalition emerges between monarch, aristocracy, and merchant, figured in the respective characters of the king, Lacy, and Eyre. At the same time, most of the journeyman and apprentice shoemakers who are the ostensible celebrants of the play's "holiday" are noticeably absent in the final scene. And those who remain, most notably Firk and Ralph, become clear examples of the laborers' exclusion from English gains at foreigners' expense through trade and war. Firk's ignorance about foreign coins and the magnitudes of global trade leaves him a mere spectator in Eyre's and Lacy's transaction. And Ralph's lame body on stage, which appears simultaneously with the king's call for a troop surge in the military campaign against France, reminds the audience of who pays the true cost of foreign wars. Such noticeable exclusion at the end sheds light on Hodge's exhortation at the start for Ralph to "cram thy slops with French crowns" (1.225) when he heads off to war. The only opportunity for laborers to gain at the expense of foreigners is to appropriate their coins after killing them. Thus, English response to foreign coins should be read within a broader context of the coins' significance to domestic social relations and a history of economic and military exploitation by the state.

In my examination of the politics and poetics of coinage, I am indebted to Marc Shell and Jean-Joseph Goux. My chapter on counterfeiting in *Measure for Measure* in particular is influenced by their work on the relationship between money and language.[34] But whereas Shell and Goux typically assume smooth processes of metaphoric exchange, my argument that the underlying "currency" in this exchange might be counterfeit, clipped, or debased disrupts the ideal exchange conditions. While Mark Osteen and Martha Woodmansee correctly indicate the critics' desire to "historicize money and to reattach it to the broader social world," Shell and Goux nonetheless rely on a stable conception of how money and exchange function. For example, Goux relates gold, the "universal equivalent" to the phallus, the Father, God, and all versions of the transcendental signifier. He finds that between these categories, "a single structural process of exchange, one and the same 'mode of substitution,' could explain (with no need to establish any causal priority) both a signifying process and an economic process."[35] Money is the tool that effects this mode of substitution, but Goux relies on the assumption that money functions as an unproblematic "universal equivalent" for exchange. Similarly in his concept of "money of the mind," Shell associates processes of exchange with signifying processes. Arguing that all metaphors are in a sense economic, he writes, "money, which refers to a system of tropes, is also an 'internal' participant in the logical or semiological organization of language, which itself refers to a system of tropes." Osteen and Woodmansee declare this to be "the major assumption upon which economic criticism has been built."[36] Indeed, the "new economic criticism" has a tendency to employ modern economic concepts to the past when the past bears its own logic with respect to categories we would classify as "economic." Applying notions of fiat money to the early modern period, for example, glosses over the political tensions arising from the persistence of coinage as an unstable measure of exchange. What typically remains missing from such "new economic" analyses is the problem of materiality.

For this reason, *Coinage and State Formation in Early Modern English Literature* is partially an intersection between the new economic criticism and what has been called the "new materialism."[37] However, because I emphasize the political valences of coinage, it diverges somewhat from both. The "new materialism" has been recently criticized for eliminating the political edge of historicist and older materialist criticism, so I see my project as a recovery in that desired direction.[38] The book works toward politicizing criticism on the object while considering the role of the "everyday" in processes of state formation. Nevertheless, the book retains an emphasis on materiality: the social functions and meanings of money in early modern England, I contend, cannot be considered distinct from its physical matter. However, the inextricability of use and meaning in the above examples suggests that the malleability of money is as much in its representational "matter" as in its physical matter, and both dimensions should be considered simultaneously. John Guillory has recently expressed concern that the economic has become "merely metaphoric" in literary studies. He believes critics should consider social space as "non-Euclidean," meaning that "all fields are *present* in any given social action, and that the identity of any particular field is defined in part by the *mode of presence* of other fields within it." All the binary terms (economic/cultural, material/symbolic, literal/metaphorical) should then be thought of "as aspects of *one* social world," and they should, therefore, be analyzed together.[39]

Each chapter of *Coinage and State Formation* considers at once the economic and cultural, the material and symbolic, the literal and metaphorical aspects of coinage. Throughout the book I hope to exhibit the rich potential of coinage as a relatively new territory of exploration within early modern studies and shed new light on these objects that scholars will recognize as being ubiquitous in literature of the period. My particular study demonstrates how coins inform "everyday" interactions between subject and state within the dynamics of state formation, but I can imagine studies that elucidate other dimensions of coinage. Moreover, I hope to establish a new approach for examining the role of the political and for reassessing the role of the economic in literary scholarship on objects and material culture. I believe such interdisciplinary approaches to material culture in literary studies can open the field up to new avenues of inquiry as the larger stakes of such studies become evident.

Chapter I

Dimensions of State Formation

In my introduction, I argued that as circulating signs of state authority, coins assume a key political dimension. But while the materiality of coins helps to pinpoint these particular objects of inquiry, the more abstract quality of "state" introduces additional complexity for its study. So in order to analyze the relation between coinage and state formation, I should first clarify what I mean by the "state," which as a key political concept has been a subject of scrutiny within several disciplines, including philosophy, anthropology, sociology, political science, and history. Within and across these disciplines, approaches vary: from analyses of the historical development of particular institutions; to comparative studies of states employing different models of governance; to intellectual histories tracing the usage of the term "state," or the underlying concept, within discourse at various points in time[1]; to Marxist analyses of the state as a manifestation of class conflict.[2] Despite the diversity of definitions and historical accounts of state formation, some common factors do emerge.

First, although for many scholars underlying political power—whether as a version of social power, a manifestation of class relations, or another form—is the basis of state formation, the actual maintenance and concretization of state functions require the development of *centralized institutions* run by various agents. Second, state formation typically requires some designated limits of state authority vis-à-vis "the law," whether divine, natural, positive, or customary. Third, state formation comprises methods by which agents produce and transform positive law to expand and extend its reach. Fourth, state formation includes politico-theological factors that both mystify and personalize state authority, whether in the person of the king, the body of the commonwealth, or some independent entity of "state." This fourth factor is less pronounced in the various approaches to state that are typically discussed, but it has an important function for the affective dimension of state formation, such as in inspiring feelings of loyalty in subjects. The final key factor, territorialization of state authority, designates geographic boundaries of influence and control. Two prominent political categories related to the state—sovereignty and the threat of physical violence—cut across several of these dimensions. Sovereignty relates to all of the dimensions in some manner while the threat of violence is most pronounced in the second, third, and fifth factors: the state's relation to law, expansion of law, and territorialization.

Before describing each of these factors in more detail, I first situate my general approach within the context of recent scholarship on the state, which emphasizes state formation over state building; the state as a more open, contingent category dependent on cultural and economic as well as political factors; and a state indistinct from "society," which must, therefore, rely on negotiation over coercion, although its agents have various modes of "social power" at its disposal. I then move to the five dimensions of state formation, each of which has particular relevance to some element of coinage, a premise that establishes the framework for *Coinage and State Formation*. Both material practices and representations of coinage were ingrained in various components of state formation in early modern England, which, as I argue throughout the book, introduced a destabilizing force in relations between state and economy. In the final section of this chapter, I consider coinage in relation to the first dimension, centralized institutions, in particular the establishment and development of the royal mint as a key resource of state.

I. The State and Social Power

In examining various forms of social organization, sociologists generally start with the notion of "social power" and consider the various ways in which that power becomes evident; the specific manifestations of power are often less important than the underlying means employed to produce them. Max Weber's famous definition in "Politics as Vocation" of a state as "a human community that (successfully) claims the *monopoly of the legitimate use of physical force* within a given territory" has been especially influential in this regard. Weber insists that the state must be defined sociologically "only in terms of the specific *means* peculiar to it," which is this use of physical force; he asserts that without this ability to use violence, the state would not exist.[3] Weber's definition continues to inform recent theories of the state. For example, although he recognizes that his approach is controversial, Charles Tilly defines states as "coercion-wielding organizations that are distinct from households and kinship groups and exercise clear priority in some respects over all other organizations within substantial territories."[4] The key elements of force ("coercion"), territorialization, and monopoly (or at least "priority") remain intact within Tilly's definition.

Historian Michael Braddick slightly modifies Weber's definition but still uses it as the basis for his own recent examination of the early modern state according to the concept of "political power." Braddick first modifies the designation of a "monopoly" on legitimate violence: because parents can wield legitimate uses of physical force within the household, the state does not, in fact, have a monopoly. What is critical to the definition is that the state is the "ultimate arbiter of what *constitutes* legitimate force within its territory" and has the capacity to employ force as "its own ultimate sanction."[5] For example, the state can judge the parent's right to employ excessive violence, as in the murder of a child. If the state determines that the parent did not have that right, it can without repercussion exact physical punishment against the offending party, even execution. Gianfranco Poggi calls the latter condition, the use of violence as a last resort, "ultimacy," a distinctive characteristic of political power for Poggi.[6]

Braddick also modifies Weber's definition in terms of the state's source of legitimacy. He argues that the power that state agents can exercise exists not in particular persons but in *offices*, which are defined by and, therefore, limited to designated functions and territories. The state differs from other forms of social regulation such as tribes and lineages in that within the state, "authority is divorced from the personality of the leader."[7] So although the state's ability to use force legitimately empowers certain groups, there remain clear restrictions on the use and abuse of this power. An important example is the monarch, whose responsibilities, even under the divine right of kings, could actually serve to limit power. As Constance Jordan notes, early modern constitutionalist theories could represent monarchy as divine and yet keep any monarch from assuming absolute power since monarchical power, which resided in the *office*, would move to subsequent inheritors of the office.[8]

Nevertheless, Braddick follows Weber in arguing that the particular forms or functions that states assume are not the crucial elements, but the "kind of power that is distinctive to it."[9] The particular "kind of power" wielded by the state is one form of "social power" discussed by sociologists such as Michael Mann and Gianfranco Poggi.[10] For Poggi, "social power" is the ability to mobilize the energies of others in the pursuit of some objective, even against competing objectives from other parties in a collective. Following the political philosopher Norberto Bobbio, Poggi designates three types of social power: economic, normative (or what Bobbio calls "ideological"), and political. Poggi's state is primarily concerned with the mobilization of one type—*political* power—which is distinguished from the other types of power first by the condition of "ultimacy," using violence as a last resort (described above), and second by that of "paramountcy," functional priority over the other types of power for the purpose of maintaining order, against threats from both outside territorial boundaries and within, by individuals or groups.[11]

Mann similarly distinguishes political power from three other types of social power: ideological (similar to Poggi's "normative"), economic, and military. Political power denotes "centralized, institutionalized, territorialized regulation" within social relations. Ideological power refers to control over categories of meaning, social norms, and aesthetic or ritual practices. Economic power means control over "extraction, transformation, distribution, and consumption" of various objects within nature. And military power "derives from the necessity of organized physical defense and its usefulness for aggression." While political power "heightens boundaries" between geographical units and concerns "one particular area, the 'center,'" the other forms tend to transcend boundaries and can be located anywhere. However, although it is based in the center, political power spreads outward. Mann ultimately defines the state in terms of political power, while maintaining the Weberian notion of the threat of physical violence: *"a differentiated set of institutions and personnel embodying centrality, in the sense that political relations radiate outward to cover a territorially demarcated area, over which it claims a monopoly of binding and permanent rule-making, backed up by physical violence."*[12]

While the concept of social power proves useful for delineating the various dimensions of state formation, the emphasis on political power alone seems to limit the scope of the state. As Steve Hindle suggests, historians of the state should consider not only "political or institutional innovation, but also...social, economic and cultural developments."[13] One could make a case that the state mobilizes all four types of social power described by Mann. For example, Louis Althusser has demonstrated the state's efficient employment of "ideological state apparatuses" within education, church, ritual, and other institutions, which complement more traditional "repressive state apparatuses" for the reproduction of social order. In terms of economic power, the state maintains the prerogative of money production to regulate financial transactions as well as the granting of monopolies within certain industries. And, of course, as the ultimate arbiter of physical force, the state maintains control over the use of military power. A fiscal/military conception of the state in particular would envision the entity utilizing economic power derived from tax revenue collection to support its use of physical force via military power.[14] Therefore, though "political power" may be the primary source permitting state excursions into these other territories of power, all four forms of social power remain crucial for state maintenance.

Indeed, as Hindle argues, the state is as much a "cultural" as a political creation. In addition to being an "'instrument' (or 'resource') of power," the state was a "'symbol' of (or 'claim' to) authority." Consideration of this two-dimensional model of state development, the "symbolic" and "instrumental," is a way to reconcile approaches to state formation that emphasize structures of power with those that emphasize legitimation through ideology and the idea of state.[15] Interactions between the two dimensions are particularly informative. For example, state agents such as magistrates, constables, and jurors could "appeal to the state itself as a symbol of their instrumental authority, justifying and legitimating their activity in political and moral terms."[16] This dynamic between cultural and instrumental dimensions informs my own emphasis throughout *Coinage and State Formation* on interactions between material and representational factors of coinage. The coin as instrument is often inseparable from the coin as symbol, and its intimate connection with state authority offers a compelling case study for considering the nature of this dynamic.

Because of these important cultural elements in state formation, recent approaches have tended to break down the distinction between state and society. For example, Jeremy Black sees revisionist approaches as emphasizing "the extent to which the state is not outside society." What he calls "more subtle" analyses of the early modern state draw on social and cultural history in addition to political history.[17] Hindle similarly argues that "state" and "society" should be considered "points on a continuum of interest and identity" rather than as binary oppositions. In particular, the authority of the early modern state increased *because of* rather than *in spite of* social need. Moreover, not only agents of the state but also members of society could appeal to the state as a "reservoir of authority on which the populace might draw, a series of institutions in which they could participate, in pursuit of their own interests."[18] In this sense the state is a tool as much for its subjects as it is for its various agents.

Recent approaches, especially by historians, also tend to emphasize "state formation" rather than "state building."[19] That is, critics consider the state to be an experimental process of trial and error rather than a linear teleological development toward rational bureaucracy. Braddick explains that since the process of state formation "was undirected, there was no defined end in view,... the term 'state building' seems inappropriate," which is why he prefers "the more neutral term 'state formation.'" Rather than a solitary or unified will driving all institutional developments, various groups utilized any and all available resources, both instrumental and ideological, in order to negotiate and renegotiate their positions. Similarly, Hindle emphasizes the "*experimental* nature of early modern governance" in the process of centralization. Numerous techniques were attempted and revised in order to produce a system of "compliance between central initiatives and local interests," an observation that has led historians to question the efficiency of the centralized institutions. For this reason, Hindle believes that state formation should be construed "as a continuous, though not necessarily linear, process in the development of institutionalised power relations."[20]

Such uneven formation has induced historians such as Jeremy Black to emphasize "negotiation" over "coercion" as the operative mode for relations between ruler and (especially elite) subjects. Citing C. B. Herrup, Hindle exhorts historians to "think less of *government* as an institution or as an event, than of *governance* as a process, a series of multilateral initiatives to be negotiated across space and through the social order: 'ruling was a repeated exercise in compromise, co-operation, co-optation and resistance.'" Corrigan and Sayer emphasize how states "encourage" certain activities, rather than constantly coercing subjects, although they do also engage in "suppressing, marginalizing, eroding, undermining others." Even among agents of the state, negotiation proved a key operative mode. Claiming that there was "much more to the agency of the state than monarchical will," Braddick finds within the state "government through, rather than by, the monarch" since "the impetus for political action could come from a variety of sources."[21] Although what appeared publicly as desires of "the state" may have been the smooth end product of consensus, the underlying machinery that produced this consensus consisted of a series of divergent private motives.

The state, then, has become a more open category in recent scholarship. Although based in political power, the state also deploys ideological, economic, and military power. While emerging in relation to society, it often remains indistinct from society. While appearing to be the culmination of teleological development, it typically reveals a contingent existence. Although usually considered a coercive entity, it must also rely on negotiation and cooperation. In general I follow this line of recent scholarship in considering the state as a political phenomenon that is also cultural and economic, as a resource available to both state agents and society, as a contingent and negotiable entity rather than a rigidly progressive development. Throughout *Coinage and State Formation*, therefore, I emphasize an open and contingent early modern state, especially open and contingent responses to a coinage inextricably bound with state authority.

II. A Framework for Analysis of State Formation

Despite the openness of recent approaches to state formation, however, we can identify five core dimensions, all of which relate to some key element of coinage and, therefore, serve as the basis of the book's organization.

Nevertheless, the open and contingent quality of state formation pertains within each of the dimensions, which I now discuss in more detail.

A. Centralized Institutions

G. R. Elton's influential, albeit controversial thesis of a "Tudor Revolution" during the reign of Henry VIII provoked a range of scholarship focusing on the development of institutions within English state formation. Elton argued that administrative changes by Henry VIII during the 1530s began the process of modernizing the English state.[22] His timeframe seems to align with the etymology of the term. According to *The Oxford English Dictionary*, the word in the sense of "the supreme civil power and government vested in a country or nation" first appeared in 1538, within Thomas Starkey's *England in the Reign of Henry the Eighth*, a work that was actually composed a few years earlier.[23] Elton started from the common assumption that the concept of the "modern sovereign state" emerged in the sixteenth century, primarily because the state and crown proved victorious over their counterparts the church and abstract Christendom, and the "self-contained national unit" became an intentional goal rather than being perceived as a necessity. Essential to the emergence of this new concept was "a revised machinery of government," created primarily under the influence of Thomas Cromwell and based on bureaucracy rather than individual control, management of the entire nation rather than solely of the king's personal estate. According to Elton, the moment "when Henry VIII accepted Cromwell's advice to consolidate the territory he governed under the exclusive sovereignty of the king in parliament" and statute law assumed power to enact legislation beneficial to state development, we witness the replacement of "an attitude to the state that can only be called medieval" with "one that can only be called modern." While older methods of household management could serve the medieval state, the modern nation state required "modern national methods" and organized departments. Although Elton concedes that there were changes prior to 1530 and that all the work of reorganization was not complete by the end of the decade, nevertheless the "rapidity and volume of change, the clearly deliberate application of one principle to all the different sections of the central government, and the pronounced success obtained in applying that principle, justify one in seeing in those years a veritable administrative revolution."[24]

Numerous scholars have responded to Elton's thesis of a "Tudor Revolution" by critiquing especially the idea that Henry manufactured his state *ex nihilo*. Some have argued that a framework for coordinated power throughout the realm had been in place for a long time, that England in particular had been precocious in its establishment of state authority. Many of the permanent, stable institutions in a centralized bureaucracy, a critical component of Elton's process of state formation, already existed in England during the medieval period. A key change occurred when certain administrative branches evolved into what Corrigan and Sayer describe as "specialized institutions, independent of the King's immediate household and Curia Regis, and permanently based in London, rather than being peripatetic with the King." Marc Bloch points to Henry II's tight control on officers throughout the realm, especially his removal in 1170 of all sheriffs from office and subsequent reappointment of a select few. Bloch argues that since "the public office was not completely identified with the fief, England was a truly unified state much earlier than any continental kingdom." David Starkey instead focuses on a later period, the War of the Roses, when the need for political reform, a key factor signaling state consciousness, was clearly acknowledged, anticipating later sixteenth-century thought. Parliamentary debates about the nature of monarchy and government efficiency prompted transformation in crown revenue collection and administration.[25]

Locating the basis of the modern state in medieval innovations, Joseph Strayer argues that the period between 1000 and 1300 experienced the emergence of several key elements, including the legitimization of political entities comprising their own people and territory, the establishment of permanent financial and legal institutions (the exchequer, high court, and chancery), and the development of professional administrators and skilled clerks. The centralized accounts of the exchequer, founded in the twelfth century to collect from royal officials and to audit accounts of funds from all over England, relied on what Strayer calls the "first permanent functionaries": estate managers such as the reeves and shire-reeves (sheriffs) of England, who used record keeping and systems of accounting to keep track of revenues from across their masters' territories. Since the king maintained royal lands throughout the realm, he needed sheriffs to keep track of his income and eventually developed a centralized office to maintain accounts. The exchequer maintained meticulous records, had a skilled, professional staff, and, most importantly, developed autonomous operations that could persist during times of civil war.[26]

At the end of this chapter I discuss the royal mint, another key institution whose structure and authority changed during this period, 1000–1300. Henry II, who had established stricter control on officers throughout the realm, also strengthened central control over coin production by hand picking moneyers, closing provincial mints, tightening monarchical control over those remaining mints, and most importantly increasing and stabilizing the weight of the penny. While operations of the exchequer connected key personnel and kept track of revenues throughout the realm, the products of the royal mint personally touched all subjects utilizing money, a persistently increasing group over this period and essentially the entire body politic by the early modern period.

In addition to such material changes, rhetorical conventions for discussing the good of the "commonweal" and "good governance" were already well established by the time of the alleged Henrician revolution.[27] Even in his "transformations," Henry appealed to a long history of state consciousness when developing a vision for the English state. For example, the 1533 Act of Appeals begins, "Where by divers sundry old authentic histories and chronicles it is manifestly declared and expressed that this realm of England is an empire."[28] Corrigan and Sayer note that many of the major Henrician statutes of 1530 appeal to an "unbroken evolutionary link with the past," typically beginning with some variant of " 'It has always been the case that.' " Elton subsequently conceded the importance of work predating the 1530s but continued to insist that Cromwell was instrumental in consolidating various established parts of state machinery. He credits Cromwell with understanding "the roots and long established realities of the polity he wished to transform."[29]

Despite the debate over the *timing* of Elton's modern state, scholars of English history continue to regard key centralized institutions as critical to state formation. For example, Bob Jessop has recently defined the "*core of the state apparatus*" as "a distinct ensemble of institutions and organizations whose socially accepted function is to define and enforce collectively binding decisions on a given population in the name of their 'common interest' or 'general will.' "[30] Most importantly, the institutional conception extends the idea of state beyond monarchical will. Corrigan and Sayer assert that although the rise of these centralized institutions helped to strengthen monarchical power, they nevertheless offered a framework for thinking about a state separate from the monarch.[31] What came across publicly as the will of the crown was often the product of diverse, possibly contentious, opinions. The most prominent site of such contention was at court, among the king's councilors. Michael Braddick refers to the court as "a means of integrating not just ambition but also opinion into politics."[32] Strayer identifies "an annoying dilemma" facing the early modern monarch in particular: although he needed councilors with knowledge and experience to provide sound advice, those very skills contributed to a political will independent of the monarch.[33] The threat of independent wills became especially pronounced when the inner council started becoming more professionalized, a movement Strayer locates under the Tudors. This professionalization first put pressure on policymakers to become better informed and more deliberative and second created an incentive for developing a staff of supporting "clerks, informants, and agents," that is, a new bureaucracy. Braddick refers to this group as a "proto-bureaucracy" because although the process of acquiring positions and form of remuneration were similar between institutions, both were "relatively informal" since patronage and preferment tended to confer positions, and remuneration came from fees charged to subjects rather than from salary. Although the offices of these proto-bureaucrats set certain limits on behavior, they were nonetheless granted a certain amount of power through the office.[34]

The written document was an important device for establishing the power of office, however limited, and consequently for establishing a system separate from the monarch. Michael Clanchy posits that the state tends to be built on the written record because of the latter's power to standardize.[35] Writing especially served the bureaucratic needs of record keeping. Noting that all major branches of the English state had begun keeping diligent records by the end of the twelfth century, Strayer describes the written document as "the best guarantee of permanence and the best insulator between an administrator and personal pressures." While the exchequer maintained reports from sheriffs, judges maintained records of decisions, and the chancery kept registers of all issued letters.[36]

The written record also permitted a critical flow of information between center and periphery, a flow that should not be considered unidirectional. While central agencies were important loci of information and administration, local interests maintained negotiative powers of policy initiation and reformation.[37] For this reason, several historians of the state have recently performed detailed assessments of localities as well, focusing especially on local officials such as head constables, petty constables, churchwardens, and overseers, those who according to Hindle "stood at the 'interface' of the state and society". Braddick argues that while institutions of the centralized state are not all necessarily centrally located, institutions of local government might be considered components of centralized authority. He notes that local agents maintained a certain degree of discretion in their implementation of policy and interpretation of their office as passed down from the center. How subjects experienced state authority partially depended on decisions by local officials.[38]

Communication between center and periphery was also essential for the establishment and centralization of the royal mint, which in most periods consisted of a London office as well as regional and ecclesiastical mints before the latter's closure under Henry VIII. The first line of communication included indentures between monarch (or privy council) and master moneyers to set the standards or designs of coinage throughout the realm. But with multiple mints, operational coordination was necessary to regulate standards and designs as well as to ensure appropriate paces of production, hiring of staff, and supply of bullion. In addition to helping to standardize operations, such written documents attest to various difficulties the mints experienced in regular operations.

B. Law and the Limits of State Authority

Of course, the effectiveness of various state functions such as coin production depended on the extent to which state authority was considered legitimate across its manifold operations. Corrigan and Sayer consider the state to be an entity that "seeks to stand alone in its authority [and] claims to be the only legitimate agency equally for this or that form of knowledge, provision, regulation or—that wonderfully neutral word—'administration.'"[39] In addition to having the authority to determine (according to Weber's definition of the state) what constitutes "legitimate violence," the state thus has the authority to determine what constitutes "legitimate administration." But the state's established rules as well as the conduct of all administrators, including the monarch himself, must be consistent with a standard of law, which might only consist of divine and natural law but might also include positive and/or customary law. Therefore, the legitimacy of administration depended on the extent to which the state was accountable to some system of law, but the composition of that law often remained a subject of debate.

Of particular concern in the period was the *monarch's* relation to positive and customary law, especially the question of whether the monarch makes positive law or vice versa. The two sides of the debate correspond, respectively, to the monarchical political models commonly referred to as *absolutism*, in which "the ruler unites both executive and legislative powers in his or her own person," and *constitutionalism*, in which "the legislative prerogative is shared by the ruler and a representative assembly."[40] While absolutism tends to mystify politics so that it becomes a specialized endeavor beyond the capacity of most people, constitutionalism brings politics to earth and makes it an essential activity across the members of the body politic. Typically in absolutism the monarch is subject only to natural and divine law. However, as I will show in Chapter III, even proponents of absolutism, including Jean Bodin and James I, argued that, despite an absolute royal prerogative over coinage, the state should maintain strict coinage standards that most early modern commentators on money considered to be based in custom and convention. Therefore, coinage offers a limit case for analyzing the extent of absolutist authority, which in some instances could be circumscribed by customary law despite rhetoric of superiority to that law.

Certain cases such as coinage could thus transcend the dialectic of absolutism/constitutionalism and yet, as scholars such as Quentin Skinner have shown, the dialectic remains essential for understanding the development of the early modern state.[41] Early modern historians often focus on the conflict between these views within England only during the seventeenth century, especially on the eve of the Civil War; however, Robert Eccleshall argues that the two models actually surfaced in dialectic relation much earlier. Intellectual historians had located constitutionalism in earlier periods, for example, in fifteenth-century writings such as those of John Fortescue, but they typically identified the emergence of absolutism only in the late sixteenth century, particularly in the writing of Jean Bodin. Eccleshall, however, traces the absolutist concept as a product of converging neoplatonic, biblical, Aristotelian, and juristic ideas during the Middle Ages. The neoplatonist idea of a hierarchical universe combined with biblical accounts of man's sinful nature requiring guidance from a community of the faithful to identify a ruler uniquely competent because of his link to divine grace. For Augustine, political activity within a hierarchical structure offered a partial, coercive solution for approaching the harmonious social order found within the natural world prior to human transgression by limiting the malignant social effects of sin.[42]

A side effect of this view was that it moved the bulk of political activity beyond the intellectual and moral capacity of the common person: only a select few were born politicians. The Aristotelian emphasis on reason, especially in thinkers such as Aquinas, bolstered the view that the ruler was the principal locus of reason and social justice.[43] Eccleshall believes that the absolutists' case "hinged on the assumption that regal authority was an adequate embodiment of reason, that his [the monarch's] enactments were acceptable because they were the product of a will that had been informed by reason." For example, in his political analogy to a community of bees, Sir Thomas Elyot suggests that the king alone embodies more wisdom than the rest of the body politic: "who hath amonge them one principall Bee for their governor, who excelleth all other in greatness, yet he hath no pricke or stinge, but in him is more knowledge than in the residue."[44] An organic conception of community implied the necessity of all members within the body politic to play their parts and even offered a rationale for the justifiable sacrifice of members who threatened harmony within the state.[45]

Proponents of both absolutist and constitutionalist thought identified authoritative sources in Roman law, in particular Justinian's *Corpus iuris civilis* (527–534 C.E.).[46] According to one common line of interpretation, the will of the emperor, who is *dominus mundi* (lord of the world), determines law: *quod principi placuit legis habet vigorem* [what has pleased the *princeps* has the force of law]. The emperor is *legibus solutus* [freed from the laws], meaning he is above the same human laws that he has derived from his authority. Indeed, drawing on the Hellenistic concept of the ruler as *nomos empsychos* [living law] the emperor was considered the *lex animata* [living law]: "Let the imperial rank be exempted from all our provisions [in this constitution], because God has subjected the laws themselves to the emperor, by sending him as a living law to men."[47] This mystical conception of the ruler as *lex animata*, the ruler *as* the very law itself, presents the most explicit example of the absolutist notion that politics transcended the capacity of the multitude.

Despite the extensive influence of Justinian's *Corpus iuris*, many of its precepts, including that of the *lex animata*, lay dormant for several centuries. Ernst Kantorowicz believes that the idea reemerged through "the revival of scientific jurisprudence and the literary style of Bologna" in the twelfth century after being mostly forgotten in the West during the early medieval period. Around the same time, the Aristotelian revival included an interpretation of *Nicomachean Ethics* that influenced the notion of the judge as "living justice," an epithet that by around 1300 became applied to the prince as well. Therefore, by the late thirteenth century, Aegidius Romanus would write in *De regimine principum* (1277–79): "the king or prince is a kind of Law, and the Law is a kind of king or prince. For the Law is a kind of inanimate prince; the prince, however, a kind of animate Law. And in so far as the animate exceeds the inanimate the king or prince must exceed the Law." Aegidius's pronouncement partially explains the peculiar belief that the king could at once *be* the law and *be above* the law.[48]

But in addition to supporting the absolutist case, Justinian's *Corpus iuris* was also mined, during the late medieval period, for passages in support of *constitutionalism*. A key concept buttressing constitutionalist thought was the *lex regia* [royal law], passages on which suggest that the Roman people had at some point transferred their authority to the emperor. Interpretation of this transfer of authority, however, became a subject of dispute. While some classical jurists explained it as a one-time shift in sovereignty from the early republic to the first emperor Augustus—that is, as a legitimization of imperial authority—others interpreted it as the perpetual process whereby the people transfer power to each emperor at the start of his reign. The *lex regia* could, therefore, imply that the emperor derived his power and authority from the people, and not from a divine source (though the latter origin of authority also could be interpreted through the *Corpus iuris*), offering a precedent for the emergence of republican ideas in the late Middle Ages and early modern period. Moreover, if the emperor derives his power from the law as *lex regia*, an argument could be made that he should likewise obey the laws, although according to some interpretations the emperor's obedience to the law was purely voluntary.[49]

The ambivalence of Roman law interpretations during the Middle Ages is evident in the writings of the important thirteenth-century English jurist Henry of Bracton. Scholars frequently cite Bracton as an early example of English constitutionalist thought, especially since he wrote in *On the Laws and Customs of England* that the king of England was "under God and the law, because the law makes the king."[50] Eccleshall argues that for Bracton, the king had to submit to the force of law because he was obligated to "fulfil the functions of his office in the presence of his magnates," so that "he was required to associate the barons with him in undertaking the task." A ruler who did not follow his own laws could be considered a tyrant spreading corruption through the realm. Bracton's comment on the *Corpus iuris*'s pronouncement *"quod principi placuit legis habet vigorem"* offers a compelling example of this consiliar view: "that is, not what has been rashly presumed by the [personal] will of the king, but what has been rightly defined by the *consilium* of his magnates, by the king's authorization, and after deliberation and conference concerning it." Kantorowicz notes the importance of "Bracton's constitutionalist qualification of the dangerous word *placuit*," especially to "contemporary and later constitutional struggles in mediaeval England whose focus was, over and over again, the problem of the king's council and its composition."[51]

However, Kantorowicz ultimately argues that Bracton exemplifies the paradoxical medieval belief that the king is at once *above* and *below* the law. Although for Bracton "the law makes the king," the same law that made him king—that is, the *lex regia*—"enhances also his royal power and bestows upon the ruler extraordinary rights which in many respects placed the king, legally, above the laws." The most extraordinary right bestowed on the king by the *lex regia* is represented in the famous passage *quod principi placuit legis habet vigorem*. The *lex regia*, according to which the people had conferred power in the king, in effect legalizes the notion of the king's will *as* law. Kantorowicz concludes from this that Bracton's position ultimately upholds *both* the royal prerogative and royal submission to the law in dialectic relation to each other:

> the king's power to legislate derived from the Law itself, more precisely, from the *lex regia* which made the king a king. Thus a king-making Law and a law-making King mutually conditioned each other, and therewith the well-known relations between the king and the Law reappear in Bracton: the king, Law's son, becomes Law's father.

Kantorowicz finds throughout medieval political theory this dialectic relation of a ruler who was at once "under and above the Law," or at once "father and son of Justice."[52]

By the fifteenth century, however, English constitutionalist ideas had become more clearly differentiated from absolutism. David Starkey notes that the 1450s in particular "marked the birth of a new political language," especially the emergence of the term "commonwealth" during the crisis of that decade, a term that was a "new word...used to express an old idea," that of a distinction between king and kingdom and a mutual obligation between king and subjects dating back at least to Magna Carta. A key political concept from the century was "mixed monarchy," which was articulated by Sir John Fortescue in *De laudibus legum anglie*, written some time between 1468 and 1470 and later translated into English by Richard Mulcaster in *A learned commendation of the politique lawes of Englande* (1567). Fortescue drew from Aquinas's distinction between regal and politic government in order to differentiate the English from the French form of monarchy. While in France "the princes pleasure hath the force of a lawe" within what he terms a "royall" monarchy, in a "politique" monarchy the ruler is governed by positive law as well. England had what Fortescue calls a "mixed" monarchy: it was "royall" since the monarch maintained prerogative in areas not covered by positive law, but it was also "politique" since the monarchy must act in and through parliament, that is, with the theoretical consent of all subjects. Starkey writes that according to Fortescue, while the French version combined king and kingdom, the English version in effect separated the king from the "polis" or commonwealth so that while in France "the king has no duty to his people, and indeed the French are poor and oppressed," in England "the king has such a duty and the English are rich and free." Eccleshall believes it was largely through Fortescue "that the theory of limited monarchy was given a specifically English connotation and transmitted to the early modern period."[53]

Despite Fortescue's important influence in the fifteenth and into the sixteenth century, Eccleshall contends that the concept of limited monarchy "all but disappeared" by the middle of the sixteenth century—especially after Sir Thomas Smith's *De Republica Anglorum* of 1565—although its key conviction that communal wisdom should govern the country would reemerge in advocates of common law restrictions on royal prerogative. Moreover, soon after the "disappearance" of limited monarchy, Jean Bodin's *Les six livres de la république*, the definitive work on absolutism in the period, was published in Paris in 1578 and eventually translated into English as *Six Bookes of a Commonweale* by Richard Knolles in 1606. Chapters 8 through 10 of the first book, the section on sovereignty, became especially influential for absolutist thought. Like other legal scholars, Bodin drew from principles of Roman law, especially the *lex regia*, in defining the extent of sovereign power. Unlike advocates of constitutionalism, however, he interpreted the *lex regia* as a permanent transfer of power from the people to the sovereign. Sovereign power, he writes, "ought to be perpetuall, for that it may bee, that that absolute power over the subjects may be given to one or many, for a short or certaine time, which expired, they are no more than subjects themselves." Moreover, in an intellectual move reminiscent of what Kantorowicz describes as a dialectic relation of a ruler at once "under and above the Law," Bodin writes, "unto Majesty, or Soveraignty belongeth an absolute power, not subject to any law," despite the basis of sovereign authority being in the *lex regia*. Sovereign power is subject to no human law, not even that of the sovereign authority's own making, although it remains subject to the laws of God and nature just like all other human authorities.[54]

Bodin had a clear impact on English political thought, most notably in the writing of King James I for obvious reasons. In "The Trew Law of Free Monarchies," which he wrote prior to assuming the English throne, James appropriated Bodin's concept of absolute sovereignty for his own promotion of absolutist monarchy. Although he asserts that "a king that governes not by his lawe, can neither be countable to God for his administration, nor have a happy and established raigne," and "a good king will not onely delight to rule his subjects by the lawe, but even will conforme himselfe in his owne actions thereunto," he nonetheless claims to have "prooued, that the King is above the law, as both the author and giver of strength thereto." James does acknowledge the role of parliament in producing statute law, but he contends that the king may either "interpret" or "mitigate" any laws that he finds "doubtsome or rigorous," and so "generall lawes, made publikely in Parliament, may upon knowen respects to the King by his authority bee mitigated, and suspended upon causes onely knowen to him."[55]

Once he assumed the throne of England, James continued to promote and attempt to extend the royal prerogative,[56] but his claims to sole legal prerogative were vehemently contested by proponents of the common law, especially Sir Edward Coke. In his *Reports*, Coke echoes Bracton in proclaiming, "The King is under no man, but only God and the law for the law makes the King: Therefore let the King attribute that to the law, which from the law he hath received, to witt power and dominion: for where will, and not law doth sway, there is no King." Coke famously appealed to the authority of common law and the notion of an "ancient constitution"—the customary set of governing laws dating back to "time immemorial"—in order to challenge early Stuart absolutism.[57] He insisted that interpretation of the law depended on "artificial reason" available only to elite judges who had long studied particulars of law. While this emphasis on the "artificial reason" of judges across several generations removed the law from the purview of commoners, it also removed it from that of the king. Coke's emphasis on the priority of English customary law helped to initiate a system of checks and balances—indeed, Coke's opinion in *Bonham's Case* (1610) is considered the origin of our modern concept of "judicial review"—against assumptions of monarchical prerogative and even parliamentary sovereignty.

Although the political challenge from common law reached its zenith under the Stuarts, the power of custom and customary law had long roots. The concept of unwritten, customary law had an important Roman law precedent in the category of *ius non scriptum*, which appears to trump *lex*, or written law, in one passage of the *Digest*, written by a second-century jurist Julian: "What does it matter whether the people declares its will by a vote or by its actions? It is, therefore, most correctly accepted that laws are abrogated not only by the vote of the legislator, but also by the tacit consent of all through disuse." Joseph Canning notes that although there is "no suggestion in the *Corpus iuris* that custom can revoke imperial law," the passage from Julian "through its understanding of the power of consent [nevertheless] provided ammunition for the elaboration of theories of the autonomy, and indeed sovereignty of the people" for juristic scholars of the Middle Ages.[58] As with the *ius non scriptum* and *lex* implicit in the passage from Julian, according to some commentators, English common law in judicial decisions based on custom could override statutes that were inconsistent with its dictates.

The power of custom helps to explain the authority of coinage standards in early modern England. While coinage had been considered a customary tool rather than a natural development—despite an attempt in the fourteenth century by Nicole Oresme to link coinage standards to natural phenomena, as I discuss in the next chapter[59]—English coinage standards became a form of unwritten law that not even an absolutist monarch should defy. Despite general acceptance of a royal prerogative over coinage, proponents of absolutism such as Bodin and James I continued to insist on maintaining standards.[60] This key exception to absolute prerogative may have resulted from Bodin's and James's observation of public outcries against historical debasements in France, Scotland, and England. Therefore, arbitrary manipulation of the coinage was proscribed even by those who considered the monarch to be above the law.

C. Statute and the Legal Expansion of State Authority

In the previous section I discussed various limitations placed on monarchical authority by positive and customary law within constitutionalist theories. However, positive law was not static despite certain claims that statutes were merely articulations of immutable common law. The king and parliament, acting as the composite institution of king-in-parliament, had the power to transform law or make new law through the creation and promulgation of statutes.

As a representative entity, parliament, in theory, represented the will of the entire body politic. Magna Carta had established the king's need to get consent of the "common counsel of the realm," initially a *magnum consilium* comprised of an elite group of peers and church officials, which would later become the basis of the House of Lords. However, by the middle of the thirteenth century, the council's exclusive right to represent the will of all subjects was called into question, and eventually—especially in the 1290s with Edward I's need to finance military campaigns—a House of Commons was added, consisting of representatives from the shires and boroughs. Thomas Ertman attributes the establishment of a national representative institution in England—in contrast to continental Europe's tricurial assembly of estates, which comprised members from various classes—to an earlier structure of relations between "communities of the shires" at both local and centralized authority levels. This established parliament assumed the *magnum consilium*'s earlier role in legislation so that by the middle of the fourteenth century it was widely held that new statutes, which could be promulgated only with the consent of parliament, would have the capacity to alter common law.[61]

Because parliament theoretically represented the will of the people, it was considered infallible by early commentators. For example, John Fortescue identifies collective wisdom in an institution with more than three hundred of the best minds of England, a number that not coincidentally mirrored the size of the Roman senate:

> But statutes cannot thus passe in Englande, forsomuch as they are made not onlye by the Princes pleasure, but also by the asse[n]t of the whole royalme: so that of necessity they must procure the wealth of the people, and in noe wise tende to theire hinderaunce. And it cannot otherwise bee thoughte, but that they are replenished with muche witte and wisedome, seeinge they are ordained not by the devise of one man alone, or of a hundrethe wise counsellers onelye, but of mo then three hundredth chosen menne, much agreeinge with the number of the aunciente senatoures of Roome.[62]

Statute as the "asse[n]t of the whole royalme" reveals the underlying assumptions about parliamentary infallibility. According to Fortescue, since parliament represents the people, it always acted on behalf of the people, who would never act against their own interests. Therefore, since parliament always intended the good of the people, it could not be anything but just in its decisions.

Eccleshall notes, however, that this sense of infallibility did not imply sovereignty in the sense of a "voluntarist conception of law." Not until the sixteenth century did a notion of parliamentary sovereignty—or the sovereignty of king-in-parliament—emerge. In his thesis of a Tudor Revolution in government, G. R. Elton notes that while "lack of true sovereignty was at the heart of the earlier dispensation...supremacy of the king in parliament was at the heart of the new." Moreover, around the same time as the Henrician Reformation, a theory of parliamentary sovereignty was being articulated by the lawyer Christopher Saint German, who followed the line of argument concerning the infallibility of parliament by noting its representative function. He describes parliamentary decision making as if the entire realm were present to give their assent to transform common law:

> There is no Statute made in this Realme but by the Assent of the Lords Spiritual and Temporal, and of all the Commons, that is to say, by the Knights of the Shire, Citizens and Burgesses, that be chosen by Assent of the Commons, which in the Parliament represent the Estate of the whole Commons: and every Statute there made is of as strong Effect in the Law, as if all the Commons were there present personally at the making thereof.[63]

As long as parliament continued to demonstrate its service as a representative assembly—especially as long as parliament remained unswayed by the singular influence of the monarch, who constituted only one member of the larger political body—neither its infallibility nor sovereignty would be questioned.

However, Ertman finds a peculiarity in that the power of parliament depended on whether or not England was at war. In particular, with the end of the Hundred Years War in 1453, parliament began to meet less frequently—Henry VIII, for example, called only four parliaments in the first twenty years of his reign—and for shorter sessions because there were no issues of taxation and war finance to discuss.[64] During the sixteenth and early seventeenth century, England remained mostly at peace compared to continental countries, and so the lack of financial pressure induced a decline in the position of parliament. As a result, parliament no longer enjoyed the power of governmental oversight over the royal bureaucracy, and "proprietary officeholders were able to consolidate their position and financiers to gain a new foothold within the English state apparatus."[65]

Sixteenth-century political commentators such as Thomas Starkey began to express concern that despite the theoretical check on royal prerogative posed by parliament, statutes appeared to be promoting the royal prerogative to such an extent that the king had the power to abrogate laws. Parliament was seen more and more as merely a tool of the monarchy.[66] As a result, confidence in parliament to represent the interests of the commonwealth began to deteriorate. Many understood that a considerable portion of government activity involved private petition to the king's privy council rather than deliberation before a representative body. Eccleshall believes it was for this reason that the earlier emphasis on limited monarchy through the power of parliament started to shift toward the upholding of common law, which neither king nor parliament could abrogate: "custom was now viewed in the same perspective as parliament had been in the sixteenth century."[67]

Despite general disapproval of parliament's complicity with the monarch, several new statutes were produced in the sixteenth and early seventeenth century. Statute law began to impose itself even in an area that had been previously left to ecclesiastical or communal regulation: moral reform. Saint German had established a precedent for moral reform by parliament, arguing in *Doctor and Student* that the king-in-parliament "hath the Rule and Governance over the People, not only of their Bodies, but also of their Souls." And in *An answere to a letter* he writes that statutes are

> made by all the people/for the parliament so gathered togyther... representeth the estate of al the people within this realme/that is to say of the whole catholique churche therof. And why shuld nat the parliament... whiche representeth the whole catholike churche of Englande expounde scripture rather than the convocacion whiche representeth onely the state of the clergy.[68]

Because parliament encompassed not only the clergy but the whole "catholyke churche" consisting of all English people, it should have the capacity to "expounde scripture" by producing legislation covering spiritual matters as well as secular concerns.

But as Steve Hindle notes, it was not until the late Elizabethan and early Stuart period that we see a significant increase in parliamentary activity focused on moral reformation, including attempts to mitigate "drunkenness, fornication, swearing, blasphemy, gaming, dancing, revelling and profaning the sabbath." An "emerging consensus" of historical scholarship has demonstrated that there were other, even earlier, periods—including the 1290s, the 1470s, the 1660s, the 1690s, and the 1750s—that were characterized by an impetus of moral regulation, suggesting that such movements were, as Martin Ingram puts it, "a recurrent, indeed almost continually persistent, feature of English social life over several centuries."[69] Moreover, Ingram points to evidence that the late fifteenth and early sixteenth century experienced common public regulation of morality through legal action. But what distinguished the late Elizabethan and early Stuart period was its "unprecedented *statutory backing*" of moral reform, which suggests to Hindle that "personal morality was now a legitimate public issue."[70]

Historians have used the phrase "reformation of manners," a term that appears in the discourse of the period, to describe such movements in general. For example, Phillip Stubbes concedes that "some kind of playes, tragedies and enterluds... containe matter (such they may be) both of doctrine, erudition, good example and wholesome instruction: And may be used, in time and place convenient, as conducible to example of life and reformation of maners." Although not a direct spokesman for the state, Stubbes and other pamphleteers who expressed outrage over moral lapses could nevertheless contribute to the state's cause of moral reform. Ingram notes that the state's reformation of manners initiatives between 1560 and 1660 received crucial support in the print marketplace through pamphlets and printed sermons, circulating texts that helped to spread the movement to a national level.[71]

In Chapter IV I consider a specific example of statutory law, the categorization as treason of coining crimes, including counterfeiting, clipping, shaving, or any method of removing precious metal from coins. Although coining was mainly considered an offense against the state—indeed, there were no explicit biblical prohibitions against it—the state employed discourses of moral regulation and used metaphors derived from biblical and classical sources in an attempt to proscribe the various practices. As a result, coining crimes assumed the connotations of other crimes targeted by the "reformation of manners," especially bastardy, connotations that partly explain the peculiar use of coin imagery in Shakespeare's *Measure for Measure*.

D. Political Theology of State

The "reformation of manners" represented an important bridge between secular and religious authorities, but such a bridge had already been evident in the body of the king.[72] My earlier discussion of the monarch as *lex animata* or "living law" within the "body politic" also indicates a mystical conception of state authority that takes us into the realm of what Ernst Kantorowicz calls, following Carl Schmitt, "political theology." In his influential study *The King's Two Bodies*, Kantorowicz traces the development of the eponymous early modern theory to its "Royal Christological" roots in Medieval Europe. The most famous statement of the theory appears in *Plowden's Reports*, from which Kantorowicz begins his investigation:

> [The king] has a Body natural, adorned and invested with the Estate and Dignity royal; and he has not a Body natural distinct and divided by itself from the Office and Dignity royal, but a Body natural and a Body politic together indivisible; and these two Bodies are incorporated in one Person, and make one Body and not divers, that is the Body corporate in the Body natural, *et e contra* the Body natural in the Body corporate. So that the Body natural, by this conjunction of the Body politic to it, (which Body politic contains the Office, Government, and Majesty royal) is magnified, and by the said Consolidation hath in it the Body politic.

Kantorowicz links the theory to the concept of Christ's two natures, especially in the evolution of the *corpus mysticum*, which initially signified the real presence of Christ in the Eucharist, but after 1150 it was increasingly used to describe the Church.[73]

Around the same time, secular authorities also appropriated the concept of *corpus mysticum*. Since the conversion of Constantine, emperors and kings had received official sanction from the Church. After Charlemagne, Holy Roman Emperors were consecrated by anointment with holy oil. Royal promoters soon argued that this consecration converted the emperor into an image of Christ, and that he claimed sacred authority directly from God, not from the pope.[74] Other consecrated kings could claim similar authority. Like Christ, the king became a "*gemina persona*, human by nature and divine by grace," a belief that foreshadowed the later theory of the king's two bodies. Of course, this bred resentment among Church authorities. In 1159 John of Salisbury presented a compromise between Church and secular authorities by designating two mystical bodies: the *corpus ecclesiae mysticum* [mystical body of the church] and the *corpus reipublicae mysticum* [mystical body of the republic]. The king could now be designated as the head of this second mystical body, but Paul Kléber Monod argues that this political compromise "was shaky from the first, because it subordinated the ruler to the church and to the corporate polity of which he was the head." The sacredness of royalty was seen not in the body of the king per se, but in the collective *corpus reipublicae mysticum* that was somehow attached to the king's body.[75]

The implications of the two bodies theory clearly represented what Eccleshall calls "a tendency to mystify political activity by removing it from the range of normal human competence" and, therefore, assumed connotations of absolutism. A related theory supporting the absolutist case was the divine right of kings: the belief that an infallible ruler was divinely appointed to lead a community and maintained this direct divine connection over the period of earthly rule. Expressions of divine right became more prominent in the late sixteenth and early seventeenth centuries, but as early as 1536, Stephen Gardiner expressed the belief that God appointed princes "whom/as representours of his Image unto men/he wolde have to be reputed in the supreme/and most highe rowme/and to excelle amonge all other humayne creatures/as Saint Petre writeth." Articulations of divine right tended to surface in the face of rebellion as well, as in this homily delivered after the 1569 Northern Rebellion:

> As in reading of the holy scriptures, we shall finde in very many and almost infinite places, as well of the olde Testament, as of the new, that kinges and princes, as well the evyl as the good, do raigne by Gods ordinaunce, and that subjectes are bounden to obey them; that God doth geve princes wisdome, great power, and aucthority: that God defendeth them against their enemies, & destroyeth their enemies horribly: that the anger and displeasure of the prince is as the roaring

of a lion, and the verye messenger of death: and that the subject that provoketh him to displeasure sinneth against his owne soule.

Steve Hindle notes that such expressions turned punishment of malefactors into a "godly act, for the simple reason that the authority which justified it was divinely constituted."[76]

But although divine right theory surfaced only occasionally in the Tudor period, it positively flourished within the absolutist rhetoric of early Stuart England. Bodin had written that "he which speaketh evill of his prince unto whome he oweth all duty, doth injury unto the majesty of God himselfe, whose lively image he is upon earth." James I espoused such ideas in his speeches before parliament. For example, in his March 1609 speech at Whitehall, James famously asserted, "The State of MONARCHIE is the supremest thing upon earth: For Kings are not onely GODS Lieutenants upon earth, and sit upon GODS throne, but even by GOD himselfe they are called Gods." James's supporters also promoted the theory. In a sermon celebrating the king's inauguration, Richard Crakanthorpe states that he had been "placed in the steede of God himselfe among us."[77]

For Joseph Strayer, belief in divine right doctrine represented the peak of personal loyalty to the monarch. Even skeptics of divine right theory tended to believe that sovereignty was essential for the existence of the state, which protected the welfare of the people. The necessary survival of the state permitted an array of actions that might otherwise be deemed unjust or even idolatrous.[78] In Chapter V I interpret James's insistence on continuing to distribute gold coins in a healing ceremony, an event with clear idolatrous implications, as a recognition of the practice's ability to strengthen the state and increase personal loyalty to James even when the king denied he had miraculous healing powers. But James relied on a political transformation that had occurred long before his time. Strayer locates a shift in basic loyalty from family, community, and church to the state during the thirteenth century, especially among lawyers and royal officials who began to idealize the state and gave state functions moral authority.[79] The highest duty of every subject became the preservation and health of the state: "policies might be attacked; governments might be overthrown; but political convulsions could no longer destroy the concept of the state."[80] Even when barons rebelled, such as in 1215 or 1258, or nearly did so, as in 1297, there was no intent to fracture England or discontinue English institutions, but rather to use central government to make the changes they desired. Hindle concurs that, especially in the Elizabethan period, an obsession with the possibility of social and political chaos manifested in a focus on obedience in common law thought.[81]

Divine right advocates could also rely on the concept of *charisma* to promote personal loyalty. Weber had defined charisma as "a certain quality of an individual personality by virtue of which he is considered extraordinary and treated as endowed with supernatural, superhuman, or at least specifically exceptional powers or qualities." He opposes it to the other "pure types of legitimate domination": "rational" (or "legal") and "traditional" authority. The charismatic authority stands clearly distinct from the masses and must routinely display this distinction in order to maintain legitimacy. Stuart Clark notes that although the divine right theory "was not derived entirely from considerations of charisma...nowhere *else* is the charismatic element to be found." Indeed, Clark points out that Weber spoke of the "genuine meaning of the divine right of kings" under the heading of charismatic and not traditional authority.[82]

But beyond the "individual personality," charisma may exist as an "objective, transferable entity" transmitted from one individual to another (especially, for kings, through the ritual of anointing and coronation), constituting what Weber terms the "*charisma of office*," according to which "the belief in legitimacy is no longer directed to the individual, but to the acquired qualities and to the effectiveness of the ritual acts." As I discuss in Chapter V, such a combination of the mundane and the mystical in "routinized charisma" permitted a flow of coins to represent the "blood of the social body" maintaining the health of the entire body politic. Moreover, as charisma became routinized it tended to devolve on subordinate state officials as well as the king's coinage. For example, Hindle notes that all "who wielded the sword of Justice" would embody this charismatic authority since the "logic of descending authority ensured that the rhetoric of mystical politics was transferred from the prince to his judicial subordinates." This characteristic of "descending authority" to subordinates, as well as its linkage to the monarch's coin, plays an important role in *Measure for Measure*, which I discuss in Chapter IV. William Pemberton describes a circle of justice beginning with God, moving through the king, various judicial officials, and people receiving justice, and eventually returning once again to God:

> God is the ordeyner of our King, the King the image of God, the Law the worke of the King, Judges interpreters of our Law; Magistrates with them dispensers, Justice our fruit of Law dispensed, this fruit of justice the good of the people, the good of the people the honour of our King, this honour of our King, the glory of God, the ordeiner, orderer and blesser of all. And so in this regular and circular revolution, all motion begins in God, and ends in God.

But again such mystical ideals of justice had their more mundane counterparts in bureaucratic routine. Monod describes Weber's notion of routinized charismatic authority as a "stable and routine" form of what had been "revolutionary and irrational." What had started as "divine grace" eventually became "human discipline." As a result, the state maintained a sacred (and hence "irrational") quality while the divinity of the ruler connected to the development of rational authority.[83]

Weber reminds readers that "the basis of every authority, and correspondingly of every kind of willingness to obey, is a *belief,* a belief by virtue of which persons exercising authority are lent prestige." Although much consideration of state formation focuses on the rational process and conceives of religion as primarily an instrument of conformity, ignoring the mystical and what we would call "superstitious" belief systems of the period leaves only a partial view of political culture. Clark notes that without considering the "ethical, mystical, and even quasi-magical aspects" of the culture, " 'the coming of the modern state' is just as partial and anachronistic a concept as 'the coming of the scientific revolution' " without "the magical and 'hermetic' dimension in early modern science."[84] Most importantly, it would ignore the state's affective qualities, the public's belief *in* the state, especially in the king, to use its God-given powers to maintain order within an often fragile body politic.

E. Territorial Boundaries of State

Of course, the body politic existed only in geographic relation to other competing body politics. Especially in the context of an inter-state system in early modern Europe, all four of the earlier dimensions of state formation previously described pertain only, as Weber specifies, "within a given territory." Yet, the existence of territory-based state power suggests, in the ideal, an apparent paradox of coexistent centrality and homogeneous dispersion, a central power without a center or with centers everywhere. In reality, however, state power tended to radiate outward from a relatively stable center to the relatively unstable margin, the degree of stability depending primarily on internal social relations and external political situations.[85] Strayer notes that in state formation there must be a stable core geographic area in order to build a political system and establish permanent institutions, although a certain amount of "fluctuation along the fringes is permissible." A monarch traveling regularly throughout the realm helps to establish sovereignty over a given area. Strayer believes that the relatively compact geography of England made it easier for the monarch to conduct such tours and, therefore, the English had an easier time than the French at achieving internal sovereignty.[86]

From a legal perspective, a crucial historic step in the establishment of territorially sovereign states was to equate the relationship between monarch and state to that between emperor and empire, since the imperial model was initially the only model of territorial sovereignty recognized in Europe. In the thirteenth century, English, French, Spanish, and Neapolitan jurists adopted the statement *rex in regno suo est imperator regni sui* [the king in his kingdom is the emperor of his kingdom] from canonist writings of Bologna from around 1200 (especially those of Alanus Anglicus and Azo), in order to argue that kings maintained sovereign independence within their territory just as the emperor had across imperial territory. Moreover, they espoused the idea of the *rex qui superiorem non recognoscit* [the king who does not acknowledge a superior] from Innocent III's *Per venerabilem: quuum rex ipse [Francorum] superiorem in temporalibus minime recognoscat* [since the king himself [i.e. of the French] does not recognize a superior in temporal matters] in order to establish independence from the empire, although interpretation of the phrase as either de facto or de jure independence was debated among canonists. Similar ideas were later employed by Bartolus of Sassoferrato in the fourteenth century to establish the sovereignty of city-states as well.[87]

The existence of alternative models of territorial sovereignty such as the city-state prompted scholars to consider various theories of why the "sovereign, territorial state" ultimately triumphed throughout Europe. The 1648 Treaty of Westphalia in particular established a formal system of recognized sovereign states divided by territory.[88] Among its conditions, Westphalia granted sovereign authority over specified territories while weakening local estates within these territories; described Europe as a self-regulating balance of such sovereign authorities superseding the earlier pan-European models of papacy and empire; established in Germany a confederation of independent principalities or city-states; and recognized religious diversity within sovereign political entities.[89] Despite the recognition of principalities in Westphalia, the sovereign, territorial state would eventually displace all other models. Thomas Ertman says that it is "now generally accepted" within recent work (by scholars such as Charles Tilly, Stein Rokkan, and Hendrik Spruyt) that the territorial state model superseded other political forms such as empire, city-state, and lordships because of its efficiency at mobilizing resources for war, including both financial resources from its urban centers and tax base and human resources from its capacity of military recruiting.[90]

Hendrik Spruyt compares three models that emerged in the late Middle Ages: the sovereign, territorial state, the city league (such as the Hanseatic League), and the city-state.[91] He finds that the sovereign, territorial state triumphed because of its institutional efficiency at decision making that could better mobilize resources; the sovereigns' ability to "credibly speak on behalf of their constituencies"; and compatibility (because of territoriality) with other states allowing sovereigns to "precisely specify who their subjects were" and "to specify limits to their authority." City-leagues, which were not based on contiguous territories, however, had difficulties being incorporated into an inter-state system. City-states were compatible with such a system and, therefore, persisted in the German principalities after Westphalia, but they were less competitive than territorial, sovereign states because they were imperfectly integrated into the system and had no "fully articulated sovereign authority." Ultimately, Spruyt argues, the "evolution of the state and the development of a state system were mutually reinforcing processes." While the state system "selected out those types of units that were, competitively speaking, less efficient," individual sovereign states "preferred a system that divided the sphere of cultural and economic interaction into territorial parcels with clear hierarchical authorities."[92]

Spruyt believes that it was especially the emergence of the concept of sovereignty in the late Middle Ages, with its characteristic emphasis on both "internal hierarchy and external autonomy" or "territorial exclusivity," that permitted the development of the modern state. But an "economic renaissance" in the same period, including an increase in long-distance trade and growth of towns, also led to a transformation in institutions and political alliances within key territories. Spruyt sees the emergence of states as a result of increasing coalitions between incipient monarchy and burghers. He notes in particular that early modern kings' "interest in rationalizing and improving the overall economy coincided with the interests of the mercantile elements in society." Therefore, political and economic innovations became inextricably linked, giving rise to Max Weber's observation that the early modern West differed from "other great civilizations" in its polity, which uniquely combined the sovereign, territorial state with a dynamic market economy.[93]

But not all members of the polity benefited from this "economic renaissance" and the establishment of a sovereign, territorial state; although coalitions may have been formed between kings and mercantile elements, other segments of society, besides the aristocracy, were clearly excluded. Perry Anderson argues that the "gradual disappearance of serfdom" in the shift toward capitalism restricted the power of feudal lords, or the aristocracy, a change that would ultimately lead to the more centralized absolutist state with power concentrated at the national level. However, far from diluting aristocratic power the "State machine and juridical order of Absolutism" would ultimately "increase the efficacy of aristocratic rule in pinning down a non-servile peasantry into new forms of dependence and exploitation." Moreover, at the same time that absolutism protected "aristocratic property and privileges," that same device (the State) "could *simultaneously* ensure the basic interests of the nascent mercantile and manufacturing classes." In effect, the absolutist state in Anderson's view— which "was never an arbiter between the aristocracy and the bourgeoisie, still less an instrument of the nascent bourgeoisie against the aristocracy" but was, in fact, "the new political carapace of a threatened nobility"— entailed a new coalition of power between monarchy, aristocracy, and bourgeoisie.[94]

We should question Anderson's presumption about the rise of the absolutist state, given its resistance by the common law and alternative models of sovereignty as I described earlier, but this perception of emerging coalitions of power in the period proves useful. For example, although the logic of absolutism is mostly absent from Thomas Dekker's *The Shoemaker's Holiday*, I argue in Chapter VI that this late Elizabethan play represents just such a coalition that excludes common laborers, the shoemakers, whose "holiday" the play purportedly celebrates. Moreover, their exclusion is directly tied to the establishment of national boundaries, for foreign trade whose benefits they cannot reap and for foreign wars of which they become victims. Although the play begins with tension between the aristocratic and merchant classes, a coalition of state interests emerges in the ultimate marriage between Lacy and Rose, Lacy's comradery with the newly made merchant Simon Eyre, and the scene of joint celebration between Eyre and the king. However, the ignorance of the shoemaker Firk about the nuances of trade, as well as the body of Ralph made lame in the same war for which the king requests more troops at the end of the play, makes clear that the laborers remain at best outside and at worst exploited by this coalition of power. This non-traversable boundary between the powerful and the powerless, I argue, manifests in different parties' use of coins, whether gold or silver, foreign or domestic.

III. The Royal Mint

Having surveyed the five key dimensions of state formation that serve as a framework for the remainder of *Coinage and State Formation*, I turn now to the relation between coinage and the first dimension, centralized institutions. The history of the royal mint, which was responsible for the production of all English coinage, offers an instructive case study for understanding the importance of institutional structures in the promotion of state power as well as the inherent instability of state formation owing to its reliance on such institutions.

Although historians such as Joseph Strayer have noted the exchequer's importance in state financial administration, mention of the royal mint has been noticeably marginal if not entirely absent in analyses of state formation, though the mint provided the key resource necessary for a burgeoning economy. Exceptions include the work of economic historians such as C. E. Challis and Glyn Davies as well as numismatists/curators such as Nicholas Mayhew, who have articulated clearly the institution's significance. Nevertheless, studies of the mint in the context of state formation remain the exception rather than the rule. The general exclusion may be due to a long history of mint production, dating back to ancient states, and thus not considered applicable to the *modern* state alone. For example, Davies, whose history covers "From Ancient Times to the Present Day," declares that "right from the inception of money, from ancient down to modern times, the state has a powerful, though not omnipotent, role to play in the development of money." In the remainder of this chapter I briefly trace the "powerful, though not omnipotent" role the state played in monetary development, and conversely the role the mint played in state formation.[95] While the general trend for coinage through the sixteenth century was toward institutional centralization, the "success" of which is evident in Henry VIII's ability to implement the "great debasement" without initial public interference, the path toward centralization was far from smooth.

Most scholars date the origin of Western modern-type coinage—that is, a relatively flat disk stamped on both sides with some iconic design—to the kingdom of Lydia in the seventh century B.C.E. As early as 2250 to 2150 B.C.E., we find in Cappadocia a state guaranteeing weight and purity of silver ingots, which gradually became smaller and thus more convenient for exchange.[96] However, it took several centuries for these objects to assume a form we would recognize as modern coinage. The most significant change occurred in Lydia and Ionia, in modern day Turkey. Archeological finds from the region indicate a clear transformation from the metallic blobs or "dumps" at the start of the seventh century B.C.E. to recognizable coins by the end of the century. Lydians and Ionians made their coins of electrum, a natural mixture of gold and silver panned from local rivers, but they later learned how to separate the two metals into a system of bimetallic coinage. For many years scholars disputed the relative importance of Lydia, Ionia, and Greece in the development of coinage, but a series of coin hoard findings in 1951 beneath a temple of Artemis at Ephesus in the Ionian mainland offered a clear picture of a developmental trajectory. The hoard includes a range of coin types, from unstamped dumps, to dumps punched on one side only, to other variations, all the way to double-struck coins displaying a lion's head, the badge of the royal house of Lydia.[97] From these and other archeological findings scholars now attribute the first true modern-type coins to Lydia, around 640 to 630 B.C.E. Shortly afterward, the Ionians probably adopted the Lydians' technology of coin production, which passed quickly westward through the Greek islands to the Greek mainland, so that various regions of Greece were producing modern-type coins by around 595–570 B.C.E. In addition to this westward movement, the coinage technology of Lydia appears to have spread quickly in other directions as well—eastward through the Persian Empire and northward to Macedonia, Thrace, and the Black Sea.[98]

It is not clear, however, that the state initially held a monopoly on coinage. While many early coin designs bear insignias associated with a particular city-state, some contain only personal names.[99] Also, the variety of symbols on punch marks from the earliest coins, many of which cannot be identified in connection with a civic authority, suggests private issue.[100] David Glassner believes that the earliest coinage may have been minted privately because even coins with the insignia of the city-state do not bear names of specific Lydian sovereigns. He hypothesizes that the state monopolized coinage production for political reasons, in order to control a key source of revenue (seignorage, or charge levied by mints for the service of coining) while the power to tax was just being established. Indeed, control of coinage may have enabled control of the state itself. Several scholars have observed that both coinage and tyranny (under Gyges) developed in Lydia. P. N. Ure argues that early Greek tyrants assumed power by recognizing coinage's political potential—that is, coinage created the conditions for tyranny. Arthur Burns refutes this causal interpretation, seeing coinage and tyranny as "probably both rooted in the revolution in conditions of life in the Mediterranean." Nevertheless, once he achieved power, the tyrant would have wanted to monopolize coin production in order to gain financial advantage over his rivals and, therefore, "kicked away the ladder by which he had risen lest others might attempt to use it."[101]

So shortly after the technology of modern-type coinage had been established, states assumed the prerogative of coin production for financial power. Moreover, they recognized propagandistic possibilities in the visual properties of coins. While insignia of city-states, from the Lydian lion's head to the Athenian "owl," ostensibly served to guarantee weight and quality of coins, they also promoted the particular state's authority.[102] The nearly universal desirability of precious metals made it easier for the state either to coerce or to persuade subjects into using its coins, a usage that could signal political allegiance, especially in times of military rivalry. Michael Mann notes that the "strong civic consciousness" of the democratic Athens "used coin design as a badge, a kind of 'flag.'"[103] In Rome after the assassination of Julius Caesar, Brutus stamped his image on the obverse of coins, and on the reverse he portrayed a cap of freedom flanked by two daggers to signify the action that brought him to power.[104] Michael Grant even argues that in particular instances, "the primary function" of certain Roman coins was "to record the messages which the emperor and his advisers desired to commend to the populations of the empire."[105] Early modern monarchs clearly understood this propagandistic potential. For example, James I promoted his plan to unite England and Scotland by issuing the "unite," a coin that prominently displayed the arms of Great Britain.

But the most potent form of propaganda was to personalize coins by portraying particular rulers—in effect, coins routinized charismatic authority. Economic forces, especially the sheer convenience of a standardized medium of exchange, thereby permitted rulers to circulate in effigy across the space of their territory and among the multitude of their subjects. The practice of stamping coins with the ruler's portrait probably began under Philip of Macedon, whose coins bore the head of Zeus, but the imprint could easily have been mistaken for an image of the ruler himself. Philip's son Alexander adopted this idea of portraying his likeness on coins; though the image was ostensibly the head of Heracles, it was clearly intended to resemble an idealized image of Alexander himself, who some believed was descended from the demigod. Persian kings after Alexander depicted themselves armed with spear, bow and arrows and boasting on their coinage, "I will conquer Greece with my archers," the term "archers" referring also to the coins themselves.[106] And with the rise of Rome, Julius Caesar adopted the practice of portraying his likeness without any pretense of the image representing some deity. Just such an image on a coin of a later Caesar (perhaps that of the contemporary Tiberius or an earlier issue from Augustus) prompted Jesus to declare, in response to the question of whether tribute should be paid to the emperor, "Render unto Caesar the things which are Caesar's and unto God the things that are God's."

Roman coins, as well as Celtic imitations of them, appeared in Britain even before the Roman conquest. By the time of Julius Caesar's invasions in 55 and 54 B.C.E., some Celtic tribes were already producing coins that circulated along with Roman coins and local sword-blade currencies.[107] Once Rome established colonial control, especially under Claudius in 40 C.E., Roman coins became common throughout the region. However, coin use virtually disappeared with the Roman army following the empire's collapse. Peter Spufford notes that after the breakdown of administrative contact with the rest of the empire, coinage ceased to enter Britain, and by around 435 C.E. coins were no longer employed as a medium of exchange there.[108] Although other regions saw a decrease in monetary circulation as a result of imperial dissolution, only Britain experienced complete collapse of the monetary economy. Coins would not circulate again until approximately two hundred years later, when a surge in trade prompted once more the need for a suitable medium of exchange.

Based on key coin hoard discoveries, including that of Crondall in 1828 (major studies of which have only recently been published) and Sutton Hoo in 1938, numismatists have concluded that some time between 620 and 650 C.E.—probably 630—England began once again to mint its own coins for general circulation.[109] Early English coins were produced by both local rulers and ecclesiastic authorities and typically included the name of the moneyer. However, when the seven kingdoms came under the coercive overlordship of Mercia in the south and Northumbria in the north, kings began to assume the royal prerogative of coinage once again, suppressing regional and ecclesiastical mints and stamping their issues prominently with heads and names of kings. From this period on, English coinage generally remained a special privilege of the monarchy as in other areas of Europe.[110]

The monetary system also started to become more uniform within England. The most significant development during this period was the creation of the penny, which became virtually the only English coin produced for the next five hundred years.[111] The penny was based on the French *denier*—introduced by Pepin the Short around 752 and adopted by his son Charlemagne—which was itself modeled on the Roman *denarius*. It was first produced around 765 by Heaberth, the independent king of Kent. Once the king of Mercia Offa (757–96) conquered Kent, he assumed the services of the moneyers (who had produced the first pennies) and increased the production and circulation of coins; the English coin was soon considered superior to its continental counterparts.[112] Offa followed the standard of Charlemagne in dividing a Roman pound weight of silver into 240 pennies. Although the penny was the only coin actually produced, around this time people adopted the Roman practice of maintaining accounts in terms of pounds (*libra*), shillings (*solidus*, 12 pence or 1/20th of a pound), and pence (*denarius*).[113]

Subsequent rulers continued the process of centralizing control over coin production. Through the ninth century, archbishops could maintain their own moneyers and issue money in their own name.[114] But in 928 Athelstan (925–40) established at the Council of Greatley a legal framework for a solitary coinage, issued by the king's authority and bearing his image and struck only within towns, with a specified quota of moneyers for each city or town. Later, Edgar (959–70) increased the number of mints and maintained strict control over moneyers and coinage dies. Moreover, he established a precedent for a regular cycle of recoinage—at first every six years—to maintain the coins' quality, to enforce continued acceptance of the coinage as legal tender, to obtain regular profits from minting, and to continually reassert the royal prerogative of coinage.[115] Athelred II (979–1016) established a centralized system of die production, all dies used by mints throughout England (which had increased to seventy five by this time) being produced by the central mint of London.[116] Each mint paid fees for using these dies, so coin production became a significant source of monarchical revenue. Although persistent incursions by Danes would impede progress toward a true national currency until William I in 1066, England became the first major European country to establish a single currency after the fall of Rome, 600 years before France and 900 years before Germany and Italy.[117] In order to establish monetary continuity, William adopted the Saxon penny as national currency. More importantly, he established the standard of 92.5 percent purity for silver, later designated as "sterling," with his recoinage in the 1080s.[118] English "sterling" would subsequently become the envy of European currencies, as I discuss further in Chapter VI.

However, upholding a uniform coinage standard depended on the skill and integrity of moneyers, whose names continued to appear alongside monarchs on coins, presumably to indicate their responsibility for the coins' weight and fineness.[119] And, of course, the more mints established, the greater the danger of losing monetary control.[120] Licensed moneyers—who typically came from privilege, maintained jurisdiction over workmen, and sometimes had official residence—were allowed to purchase silver and pay out new coins at specified rates. Typically moneyers paid the monarch a fee upon appointment and for each subsequent recoinage.[121] The monarch would usually place his faith in the integrity of moneyers to produce coinage according to commissions but occasionally intervened in money matters when the public scrutinized coin quality. For example, during the reign of Henry I the coinage had deteriorated such that it became common public practice to nick coins for verification that they were silver throughout. In response, during Christmas of 1124, Henry had all of the approximately 200 mint masters of the kingdom attend the Assize of Winchester. One report attests that 94 of them had their right hands cut off.[122] The willingness of Henry (and other monarchs) to employ state violence against offending moneyers demonstrates the importance monarchs placed on these circulating forms of routinized charisma.

Coinage quality and uniformity suffered even more during the civil war between Stephen and Matilda (1138–1153), when both rival monarchs and several lesser barons produced their own coins.[123] In order to establish tighter control over coinage production, starting around 1158, Henry II undertook a number of monetary initiatives, including replacing all moneyers with a self-picked staff; eliminating several mints and bringing remaining ones under tight monarchical control; increasing and stabilizing the weight of the penny at 1.4 grams, a weight maintained into the fourteenth century; and abandoning the common practice of frequent recoinages. According to Nicholas Mayhew, Henry "inaugurated a period of 200 years of stability that laid the foundations for sterling's reputation for stability and strength."[124] By contrast, coinage of medieval France lacked standard weights and purities as a weaker monarchy devolved the right to produce coinage to various counts. The closing of provincial mints especially helped to establish the dominance of the London mint and started the move toward the Tower of London becoming the central location of coin production.[125]

By the thirteenth century, mint production was mostly limited to London and Canterbury. However, it was not until the reign of Edward I (1272–1307) that the London mint was officially established at the Tower of London. Before this, the mint had been located in Westminster, in the same building as the treasury and exchequer. To house the mint, a new building 400 feet long was constructed between the inner and outer walls of the Tower of London. Coin production for the entire country became concentrated mostly at the Tower mint, although episcopal mints at Canterbury, York, and Durham continued to produce coinage at various times.[126]

The appointment of William de Tunemire in 1279 as the first "master-moneyer" or "master of the mint" for the whole of England accelerated the process of subordinating regional mints. The master of the mint contracted with the monarch to receive specified coinage charges—the value of coinage he produced less the amount he could pay individuals bringing in silver and gold, the so-called "mint rate"—from which he paid all costs, especially for labor and tools. Any remaining profit, or "seignorage," would normally go to the master. Elton states that the mint's "profits were ordinarily so negligible as to make it less a revenue department than a coin manufactory." Nevertheless, as J. D. Gould notes, any profits from the mint became "a form of non-Parliamentary revenue, which at times made it a doubly attractive source to tap." As we will see in Chapter III, the mint did indeed become a substantial source of non-parliamentary revenue for Henry VIII during the "great debasement," which would singlehandedly destroy confidence in English coinage both at home and abroad for several years.[127]

What made Henry VIII's debasement especially offensive to Tudor subjects and modern numismatists alike was that Henry's father had produced some of the most magnificent coinage in English history. Henry VII inherited from Richard III a coinage that had suffered during the War of the Roses, whether just from general wear and tear or from illicit coin alterations and culling of good coins by the public. Henry tightened the reigns on the mint and would not tolerate any corruption among mint workers; in 1505 he made an example of one counterfeiting mint worker by having him hanged at Tyburn. Glyn Davies concludes about the monarch, "To Henry sound money was essential to sound government."[128]

In addition to tightening control over mints, Henry encouraged coinage innovation. He introduced a shilling coin (unofficially called the "testoon") and a pound coin, the sovereign. Both of these coins were designed by the German Alexander of Bruchsal, who has been dubbed "the father of English coin portraiture."[129] The design of the sovereign, first produced in 1489, was especially significant. In addition to imitating heavier gold coins of the continent, its portrayal of the imperial crown connoted English power and the establishment of the Tudor dynasty to continental countries. C. E. Challis notes the relevance of 1489 as the release date because that was the "year that the new dynasty effectively made its diplomatic entrée into Europe."[130] The shilling or "testoon" was also important because it had "by far the best profile portrait of the monarch produced up till then on any English coin." Overall, Henry VII had clearly transformed the quality of English coinage by the first decade of the sixteenth century.[131]

For the first years of his reign, Henry VIII made few coinage changes, even retaining his father's portrait on coins and merely replacing "VII" with "VIII."[132] However, his break with Rome and the consequent closing of ecclesiastical mints intensified mint centralization. Church officials at York, Canterbury, and Durham had previously been granted permission to produce coins, although coinage prerogative always remained the king's. But this practice stopped under Henry VIII. Wolsey appears to be the final such official to have produced coinage. Although there is no documentation of the ecclesiastical mints being officially closed, George Brooke attributes it to Thomas Cromwell's administration around the time of the dissolution of the monasteries.[133] As with all other revenue-generating departments, the mint was scrutinized by Cromwell, who appointed his friend Stephen Vaughan as undertreasurer.[134]

But Henry VIII's biggest impact on coinage was the "great debasement," when he systematically reduced English coinage standards for fiscal purposes. The event demonstrated the extent to which control over coinage production had become centralized. Without a coordinated effort to maintain a sufficient inflow of bullion, sustained minting of a large quantity of coins, and absolute secrecy about all the effort, the debasement would have failed before the first debased coin could be circulated. However, all functions were sufficiently coordinated and the debasement became an initial "success" for Henry, bringing in over £1 million of revenue at the public's expense. But as we shall see in Chapter III, Henry took into consideration only coinage supply, over which the state maintained a monopoly. Monetary demand and persistent beliefs in an intrinsic value theory of money would, however, come to hamper the English economy as a result of debasement. For generations thereafter, the English public would remember the traumatic event and continue to distrust the state's economic role, placing a significant constraint on the state's ability to function within a rapidly changing economy.

The history of the royal mint demonstrates that attempts at establishing centralized institutions often experienced fits and starts, moments of irrationality as well as rationality. The assumption that state formation in general and the establishment of institutions in particular constituted a linear process toward rationalized bureaucratization should be qualified and nuanced by tracing specific histories of particular institutions. Moreover, such histories should consider interactions between the institution and a concept of "state authority." To what extent did institutional agents employ, reject, or abuse the authority provided by this abstract concept, and to what extent did their actions expand the bounds of authority or redefine the concept? Finally, in the specific case of the royal mint we must acknowledge that the institution controlled only supply of these devices of state authority and had limited, if any, control over demand. The royal mint produced and distributed coinage—whose portraits, iconography, and mottoes bore the routinized charisma of monarchs and transmitted state authority through commercial transactions—but was generally powerless to control how the public actually used the coinage. Other state agents such as justices of the peace would attempt to regulate this use, for example, through prosecution of counterfeiters. But even this extended framework for state control of coinage had limited powers. The remainder of this book examines such uses and abuses of coinage and the various responses to such activity in terms of both its material and representational circulation.

Chapter II

More's *Utopia* and the Logic of Debasement: Reason, Custom, and Natural Laws of Coinage

a man may change the name of things, but the value he cannot in any wise to endure for any space, except we were in such a country as Utopia was imagined to be that had no traffic with any other outward country.

—A Discourse of the Common Weal of this Realm of England (1549)

Monarchical control over coinage supply produced constant temptation of debasement, which would provide immediate fiscal revenue at the expense of long-term economic stability. But the possibility of debasement also raised important questions about the extent of state and especially monarchical authority in England. If the monarch maintains the exclusive right to stamp coinage, does he or she not have the privilege to determine coinage quality? And if monetary value was merely conventional, as Aristotle had argued, might not the state justify altering its value in times of need through enhancement (increasing the ascribed value of a particular coin) or debasement (decreasing the quantity of precious metal in each coin)? The answers to these questions depend on the extent to which coinage standards constituted written or unwritten *law*, and the extent to which the monarch was accountable to this law.

Until the fourteenth century, it was generally understood in continental Europe that the monarch had sole privilege to choose coinage quality. However, in the fourteenth century, Nicole Oresme invoked the authority of natural law, reason, and custom in order to censure the practice of debasement, thereby transforming political thought on relations between coinage and state. Drawing on contemporary Aristotelian scholarship concerning the significance of law and custom for setting limits on monarchical prerogative, Oresme influenced strong monetary policy in medieval Europe based on the belief that money had developed a rational and "natural" form despite its original purpose of providing "artificial riches" for the community's exchange of "natural riches." As guarantor of coins' value, the monarch was consequently bound by custom and/or natural law governing monetary value.[1] By the early modern period, coinage production had, therefore, become inextricably linked with questions about relations between monarchy and the law, about royal prerogative in light of theories of absolute and limited monarchy.

However, the discovery of the "New World," as well as its resemblance to the classical Golden Age described by writers such as Ovid, called into question the idea of monetary standards as "rational" and "natural." In particular, Thomas More's *Utopia*, a text clearly influenced by New World accounts, reexamines relations between monetary value, custom, and natural law and, therefore, represents an important response to Oresme's legal argument against debasement. By making monetary value arbitrary, especially by refuting the intrinsic value theory, More established a case for the state's prerogative to deviate from established norms based on European custom. Nevertheless, a European-type monetary custom persists at the boundaries of Utopia, at the limits of the territorial delineation of state authority. Indeed, territorial boundaries constitute the main purpose for maintaining monetary logic in Utopia: the need for military defense of the commonwealth financed by the same gold and silver devalued by the public. Therefore, despite its seeming absence, the logic of money persists and even thrives within More's ideal commonwealth. Drawing from New World accounts and Golden Age topoi, More articulates not only a moralistic critique of monetary dependence, but also a pragmatic solution to meet the state's monetary needs. In fact, the critique *is* the solution: public indifference or even hostility toward money provides the state with all the resources it needs, revealing a clear fiscal motive for establishing a system of arbitrary value. More, in effect, incorporates the logic of European debasement in his fictional commonwealth.

Oresme and the Legal Case against Debasement

Although European experience with debasement dates back to the classical world, most prominently under the Roman Empire, a legal case against the practice was not produced until the dramatic debasements in

Medieval France. Under Philip IV, who acquired the infamous epithet "Le Faux Monnayeur" [The Counterfeiter], the value of French coins decreased by around 80 percent between 1295 and 1305. A temporary respite during the following decade returned the currency to its original value, but the subsequent reign of Charles IV (1322–8) saw another substantial decrease in value.[2] Philip IV's legal scholars had boldly proclaimed, "Abaisser la monnaie est privilege seul et special au roi, de son droit royal, et n'appartient a nul autre, mais a lui seul" [To debase the money is the sole and special privilege of the king, from his royal right, and does not belong to any other but to him alone]. It was widely held in this period that a monarch had the exclusive right to alter the coinage in whatever manner he or she saw fit. Princes in France, Spain, and the Low Countries often made bargains with subjects to give up this right in exchange for an alternative form of tax, hearth-taxes or tallages of bread and wine.[3] Such bargains implied that the princes possessed the privilege of debasement in the first place, and so this right could be used as a negotiating tool to gain other concessions.

However, this privilege began to be questioned at the start of the fourteenth century and culminated in Nicole Oresme's influential treatise from the 1350s, *De moneta*. Oresme first articulated what would become a new orthodox perspective on money: the prince had no right to alter coinage because it belonged solely to the people, those employing money in the exchange of goods.[4] A famous nominalist scholar associated with the University of Paris and eventually the court of Charles V, Oresme was primarily writing in support of the aristocratic perspective in *De moneta*. The treatise first appeared in 1355 under the title *De origine natura jure, et mutationibus monetarum* and consisted of twenty-three chapters; a longer version containing twenty-six chapters was subsequently released in 1358. It appeared in print for the first time in 1477.[5] Spufford believes that the treatise circulated widely and became quite influential during Oresme's lifetime because copies appeared in libraries of the most powerful European rulers and frequent allusions were made to the text within academic discourse of the time. Joel Kaye notes that Oresme took the unusual step of translating *De moneta* from the Latin to vernacular French so that it could be read by members of the royal court in addition to scholars, presumably to have a direct political impact on monetary policy.[6] The strategy appears to have been effective since the treatise was clearly instrumental in transforming ideas about the prince's prerogative of coinage.

De moneta was primarily a response to the debasements by two French kings and the consequent effects on trade and social relations. The English and French having engaged in the first phase of the Hundred Years War for about twenty years, Philip VI and then John II, feeling immense financial strain from war expenses, decided to execute a series of debasements. In response, some time in late 1355 Oresme released *Traictie des monnoies*, the shorter French version of what would become *De moneta*. Around this same time the French nobility and upper clergy were pressing John II for reform, especially for a stronger monetary policy. In 1357 the group requested the same reforms from the dauphin Charles, the then regent while his father John II was prisoner in England. During the next meeting of the estates in 1358, another group led by Etienne Marcel gained significant power, even calling together a rival assembly, which Charles supported, at Compiègne in May of that year. Around this time Oresme wrote the longer version of *De moneta*, initially as a tract on strong monetary policy in support of the rival party's proposals. Oresme was rewarded for his efforts by being named Bishop of Lisieux once the party triumphed. Being profoundly influential, *De moneta* eventually became the standard statement not only of French monetary policy, but also of policy in the Netherlands and possibly Castille. Spufford concludes that as a result of Oresme's influence, after 1360 "debasement was largely a thing of the past in France."[7]

In order to understand how Oresme had produced such a convincing case against debasement, we should examine the text, especially its underlying assumptions about the relationship between monarchical authority and the law. Oresme begins *De moneta* by describing the origin and purpose of money. He explains the necessity in ancient times for a more convenient instrument in the exchange of "natural riches," the various commodities "which of themselves minister to human need." People, therefore, invented money as a form of "artificial riches," which do "not directly relieve the necessities of life" but serve to transfer such necessities from person to person. Implicit in Oresme's description are money's two main purposes: to serve as a medium of exchange and to offer a store of value. Although in itself money does not fulfill a "natural" need because it cannot be consumed, its use permits a transfer of one "natural" good to another without the need for a comparable "natural" good at the time of exchange, as in barter. Rather, the person can exchange the "natural" good for "artificial" money, which will retain a certain value until the person desires to trade the money for another "natural" good. Therefore, as a medium of exchange and store of value for the transfer of "natural" needs, money provides an essential service "for the good of the community" engaged in trade.[8] This explanation of how money functions in relation to "natural" needs will be important for understanding why the question of who *owns* money becomes essential for Oresme, and it highlights the terms in a debate over whether monetary value is based in natural law or convention.

Initially, money was just a given weight of silver or bronze (gold, according to Oresme's history, was apparently employed at a later time), but because it became "tiresome" to weigh and check the purity of the metal for each transaction,

> it was wisely ordained by the sages of that time that pieces of money should be made of a given metal and of definite weight and that they should be stamped with a design, known to everybody, to indicate the quality and true weight of the coin, so that suspicion should be averted and the value readily recognised.[9]

I argue below that the obscurity of this "history" has an important connection to the relation between immemorial custom and the law, as well as to the Aristotelian ideal of collective wisdom. A specific historicization of money's invention might make the process appear more arbitrary rather than a natural or rational progression of cultural development. This system of standardization, whenever it emerged, made trade more convenient, but it also offered opportunities for corruption: those who had little concern about their reputation might cheat others by producing inferior coins. To curtail this problem, "it was ordained of old, with good reason, and to prevent fraud" that only "one or more public persons deputed by the community to that duty" should have the right to stamp coins with a chosen impression. And since "the prince is the most public person and of the highest authority, it follows that he should make the money for the community and stamp it with a suitable design," that is, one difficult to counterfeit (ibid., 9–10). Unlike the typical community member, the prince has a powerful incentive to maintain reputation, and more importantly, he or she must answer to the community if coinage quality deviates from the standard.

Although the prince provides the legitimating stamp on coinage "for the common good," Oresme cites biblical authority, Aristotle's *Politics*, and Cicero's *Rhetoric* to argue that the prince is not the "lord or owner" of the money produced. First locating individual property rights in scripture—"for it was not to princes alone that God gave freedom to possess property, but to our first parents and all their offspring, as it is in Genesis"—Oresme extends these rights to include artificial measures of natural riches: "money, therefore, does not belong to the prince alone." Since money is a "balancing instrument for the exchange of natural wealth," and a person exchanges either commodities or labor for it, money remains "the property of those who possess such wealth" (ibid., 10–11). In order to foreclose any objections from another oft-cited biblical passage, Oresme clarifies the intention of Christ's famous statement, "Render therefore unto Caesar the things which are Caesar's, and unto God the things that are Gods," which is typically understood as, "'The coin is Caesar's because Caesar's image is stamped upon it'" (ibid., 11).[10] He argues instead that the passage means money was due to Caesar, the "person who fought the battles of the state," only as *tribute*, not because it bore his image. That is, this specific coin belongs to Caesar as tax revenue—which was the question asked of Christ, whether taxes should be paid to Caesar—not because it was produced by Caesar and bears his mark. The mark is merely a sign of authenticity, not of ownership.

Establishing ownership of money is critical for Oresme because it legitimizes his claim that the prince has no right to alter money in terms of value, denomination, quantity, weight, or material substance (ibid., 13). That is, the prince has no authority to debase or devalue the coinage. There *are* permissible occasions for changing the money's "form or shape," such as when a foreign prince or counterfeiter copies the prince's dies in order to forge coins that resemble the official coinage but with less precious metal. Similarly, the prince can change the money if the old coinage becomes too worn with age. In both cases, the prince should change the stamp and molds to produce a new form of money, so that the public can tell the difference between the new and the old, while demonetizing the old form (ibid., 14). However, any other transformation would be unauthorized. Since the prince's stamp is supposed to "guarantee the weight and standard of the material," any such alteration would be construed as "a foul lie and a fraudulent cheat," and it would be "unjust" and "detestable" to reduce the weight of a coin without changing the stamp to indicate this reduction (ibid., 19).[11] The most heinous form of alteration is to change the composition of the mixture (technically the only true form of debasement), which is worse than changing the weight "because it is more cunning and less apparent and does more harm and injury to the community" (ibid., 22).[12]

Oresme audaciously proclaims that any prince "who seeks to profit from such changes of money" not only transgresses human law but also "sins against God and against nature" (ibid., 26). As with usury, debasement is "an unnatural act of injustice" because an "unfruitful thing" multiplies itself: it "causes money to beget money, which, as Aristotle says, is against nature" (ibid., 25–26). Yet the wickedness of debasement surpasses even that of usury. Although there are times when "from necessity or for convenience, some contemptible business like money-changing is permitted, or some evil one, like usury," there is "no earthly cause" to permit profitable alteration of coinage (ibid., 29). While with usury the person borrowing money "takes it of his own free will, and can then enjoy the use of it and relieve his own necessity with it," and the terms of the transaction are "determined by free contract between the parties," with debasement a prince "plainly takes the money of his subjects against their will" (ibid., 28). Aristotle neglected to mention debasement only "because in his times such wickedness had not yet been invented"; in fact, debasement's very modernity attests to its evil (ibid., 27). He considers the act to be theft, as "robbery with violence or fraudulent extortion" (ibid., 28). Moreover, since some coins are inscribed with God's name or with a cross, to serve as witness to the coin's authenticity, any prince who should alter such coins "would seem to be silently lying and forswearing himself and bearing false witness, and also transgressing that commandment which says: 'Thou shalt not take the name of the Lord thy God in vain'" (ibid., 22). Indeed, since the prince detracts "from the honour of his ancestors when he cries down their good money," debasement could likewise be considered a violation of the "Lord's commandment to honour our parents" (ibid., 31).

More than damaging his or her own soul, however, the prince does significant damage to the commonwealth by debasing the coinage. Oresme employs the trope of the body politic to describe a commonwealth in which the "wealth, power and position" are concentrated in the prince from the act of debasement as "a monster, like a man whose head is so large and heavy that the rest of the body is too weak to support it," and thus the body cannot survive for very long (ibid., 44). The moral and political dimensions converge especially in the claim that debasement is an act of *tyranny*, performed out of pure self-interest (ibid., 42). Citing Aristotle's *Politics* and *Ethics*, Oresme declares that "whatever loss the prince inflicts on the community is injustice and the act of a tyrant and not of a king" (ibid, 24). Since unwarranted monetary alteration "involves forgery and deceit," the prince "unjustly usurps this essentially unjust privilege"; any profit he or she receives cannot be obtained "justly" because the gain is made at the community's expense. Moreover, any act of alteration might prove a slippery slope. If the prince is permitted a small alteration, he could also justify a slightly larger alteration, and through a continual process of gradual increases, he would be able to "draw to himself almost all the money or riches of his subjects and reduce them to slavery," which would be "tyrannical, indeed true and absolute tyranny, as it is represented by philosophers in ancient history" (ibid., 24–25).[13]

Because of the particular experience of France in the fourteenth century, Oresme focuses mostly on debasement by the state. However, at one critical point he extends the argument to a more general statement that *no one*, not even the "people," has the right to alter the coinage. In so doing, he enunciates a monetary *law* standing above both ruler and subject. Although money belongs to the people, who use it as an artificial measure to exchange for natural riches, "neither the community nor anyone else has the right to misuse or unlawfully use his own property, as the community would be doing if it made such an alteration in the coinage." Coinage should be restored to its *"due and permanent state*, and all taking of profit from it must cease" (ibid., 37; emphasis mine).

Surprisingly, Oresme only briefly alludes to counterfeiting, a practice that plagued states throughout the Middle Ages, and he does so primarily in the case of a foreign state imitating the money of a given state. That is, he is less concerned about an individual subject altering money than about the collective decision to do so. He seems more anxious about the possibility that the people might collectively transfer property rights to a ruler who wants to debase the money, especially in a state of emergency. Later comparing the granting of privilege to alter coinage to permitting the prince "to misuse the wives of any of its citizens he will," Oresme establishes that "anything belonging to anyone as of *natural right* cannot justly be transferred to another; but that is how money belongs to the *free* community" (ibid., 40; emphasis mine). Although money always belongs to the people, they cannot use it any way they so choose since they cannot alienate their natural rights. Such statements that money is a "natural right" within a "free" community and that coinage should be maintained at its "due and permanent state" suggest that even though money had been invented at some point in history for the benefit of the community, its characteristics are based in irrevocable law that must be obeyed by both ruler and subject.

Oresme's "law" integrates two related strands within Aristotelian political thought: the ideal of rational collective decision making and the relationship between custom and law. Both political strands relate to Oresme's obscure monetary history: although he acknowledges that money was invented at some time in the ancient world, he leaves all particulars of this invention vague. The closest he comes to a timeframe is in citing a passage from Cassiodorus' *Variae*, which attributes the discovery of gold and silver to Aecus and Indus, king of Scythia, respectively (ibid., 6). But allusions to such figures allow as much room for myth as for history. Otherwise, he uses phrases such as "when men first began to trade," "it was wisely ordained by the sages of that time," and "it was ordained of old, with good reason" in his recounting of events leading up to the use of state-issued coinage (ibid., 8, 9). It may be that Oresme does not know the particulars of monetary history and so is forced to leave it vague.[14] Nevertheless, the obscurity of his account of history helps establish a law for coinage. It suggests that money's invention was a result of a natural development of collective wisdom, especially in its interpretation of natural and divine law, rather than an arbitrary, ad hoc artifice created for the benefit of some particular party. Moreover, because the laws that emerged from this obscure history have stood the test of time, every generation should refrain from altering them in any manner.

His emphasis on the collective wisdom of monetary development reminds us that Oresme was writing at the height of an Aristotelian revival, beginning in the thirteenth century. In particular, Oresme engages with what Robert Eccleshall describes as an Aristotelian emphasis on the political society consisting of rational and "moral agents able to regulate their actions in accordance with natural law." Typical

Aristotelian arguments of the period, which Eccleshall sees as "reinforced by the Thomist clarification of natural law as the repository of an absolute justice accessible to rational agents," held that the king should govern with the aid of communal wisdom and collective interpretation of natural laws. Although such a political society might uphold monarchical rule—indeed Aquinas had sanctioned monarchy as the best form of government—it would also consider those beneath the monarch to be "sufficiently rational to engage in political activity" for the good of the commonwealth. Despite its potential for sanctioning monarchy, the Aristotelian revival "cast an element of doubt on the supposition that a communally unrestrained monarch was an adequate guarantee of the public good."[15] Moreover, this line of thinking would prompt consideration of alternatives to monarchy, especially republican theories based on the concept of popular sovereignty.

Because Aquinas was influential in his argument about the relation between natural and positive law—as well as an instigator of various arguments about what form of government should arise from this relation—it would be worthwhile to briefly review Aquinas's conception of law. In *Summa Theologica* Aquinas establishes a hierarchy of laws: the *lex aeterna* [eternal law], the law through which God acts; the *lex divina* [divine law], which, revealed by God through scripture, governs the formation of the Church; the *lex naturalis* or *ius naturale* [law of nature], law "implanted" by God so that people might understand His design and intentions; and finally the *lex humana*, *lex civilis* or *ius positivum* [the positive human law], which provides order to the commonwealth.[16] For early realist Thomists, the natural law is *intellectus*, intrinsically just and reasonable, for later nominalists it is *voluntas*, the will of God, and for those assuming a position in the middle it is both. For all mainstream Thomists, however, positive laws should always be compatible with ideas of justice according to this "implanted" natural law, and they should serve to enforce within the world (*in foro externo*) a higher law that is always already present within human conscience (*in foro interno*).[17]

In typical Thomist fashion, Oresme emphasizes that the collective wisdom of the ancients relied on perceptions of natural law. For example, he notes the logic of using gold and silver for money because of their relative rarity in nature: "Providence has ordained that man should not easily obtain gold and silver, the most suitable metals, in quantity." The reference to Providence suggests Oresme's nominalist view of the will of God found within characteristics of nature. He also sees God's/nature's hand in preventing artificial production of these metals through alchemy, practitioners of which "vainly try to outdo" the work of nature. Moreover, he finds a "natural relation in value of gold to silver" governing the bimetallic ratio, which "should be fixed, not to be arbitrarily changed, nor justly varied except for a reasonable cause and an alteration arising from the material, a thing which rarely happens."[18] Even monetary designations have their basis in natural phenomena. Oresme quotes Cassiodorus's *Variae* to demonstrate how the "ancients" produced a "rational" plan for money based on characteristics of nature. They had designated that each talent consisted of six thousand drachms,[19] each a "round shape of radiant metal, like a golden sun," in order to "correspond numerically with the age of the world." Also, the pound was equated to twelve ounces (the Roman pound) in order to correspond to the months of the year. All of the key conventions of monetary value, therefore, showed correspondence to nature. Cassiodorus ends the passage by extolling the wisdom of the ancients in their comprehension of nature: "What a wise invention! How far-seeing were our elders! It was most ingenious to devise measures for human use and at the same time symbolize so many of the secrets of nature."[20]

Oresme establishes such correspondences within natural law to assert that inventions of communal wisdom based on natural law, especially as they relate to coinage, should be fixed according to positive law: "the course and value of money in the realm should be, as it were, a law and a fixed ordinance." Given this collective establishment of monetary law and Oresme's belief that money belongs to the people by right—although they cannot transfer this right to another—it is tempting to consider money in light of *sovereignty*, especially since a concept of popular sovereignty (in defense of emergent republicanism) was being articulated within scholastic thought by Bartolus of Sassoferrato and Marsilius of Padua at the beginning of the fourteenth century.[21] These political theories partly responded to Aquinas, who had argued that monarchy was the best form of government and that although the people initially held sovereign authority over the formation of political society, they *alienated* this sovereignty—not merely delegated it—in the process of designating a ruler. Moreover since sovereignty had been alienated from the people, rulers are *legibus solutus*, that is, free from following the system of positive laws established in the community.[22] Such convictions would contribute to the development of absolutist thought.

In opposition to Aquinas, Marsilius contended in *Defensor Pacis* (1324) that "the legislator, or the primary and proper efficient cause of the law, is the people or the whole body of citizens, or the weightier part thereof, through its election or will expressed by words in the general assembly of the citizens." Even when this body of citizens "entrusts the making of it to some person or persons," that body remains the sole legislator because the entrusted people "are not and cannot be the legislator in the absolute sense, but only in a relative sense and for a particular time and in accordance with the authority of the primary legislator." Therefore, "the human authority to make laws" always belongs "only to the whole body of the citizens or to the weightier part thereof."[23] Sovereign authority ultimately rests in the people, who can remove any ruler defying their will.

Emphasis on the people as the ultimate legislator intimates Marsilius's conviction that law must remain beyond the ruler's control. At one point he argues—following the Aristotelian counsel that "no judge or ruler should be granted the discretionary power to give judgments or commands without law"—that all rulers "must be regulated by the law in judging, commanding, and executing matters of civil justice and benefit, for otherwise the ruler would not act toward his proper end, the conservation of the state."[24] Like Aristotle, he is most concerned about prioritizing a historically established, relatively fixed body of law over the discretion of a particular judge at any given time. He articulates this most effectively in the image of law as "an eye composed of many eyes," or "the considered comprehension of many comprehenders for avoiding error in civil judgments and for judging rightly." The long history of eyes and minds contributing to production of sound law makes it a "safer" basis of judgment than "the discretion of the judge" since civil judgments would then be "preserved from the ignorance and perverted emotion of the judges." A similar concern may be found in *The Politics*, when Aristotle argues that justice would more likely be found in a community regulated by rule of law determined by numerous people because there would be less chance of rule influenced by passion and desire. But in addition to emotion, Marsilius mentions the "ignorance" of judges to preclude skeptical claims that he merely mistrusts particular arbitrators. One individual or even all the individuals of an era, no matter how intelligent, could not improve on the collective wisdom of generations of investigators. Aristotle serves again as the primary source for this rationale, and Marsilius himself points to the philosopher's statement in Book I of *Rhetoric*—"'Laws are made after long study'"—in order to argue that the "making of laws requires prudence..., and prudence requires long experience, which, in turn, requires much time."[25]

Oresme's defense of a monetary law is clearly based on a similar Aristotelian rationale. For example, he also cites Aristotle's *Politics* to assert that a ruler should employ only "power regulated and limited by law and custom." However, the emphasis on law *as* custom becomes more pronounced in Oresme, perhaps because monetary practices depended primarily on custom and were not governed strictly by positive law.[26] Moreover, he is more concerned about establishing unalterable law than about providing a rationale for the notion of popular sovereignty. That is, fixity of law is more important than empowering "legislators" who had established it. Although Marsilius's distrust of designated authorities seems congruent with Oresme's concern about debasement, the stringency of Oresme's law suggests distrust even of popular will, or at least the will of a certain group of people at a given point in time. Like Marsilius, Oresme paraphrases statements from Aristotle's *Politics* on the necessity of a relatively fixed body of law, but his emphasis is more on preventing changes in law than on precluding the discretion of a particular judge at any given time: "an ancient positive law is not to be abrogated in favour of a better new law, unless there is a notable difference in their excellence, because changes of this kind lessen the authority of the laws and the respect paid them, and all the more if they are frequent." He even extends Aristotle's advice beyond the strict notion of positive law in order to conclude that "existing laws, statutes, customs or ordinances affecting the community, of whatever kind, must never be altered without evident necessity" because doing so might lead to "scandal and murmuring among the people and the risk of disobedience."[27] Oresme purposely distinguishes "customs" from "laws" to emphasize inclusion of both and adds the qualifier "of whatever kind" to support his argument that such rules should apply to coinage production.

Like advocates of common law in early seventeenth-century England, Oresme in the fourteenth century upheld a rule of law based in custom and reason in order to prevent arbitrary measures by the monarch. Although concerned particularly with coinage, Oresme's method of argument clearly engages with the political dialectic of absolute and limited monarchy at a time when the Aristotelian emphasis on collective wisdom was being used to challenge absolutist tendencies. Despite an origin based primarily in convention, the development of monetary standards assumed the status of law. The collective wisdom of numerous generations had validated the rationality of these "ancient" standards, and any deviation from them could be construed as the arbitrary act of a tyrant working against the interest of the community.

Pragmatic Morality in More's *Utopia*

However, if ancient standards of monetary value are grounded in custom and the historical experience of a particular culture, what happens when the conventions of an entirely new culture, and hence new responses to the problem of value, enter the picture? Even within the European context, laws varied across countries despite common claims that laws were all grounded in reason. In outlining the relative importance of reason and custom for common law, Glen Burgess raises the question of "how laws could differ from place to place" if reason should be "both synchronically and diachronically" immutable. One answer was offered by the seventeenth-century English jurist John Selden, for whom "all laws in generall are originally equally ancient. All were grounded upon nature, and no nation was, that out of it took not their grounds; and nature being the same in all, the beginning of all laws must be the same."

Therefore, despite being diverse, all laws are equally valid because each of them is based on reason and natural law. Diversity arose because laws of particular regions were, as Burgess describes it, "adaptations of the essence of natural law to local circumstance."[28] Of course, by "all" Selden means all *European* systems of law, but given the universal quality of "natural law," could we not extend the logic to include *non*-European systems also? Should not natural law intuited by reason be synchronically immutable across the Atlantic as well?

The question is of particular relevance for considering the European discovery of New World cultures, especially because unlike European—and even African and Asian—cultures, those of the New World tended not to use precious metals for monetary purposes. How then would this affect Oresme's argument about the rational development of customary ancient standards? Could the "local circumstance" of the New World be so different that a concept of money would be entirely absent? Could there be a rational state whose principles are grounded in natural law—even with a system of common law as in England—that nevertheless did not use money? This is exactly the thought experiment developed in *Utopia* by Thomas More, who later in his career controlled the coinage as chancellor.[29] Exploiting the absence of money in the New World, as well as in Golden Age topoi that informed New World accounts, More complicated the natural/rational conception of monetary development by describing a non-monetary economy within a rational state.

However, despite its apparent absence, the logic of money persists and even thrives within Utopia. More has difficulty thinking beyond monetary systems though his whole state seems based on the principle that private property and money can only lead to social problems. Indeed, he produces a vision of a commonwealth that debases the category of money—although it does not produce debased money for circulation—even as it depends entirely upon it. More, in effect, realized that the moral state was not possible without money. Although gold and silver are not used as currency within Utopia, they are essentially held in reserve in case they are needed for military defense. And the supply of these metals in Utopia seems unbounded. The state accumulates gold and silver through trade with other countries primarily for the purpose of hiring mercenary soldiers and bribing other nations. Moreover, despite its professed hatred of war, Utopia profits from waging war against other nations. Hythloday describes how the commonwealth has amassed great wealth by forcing enemies from past wars to pay reparations in the form of precious metals, income-generating property, and credit. They even employ financial agents or "factors" abroad to oversee their foreign investments.

Rather than appropriating from New World accounts idealistic beliefs that the withering away of the state would restore virtuous nature free from problems associated with money, More learns that money and the moral state are not necessarily inconsistent. Although it initially seems that he must negotiate between the moral commonwealth's monetary reliance and its insistence that money is immoral, he discovers in the immorality of money a source of strength. In addition to a prodigious quantity of gold and silver, the New World provided Europe with a practical way to guarantee state access to these metals: public indifference or even hostility toward them. The state could guarantee a ready supply of gold and silver by devaluing the substances in the eyes of its citizens, so that Utopian citizens would be willing to relinquish them when the state requires military funds. Thus, while the ostensible purpose of abolishing money from Utopia is the production of a moral community, the abolition has more to do with strengthening the state's financial position. That is, the debasement of gold and silver is not merely a disinterested moral position against money; rather, it serves a pragmatic purpose for the preservation of the moral state, which depends not only on immoral money but also on the very *immorality* of money.

A key to the political implications of this pragmatic solution may be found in the "Life of Lycurgus," in which Plutarch describes how the Spartan law-giver discovered a solution for rampant avarice in Sparta: he "commanded that all gold and silver coin should be called in, and that only a sort of money made of iron should be current." As a result of this plan, "at once a number of vices were banished from Lacedaemon; for who would rob another of such a coin?" Although Lycurgus did not eliminate money from the state entirely, he refashioned the system so that money was acquired for utility rather than signification of status. He thereby prevented crimes motivated by monetary greed, for "who would unjustly detain or take by force, or accept as a bribe, a thing which it was not easy to hide, nor a credit to have, nor indeed of any use to cut in pieces?" What Plutarch does not mention, however, is the benefit to the state from this appropriation of all the gold and silver in the commonwealth. He does note that the iron money "was scarcely portable" and so if the citizens "should take the means to export it," it would not "pass amongst the other Greeks, who ridiculed it." As a result it would help the balance of trade because for Spartans "there was now no more means of purchasing foreign goods and small wares...so that luxury, deprived little by little of that which fed and fomented it, wasted to nothing and died away of itself."[30] But the state *could* deploy its gold and silver extraterritorially, and so despite the fact that his plan was primarily concerned with ridding vice in Sparta, Lycurgus found a way to strengthen the state's fiscal position by eliminating competition for the accumulation of gold and silver. As a result, Sparta was at once strong and moral; indeed its strength—at least its financial strength—was a byproduct of its morality.

This example sheds light on the logic of the commonwealth's attitude toward money in More's *Utopia*.[31] But while Lycurgus merely transforms the monetary system, More ostensibly eliminates money altogether. He found the potential of a moneyless economy in other classical accounts, those of the Golden Age before the invention of money, and especially in New World accounts that had close affinities with Golden Age topoi. Let us recall *Utopia*'s connection to New World accounts. In Book I More places his characters within the context of New World exploration. The Portuguese Raphael Hythloday, "being eager to see the world, joined Amerigo Vespucci and was his constant companion in the last three of those four voyages which are now universally read of" (51/5–7). Vespucci's voyages were "universally read of" in a 1504 letter to Piero Soderini, which inspired certain characteristics of Utopia, although it is now generally considered a forgery.[32] On Vespucci's final voyage, Hythloday asks to be one of the twenty-four men "who at the farthest point of the last voyage were left behind in the fort" (51/10–11)—a detail from the Soderini letter. He recounts how after Vespucci's departure, he and his companions "began by degrees through continued meetings and civilities to ingratiate themselves with the natives till they not only stood in no danger from them but were actually on friendly terms and, moreover, were in good repute and favor with a ruler" (51/30–34). Hythloday adds that he has forgotten the natives' name and their country, but the Soderini letter provides an exact location of the twenty-four men left behind: "eighteen degrees south of the equator, and 35 degrees west of the longitude of Lisbon," which Franklin McCann locates in eastern Brazil near the present town of Diamantina.[33]

Hythloday decides to explore the region further, and on these additional travels he eventually comes upon Utopia. For their voyage the unnamed ruler supplies Hythloday and his companions with "travel resources and, moreover, with a trusty guide on their journey...to take them to other rulers with careful recommendations to their favor" (51/36–39). They pass the equator, around which lies in all directions a "gloomy and dismal region...without cultivation or attractiveness, inhabited by wild beasts and snakes or, indeed, men no less savage and harmful than are the beasts" (53/5–8), a reference to the supposedly uninhabitable "torrid zone" from zonal maps of the classical and medieval periods. But eventually as they move farther beyond the equator, the environment "assumes a milder aspect, the climate is less fierce, the ground is covered with a pleasant green herbage, and the nature of living creatures becomes less wild" (53/9–11). Eventually, Hythloday finds civilization with "peoples, cities, and towns which maintain a continual traffic by sea and land not only with each other and their neighbors but also with far-off countries" (53/11–13). Surprisingly, Hythloday mentions the dismal region as "under the equator and on both sides of the line," which suggests he passes the equator from the north. But if he indeed intended to use the Soderini letter as a reference point, he would have started out already south of the equator, and his travels would have taken him past the equator from the south. Utopia should then lie in the northern hemisphere, like England, if More had any specific location in mind for his ideal state.[34] The contradictory details constitute a deceptive move on his part to disorient the reader while subtly proving that Utopia is in fact "Noplace."

Regardless of whether More intended to locate, or dislocate, Utopia via the Soderini letter, however, he was clearly influenced by the letter's description of the territory, especially details of New World inhabitants' attitudes toward things considered valuable in Europe. The letter describes how, among the local inhabitants, "the wealth which we affect in this our Europe and elsewhere, such as gold, jewels, pearls, and other riches, they hold of no value at all; and although they have them in their lands they do not work to get them, nor do they care for them."[35] Such accounts were first used to show how New World peoples' indifference toward riches provided a moral argument against European vices; indeed, certain accounts represent local inhabitants as morally superior to Europeans. For example, the first Italian chronicler of the Columbus expeditions, known in English as Peter Martyr, recounts how the eldest son of King Comogre, a local cacique, rebuked gold hungry Spaniards, telling them of other nearby cultures that "used kitchen and other common utensils made of gold; 'for gold,' he said, 'has no more value among them than iron among you.'" And Martyr later describes how Vasco Balboa, having been presented with thirty plates of gold from a delegation of King Chiorisos, a local cacique who had sought aid against a rival cacique,

> encouraged their hopes and sent them away satisfied. In exchange for their presents he gave them some iron hatchets, which they prize more than heaps of gold. For as they have no money—that source of all evils—they do not need gold. The owner of one single hatchet feels himself richer than Crassus. These natives believe that hatchets may serve a thousand purposes of daily life, while gold is only sought to satisfy vain desires, without which one would be better off.

The comparison of useful iron hatchets to useless gold recalls the Utopians' use-based value system. Martyr's stories provided More with real-world examples of cultures that eschewed the vain allure of gold and offered the possibility for European reform.[36]

New World accounts also coded the moral superiority of New World peoples in allusions to the Golden Age, the paradisal period from which Europe had putatively fallen as described especially among the four ages in Ovid's *Metamorphoses*. Harry Levin lists common parallels between the New World and the Golden Age: relative lack of clothing and use of artifacts, lack of iron, and relatively little labor needed to produce corn because of favorable climate and soil. He argues that New World discoveries led to a revival of interest in Golden Age topoi because, whereas in earlier periods Europeans had nowhere else to look for the "cult of the simple life" than in the "inscrutable past... an expression of chronological primitivism," with the discoveries, Europe found a "manifestation of cultural primitivism" in that they could now confront "genuine primitives." Moreover, the terms of chronological primitivism were thought to be applicable to cultural primitivism as well, so texts by writers such as Ovid could help to explain the New World. In the marginalia to Martyr's *De Novo Orbe*, the Elizabethan translator Richard Eden notes, "Fables muche lyke ovide his transformations." In attempting to understand the New World, Levin argues, Europeans "could draw upon a rich backlog of fabulous lore about aborigines" in the Golden Age, and it is not surprising that allusions to Ovid were "likely to come into play, almost as if it had been touched off by a reflex action."[37] For many Europeans, the New World seemed to bring to life the wondrous world of *Metamorphoses*.

In fact, the wonder of the New World offered a stark contrast to the corruption of the Old, and some New World attributes offered models for European economic reform. For example, Golden Age topoi provided a rationale for communism, the abolition of private property, such as in Ovid's explanation of the land being subdivided during the Iron Age: "the ground, which had hitherto been a common possession like the sunlight and the air, the careful surveyor now marked out with long-drawn boundary-line."[38] Whether or not a cause-effect relationship existed between communism and virtue, there nevertheless appeared to be a strong correlation between the two in the New World. Martyr sees the absence of possession among the people of the Lucayan islands to be a key element of the Golden Age the natives inhabit: "These natives, therefore, enjoy a golden age, for they know neither *meum* nor *tuum*, that germ of all discords." Such critical commentary had a clear impact on English audiences as well. In his marginalia to Martyr's *Decades*, the translator Richard Eden calls "mine and thine the seedes of al mischeefe." Since a concept of possession helped produce many of the vices rampant in Europe, some believed that these vices would disappear with the elimination of private property.[39]

Might references to the Golden Age topoi within the New World, therefore, have influenced More's own call for political reform in *Utopia*? There is one key problem with this hypothesis: Utopia is decidedly *not* a Golden Age commonwealth. First, there is no war in the Golden Age while Utopians seem to have developed an elaborate rationale for war.[40] Second, Golden Age inhabitants need not labor while the Utopian government *regulates* the daily labor of citizens. In fact, Utopian labor replaces nature as the great provider of all necessities.[41] Labor regulation is one of many implicit laws in Utopia, which constitute another key and perhaps the most important differentiator: laws do not exist in the Golden Age. "Golden was that first age," Ovid writes, "which, with no one to compel, without a law, of its own will, kept faith and did the right. There was no fear of punishment, no threatening words were to be read on brazen tablets; no suppliant throng gazed fearfully upon its judge's face; but without defenders lived secure."[42] Because Golden Age inhabitants followed the strictures of nature, which in itself is virtuous, there was no need for laws—the presence of law signals human corruption. Indeed, for Hythloday, law frequently *contributes* to human corruption. For example, he notes that laws, which are supposed to curb vicious tendencies, are often used to benefit the rich at the expense of the poor (241/19–24). Moreover, Utopians mistrust lawyers' capacity to manipulate the law so they have banished them from the state (195/15–17).

Nevertheless, Utopia seems to be governed by a notion of common law. Like common law, the Utopian system is based in custom, developed over a long period, and thus subjected to rational consideration by several generations. Alistair Fox notes that the Utopians maintain historical records over the 1,760 years from the time of Utopus, who had not attempted "to institute a perfected state, but left Utopia in a condition to be embellished and developed through the course of future history, like the gardens of which he was so fond."[43] In order to keep laws free from abuse and simple enough so that all citizens can represent themselves in court, Utopia has "very few" laws; indeed "very few are needed for persons so educated" (195/8–9). But despite their minimal "written record" of laws, there are clear rules that Utopians must abide by or suffer punishment such as slavery.[44] Although Hythloday acknowledges that laws may support corruption, he admires the Utopians for instituting the *right* laws, those that serve to enhance virtue. Rather than do away with laws and the state altogether and return to a pure state of nature, the Utopians attempt to achieve moral perfection by instituting *pragmatic* laws that strengthen the moral state.[45]

Sir Thomas Smith criticizes More and other philosophers such as Plato and Zenophon for producing "feigned common wealths such as never was nor never shall be, vaine imaginations, phantasies of Philosophers to occupy the time and to exercise their wittes," in contrast to his own "realistic" picture of the political state of England. But the three key differences between Utopia and the Golden Age—war, labor, and laws—suggest that More also presents a realistic model of reform, a political plan of action, rather than a mere fantastic vision of an ideal commonwealth. Fox notes the enthusiasm of More's 1509 epigrams to Henry VIII as proof that he "was sincere in speculating upon the best state of a commonwealth in 1515 when almost all things still seemed possible under the mirror of Christian kings." George Logan argues that More's "realism" is "one of the ways in which *Utopia* differs from the products of most utopian writers, who assume that, once their splendid constitutions are in place, human nature will no longer present any problems." More seems rather to anticipate several potential problems and to incorporate contingencies in his structure. As what Richard Halpern calls a "product of labor, not cognition," Utopia is no mere "utopian" daydream.[46] More did not uphold the idealistic belief that the withering away of the state would return the world to virtuous nature. Rather, he chose to use the tools we had acquired after the fall— specifically the state, gold and silver—in order to produce a second best solution: the rational, sustainable moral state.

An abundance of the latter tools, gold and silver, represents not only the widest gulf between Utopia and the Golden Age but also one of the strongest links between Utopia and the New World. Ovid describes how metals were not discovered until the Iron Age, when men began to delve

> into the very bowels of the earth; and the wealth which the creator had hidden away and buried deep amidst the very Stygian shades, was brought to light, wealth that pricks men on to crime. And now baneful iron had come, and gold more baneful than iron; war came, which fights with both, and brandished in its bloody hands the clashing arms. Men lived on plunder.[47]

Hythloday alludes to the Ovidian trope in his description of Utopia: "like a most kind and indulgent mother, [Nature] has exposed to view all that is best, like air and water and earth itself, but has removed as far as possible from us all vain and unprofitable things" (151/26–29). And yet surprisingly, gold and silver, which are supposed to be "removed as far as possible," seem to be everywhere in Utopia. Despite its devaluation of the "precious" metals, or (as I suggest below) perhaps *because* of their devaluation, Utopia seems to have no shortage of them.

But the same may be said for the New World. Richard Eden, the Elizabethan translator of Peter Martyr, appears to be obsessed with his description of gold's abundance, simply writing in one marginal note, "Golde every where." The contrast between the absence of gold and silver in the Golden Age and the ubiquity of the metals in New World accounts indicates the enormous gulf between fantasies of communal return and realities (or at least realistic possibilities) of global commerce in the sixteenth century. According to various historians' estimates, from 145,000 to 165,000 tons of silver and from 2,739 to 2,846 tons of gold were shipped to Europe from the New World. Ward Barrett estimates that the Americas contributed around 70 percent of the world's output of gold and 85 percent of the world's output of silver from the discovery to 1800. The prodigious quantities of the metals imported into Europe expanded monetary economies and supported the emergence of global commerce, while also contributing to the first occurrence of inflation, which economic historians often refer to as the "price revolution."[48]

But although the material wealth from New World precious metals was by far the most important import into Europe, Europeans also brought back important knowledge about how one might obtain relatively easy access to these metals: indifference on the part of native inhabitants. Besides providing a lesson about European greed, the various accounts attesting to the natives' indifference or hostility toward gold and silver served as propaganda encouraging further exploration. The promise of gold, with very little concern by natives about its disappearance from their territories, presented a great opportunity for those interested in New World exploration and exploitation. Moreover, it suggested a way that European states might take advantage of attitudes toward gold and silver in order to guarantee a ready supply of the metals for fiscal needs. If the state could reproduce in Europe New World attitudes toward gold and silver, it would strengthen its fiscal position. More learned this lesson well in constructing his ideal commonwealth. The devaluation of gold and silver in Utopia is a way of preserving the moral state, rather than merely a disinterested moral position against money. Both "evil money" and the evil *of* money are necessary for the Utopian state.

In order to deprive the metals of their advantage and honor, the Utopians famously use gold and silver to make chamber pots and "the humblest vessels for use everywhere," while they "eat and drink from earthenware and glassware of fine workmanship but of little value," a contrast that has become emblematic of Utopia's entire value system (153/4–7). Halpern calls the ritual debasement of gold and silver "*the* quintessentially Utopian act," because it "signals the ascendancy of use value over exchange value and demonstrates that the production of goods in Utopia aims at satisfying needs rather than extracting profit." Yet the specific forms used to debase precious metals are significant in themselves: for example, the evils of gold and silver are made visceral in the form of chamberpots by associating them with excrement.[49] The metals are also used to humiliate both slaves, who are bound with gold and silver chains, and criminals, who "have gold ornaments hanging from their ears, gold rings encircling their fingers, gold chains thrown around their necks, and, as a last touch, a gold crown binding their temples" (153/8–14).[50] Instead of critiquing subjects for their reliance on precious objects, as is common in classical satire,[51] More targets the objects themselves, reevaluating the system so that the most useful materials become the most precious.

But why does More allow gold and silver even to remain in Utopia? Although the relevant question to ask about the Utopian economy would seem to be, "Why is there no money in Utopia?," we should rather ask, "Why *is* there money in Utopia?" The most telling evidence that the logic of money persists in Utopia is that despite their disdain for gold and silver, the Utopians have an extraordinary abundance of these metals—"more than would be believed," according to Raphael—and surprisingly, through *trade*, they accumulate gold and silver even beyond their natural endowment. In Ovid, Golden Age people had not yet wandered the seas: "men knew no shores except their own." It was only during the Iron Age that they embarked on maritime voyages: "Men now spread sails to the winds though the sailor as yet scarce knew them; and keels of pine which long had stood upon high mountain-sides, now leaped insolently over unknown waves." Utopia, however, is not only well aware of its geographic neighborhood but also trades surplus goods: "when they have made sufficient provision for themselves..., then they export into other countries, out of their surplus, a great quantity of grain, honey, wool, linen, timber, scarlet and purple dyestuffs, hides, wax, tallow, leather, as well as livestock" (149/5–11).[52] In exchange for these exports, Utopians "bring into their country not only such articles as they lack themselves [especially iron]...but also a great quantity of silver and gold" (149/14–16). Therefore, the Utopians, who supposedly disdain gold and silver, trade valuable commodities to acquire them.

Moreover, they have contractual promises for even more gold and silver in the future. Since the Utopians do not value the metals for everyday use, they have devised elaborate credit instruments to guarantee their financial position vis-à-vis their trading partners:

> they now care little whether they sell for ready cash or appoint a future day for payment, and in fact have by far the greatest amount out on credit. In all transactions on credit, however, they never trust private citizens but the municipal government, the legal documents being drawn up as usual. When the day for payment comes, the city collects the money due from private debtors and puts in into the treasury and enjoys the use of it until the Utopians claim payment. (149/19–28)

Although such arrangements would be unlawful in Utopia, the Utopians willingly employ legal structures of other countries to bolster their trade balance of payments.[53] Extensive involvement in these transactions suggests financial sophistication on the part of Utopians. If most Utopians do not comprehend the logic of money, how are they to understand the nature of credit? Moreover, if they place such little value on gold and silver, why are they not willing to trust private citizens to reimburse them and instead deal only with governments? Despite their eschewal of riches and basic financial instruments such as money, Utopia has become exorbitantly rich from mercantile trade while becoming quite adept at mercantilist practices.

Why do the Utopians accumulate so much gold and silver, and why have they developed financial instruments in order to guarantee access to funds in the future? Commenting on the devaluation of precious metals and the potentially divisive threat of abundant treasure in mercantilist trading, Robert Shephard calls its practices "perverse."[54] But Hythloday rationalizes the practice by claiming that "the Utopians never claim payment of most of the money" since they "think it hardly fair to take away a thing useful to other people when it is useless to themselves" (149/29–31). Nevertheless, they keep a careful watch on whoever owes them money because

> if circumstances require that they should lend some part of it to another nation, then they call in their debts—*or when they must wage war*. It is for that single purpose that they keep all the treasure they possess at home: to be their bulwark in extreme peril or in sudden emergency. (149/31–36, emphasis mine)

Here in what is almost an afterthought—"or when they must wage war"—is the rationale for Utopia's accumulation of gold and silver and for the development of credit instruments: the state needs the metals to defend the commonwealth. Meanwhile, the commonwealth needs the state to defend its citizens' moral prerogatives. Indirectly, then, money, the "root of all evil," is needed to defend the moral principles of Utopia.

The state has a pragmatic rationale for the specific repression of monetary desire: individual desire for gold and silver would compete with the state's fiscal needs. However, since any such need may quickly transform into desire, the state must conceal any evidence of its own financial requirements. For this reason, they keep the metals out in the open, rather than behind walls controlled by the state, in order to eliminate any suggestion of deception: "If in Utopia these metals were kept locked up in a tower, it might be suspected that the governor and the senate—for such is the foolish imagination of the common folk—were deceiving the people by the scheme and they themselves were deriving some benefit therefrom" (151/30–34). The state worries that its own hoarding of gold might be construed as a plot against the people. In Book I of *Utopia*, Hythloday outlines various methods not merely in the "foolish imagination of the common folk" by which European states might contrive to accumulate treasure at the expense of the populace. He imagines councilors to some king "'devising by what schemes they may heap up treasure for him'" (91/33–34). One councilor advises strategic enhancements and depreciations: raise the value of money whenever the king must pay any and lower the value of money whenever he is to receive any (91/34–36). Another councilor suggests pursuing a fake war to raise funds and then declaring peace, with a great show of compassion in not shedding human blood after the funds have been raised (91/39–93/4).

Revelation of such devious schemes justifies the people's concern that the king may plot against them to accumulate treasure, and thirty years after *Utopia* was written, Henry VIII offered a real world example, which I discuss in the next chapter. Hythloday gives a counterexample of a virtuous king who institutes a policy to guarantee against royal accumulation of excessive treasure at the people's expense. The king of the Macarians, Hythloday informs,

> "on the day he first enters into office, is bound by an oath at solemn sacrifices that he will never have at one time in his coffer more than a thousand pounds of gold or its equivalent in silver...He saw that this treasure would be sufficient for the king to put down rebellion and for his kingdom to meet hostile invasions. It was not large enough, however, to tempt him to encroach on the possessions of others." (97/18–28)

The Utopian state similarly worries that if it accumulates too much gold and silver, the people may suspect monetary desire on its part. But instituting a policy such as the King of the Macarians' would still grant internal value to gold and silver. Therefore, the state must not only repress citizens' desire for gold and silver but also repress any potential perception of its *own* intention as desire, even limited desire, for the metals.

Moreover, the particular forms the metals take—chamberpots, slave chains, and stigmatized ornaments for criminals—assure easy access to them when needed. Since the state maintains control over slave chains and ornaments for criminals, they can appropriate them for war funds and provide suitable replacements. However, households maintain some of the metal, which must assume a form to which householders will not become attached. If, Raphael supposes, gold and silver were used as in Europe for "drinking vessels and other such skillful handiwork, then if occasion arose for them all to be melted down again and applied to the pay of soldiers, [the Utopians] realize that people would be unwilling to be deprived of what they had once begun to treasure" (151/34–38). Halpern points out that despite the inconvenience of their seizure, chamber pots and especially chains on slaves "occupy a low rung on a scale of invidious differences and thus are expendable in the end."[55] The state finds a brilliant solution to the dilemma: store gold and silver in particular forms that will not be missed if they must be reclaimed.

In addition to serving moral ends—the devaluation of gold and silver in order to sap the "root of all evil" of its vigor—keeping the metals in these forms, out in the open, also serves a *pragmatic* function: it guarantees a ready supply of money in case of war. In *The Discourses*, Machiavelli describes the ease of maintaining a state when the masses are uncorrupt, by which he means that they voluntarily pay their appropriate share of taxes. He provides two examples of "goodness," both involving proffered money. In the first example, a ruler (Camillus) vows to give one tenth of the booty taken from an enemy town (Veientes) to Apollo. But the booty is seized individually by the plebians. Therefore, the senate passes an edict that everyone should bring the state one tenth of what they had seized. Machiavelli concludes that the edict showed how much trust the senate had in the "goodness of the plebs [and especially their 'respect for religion'] in that it felt sure that no one would fail to bring forth immediately all that the edict prescribed." In the second example, Machiavelli mentions certain republics that, when they require tax revenues, ask its inhabitants to pay one or two percent of their property value. The taxpayer takes an oath to pay the appropriate sum and puts it into a chest: the only witness to the act is the taxpayer. Machiavelli sees this as

> an indication of how much goodness and how much respect for religion there still is in such men; for presumably each pays the correct sum, since, if he did not do so, the tax would not bring in the amount estimated on the basis of previous collections made in the customary way, and failure to realize it would reveal any fraud, and in that case some other method of collecting the tax would have been adopted.[56]

Subjects who are "good" or have "respect for religion" are more likely to pay their fair share of taxes than the subjects of countless "corrupt" commonwealths. One would think that virtuous Utopians would resemble the dutiful taxpayers in Machiavelli's examples, but More remains distrustful of individual temptation. Therefore, rather than depend on the inherent goodness of its subjects, the Utopian state in effect institutionalizes "virtuous" taxpaying by regulating its citizens' attitudes toward gold and silver. The subjects do not realize that they are, in fact, paying taxes when the state appropriates these worthless objects for their defense, but a tax system nonetheless inheres in Utopia.

When the gold and silver is reclaimed, the Utopian state uses it to wage war against enemies, which is the "single purpose that they keep all the treasure they possess at home: to be their bulwark in extreme peril or in sudden emergency" (149/33–36). The abundance of precious metals in Utopia follows Crassus's dictum, cited by Hythloday in Book I, that "'no amount of gold is enough for the ruler who has to keep an army'" (93/38–39). But rather than describing the war funds as keeping an army *with* money, the state seems to employ money itself to fight its wars, both in bribery and in the hiring of mercenaries. They realize that "by large sums of money even their enemies themselves may be bought and sold or set to fight one another either by treachery or by open warfare" (151/1–3). The first line of defense is an attempt to distribute placards promising "huge rewards to anyone who will kill the enemy king" and "smaller sums, but those considerable, for the heads of the individuals... whom, next to the king himself, they regard as responsible for the hostile measures taken against them" (203/39–205/5). The strategy relies on the non-Utopians' avarice, which creates distrust in the enemies, who "suspect all outsiders and, in addition, neither trust nor are loyal to one another" (205/10–11). Money thereby becomes a powerful weapon for creating dissent within enemy territory. If this strategy is insufficient, they undertake a second line of defense, offering monetary support to their enemy's neighbors for reclaiming historically disputed territory. They try to "stir up and involve the neighbors of their enemies by reviving some forgotten claims to dominion," promising their assistance, especially by "supply[ing] money liberally," though they "are very chary of sending their own citizens" (205/36–207/1). While Raphael calls the first strategy of offering rewards for the enemy leaders "bidding for and purchasing an enemy" (205/22), the latter strategy of supplying money for neighbors to fight the enemy might be called "bidding for and purchasing an ally."[57]

The Utopians seem to wage war frequently despite the fact that they see it "as an activity fit only for beasts" and "regard [it] with utter loathing" (199/37–38). Hythloday describes several reasons for going to war including protection of themselves or allies; freeing a people from tyranny; acquisition of colonies when land is needed and foreign land is not being used properly; and vengeance for prior injuries to allies, including financial injuries to the ally's merchants (201/5–20).[58] However, an implicit reason why Utopians wage war so frequently is that they profit from it: war is generally a good investment for Utopia. Although it requires a great outlay of funds for mercenaries and plots against enemy governments, war also presents a substantial source of monetary income since the Utopians make the "conquered" pay for all incurred expenses:

> they make them not only pay money, which they lay aside for similar warlike purposes, but also surrender estates, from which they may enjoy forever a large annual income. In many countries they have such revenues which, coming little by little from various sources, have

grown to the sum of over seven hundred thousand ducats a year. To these estates they dispatch some of their own citizens under the title of Financial Agents to live there in great style and to play the part of magnates. Yet much is left over to put into the public treasury, unless they prefer to give the conquered nation credit. (215/26–35)

Utopians, who purportedly despise both money and war, have profited so much from past wars that they have accumulated a great amount of wealth held in gold, property income, and credit. Moreover, their own citizens, who supposedly have no conception of money, become "Financial Agents" to oversee their investments in the war industry. And although they live very modestly in Utopia, they have the chance to live "in great style" abroad.

For a commonwealth that allegedly rejects money, Utopia has developed a strong and elaborate financial position with respect to other commonwealths. A passage from *A Discourse of the Common Weal of this Realm of England* provides a rationale for a country to establish such financial strength. The doctor in *Discourse* notes that if England

> alone should cast away our gold and silver because of the harm that comes...and other countries should retain them still, we should weaken ourselves and strengthen them much. Though it be commendable in some private man for contemplation's sake to set aside as much as he may well use of money, it is not necessary for the Commonweal that all men should do so, no more than for all men to be virgins though privately in some it is very commendable.[59]

More's resolution to this dilemma is to have *all* private men in Utopia eschew the use of money while agents of the state retain access to gold and silver in order to defend the commonwealth. His solution permits a "commendable" life for the citizens while establishing the necessary defense for this way of life. In effect, the morality of the state, at least in terms of its employment of "evil" money, gets sacrificed for the morality of individual citizens. And yet the more "commendable" the life of its citizens, the stronger is the state. Maintenance of the moral state depends on the state's financial strength, which in turn depends on the morality of its citizens, who must lack desire for gold and silver. Conversely, by devaluing gold and silver, the state can guarantee ready access to exorbitant supplies of them, and by having access to the gold and silver, the state can maintain its moral program. The moral lesson that the New World offered to More may be read and has often *been* read as a virtue in itself from eschewing riches. But there is also a pragmatic element to this morality: by eschewing riches, New World inhabitants leave all the gold and silver to Europeans. In a similar vein, if the Utopian citizens are indifferent or hostile toward gold and silver, the Utopian state guarantees easy access to the metals. The Utopian state, in effect, colonizes its own citizens.

What an appealing prospect for a state: to strengthen its financial position *and* increase the virtue of subjects! Lessons from the New World offered European states a new perspective on monetary value. In response to Oresme's argument that monetary value is rational and natural, More utilized New World experience to present a convincing case that it was merely an arbitrary convention that, in fact, constituted a danger to public morality. However, convincing the European public of this new perspective was another matter. As we will see in the next chapter, by its stark contrast to contemporary England, *Utopia* also reveals how powerful this customary notion of intrinsic value had become, too powerful indeed to be negated by rational argument. That is, although *Utopia* refutes the intrinsic value theory of money, it nevertheless exposes (by its divergence from Henry VIII's England in particular) the inability of the state to control the *demand* side of the money equation despite its monopoly on *supply*. While More's text offers a fantasy of fiscal abundance within a moral state for Henry VIII, it also sheds light on the very problems the king experienced as a result of debasement. Although Henry could transform the coinage, he could not impose a new system of value in England. In fact, this problem of value explains why Henry's state had to carry out devaluation in secrecy in contrast to the Utopian state that left its gold and silver out in the open so that its citizens would not suspect the state's own desire for these resources. Neither the real nor fictional state employed transparency, but the Utopian state presented at least an *illusion* of transparency.

In order to understand "the economy of state," we should, therefore, consider not only material factors within the economy (e.g., taxes, fiscal spending) but also representational factors (e.g., cultural attitudes toward money). Alistair Fox notes that at the same time that More "created an image of the happiest world in which men might live, he subjected it to a penetrating critique, in which he contemplated the frustration of his own utopianism."[60] Although Fox's comment is concerned with More's pessimism about human behavior, it also points to the difficulty of instituting a new system of value by transforming representations of money. The New World example had suggested to More how representation may have a direct impact on material distribution. Because New World inhabitants seemed indifferent to the gold and silver the Europeans so desired—that is, the metals had very different cultural representations—an enormous quantity of these metals was redistributed by global commerce throughout Europe and Asia. More recreated this cultural discrepancy in Utopia, which explains why money at once exists and does not exist in the commonwealth. The Utopian state can regulate representations of gold and silver in order to guarantee access to the material resources when needed. So while early modern money was itself a vital technology of state in addition to being an important tool for commerce, state *representations* of money constituted another essential component of this technology. In the next chapter I demonstrate that the power and persistence of these representations explain why Henry's debasement was a failure and why subsequent monarchs generally refused to even broach the subject of reducing the quantity of precious metal in their coinage.

Chapter III

The Great Debasement and Its Aftermath

Between 1544 and 1551 Henry VIII and Edward VI systematically debased the currency—replaced precious metal content of coins with base metals—for the sake of fiscal profit. With rapid population growth in the early sixteenth century straining the money supply, and with his military endeavors in France, Scotland, and Ireland producing fiscal pressure, Henry turned to exploitation of his coinage after he had already exhausted the bounteous resources he had acquired from the dissolution of the monasteries.[1] Debasement had been common and quite severe throughout much of medieval Europe, especially in France, but it had been essentially nonexistent in England from the thirteenth to the sixteenth century. For approximately 400 years, England had maintained 92.5 percent purity for sterling, but with Henry's debasement, the purity of coins gradually dropped to 75 percent, then to 50 percent, to 33 percent, and finally to 25 percent. A 1551 issue under Edward VI contained only 17 percent of the silver contained in pre-debasement issues.[2] As a result, the earlier prestige of English coin, which at times had been the envy of northern Europe, quickly disintegrated over a brief period.

Public response, once the debasement was recognized, demonstrated the continuing importance of the intrinsic value theory of money despite More's implicit argument that coinage values and standards were merely conventional, which provided an ostensible rationale for a state to issue coinage of whatever quality. Unlike *Utopia*, however, Henry could not transform public perceptions of gold and silver, and thus his experience ultimately exposed the English state's lack of monetary control. Moreover, fears of associating their coinage policies with Henry's debasement would force subsequent rulers to adopt a new conception of the relation between coinage and royal prerogative, to uphold customary laws of coinage standards and prevent any deviations from such standards with immediate reform. Even James I, who otherwise promoted an absolutist political agenda, understood that the coinage must be protected if he wanted to maintain peace and stability within England and avoid associations with a decadent Rome, which had debased its currency, leading many to believe the debasement had caused its fall. The persistence of the intrinsic value theory and its implications for coinage standards would serve to limit state power within a rapidly expanding commercial economy.

THE TRAUMA OF DEBASEMENT

The "great debasement" brought to an abrupt end a period of approximately four hundred years during which English currency had become the envy of other European states.[3] Continental currencies—especially those of France, Spain, and various states within modern Netherlands, Italy, and Germany—experienced frequent debasements and resulting depreciations, or reductions in value relative to other currencies.[4] Once other countries understood that the level of precious metal in the countries' currencies had decreased, its value immediately declined. Rulers resorted to debasement usually to fund military endeavors when other funds could not be obtained. In effect, debasement constituted a tax on all subjects that could be collected quite rapidly, even in the face of political opposition or rebellion.[5] For the most part, England had eschewed this drastic measure and instead become—and remained so for several centuries—a model of stability made evident in the reputation of "sterling."

As with other countries, there had been gradual reductions in *weight* for English coins. From the thirteenth to the fifteenth centuries the English penny was reduced by a fifth or sixth of its weight with each recoinage, every two generations or so. However, such weight reductions corresponded to the general wear and tear typical of coins, which even without clipping or other methods of extracting precious metal could be substantial, plus the extra costs of recoinage, which kings typically refused to subsidize.[6] By the later Middle Ages the pound sterling, initially equivalent to a Roman pound in weight of sterling silver, was gradually reduced to approximately half as much silver so that the "pound" measure of currency became divorced from the "pound" measure of weight. While a pound of sterling silver had originally produced around 240 to 243 pennies, approximately 450 pennies were minted by 1464. Nevertheless, such transformations should be put into context of the rest of Europe, since the currencies of all other European countries saw much larger reductions in precious metal content.[7]

Most importantly, English kings usually never profited from recoinages, other than collecting fixed fees from moneyers for the right to produce new currency. They would instead rely on direct taxation granted by parliament and customs revenues, especially from the wool trade. One problem with this system was that coins tended to circulate in England much longer than typical coins on the continent, so they deteriorated considerably by the time they were recoined. Recoinages at cost would not permit the king to offer a "mint price" (the price in terms of newly minted coins in exchange for bullion brought to the mint) much higher than face value, so there was little incentive for subjects to turn old coins in for new ones. There was more incentive to clip heavy older coins—even though clipping was illegal—so that they matched the weight of the new coins, and to keep the gold or silver clippings as personal profit.[8]

Because of the frequency of debasement on the continent, rumors of debasement sometimes surfaced in England also, despite its reputation for high-quality coin. For example, the English public believed coinage weight reductions from 1344 to 1351 to be the beginning of a much larger debasement rather than merely a reflection of rising bullion costs. As a result, in 1352 Edward III cooperated with parliament on issuing the Statute of Purveyors, which stated that coinage standards could be changed in the future only by acts of parliament, and that any reduction should be restored to its "ancient" state as quickly as possible.[9] Nicholas Mayhew finds that during the events leading up to the Statute of Purveyors, parliament's interest in coinage, which had been a royal privilege since Anglo-Saxon times, "marks a milestone in the evolving relationship between king and Parliament." After this date, the House of Commons "spoke increasingly freely on the subject," debating monetary policy in 1381 and causing a delay in Henry IV's recoinage to adjust for rising bullion prices.[10]

Nevertheless, parliament recognized the need for occasional coinage adjustments due to changing international market conditions. So when in 1526 Cardinal Wolsey, at the direction of Henry VIII, ordered mint authorities to reduce the metal content of gold coins by 10 percent and of silver coins by 11 percent, in order to make the coinage standards equivalent to those of foreign countries, not many were surprised because such devaluations had been common since the thirteenth century.[11] They recognized that Henry was merely responding to similar reductions in silver coins of France and Burgundy.[12] In fact, Henry publicly justified the weight reduction by claiming that the higher value of English money induced people to bring money out of the realm. Only by lowering the intrinsic value of the coinage to that of continental coins would he be able to deter money exporters.[13] However, his subsequent introduction of a new coinage of gold crowns only 22 carats pure was "innovative" and perhaps should have sparked concern for future such changes. Although changing the weight of English coins was not new, reducing their purity was. Nevertheless, because the purity of this new gold coin was not kept secret, the coins did not cause much of a stir.

The "great debasement" of the 1540s was something quite different. While previous changes in weight for coins had been publicly announced, usually following parliamentary debate and approval after the Statute of Purveyors, the 1540s debasement was executed secretively. Although there is no direct evidence that Henry was *personally* involved in the debasement, a letter in September 1545 from one of his two principal secretaries of state, Thomas Wriothesley, declares about the debasement, "That office hath marvellously served the King's Majesty." In the same letter Wriothesley advises the teller of the Bristol Mint, James Paget, to keep all information about the mint to himself: "for if it should come out that men's things coming thither be thus employed, it would make them withdraw and so bring a lack," that is, the public would refuse to bring to the mint new bullion, which was necessary for the new coinage to be produced, if they knew what was being done. Wriothesley does seem to express some regret about the scheme—"God help us; for, for mine own part, it maketh me weary of my life"—but apparently not enough to prevent the extortion of the public.[14] Glyn Davies concludes that the debasement "became literally a *hidden* form of taxation from its inception," and Mayhew suggests that "any public debate [in parliament] would certainly have exposed its fraudulent nature."[15] In direct violation of the Statute of Purveyors, Henry and/or his officials had, without parliamentary approval, arbitrarily levied on the general public a tax that they would only gradually come to realize, once the surface of the new coins had worn off to reveal base metal, usually brass.

Technically the first "experiment" in debasement was an Irish harp produced in 1536 with only around 90 percent of the silver in equivalent English coins. Members of the English army in Ireland were among the first to receive these coins.[16] With little stir from this pilot project, the mint produced another Irish coin in 1540, which was only 75.8 percent pure in contrast to the 92.5 percent purity of sterling. In 1542, a similar English version was produced. Initially, neither of these two latter coins was introduced into public circulation—they were being held by the king's officers, who prevented any information leak about the issue to the public.[17] The coins were primarily made of copper alloy (usually brass) and after 1546 were "blanched" or given a thin silver coating to hide the material underneath. While silver coins eventually became severely debased, gold coins remained close to their original purity throughout the period.[18]

The initial debased English coins were finally released in May 1544 to an unsuspecting public. The public may have caught on quickly because of the high mint prices needed to bring in a sufficient quantity of bullion.

Moreover, those who exchanged large quantities of bullion for the new coins likely understood the extent of the fraud by assaying some samples. Nevertheless, the initial debasement proved a moderate success and, therefore, induced further debasement. In order to produce sufficient output, the mint needed more bullion, and the only way to get it was by increasing mint price. However, financing an increase in the mint price required coins being exchanged for the new bullion to have even less precious metal content. Therefore, after the initial reduction in purity of 1544, three further reductions—in 1545, 1546, and 1549—were made for the gold coinage alone. Eventually the public stopped financing the government's endeavor, and the mint had to find other means of bringing in bullion, including recoinage of some of the already debased coins, manipulation of bimetallic ratios, and special deals with continental bankers and mines.[19]

Between 1544 and 1551 Henry and his son netted £1.27 million from debasement, a profit higher than from either taxation or the dissolution of the monasteries (each netting approximately £1 million over the same period). Of course, given Henry's notorious profligacy the money was rapidly spent.[20] From this exercise, the crown appropriated approximately half of all the base silver coins produced or about 10 percent of gross domestic product. For this reason, Mayhew declares that the debasement "remains the single greatest fraud deliberately carried out by any English government on its own people," and the "trauma scarred the collective memory for generations to come." In a 1626 speech before parliament on a proposed depreciation, Sir Robert Cotton demonstrated that memories of the event lingered: "When *Hen.* the 8. had gained as much of power and glory abroad, of love and obedience at home, as ever any; he suffered Shipwrack of all upon this Rock," by which he means the debasement. Davies concludes that the "public never forgot the lesson and subsequently, until the coming of modern paper money, never allowed the monarchy to profit substantially again through debasement or reform."[21]

The debasement clearly transformed public perception of the king's stamp as guarantor of value. Once the debasement was publicly known, the English state literally had to force subjects to use its coins. During the reign of Mary in 1556, Henry Machyn describes a proclamation of December 23, stating

> that watt man somover thay be that doysse forsake testorns and do not take them for vjd. a pesse for corne or vetelles or any odur thinges or ware, that they to be taken and browth a-for the mayre or shreyff, baylle, justus a pesse, or constabulle, or odur offesers, and thay to ley them in presun tyll the quen [Mary] and her consell, and thay to remayn [at] ther plesur, and to stand boyth body and goodes at her grace('s) plesur.[22]

The situation had apparently gotten so bad that the queen herself had to become directly involved in enforcing continued use of testoons at their nominal value for common transactions. Rather than representing the state's guarantee that the coins contained a given quantity of precious metal, the stamp now signified a legal value imposed upon the public with the threat of state violence. This case offers clear evidence that both intrinsic and extrinsic value theories were operative in the period, although in this particular instance extrinsic value had to be coerced through legal channels. Indeed, the only factor making the coins a suitable medium of exchange was this threat of legal action. Moreover, in addition to damaging money's dependability as a medium of exchange, debasement destroyed its role as a store of value. In 1551 the Clerk of the Council, in a meeting about coin reform, said that people "esteem [the current money] so little that they will employ it to great disadvantage rather than keep it."[23] Those who held coins wanted to spend them as soon as possible, believing they would decrease in value, while others refused to accept the coins at face value.

The economic consequences were recognized almost immediately, for example, in *A Discourse of the Common Weal of This Realm of England* (written in 1549 but first printed in 1581), whose authorship remains under dispute but which several scholars have attributed to Sir Thomas Smith.[24] In the third dialogue, a knight, a merchant, and a learned doctor are trying to explain a recent dearth in most commodities. The merchant initially blames foreigners, who have driven up relative prices of commodities: "as we now sell dearer all things than we were wont, so we buy dearer all things of strangers. And therefore let them put the matter from them there; we disburden ourselves of this fault." However, the doctor responds that there must be a reason "why they sell their wares dearer now than they were wont to do." The merchant realizes that because of debasement, English coin has depreciated so that foreign merchants require more coin for their products than previously, "saying they cared not what names we would give our coins, they would consider the quantity and right value of it that they were esteemed at everywhere through the world." The doctor concurs, rhetorically asking, "why should they not esteem our coin after the quantity and value of the substance thereof, both after the rate it was esteemed among us and also every other where?"[25] Foreign merchants should not be blamed for the dearth because commodity price increases were merely a response to the deterioration of the English coin.

Henry should not have been surprised to see the reputation of English coin suffer so quickly abroad. Foreign exchange markets kept careful watch on intrinsic values of circulating coins, especially because of the history of debasement in Europe, so Henry's scheme led to an immediate drop in the value of the pound.[26] Sir Robert Cotton later noted that "it is not in the power of any State to raise the price of their own, but the value that their Neighbour Princes acceptance sets upon them." On January 18, 1551, William Lane wrote to Cecil: "The exchange as well for flandars, france as spaine amonge the mercha[n]tes is fallyn abowte vij in C [7%] by Resonn of the newys of the new quyne commi[n]ge furthe." Even Englishmen abroad did not want to be paid in sterling. In 1546, Stephen Vaughan, the royal agent in Antwerp, wrote to Lord Cobham:

> if ye send me any money, let it not be neither in new crowns nor new angels, for I can put neither of both away without great loss. I have much money even now to be paid here for the king, and I would fain have you send it me in such money as I may pay again, or else I must take up so much by exchange here to great loss, the exchange going now very evil.

Mayhew notes the irony in Vaughan's complaint since he served as the undertreasurer of one of the mints used for the debasement and so was personally involved in the endeavor.[27]

The knight in the *Discourse*, therefore, understands that if the fault is not in foreign merchants, "it must be in the coin and consequently in the King's Highness by whose commandment the same was altered." Interestingly, at this point when the author could directly criticize the king, he retreats from this conclusion; instead the doctor attributes the debasement to a mistaken notion by the king's counselors, an approach reminiscent of the evil counselors blamed for the failings of usurped kings such as Edward II and Richard II. He uses a medical analogy to excuse both the current king Edward VI and his father:

> As a man that intends to heal another by medicine that he thinks good, though it prove otherwise, is not much to be blamed, no more is the King's Majesty in no wise, in whose time this was not done, nor His Highness' father, which is not to be supposed to have intended thereby no loss but rather commodity to himself and his subjects, to be herein reprehended albeit the thing succeeded beside the purpose.

Surprisingly, the doctor interprets Henry VIII's intention to have been for the "commodity to himself *and his subjects*." He compares the debasement to bad medicine that was initially thought beneficial to the body politic. Nevertheless, the author seems hesitant to make public his own diagnosis and prescription for the problem. In response to the knight's exhortation for the doctor to let his solution be publicly known, the Doctor proclaims, "It is dangerous to meddle in the King's matters and specially if it may have any likelihood to diminish his profit."[28]

While the author of the *Discourse* avoids blaming Henry and Edward directly by pointing to the bad medicine advised by inept counselors, other writers of the period instead insult Henry's coins, especially those bearing his image. In his epigram "Of Brasse," John Heywood jokes about how

> brasse is waxen proude
> Because brasse so much with Silver is aloude.
> And being both joynde, sins they most by brasse stande,
> That maketh Brasse bolde, to stand on the upper hande.

More pointedly, in his epigram "Of redde Testons," Heywood decries such "testons [that] looke redde," because of the dominance of brass within the coins, which is "a tooken of grace: they blushe for shame."[29] The testoon was an informal name for the shilling coin introduced by Henry VII toward the end of his reign. The name derived from the Italian *testone* [headpiece]—a coin introduced in Milan in 1474—because it was one of the first coins to bear a realistic portrait of the king rather than a conventional, idealized version.[30] Henry VIII's own testoons displayed a prominent and unflattering profile of the king with a large nose (see figure 3.1 at www.stephendeng.com). When the surface silver on Henry's debased testoons wore off, the red nose showing through produced a new nickname for the king: "old copper-nose."[31] Attacking the coins was a way to criticize the king indirectly. However, some commentators persisted in deflecting responsibility from Henry, blaming instead those who had produced the coins for making the king look bad. For example, William Camden recounts how one "*Sir John Rainsford* meeting Parson *Brocke*, the principall deviser of the Copper Coine, threatned him to breake his head, for that hee had made his Soveraigne Lord the most beautifull Prince King *Henry* with a redded and copper nose."[32] In the next chapter I return to this discussion of how the representation of Henry's "redded" or "bloody" noses—criticism of the coins as criticism of the state—was employed to condemn the hypocrisy of a state attempting to prevent counterfeiting and other coining crimes.

In order to restore England's reputation abroad, as well as to curb economic problems at home, Elizabeth quickly instituted coin reform. Upon assuming the throne, the queen, who, according to Sir Robert Cotton, "was happy in Council to amend that Error of her Father," formed a commission of four men—Sir Edmund Peckham and Sir Thomas Stanley (the two masters of the mint), Sir William Cecil, and Sir Thomas Smith (the likely author of *Discourse*)—to gather thoughts and opinions on reform.[33] C. E. Challis estimates the value of base coinage that Elizabeth had to cope with to be £1,065,083. On September 27, 1560 the queen proclaimed, "nothing is so grevous, ne likely to disturbe and decaye the state and good order of this Realme, as the suffraunce of the base monies...to be so aboundantly currant within this Realme, which have ben coined in the same, before her Majestys raigne, and no parte sence." She, therefore, announced devaluation of the debased coinage and plans for producing "fine monies," giving as reasons not only the "impoverish[ment]" of various parties within England, the motivation to counterfeit English coin abroad, and the problems of inflation, but also the fact that "the auncient and singuler honour and estimacion, which this Realme of Englande had beyonde all other, by plentye of monies, of golde, and silver, onely fine and not base, is hereby decayed and vanished away."[34] Between September 27 and October 9 of 1560, Elizabeth issued a series of proclamations articulating the state's plans to depreciate and call in old money in order to recoin new and admonished the public that exporting or melting coins would carry a severe penalty.[35]

The ruthless extent of devaluation reduced the old coins' value below mint price of new issues and, therefore, made it profitable to remint new coin. This was, in fact, the reform recommendation mentioned in *Discourse*. In a section included in the original 1549 manuscript but excluded from the 1581 printed edition, which instead incorporated a shorter section without a specific plan (presumably because the measure had already been carried out), the doctor recommends that

> all the coin now current should be, after a certain day, not current but as men list to take them after the estimation of the stuff; and the old coin, or new, after like value and quantity and names to be only from thence current; and so the coin thoroughly restored to the old rate, goodness, and value.

Cotton attests to having read in "a Memorial of the Lord Treasurer *Burleigh's* hand" that Burleigh and Sir Thomas Smith advised Elizabeth "that it was the honour of her Crown, and the true wealth of her Self and People, to reduce the Standard to the antient parity, and purity of her great Grandfather, King *Edw.* 4."[36] However, the restoration of the standard was not accomplished at the queen's expense. The public, especially the lower sort, subsidized the recoinage through the loss in value of their current holdings.[37] But despite the immediate detrimental effects on subjects, most commentators understood that the measure would benefit the entire country in the long term.

And yet Elizabeth's privy council discovered that subjects remained suspicious about the state's intentions in ordering devaluation and recoinage. One observer commented, "The crying down of the money made great dearth and in many places the people would not sell for money, but upon trust because they knew not the certainty of the fall, and in many places the price of things was double increased."[38] A series of proclamations attempted to reassure the public. In order for the public to make sense of the different coins circulating, Elizabeth ordered the debased testoons to be countermarked with a greyhound mark behind the king's head and the newer, better coin to display a portcullis in the front. In an adroit public relations maneuver, Elizabeth herself visited the mint in February 1561 to strike coins.[39] By November of 1560 the English mint was once again producing coins of sterling standard (92.5 percent pure), though of lower weight than before the debasement, so that William Camden would claim that by Elizabeth's good deed "England enjoyeth as fine, or rather finer sterling silver then ever it was in this Realme by the space of two hundred yeares and more; a matter worth marking and memory."[40]

The recoinage was finished by September 1561, and the reputation of English coin abroad was soon thereafter restored. The queen even received a modest profit of £50,000 from the recoinage.[41] According to Cotton, Elizabeth had issued an edict stating "that she had conquered now that *Monster* that had so long devoured them, meaning the Variation of the Standard." Cotton adds that "so long as that said Adviser [Burleigh] lived, she never (though often by Projectors importuned) could be drawn to any shift or change in the rate of her monies." Toward the end of Elizabeth's reign a draft of a proclamation announcing the introduction of copper coins for small change boasts, "Whereas in the beginning of our reign, to the great honour and profit of us and all our people, we did restore and reduce the monies of our realm from dross and base matter unto fine gold and fine silver." Elizabeth's monument at Westminster Abbey mentions the restoration of money "to its just value" among her principal achievements, in a list that includes the defeat of the Spanish Armada and establishment of religious peace in England.[42]

DEBASEMENT AND THE LIMITS OF STATE POWER

"Experience hath taught us," Sir Robert Cotton concludes in his 1626 speech before parliament, "that the enfeebling of Coin is but a shift for a while, as drink to one in a Dropsie, to make him swell the more: But the State was never throughly cured, as we saw by *Hen.* the eighths time, and the late Queens, until the Coin was made up again." Henry's bold "experiment" caused such a public outcry against the abuse of authority that Elizabeth prioritized restoring the dignity of English coin. Despite the rhetoric of monarchical prerogative over coinage production, and despite More's case in *Utopia* for monetary value as convention, the state's power in the matter of coinage was clearly limited by public perception and belief. Ancient coinage standards had become customary law that the monarch was obliged to uphold, and any deviation from such standards had to be immediately rectified.

The main reason for this limitation on state power was the persistence of the intrinsic value theory. We find articulations of the competing theories of value shortly after the debasement. For example, the knight in *Discourse* comments that he

> cannot perceive what hindrance it should be to the realm to have this metal more than that for our coin, seeing the coin is but a token to go from man to man. And since it is stricken with the King's seal to be current, what makes it the matter what metal it be of, yea, though it were but leather or paper?

Although he assumes an extrinsic value theory, the king's stamp as the ultimate source of value with the metal itself being but a "token," the knight's questioning of why England witnessed such economic results implicitly calls attention to the value of the metal itself. To the extent that value derives from the stamp and not the material, Henry's debasement should have had no impact on the economy because the stamp remained the same: only the material had changed.[43] But the fact that the debasement did impact the economy suggests that the material still clearly mattered to the public.

Another text by Sir Thomas Smith, Elizabeth's advisor in the recoinage and the probable author of the *Discourse*, includes a more explicit articulation of tension between these two competing theories. In *De Republica Anglorum* he writes,

> The prince useth...absolute power in crying and decreeing the mony of the realme by his proclamation onely. The mony is always stamped with the p[r]inces image and title. The forme, fashion, maner, weight, finenesse, and basenesse thereof, is at the discretion of the prince. For whom should the people trust more in that matter than their prince, seeing the coine is only to certify the goodnes of the mettall and the weight, which is affirmed by the princes image and marke? But if the prince will deceave them and give them copper for silver or golde, or enhaunce his coine more than it is worth, he is deceaved himselfe, as well as he doth go about to deceave his subjectes. For in the same sorte they pay the prince his rentes and customes. And in time they will make him pay rateably or more for meate, drinke and victualles for him and his, and for their labour: which experience doth teach us nowe in our dayes to be doone in all regions.[44]

The first three sentences of this passage indicate the extrinsic value theory since the value of the coin remains at the discretion of the prince. However, the fourth sentence shows a shift to the intrinsic value theory, especially when he says, "seeing the coine is only to certify the goodnes of the mettall and the weight, which is affirmed by the princes image and marke." The rest of the passage then discusses the disastrous impact of debasement on the economy, an impact that affects the king as well as his subjects. Because of a lag in the depreciation of the currency, which would occur only when the public recognizes the quality of the new coin, the king would, in fact, initially profit from the debasement. But Smith is correct that the lingering effects after depreciation would be harmful to all, king and subject alike.

In fact, many perceived debasement as having an impact beyond the economy per se; some even considered it to be a major cause for the fall of the Roman Empire. For example, Cotton notes that "the steps by which that [Roman] State descended, were visibly known most by the gradual alteration of their Coin. And there is no surer Symptom of a Consumption in State than the corruption in money."[45] Recent historians have found some basis in the argument that Roman debasement contributed to the empire's destruction. Debasement began with Nero around 64 C.E. and gradually, over a course of two hundred years, Roman coins of pure silver were replaced with coins almost entirely composed of base metal.[46] Persistent problems especially with the silver coinage over the next few centuries ultimately led to financial instability and thus vulnerability to imminent collapse. Consequently, Glyn Davies finds as a key underlying cause of Rome's collapse the "chronic economic and financial chaos" due to debasement.[47] The warning to England is clear: to the extent that the country could fulfill its promise as the successor of Roman greatness, any attempt to reenact the Roman mistakes as well would condemn them to repeat history.

James I, who often looked back to the Roman model, clearly understood this. Because of the experience of debasement and an intrinsic value theory persistent within public belief, James refused to even broach the possibility of debasement once he assumed the throne, despite his absolutist leanings in other matters. For example, although he claims that "Kings are not onely GODS Lieutenants upon earth, and sit upon GODS throne, but even by GOD himselfe they are called Gods," James in *Basilikon Doron* ultimately advises his son to avoid debasement:

> make your money of fine Gold and Silver; causing the people be payed with substance, and not abused with number: so shall ye enrich the common-weale, and have a great treasure laid up in store, if ye fall in warres or in any straites: For the making it baser, will breed your commodity; but it is not to bee used, but at a great necessity.

James had the fortune or misfortune of having seen disastrous debasements in Scotland, thus gaining experience that may have influenced his particular aversion to the practice. But he probably also learned from rulers such as Henry VIII the lesson that debasement would have a devastating impact on his reputation in posterity. Cotton proclaimed that any deviation from the "Standard, both in purity and weight... must stick as a blemish upon Princes."[48]

And yet James's own anxiety about "experimenting" with the coin created other problems. For example, there was what Thomas Sargent and François Velde have called the "big problem of small change." A market need for coins of small denomination in order to carry out common, everyday transactions had been a problem for several years, going back at least to the thirteenth century.[49] However, production of small denomination coins was generally not profitable for monarchs, so they tended not to address this problem until absolutely necessary. Therefore, starting in the sixteenth century shopkeepers attempted to allay the problem by issuing base (mostly lead) tokens. Although the practice was technically illegal, it was not at first suppressed, and Queen Elizabeth even provided the city of Bristol with a license to issue such tokens.[50] From 1572 to 1582 Elizabeth experimented with the production of three-halfpenny and three-farthing silver coins for the purpose of being able to provide change in smaller transactions while maintaining the integrity of the coinage.[51] In *King John* Shakespeare alludes to the smaller denomination coins, which depicted a rose behind Elizabeth's profile, in Philip the Bastard's remark that his face is now so thin "That in mine ear I durst not stick a rose / Lest men should say, 'Look, where three-farthings goes!'" (1.1.141–3). However, her experiment did not fulfill all the needs of the market, so the state began to consider producing copper coinage. Many proposals were drawn up, but the unprofitability of coinage as well as the traumatic experience from a debasement consisting primarily of copper coinage prevented monarchs from taking necessary action for several years.

The shortage became especially severe in the early seventeenth century, when urban growth and increased wage labor created a greater demand for money. By 1612 there were around 3,000 unofficial minters of token coins who provided no proceeds to the crown. This development of token currency indicates the rising importance of extrinsic value theories as the public was willing to employ certain "coins" as a medium of exchange without relying on their intrinsic value as a source of wealth. James decided he needed to become involved in the business but without becoming implicated in a state-produced copper coinage. Starting in 1613 he, therefore, granted licenses to outside agents—the first being Lord Harington—to produce base tokens, with half of the profit going to the king. James had hoped to make about £35,000 from the endeavor, but by the time Harington died just six months later he had netted only £300. Charles I continued the practice of granting licenses for producing base tokens to subjects such as the Duchess of Richmond and Lord Maltravers. All such private licenses were revoked by the Commonwealth parliament in 1644.[52] Once again the "big problem of small change" loomed, so again the public took matters into its own hands. Between 1648 and 1672, many private individuals again began issuing tokens, which as John Evelyn describes, "every Tavern and Tippling-House (in the days of late Anarchy among us) presum'd to stamp and utter for immediate Exchange." Finally, giving into market demands, in 1672 the mint began to produce its own official copper coinage.[53] By this point the extrinsic value theory had become prominent enough to cause the public to accept copper coins even from a state that had previously defrauded them.

In addition to facing problems establishing a base coinage for small change, James had difficulty altering the weight of currency so that it aligned with international silver market standards, a common practice of English rulers throughout history. James was willing to lower the weight of his *gold* coinage, which he did immediately in 1604 with his new unite. The weight reduction was to curb export of English money because of a discrepancy in gold-silver value ratios between England and the continent.[54] However, he refused to do the same for silver, and this neglect created problems with silver drainage. Despite various debates on measures to solve this problem from 1612 to the 1630s, nothing was done. In 1620 an advisory committee comprised of merchants wrote that "although the abasing of the standard...is...the only way at this present to draw silver into the kingdom, yet we dare not advise to put it into practice." Mayhew concludes, "More than half a century after the Tudor debasement, the trauma of a debauched currency still influenced policy...For James VI and I the memories of a debased currency in Scotland and the inflation that it brought were more painfully recent."[55]

Even his son Charles—who was otherwise happy to flaunt his authority over parliament and who was desperate for money—suppressed proposals for reducing coinage weights. In 1626 he debated the costs and benefits of weight reduction—the debate in which Cotton participated—before deciding to seek other avenues.[56] Cotton had ultimately advised parliament, "I cannot...but assuredly conceive that this intended project of enhauncing the Coin, will trench both into the Honour, the Justice, and the Profit of my Royal Master very far."[57] Facing civil war, Charles once again in 1640 considered coinage alteration after a failed attempt to seize merchants' money at the mint. Hoping to bribe the City into giving him desperately needed loans, he announced plans to issue a coin with only 25 percent silver. The City responded by refusing the loan and asserting that city merchants would refuse to accept the proposed coinage, so Charles was ultimately forced to back down without having gained any financial resources.[58]

Stuart monarchs may also have avoided debasement or weight reduction out of fear of consequent sedition. Cotton claims that the proposed weight reduction of 1626 would have reduced the wealth of both subjects and king alike by around 10 percent, which he notes "would have been little less than a Species of that which the *Roman* Stories call *Tabellae novae*, from whence very often seditions have sprung." He mentions the particular example from Livy of Marcus Gratidianus, "who pretending in his *Consulship*, that the currant money was wasted by use, called it in, & altered the Standard, which grew so heavy and grievous to the people, as the Author saith, because no man thereby knew certainly his wealth, that it caus'd a Tumult."[59] Although there had been no material sedition or tumult as a result of Henry VIII's debasement, Cotton suggests that such a response would have been feasible within the prevailing political climate.

The experience of debasement, therefore, provides a limit case for considering the historical struggle between monarchical authority and law in England. In his speech to parliament at Whitehall, on March 21, 1609, James—after claiming that "Kings are justly called Gods, for that they exercise a manner or resemblance of Divine power upon earth" and subsequently listing the God-like powers that kings have, especially to "make and unmake their subjects,"—ends with the simile of being able "to cry up, or downe any of their subjects, as they do their money."[60] James's comparison, however, reveals that his absolutist vision remained a utopian fantasy. Just as he could not arbitrarily cry up and down his money without public unrest, neither could he for any of his subjects.

In James's native Scotland the limits of monarchical authority with respect to subjects became ingrained even in the coinage itself. After the Scots had removed Mary from the throne and made James the King of Scotland, they produced new coins called "sword dollars," which have the superscription of James VI and the arms of Scotland, conventional iconography, on the obverse side, but on the reverse side the coin depicts the crown of Scotland balanced on a sword with the inscription *"Pro-me-si-mereor-in-me."*[61] In his *Rerum Scoticorum Historia* (1582), James's tutor George Buchanan described the meaning of this inscription:

> Even in those times in which the Roman republic was oppressed by the most cruel tyranny, when by accident any virtuous man was made emperor, he considered it his highest glory to acknowledge himself inferior to the people, and liable to the empire of the law. Trajan, when, according to custom, he delivered the sword of justice to the prefect of the city, is said thus to have addressed him, Use it for me, or against me, as I shall deserve.[62]

Although James was to eventually reject Buchanan's view of limited monarchy, the coin and Buchanan's explanation nevertheless constituted a reminder that the arbitrary employment of power based on absolutist belief that the monarch is above the law—especially with respect to the coinage of the commonwealth—would not be tolerated. Indeed, as we shall see in the next chapter, metaphors of debasement would be deployed to subvert even the state's own case against counterfeiting and other coining crimes.

Chapter IV

Coining Crimes and Moral Regulation in *Measure for Measure*

In *Basilikon Doron*, the same text wherein he warns against the temptations of debasement, James also lists six "horrible crimes" that his son Henry is "bound in conscience never to forgive": witchcraft, willful murder, incest, sodomy, poisoning, and "false coin." The emblem of Ganymede in Henry Peacham's *Minerva Britanna* clearly depicts James's catalogue: the "foule Sodomitan" sits astride a cock, holding a cup "topfil'd with poison," a wand, and "Meddals, of base mettals wrought, / With sundry moneyes, counterfeit and nought." The text decodes this image as a representation of Ganymede's various crimes: while the cock signifies incest and the cup and wand allude to witchcraft and murder, by the base medals and moneys, "false coine you understand." Critics have sometimes alluded to this peculiar list in investigations of sodomy within early modern England; the fact that Ganymede commonly represents the object of homoerotic desire clearly warrants such study. But thus far little attention has been given to the unusual inclusion of "false coin" within a taxonomy that Gregory Bredbeck calls "a mythology of the unnatural, the alien, and the demonic."[1] While the term "sodomy" connotes biblical prohibition of certain acts—and similar prohibitions could be cited for poisoning, witchcraft, incest, and, of course, murder—such was not the case for counterfeiting or "coining" crimes in general. The practice was neither "unnatural," "alien," nor "demonic" in early modern England, where, as Malcolm Gaskill notes, it constituted a "mundane cottage industry."[2] As James's inclusion of the term among other "horrible crimes" suggests, coining remained a persistent cause of concern for

English monarchs, but it seemed to pose more danger to the state than it did to its practitioners' souls.

Just as James's taxonomy links coinage crimes with other biblically proscribed acts, numerous coining metaphors with clear moral implications circulated within early modern England. In one version, probably originating in early interpretations of Christ's response to the question of whether tribute should be paid to Caesar, the Christian faithful receive God's stamp, whose value they must continue to recall and treasure. In another version, stemming from Aristotle's description of procreation in *De Generatione Animalium*, offspring are compared to coins that receive a stamp from the father and the material from the mother. These two prominent metaphors, I argue, partly explain the peculiar coin imagery of Shakespeare's *Measure for Measure*, in which coining is metaphorically compared to theft, illicit procreation, and the usurpation of divine authority.[3] Drawing upon these traditional tropes, the state's representatives in the play, Duke Vincentio and Angelo, "mint" a case against coining crimes by associating them with other immoral acts.

And yet besides connoting bastardy and usurpation of God's stamp, coining metaphors in the play point to another common association with coinage: that of justice. For example, a metaphor at the start of the play compares Angelo, who will become as deputy the embodiment of justice in Vienna, to a coin stamped by the duke's commission. The question of justice is, of course, a key concern in the play, and the subsequent actions of the state's representatives call into question the state's own offenses against the coin, especially debasement. Although Angelo proves false, the duke cannot avoid the fact that it was his own legitimate stamp that has permitted his judicial substitute Angelo to perpetrate his crimes.

Moreover, the deficiency of the duke's stamp, which ostensibly guarantees the integrity of his coin/deputy, induces into action a competing "mint" that associates the state's own coining crimes with other immoral acts as well. Historically, monarchs who debased their coinage were threatened with the injurious epithet "Le Faux Monnayeur" [counterfeiter], which would recall their hypocrisy in debasing the coin while actively prosecuting counterfeiters. In *Measure for Measure*, the duke's comic foil, Lucio, despite his own deficiencies, constantly interrogates the ruler's character, and he refuses to allow the duke monopolistic control over the economy of poetic exchange that equates coining with other heinous crimes. Lucio's example demonstrates the possibility of appropriating the standard; while coining might serve as a link in a chain of cultural associations with "horrible crimes," so also might debasement. Indeed, the deficiency of the coinage described by the coin imagery indicates an inability to establish a stable measure of value for assigning terms of justice within the play. The coining metaphors in *Measure for Measure* ultimately reveal both the state's strategy of equating coining crimes with other immoral acts as well as subjects' refusal to grant the state a monopoly over the terms of justice that permit such arbitrary comparisons.

COINING AND TREASON

Historians of crime such as Malcolm Gaskill and J. A. Sharpe employ "coining," a term commonly used in the early modern period, to cover all offenses against the coin—including forgery/counterfeiting and unauthorized alteration—other than the passing or "uttering" of illegal coins, which was considered a lesser crime. While the practices of coining began as soon as coinage was introduced into England, the first statute classifying some of these offenses as treasonous was instituted in 1351 during the reign of Edward III. The statute, which states that "if a Man counterfeit the King's Great or Privy Seal, or his Money...[that] ought to be judged Treason," was established to prevent the passing of coins composed of base substances—primarily tin, copper, lead, or some combination of these such as brass or pewter (*25 Edw. III* s. 5 c. 2). False silver coins were more common than false gold ones because higher-valued gold coins drew more scrutiny, and the interior metal might more easily show through as with the counterfeit Portague (a gold coin from Portugal) shown in figure 4.1 (www.stephendeng.com).

When copper was used to imitate silver it had to be "blanched." In *Eastward Ho!* the profligate coiner Quicksilver describes how he can "blanch copper so cunningly, that it shall endure all proofs, but the test," that is, the process of assaying coins by separating base metals from precious ones. He boasts that "it shall endure malleation, it shall have the ponderosity of Luna [weight of silver], and the tenacity of Luna, by no means friable." Quicksilver proceeds to explain how the blanching process works, which "every ignorant quacksalver" has perfected:

> Take arsenic, otherwise called realga (which, indeed, is plain ratsbane). Sublime 'em three or four times, then take the sublimate of this realga, and put 'em into a glass, into chymia, and let 'em have a convenient decoction natural, four and twenty hours, and he will become perfectly fixed. Then take this fixed powder, and project him upon well-purged copper, *et habebis magisterium* [and you will have the philosopher's stone].[4]

The Latin phrase points to the similarity of such processes to alchemy; indeed substances made of base metal resembling current coins were often referred to as "alchemy," or some close etymological variant. For example, in 1558 Henry Savell, a "marchaunt" from York County, was indicted for introducing from France into Norwich 66 pieces of "'half sufferens and Inglysshe crownes' of brass, copper, alcamyne (*alcameno*) and divers other mixed metals falsely counterfeited." It is no coincidence that Subtle in Ben Jonson's *The Alchemist* also offers to his clients the service of counterfeiting.[5]

But forgery was not the only coin-related crime; later statutes and proclamations were forced to extend legislation to criminalize acts involving alteration of previously legitimate coins.[6] William Fulbecke outlines the main categories of coining offenses in the late sixteenth and early seventeenth centuries. While the first three include offenses related to forgery and the last adds the "uttering" or passing of false coin, the fourth covers another category: "When the lawful & ordinary weight of the coine is falsified, & altered by one that hath no authority to alter."[7] However, there was a diversity of practices even within this one category. In 1576 the privy council sent to the warden of the mint a commission "to searche and finde out all counterfetours of money, clippers, sherers, wasshers, or any maner of ways deminishers of her Majestys coine, or any other coine curraunt in this realme."[8] Clipping, the easiest and most common form of alteration, involved cutting gold and silver from the edges of current coins, which could be done by anyone with a pair of shears (see figure 4.2, www.stephendeng.com). "Washing," which involved removing precious metal through the use of chemicals, was, of course, more complicated. In *Eastward Ho!* Quicksilver says he can take off "twelve pence from every angel, with a kind of aquafortis, and never deface any part of the image." He then restores the coins' weight by letting them lie in "*sal alchyme*" [alchemical salt] and "distilled urine" for twenty-four hours, "and they shall have their perfect weight again."[9] More ingenious coiners could remove the metal without the use of chemicals. For example, in 1696 a coiner took "the King's Effigie from off a Half-Crown as thin as a Groat, and then scooping out 20 Pennyworth of silver, filled the vacuity with base Metal, and cemented the Effigies so close thereon again, that the most curious Eye could not perceive it was a Counterfeit." Other practices not mentioned in the letter include sweating (shaking coins together in a bag to get the gold or silver dust) and filing metal off the surface of coins.[10]

Since this diversity of practices had not been made explicitly treasonous under Edward III's statute, subsequent legislation had to account for them. Acknowledging that "great Doubt and Ambiguity hath been, whether that Clipping, Washing, and Filing of the Money of the Land, ought to be judged Treason, or not," a statute under Henry V explicitly denounced practitioners as "Traitors to the King and to the Realm" who "shall incur the Pain of Treason" (*Hen. V* s. 2. c. 6). Nevertheless, the status of such crimes remained unclear for many subjects through the reign of Elizabeth, who felt the need in a 1564 statute to reiterate the law and include foreign coins current in England:

from and after the first daye of May next coming clipping washing rownding or filing, for wicked Lucre or Gaines sake, of any the proper Moneys or Coines of this Realme or the Dominions thereof, or of the Monies or Coines of any other Realme allowed or suffredd to bee currante within this Realme or of the Dominions thereof...shalbee taken demed and adjudged by vertue of this Acte to bee Treason. (5 *Eliz.* c. 11)

But this was not the end of legal niceties under Elizabeth. Apparently, the specification of "clipping washing rownding or filing" did not cover all the possibilities for altering the queen's coin. Thus, a 1575 statute laments the fact that certain "false and evell disposed persons" believe that the law "ought to bee taken and expounded strickte according to the Woorde thereof" so that "other Artes undue Wayes and Meanes to falsifie impayre deminishe and lighten" coins would not suffer the same punishment. The statute, therefore, covers even more ground in the legislation by making it clear that

if any person or persons, of what Estate Degree or Condicion soever hee or theye bee, shall by any Arte Wayes or Meanes whatsoever, impaire deminishe falsefye skale or lighten the proper Moneys or Coignes of this Realme or any the Dominions thereof, or... of any other Realmes allowed and suffered to bee currant,

the person or persons will be deemed traitorous and suffer the pains of treason (*18 Eliz.* c. 1). It was now up the courts to decide whether suspects did indeed "impaire deminishe falsefye skale or lighten" the queen's coin in any way.

The punishment for counterfeiting or coin alteration, classified as an act of treason, was hanging, drawing, and quartering for men, and burning at the stake for women. A couple, John and Jane Chapman, having pleaded guilty and having thrown themselves at the mercy of Queen Mary, were nevertheless brought by a constable to the Tower and "thence drawn to the gallows of Tyborne," where "John should be there hanged and Jane burnt to death." The couple was, however, pardoned soon thereafter, but others were not so fortunate. In February 1603 one James Browne was "hanged and drawn" merely for making two counterfeit coins: one shilling and one half-shilling. In his diary, Henry Machyn describes a number of men in the mid sixteenth century who were "drane upon a hyrdyll unto Tyburne" for "qwynnyng [coining] of noythy [naughty] money, and deseiving of the quen['s] subjects."[11]

Why, though, were these offenses classified as treason and punished accordingly? What is the relation between the designation in Edward III's 1351 statute that "if a Man do levy War against our Lord the King in his Realm" and the subsequent condition that "if a Man counterfeit the King's...Money...it is to be understood, that in the Cases above rehearsed [that] ought to be judged Treason"? Why might the state equate raising arms against the state with merely producing two false coins?

The case of Christopher Marlowe offers a potential explanation. According to his "chamber-fellow" and later informant, Richard Baines, Marlowe had claimed "that he has as good Right to Coine as the Queen of England."[12] Both Baines and Marlowe were arrested for counterfeiting in 1592. A letter to Lord Burleigh from Robert Sidney, the younger brother of Sir Philip and governor of Flushing, describes how Marlowe, along with Baines and goldsmith Gifford Gilbert, produced several false coins, including English ones, and tried to "utter" or pass as current a Dutch shilling, which according to Sidney was of "plain pewter and with half an eye to be discovered."[13] Baines, who later wrote the infamous note accusing Marlowe of atheism and other crimes, informed Sidney about the action because he apparently "fear[ed] their success" despite the poor quality of the coins. Once brought before Sidney, Marlowe and Baines accused each other of having persuaded the goldsmith to make the false coin and of intending to practice the crime thereafter.[14] Moreover, Sidney explains that Baines and Marlowe "do also accuse one another of intent to go to the enemy, or to Rome, both as they say of malice to one another." Charles Nicholl finds a clear implication here that Baines and Marlowe accused each other of intending to join a group of "renegade English" in the Low Countries—an exile community under Hugh Owen in Brussels or an English regiment under Sir William Stanley, based near Nijmegen—or defect directly to Rome. The implication is that the two charges of counterfeiting and defecting are connected since the Catholic exiles were in dire need of money.[15] If an army lacked money, why not produce its own?

Baines's 1593 note after Marlowe's death offers another allegation of coining related to sedition. He explains how Marlowe "was acquainted with one Poole a prisoner in Newgate who hath greate Skill in mixture of mettals and having learned some thinges of him he ment through help of a Cunninge stamp maker to Coin ffrench Crownes pistoletes and English shillinges." Nicholl believes this refers to John Poole, who was known not only for coining (he was imprisoned in Newgate around 1587) but, according to his contemporary Humphrey Gunson, also for his militant Catholicism since he had once been arrested as a seminary priest.[16] So in addition to being a coiner with "greate Skill in mixture of mettals," Poole held subversive Catholic views and aided seminary priests believed to be infiltrating England. Recall that Baines had famously accused Marlowe of Catholic subversion, of having stated "that if there be any god or any good Religion, then it is in the papistes...That all protestantes are Hypocriticall asses." Whether or not Baines was telling the truth about Marlowe, his accusation relies on an imagined connection between coining and political subversion.

Another case from around 1591 similarly links coining with papist sympathy. In that year, a group stole from Winchester cathedral church plate worth about £1,800, which was later "melted and coined" at Sir Griffin Markham's place in Gray's Inn. One member of the group, Edward Bushell, had been reported as saying that "when his father was dead, he would make money of all he had, and go oversea," presumably to support the cause of Sir William Stanley with whom he sympathized. Other members of the group also had grievances against the state. In a 1592 letter to Lord Burleigh, one Henry Duffield was reported to be a "discontented man, and bitter in invectives against the state," and he was believed to be plotting to sabotage the queen's fleet at Chatham. Also, the "ringleader" of the robbery, the Welsh Catholic Richard Williams, had gone with Essex to France where he deserted to join Stanley's regiment at Nijmegen. In 1594 Williams was charged with treason and hanged for planning to assassinate the queen (apparently urged on by Sir William Stanley himself). Several members of this gang of coiners, therefore, had clear ties to Catholic causes, including the rebel Stanley.[17]

Therefore, coining might have been deemed treasonous because it permitted foreign elements to corrupt the English nation. In Chapter VI, I consider the state's concern about circulating foreign coins in light of such treasonous plots. However, most coining involved English coin forged or altered by otherwise loyal English subjects. Most coiners were not involved in external plots against the government, and it would be easy enough for the government to classify as treason only those cases where coining funded external plots. A prominent example of usurping royal prerogative without necessarily intending usurpation of the throne was the infamous York groat produced by Cardinal Wolsey, which bore his initials and an image of a cardinal's hat. Recall that Wolsey was the final ecclesiastical authority to be granted permission to produce certain coins. However, Wolsey had not been commissioned to produce this particular denomination, the groat, and his coining offense was included among the other articles of accusation he was facing at the time of his death.[18]

Cases such as that of Wolsey were exceptional, of course. In his characterization of typical coiners, Malcolm Gaskill identifies two broad categories during the early modern period: a large number of "ordinary men and women" who put themselves at great risk for small return and a very small minority that put themselves at a smaller risk for much larger profits. The latter group consisted of either the "artisan-entrepreneur of some wealth and standing" working with a small family workforce or mostly plebeian "gangs and cooperatives" that benefited from pooled risks and resources, especially "safe-houses" that could guarantee the necessary privacy. Although Marlowe's and Bushell's "gangs" could be included in the latter category, most of these "gangs and cooperatives" clearly operated primarily for personal profit and not to overthrow the state. As Gaskill notes, "What became treason in the courts was in daily life a mundane cottage industry."[19]

In fact, it might be argued that coiners, or at least counterfeiters, rather than damaging the state, provided a necessary service to England because the country frequently suffered a dearth of circulating money. As I mentioned in Chapter III, there was the frequent "big problem of small change," when no, or not enough, lower-denomination currency was produced by the state. Therefore, many stepped in by producing base tokens that could circulate within local economies, such as in transactions in taverns. Technically, this was a form of counterfeiting under coining laws, so some counterfeiters might maintain that they were merely providing the money the state itself failed to supply. Although it could ultimately lead to long-term inflation, in the short term counterfeiting provided a much needed supply of coin and even helped to increase consumer demand.[20]

It is, therefore, no surprise that there was great sympathy for coiners in contrast to general hostility toward other criminals. Fellow countrymen often commiserated with many coiners who claimed that they suffered from insufficient income. For example, the coiner Abel Feckman in 1594 told his examiner that he began counterfeiting "for want of maintenance in the time of the last great infection, being then newly married and not having work to keep himself and his family." And the couple John and Jane Chapman, who had been found guilty of coining but were later pardoned, apparently committed the crime for lack of resources. The report claimed that because John "was indebted to divers subjects of the realm in diver great sums of money," a servant had "traitorously advised Jane to counterfeit divers sums of money for the use of John with intent that John should with the money so counterfeited pay his debts." Moreover, sympathy for coiners often led to disruption in conviction and trial processes. In some cases, people would tip-off known coiners as in 1577 when a Lancashire gang of coiners were warned about a search and departed before they could be captured. During trials, some witnesses would lie about suspected coiners; John Barnes, an "alehouse keeper at Salisbury," as the esquire Richard Mompesson complained, committed "false swearing" in defense of two convicted coiners. And in 1605 Attorney General Edward Coke, writing to the earl of Salisbury, worried about a group of "poor creatures" under trial for coining being tried "in the face of the country, where they will rather be pitied than misliked for their offence." Trials of notable figures might be even more complicated. For example, in the case of Richard Franklin, we find "many notable and injurious practises...used by subornation of wittnesses" in his favor as well as the "choice of partiall jurours (as it is alleaged)...wrought and attempted by his adversaries" to his detriment. The judge was warned to ensure "the choice of an indifferent and substantiall jurie who without respect of either party may geve their verdict according to the evidence."[21]

Despite the flood of proclamations, some claimed not to even realize that clipping was illegal. In 1647 a clipper was surprised to learn about the illegality of his act "bycause the times have bene troublesome, and he never heard such thinges Questioned till now of late."[22] J. A. Sharpe notes that in several recent historical works on crime in the early modern period (such as *Albion's Fatal Tree*, *Whigs and Hunters*, and *An Ungovernable People*), there is "an underlying theme...that a number of types of behaviour regarded as illegal by the authorities were thought of as legal, or at least justifiable on quasi-legal grounds, by certain sections of the ruled." He includes coining as one such "'social crime,' illegal behaviour which many of its perpetrators, and large sections of the populace, did not regard as criminal."[23]

Therefore, authorities had to find a way to explain why coining crimes were morally wrong. Gaskill contends that it offended no key tenet of Christianity and that there were no direct biblical proscriptions against it. Deborah Valenze reasons that commoners perceived the statutes to be based on "'flawed' logic" since there were no moral justifications for the inviolability of coins, and hence the law was "exposed as the naked construct of the state." "The best the authorities could do," Gaskill concludes, "was solemnly declare the sacred status of the coin and leave it at that." Yet, as I will show, a case was indeed made against coining crimes using metaphoric comparisons to other immoral acts, especially theft and the production of illegitimate children.[24] Although the state could not cite explicit scriptural proscription of coining crimes, traditions of biblical and Aristotelian interpretation that relied on coining metaphors were employed to demonize the crimes. In the next section I argue that such metaphoric relations partly explain Shakespeare's use of coin imagery in *Measure for Measure*.

God's, King's, or Man's Stamp

Silver is the Kings stampe, man Gods stampe, and a woman is mans stampe, wee are not currant till wee passe from one man to another.

—Thomas Dekker, Northward Ho

To understand first the effectiveness of this strategy of demonizing coining through metaphor, consider an entry from the mid-seventeenth-century diary of the Puritan artisan Nehemiah Wallington. One day a customer noticed that Wallington had given him a brass shilling. Apologizing, the artisan took the false coin back and restored it to his box, "intending to pay it away another time." However, as Paul Seaver explains, the coin's mere presence in his money box "became the basis of a great moral struggle" for Wallington; possession of the coin led to a battle between spirit and flesh. He becomes anxious about the false coin's presence among his other "good" coins:

> conscience did begin to chide me and said I had a *thief* in my box, a brass shilling which will *canker* all the rest. And now the battle begins and the flesh begins to baffle me, saying that being I took it [for good coin], I may pay it away again, and a shilling loss to thee is a great matter, it is more than thou will gain in a good while, ... and many such like cavils the flesh did say to me.[25]

Wallington calls the counterfeit coin a "thief" presumably because as a worthless thing it could be accepted for and, therefore, in effect "steal" valuable goods. Moreover, he worries that the mere presence of this "thief" among his other coins would corrupt them, spreading "canker" by proximity. But it would be worse for him to pass the coin along because doing so would "be to God's dishonor, for it will cause men to say, this is your religion! Men, see how he hath cozened and deceived me!" He, therefore, decided to destroy the coin the same day "a chapman came for payment." Wallington warned him about the brass shilling among the other coins, yet "the man said that they were all very good." Seeing this as a miraculous deliverance, he subsequently destroyed three other counterfeit coins he had in his possession, two brass half crowns and a sixpence, cutting the half crowns in two and nailing the sixpence to a post. "And so," he concludes, "all this trouble was at an end: all the glory be to God."[26]

Wallington's reaction to the outcome is striking. It implies his belief that God has delivered him from sin by reforming the bad coin passed along to the chapman. Clearly, the chapman merely believed he could in turn pass the counterfeit coin without any trouble. On the surface, then, Wallington sees his deliverance as a miracle of God, but subconsciously he knows his "deliverance" is from the fact that the bad coin is no longer his concern. Nevertheless, he pays tribute for his miraculous deliverance by sacrificing three other counterfeit coins in his possession in order to justify his passing of the fourth. Significantly, the particular form the sacrifice takes mirrors the state's own punishment of traitors. Cutting the coins in half resembles the prescribed punishment for counterfeits and the symbolic punishment of counterfeiters. As I mentioned in my introduction, in 1556 Queen Mary had issued a proclamation encouraging any subject who discovered a counterfeit coin to "immediately deface or cause to be defaced, and break or cause to be broken in pieces" every such counterfeit coin before turning them over to a local justice of the peace.[27] The ostensible purpose was to make the coins unusable as currency, but cutting the coins also entailed a symbolic violence that rehearsed the ensuing physical violence, drawing and quartering, against those who produced these coins. The state's prescribed action against counterfeit coins, along with the demonization of counterfeits, had worked its way into individual moral decisions such as those of Wallington.

With such an emphasis on the immorality of coining, we can understand why James placed "false coin" among the list of "horrible crimes" that his son is "bound in conscience never to forgive." We find in statutes and especially in proclamations the language of thievery and deception that Wallington had adopted. A proclamation of Elizabeth states that the passing of lower-valued foreign coins resembling English coins had led to "the derogation of the dignity of this crown and to the manifest deceit and colorable robbery of her highness' people."[28] Implicit in this intrusion by foreign coins is a fear akin to Wallington's that the "thief" in his money box will canker all other coins. The immoral passing of coins will breed disease as punishment of wicked deeds. The statutes are filled with complaints about offenses against the coin committed "for wicked Lucre or Gaines sake," and offenders are referred to as "false and evil disposed p[er]sons."[29] By employing such terms, the statutes upheld the belief that these acts are immoral in addition to being illegal; they constitute an affront to God as well as to the king. Henry VII even modified his coins so that clippers would have to violate the word of God when practicing their craft. A statute states that all gold coins "shall have the hole scripture about ev[er]y pece of the same gold w'out takking any p[ar]te therof, to thentent that his subjettis hereaft[er] may have p[er]fite Knowledge by that...scripture when the same Coines be clipped or appaired" (*19 Henry VII* c. 5). In addition to making evident that the coin has been altered, those who clip such coins would have to cut through God's words, so that an act offensive to the king could be converted into a symbolic offense against the Lord. By stamping scripture on coins, Henry aligned his cause with God's.

In *Measure for Measure* Shakespeare exploits this theological dimension of coinage in order to explore the political implications of regulating morality. For example, in a conversation with Isabella about her brother Claudio's crime, Angelo describes the production of illegitimate children—one of the concomitant problems in a community that has relaxed its enforcement of laws established to curb rampant sexuality—in terms of the fabrication of illicit coins. In response to Isabella's request that Claudio be pardoned, Angelo declares,

> It were as good
> To pardon him that hath from nature stol'n
> A man already made, as to remit
> Their saucy sweetness that do coin heaven's image
> In stamps that are forbid. 'Tis all as easy
> Falsely to take away a life true made
> As to put metal in restrained means
> To make a false one. (2.4.42–49)

Angelo begins with a comparison between murder and the production of bastards: to take a life is, in his calculus, as immoral as producing one who should not exist. However, in the midst of establishing equivalence between two acts, Angelo slips in a metaphor that incorporates a third term for comparison: that of making a counterfeit coin.[30] While the equivalence of murder should be enough to warrant justification for punishment, the reference to counterfeiting indicates that Claudio's action also transgresses against the state in its recent attempt to police sexuality. That is, the coining metaphor is employed here to remind any potential offender that producing bastards, like counterfeiting, has been explicitly forbidden by the state. But such comparisons operate in the other direction as well, so Claudio's act of bastardy also assumes connotations of coining crimes.

Indeed, Claudio's death penalty is more appropriate to the treasonous crime of coining than to bastardy. Of course, the severity of the penalty may have been designed for dramatic effect: a threat of imprisonment would not have the same narrative impact. However, if we consider *Measure for Measure* within the context of late Elizabethan and Jacobean parliamentary initiatives for the "reformation of manners," with which the play's concerns of policing sexuality have clear resonance, Claudio's punishment stands out as conspicuously excessive. As in the play, there were late sixteenth- and early seventeenth-century calls for stricter statutory measures to regulate morality because it was believed that some local communities were letting the imposition of longstanding penalties for morally transgressive acts fall into disuse.[31] However, proposed penalties for these transgressive acts were considerably milder than in the play. According to one bill written around 1584–85, those who were reputed to have produced illegitimate children were to be imprisoned for one year, whipped monthly, and required to give bond not to reoffend; penalties of death were never employed for sexual transgressions such as bastardy during the period.[32] Not until 1650 in the Commonwealth's act "for suppressing the detestable sins of incest, adultery and fornication" did sexual crimes carry a death penalty, but only in the first two instances: incest and adultery. Fornication would be punished with three months imprisonment instead. Nevertheless, the death penalty appears never to have been imposed, and even the lighter penalty of brief imprisonment for fornication was only rarely enforced. Moreover, the act was quickly repealed during the Restoration. As Martin Ingram notes, other than this Commonwealth act that had more bark than bite, all attempts by zealots to take more extreme measures against such sexual crimes as incest, adultery, and fornication were blocked by more moderate members of parliament.[33] The laws of England were clearly not as draconian as those of Duke Vincentio's Vienna.

However, a death penalty is appropriate in the context of Elizabethan and Jacobean England once Claudio becomes designated as a counterfeiter: the coining metaphor makes the penalty fit the crime. Moreover, the coining metaphor conveys the crime's severity by suggesting that bastardy is tantamount to the appropriation of God's authority. Those who "coin heaven's image / In stamps that are forbid" usurp the King of heaven's prerogative to mint His creatures. Believers in Christ receiving "God's stamp" was a common metaphor based on biblical interpretation of early church fathers, which I discuss further below. Yet, Angelo's articulation of this tradition merges two different versions of the coining metaphor. In the first, all children, whether legitimate or illegitimate, receive God's stamp because they are made in His image. In the second, the bastard receives an illicit stamp from a man who is not the husband of the child's mother. That is, the misuse of God's stamp is, in Angelo's expression, the use of an otherwise legitimate stamp, because it came from God, for illegitimate purposes. The instability of such coining metaphors becomes clear: in various versions the legitimate stamp may belong to, or at least be in the possession of, either God, king, or man. Indeed, "legitimate" versions of all three stamps are operative within *Measure for Measure*. Moreover, the metaphor of humans receiving God's stamp allows the possibility of alteration to a previously legitimate coin. This latter aspect, in the context of the *ruler's* legitimate stamp, becomes a key crux to which I will return: does Angelo represent a debased coin—that is, does the duke know that he is a bad choice from the start—or does he somehow abuse the legitimate stamp that has been given to him by the duke?

The stamp of man relates to the Aristotelian notion that in procreation "the female always provides the material," while "the male always provides that which fashions the material into shape," that is, the soul.[34] Although women may bear the legitimate stamp of their husbands, they might also receive an illegitimate stamp, for they are, as Isabella states, "soft as [their] complexions are, / And credulous to false prints" (2.4.129–30).

We have a similar sense of such procreative stamping in the play's references to "character," whose first definition in the *OED* is a "distinctive mark impressed, engraved, or otherwise formed; a brand, stamp."[35] When Claudio worries that "the stealth of" Juliet and his "most mutual entertainment / With character too gross is writ on Juliet" (1.2.154–5), he implies that he has left his own conspicuous mark on her body. These metaphors are not particular to coins—in fact, Aristotle employs the specific image of wax seals—but early modern authors were quick to extend them to coinage.[36] In *Edward III* the countess of Salisbury warns the king that by adulterously pressing himself on her, he would "stamp his image in forbidden metal" (2.1.258). And in *Cymbeline* Posthumus, believing that Imogen has been unfaithful, laments the ubiquity of adultery with a coining metaphor:

> We are all bastards,
> And that most venerable man which I
> Did call my father, was I know not where
> When I was stamp'd. Some coiner with his tools
> Made me a counterfeit.... (2.5.2–6)

Reference to "tools" of the coiner gives the metaphor a more visceral connotation than the spiritual form described by Aristotle, but the logic of the metaphor clearly follows from the Aristotelian line.

Later in *Cymbeline*, Posthumus introduces yet another coining metaphor that suggests he is a previously legitimate coin that has been altered, rather than a counterfeit coin by birth. Regretting what he believes he has done to Imogen, he asks the gods to restore her life in exchange for his own:

> For Imogen's dear life take mine, and though
> 'Tis not so dear, yet 'tis a life; you coin'd it.
> 'Tween man and man they weigh not every stamp;
> Though light, take pieces for the figure's sake;
> You rather, mine being yours; and so, great pow'rs,
> If you will take this audit, take this life,
> And cancel these cold bonds. (5.4.22–28)

In Posthumus's first speech, his own stamp is illicit because it belongs to a man who is not his mother's husband. In the second, he has received the gods' own stamp, but the manner in which he has handled his life has caused his metal to become lighter. That is, Posthumus is a coiner who admits to having altered his god-given coin and yet hopes it still passes current according to the value of the original stamp. Whereas he initially thought his mother had provided the metal to counterfeit him with another man's stamp, his guilt induces belief that he had indeed been born a legitimate, full-bodied coin but had destroyed what was bestowed upon him by his own immoral behavior.

This latter passage in *Cymbeline* indicates the second version of the coining metaphor in Angelo's speech: God stamping his image in humans. A common metaphor in biblical hermeneutics, it likely emerged from interpretations of the passage in Matthew (22:21) about Caesar's tribute money: "Render unto Caesar the things which are Caesar's and unto God the things that are God's." Identifying the metaphor in early sources such as Gregory of Nyssa and Macarius, G. W. H. Lampe suggests that early church fathers found in the passage Jesus's intention to compare the image of Caesar on the coin to the divine image and inscription of God's name engraved in the believer, who "becomes the Lord's coin and receives the royal χάραγμα [charisma]."[37] Augustine invokes the metaphor in a sermon, imploring Christians:

> Regain, therefore, the likeness to God which you lost through your sins. For as the image of the emperor on the coin is one thing and his image in his son another: for there are different kinds of images; but the image of the emperor is engraved in the coin in one way, in the son in another, and in solid gold even in a different way: so you too are a coin of God; and even better since you are God's coin with reason and life, so that you know whose image you bear and according to whose image you are made: For the coin is not aware of bearing the emperor's image.[38]

Augustine mentions all three stamps: the emperor's on his coins; the emperor as father's stamp on his son; and God's original stamp on the sinner. Like Posthumus in his second speech, Augustine intimates the idea that sin alters the coin granted by God. Only by recalling the value of the stamp can one follow the path of redemption and restore one's coin to full weight.

In a sermon preached on Christmas of 1622, John Donne devised an interesting version of the metaphor that conflates God's and the father's stamp. Donne extends the idea of a father stamping a son to describe Christ as a freshly minted coin produced by the stamp of the Holy Ghost within the Virgin's mint in order to redeem the debts of humans, who have abused the coins originally loaned to them:

> First, he must pay it in such money as was lent; in the nature and flesh of man; for man had sinned, and man must pay. And then it was lent in such money as was coined even with the Image of God; man was made according to his Image: That Image being defaced, in a new Mint, in the wombe of the Blessed Virgin, there was new money coined;

The Image of the invisible God, the second person in the Trinity, was imprinted into the humane nature.[39]

In this version the coming of Christ represents a new gift in the form of coinage with restored standards, which provides the wealth necessary to pay back the original loan. However, the emphasis on a different stamp from the Holy Ghost suggests coinage even more dear than that with the original stamp of God so that human wealth has increased from redemption, a monetary version of *felix culpa*.

The theological implications of Christ as coin of the Holy Ghost could also take on political implications for a king claiming to have been divinely appointed. As I mentioned in Chapter I, the mystification of kingship drew substantially from mysteries surrounding Christ. In the next chapter I discuss the political theology of coinage in the context of a coin used in one such mystery, healing of the sick, but here I am interested primarily in the idea of God's image stamped specifically in the king, another commonplace especially within absolutist ambitions of the early Stuart period. For example, William Pemberton writes that God has "stamped his image of Soveraignty in Kings and Caesars, set the Crowne upon their heads, put the scepter into their hands, and created them chiefe Monarches...next under himself." Henry Finch described the king as "carrying Gods stampe and marke among men, and being, as one may say, a God upon earth, as God is a King in Heaven." John Rawlinson remarks that there is an "impression or character of dreadfull Majesty stampt in the very visage of a King." And Henry Valentine describes a king as *"Imago Dei*, the bright *Image* of God, and the most magnificent and conspicuous representation of the Divine Majesty."[40] With a long tradition of biblical hermeneutics employing the metaphor of God's stamp in all believers, the burden remained on the monarch to explain the exceptional nature of his own particular stamp. Various claims as to who receives God's stamp—whether the king alone or all believers in Christ—would prefigure ensuing struggles between king and subjects, especially Puritans.

Of course, in addition to receiving God's stamp, the king used his own stamp to produce circulating coinage whose integrity must be maintained. The king had a duty to guarantee first that he not do damage to the image of God with which he has been impressed, and second that his *own* coinage bearing his image as guarantee of validity remained sound as well. In fact, both forms of coinage relate to the king's role as living embodiment of justice. Regarding the first form, God's stamp in the king, Stuart Clark notes a maxim from Plutarch, popular in the early modern period, which "spoke of justice as the end of the law, the law as the work of the prince, and the prince as the image of God." Regarding the second, the king's stamp on his coins, in his 1626 speech before parliament, Sir Robert Cotton comments that the "regulating of Coin has been left to the care of Princes," who are "Debtors and Warranties of Justice to the Subject in that behalf."[41] A just king maintains his own God-given coin as well as those coins he produces to serve his commonwealth.

An important line of Aristotelian thought associated money with justice. In Book V of *Nicomachean Ethics* Aristotle describes one form of justice in terms of "reciprocal exchange in the right proportion." Money was invented to become the "middle term" to guarantee the "right proportion" in exchange. Aquinas describes this version of justice in the *Summa* as "commutative justice," or "justice that is concerned with the mutual dealings of two private persons one with another." William Camden explains this natural progression toward the use of money from the need within "commutative Justice... to have a common measure, and valuation as it were of the equality and inequality of wares," which was designated as "*Nomisma*, not from King *Numa*, But of *Nomos*, Because it was ordained by law," a point Aristotle mentions in Book V of the *Ethics*. Moreover, the Roman tradition designated this measure as "*Moneta*" (the origin of the English term "money") "because when the Romans stood in need of money, *Juno* admonished them to use justice, and there should be no want of money: the effect thereof when they found, shee was surnamed *Juno Moneta*, & money was coined in her temple."[42] According to Camden, therefore, both the Greek and Latin terms for "money" assumed an implicit association with justice.

Joel Kaye identifies a significant shift in the Aristotelian tradition during the fourteenth century: from the need for a subjective judge to oversee "right proportion" in exchange, toward an acceptance of money within a market mechanism as objective equalizer. Kaye points out that in Aristotle's *Ethics* a judge had the primary task of subjective equalization by fixing a "just price" for goods. Indeed, Aristotle notes that although money is a measure for exchange, "the price of all goods," which should be "fixed," must be determined from the start. However, in fourteenth-century commentaries on Aristotle, the roles of the "subjective" judge and money as "objective instrument of equalization" setting its own price levels were discussed in a similar light. For example, the commentator Odonis described the functions of both judge and money as equating what had been unequal by "*reducens ad equalitatem et ad medium*." Kaye sees in the fourteenth century a move toward replacement of the judge for everyday exchange with money as an instrument of equalization in the market: "The model was shifting from the personal to the instrumental, from mind to mechanism as the basis for establishing order and equality." In fact, the scale itself—as both symbol of justice and practical device for weighing coins—eventually became "the visual symbol of equalization for both commerce and law." In the seventeenth century, Camden describes the pagan goddess *Dea Pecunia* "in the figure of a woman holding a paire of ballance in one hand, and *Cornucopia* in another." And Nicole Oresme quotes Cassiodorus in order to warn about the scales of justice becoming corrupt by fraudulent coinage: "For what is so criminal as to permit oppressors to sin against the very nature of the balance, so that the very symbol of justice is notoriously destroyed by fraud?"[43] In order to uphold justice, a ruler must guarantee that coinage standards are upheld as well.

It is ultimately this other explanation for the coin imagery—the figurative association between coinage and justice—that creates difficulties for the authority figures in *Measure for Measure*. Whereas metaphors of coining God's image in believers and coining the father's image in children could be deployed without necessarily calling attention to the state's own practices of coin production, the connection to justice, a central concern in the play, destabilizes the figurative case against coining crimes by revealing the hypocrisy of state officials. Angelo in particular, who has been granted Duke Vincentio's stamp to become the embodiment of living justice in Vienna, commits a crime even worse than the ones perpetrated by those he has condemned. The fact that Angelo abuses the duke's stamp, whether or not such abuse had been anticipated by the ruler, signals an unjust system of exchange in Vienna as the scales of justice prove inadequate to the task. The play's resolution requires Vincentio to reassume authority in order to arbitrate—whether by deploying justice or mercy—among the various crimes committed. But the earlier deficiency of the duke's issue and persistent interrogation of his "character" by his chief critic Lucio indicate the arbitrary nature of the state's case against coining crimes.

At the start of the play both Vincentio and Angelo employ coin imagery to express concerns about restoring justice in Vienna. Referring to Angelo, the duke asks Escalus, "What figure of us think you he will bear?" (1.1.16), as if anxious to finally see for himself the latest coin design issued by the master-moneyer of the mint, as if describing a freshly minted coin, like the English gold "angel" his name connotes.[44] Despite concern about Angelo's initial appearance, however, the duke knows that this figure may not persist once he has assumed deputy power, suggesting that the word "will" points not to the immediate future, when Angelo enters the chamber, but to the period after the duke has officially turned over his commission to Angelo. Vincentio asks whether Angelo will either uphold or debase the "figure" of the duke imprinted by his commission once he assumes power. This concern indicates a second meaning of the word "figure," that of *value*, related to the first meaning by Angelo's performance as deputy. The two are interdependent: since in his commission Angelo is stamped by the duke's figure, his actions will affect its value. Any injustice will constitute an alteration of the initial coin and hence devalue the figure. Thereafter, any other object stamped with the same figure will become suspect like Henry VIII's "bloody nose" sitting atop his debased testoons.

Angelo worries about this very problem of his worth and even employs similar language of minting prior to officially receiving his deputation. He begs the duke to reconsider his imminent appointment: "Let there be some more test made of my mettle / Before so noble and so great a figure / Be stamp'd upon it" (1.1.48–50). The "mettle" puns on the metal of a "blank," the initial disk that gets "stamp'd" with the ruler's image, and there may even be a pun on "noble," a common gold coin of the period. Angelo's request is reminiscent of the customary Trial of the Pyx, originating in the thirteenth century, during which a public jury of "twelve discreet and lawful citizens of London with twelve skillful Goldsmiths" assayed a sample of newly made coins from the mint.[45] The trial was an attempt by the king to assure the public of the new coins' quality through objective assessment. However ceremonial, it provided an important check by the commonwealth on the monarch's sole prerogative of coinage. As in the Trial of the Pyx, Angelo asks to be tested before being allowed to circulate with the duke's guarantee of value. This denied request raises a red flag about the duke's willingness to release this new coin based on blind faith alone and to flout a ceremony that represented a significant restraint on the ruler's authority.

Minting offers a suitable metaphor for the deputation process because early Greek coins, as *symbola*, were likened to deputies of the state witnessing commercial transactions. Prior to coinage, the validity of a trade had to be guaranteed by a third-party observer. Instead of providing a personal witness, a system was adopted whereby objects would serve essentially as witnesses—visible tokens of the proceedings. The object, known as a *symbolon*, would be divided in half, and the union of the two pieces would attest to the transaction's validity. Marc Shell points out that besides bearing a particular numerical value, coins, more importantly, served as *symbola*.[46] They thus allowed the ruler to disseminate surrogates for "observing" the workings of the economy and for guaranteeing a legal system of transactions within the state's economy. This process recalls Kaye's observation about the shift from the subjective judgment of judges to the objective measure of money. Coins assumed the role previously held by judges and thus helped realize a ruler's fantasy of maintaining by proxy the power to examine all transactions within his state—the circulation of coins as the circulation of state power. They became critical factors in the deputation process, the "power-in-absence," which Jonathan Goldberg describes as essential for achieving absolutist goals.[47]

However, the deputy circulating among subjects within the absolutist state must be a pure representation of the ruler, an extension of the ruler's will. He must have a "scope" as wide as the ruler's "own, / So to enforce or qualify the laws / As to [his] soul seems good" (1.1.64–66). Stuart Clark notes that magistrates were probably expected to function as "agent-symbols" of Tudor and Stuart monarchs, "representing these theocratic rulers both in action and in aspect." Richard Crompton comments that English justices should make decisions based on "what is meete according to honesty, and such judgment the honour of the King doth love, whose personne in judgment they represent."[48] However, if kings are also considered deputies of God, then judges are only one step removed in this holy line of deputation. In Angelo's eventual indictment, the duke articulates this required virtue in judges who assume the power of God:

> He who the sword of heaven will bear
> Should be as holy as severe;
> Pattern in himself to know,
> Grace to stand, and virtue go;
> More nor less to others paying
> Than by self-offenses weighing. (3.2.261–66)

Political discourse in the period expresses similar concern about judges. Guillaume de La Perriere argues that "Magistrates in their Judgements ought to imitate God" because the "exercise of Judgements, and authority of Magistrates, is a power from God, appointed unto man, who in this world doe hold the place of him to yield and give right unto every one." And Barnabe Barnes advises judges "to retaine a firme and venerable gravity, confirmed in his countenance with some serious kinde of awfull majesty, through his continuall meditation upon the just judgements of God with the charge upon him imposed."[49] Any deviation by a judge from at least *displays* of virtue would reflect poorly on a ruler who is the supposed living embodiment of justice.

It is "precise" Angelo's reputation for moral purity, the metric of value in Shakespeare's Vienna, that seems to attract the duke to his choice. Vincentio's advisor Escalus acknowledges, "If any in Vienna be of worth / To undergo such ample grace and honor, / It is Lord Angelo" (1.1.22–24). Although Escalus has sufficient knowledge about state matters to assume control, he is not of the immaculate material Angelo is purported to be. Angelo's appointment and circulation, especially in light of the coin imagery employed at the start of the play, might be compared to the replacement of a coinage whose quality has deteriorated. As I mentioned in the introduction, according to Alfred Sohn-Rethel, a coin's "weight and metallic purity are guaranteed by the issuing authority so that, if by the wear and tear of circulation it has lost in weight, full replacement is provided." As an "immutable substance," a coin then "stands in antithetic contrast to any matter found in nature," constituting what Slavoj Žižek calls "sublime material." Angelo is thought to be of a "sublime material", whose purity remains constant despite the number of transactions he has experienced, since, as the duke comments, "Spirits are not finely touch'd / But to fine issues" (1.1.35–36).[50] This image also connotes the prodigious talents of Angelo, whose unwavering purity, Vincentio hopes, will restore the state he has allowed to deteriorate morally. Moreover, once the duke has "lent" Angelo his "terror, dress'd him with our love, / And given his deputation all the organs" of his own power, he "has elected" Angelo with a "special soul" to supply his absence as if the immortal, immutable body politic is temporarily invested in Angelo (1.1.17–21). His faith in Angelo's immaculate material and his own stamp leads him to believe that Angelo is made of what Sohn-Rethel calls an "immutable substance...over which time has no power" and "which persists beyond the corruption of the body physical" like the immortal body politic invested in the body natural of a king.[51]

The existence of such an "immutable substance," though, like the immortal body politic invested in the current monarch, constituted merely an ideological strategy of an aspiring absolutist state. Despite the reputation of "precise Angelo," the realistic duke remains skeptical of Angelo's ability to serve as a perfect substitute for himself. Therefore, he observes the deputy's circulation, fulfilling the fantasy of a ruler, to follow his coinage across all transactions. J. W. Lever connects the duke's surveillance to James's plan to secretly visit the Exchange and watch his English merchants unobserved. As described in *The Time Triumphant*, news of the planned visit was leaked, and the resulting crowds pressing to see James caused him to cancel the visit.[52] Like James wanting to observe his merchants, the duke wishes to "behold [Angelo's] sway" and "visit both prince and people" in order to examine the mechanics of his economy (1.3.43, 45). He lulls the economy into believing that he has allowed his surrogate coin to pass unobserved, while his deputation diverts attention from his own circulation.

Yet utter lack of faith in his surrogate *calls* attention to the inadequacy of his issue, and because he distrusts the "character" of his subjects, especially Angelo's, the duke needs to test their true "mettle."[53] Early on he gives Angelo the benefit of the doubt. Even after he learns about his proposal to Isabella, he believes that "Angelo had never the purpose to corrupt her; only he hath made an assay of her virtue to practice his judgment with the disposition of natures" (3.1.161–4). The duke remains uncertain whether Angelo counterfeits his lust to test the seemingly pure Isabella, or the genuinely pure Isabella inadvertently tests the ostensibly pure Angelo. He must confirm with his own assay which of the two is base. He, therefore, informs Isabella that he has a method to teach her how she should "arraign [her] conscience, / And try [her] penitence, if it be sound, / Or hollowly put on" (2.3.21–23). That is, he first tests Isabella, and having gained confidence in her, he then uses her purity and his own power of substitution (Mariana and the bedtrick) to test the mettle of Angelo, to have "the corrupt deputy scal'd" (3.1.254–5).[54]

OF MIMICRY AND MONEY

Princes must not suffer their Faces to warrant falsehood.
—Sir Robert Cotton

At the end of 3.2, the duke expresses his frustration over Angelo's actions:

> O, what may man within him hide,
> Though angel on the outward side!
> How may likeness made in crimes,
> Making practice on the times,
> To draw with idle spiders' strings
> Most ponderous and substantial things! (3.2.271–6)

Drawing on Lever's observation that the reference to "angel" in this passage returns us to the coin imagery from the start of the play, R. J. C. Watt comments that Duke Vincentio "remembers the bright promise shown by the gold Angel, who, though stamped in the Duke's *likeness*, has turned out to be a counterfeit who is *making practice on the times.*" But although Angelo does prove base, we must remember that the duke had "stamped" Angelo as his appointed deputy without testing his "mettle."[55] Ostensibly he had thought that Angelo could in practical application prove to be more effective currency since the duke had not administered justice for so long that he now feared doing it himself. But Angelo cunningly exploits the duke's stamp as guarantee of value to argue that his reputation, his "unsoil'd name, th' austereness of [his] life," and his "place i' th' state" will "overweigh" the currency of Isabella's accusation against him (2.4.155–57). Since he has received the duke's own commission, his base mettle will appear more valuable than Isabella's pure reputation: "Say what you can," he says to Isabella, "my false o'erweighs your true" (2.4.170). Moreover, although early on we hear much about Angelo's pristine reputation, later we learn that the duke had known some shady details about his past, especially his retraction of a promise to marry Mariana. So when at the start of the play the duke tells Angelo that there is "a kind of character in thy life, / That to th' observer doth thy history / Fully unfold" (1.1.27–29), he appeases

Angelo's concern about first testing the true quality of his mettle before receiving his commission, but we wonder whether he includes in this conspicuous "history" the incident with Mariana.[56]

Mary Thomas Crane argues that Angelo's concern about receiving the stamp of the duke's authority "suggests that his 'character' is not a permanent and unchanging inscription but one capable of taking the impression of a new stamp."[57] But any new stamp would negate the duke's original commission, which endures until he finally reassumes authority. Moreover, Angelo continues to exploit his commission prior to the duke's public return. Thus, although he may be a "counterfeit" since his own pursuit of Isabella defies Vincentio's intentions to clean up Vienna, he nevertheless uses the face of authority provided by the duke to achieve his malevolent ends. In the final scene the duke attempts to recast Angelo's deeds, which deserve "with characters of brass / A forted residence 'gainst the tooth of time / And razure of oblivion" (5.1.11–13). The image recalls the brass in John Heywood's epigram, which is "waxen proude" because it has become equivalent to silver coin. The ironic show of courtesy thus employs connotations of debasement in order to eternalize Angelo's vice, but this restamping of Angelo merely replaces the original debased coin, the one the duke had minted at the beginning.

In case we overlook the ruler's implication in his choice of deputy, the critic Lucio offers a caustic commentary on the duke's initial decision. The most concise and evocative critique of all the duke's misdeeds is Lucio's statement accusing Vincentio of theft: "It was a mad fantastical trick of him to steal from the state, and usurp the beggary he was never born to. Lord Angelo dukes it well in his absence; he puts transgression to't" (3.2.92–95). Although "to steal from" here, of course, means "to flee," it also intimates the duke's having stolen something of value from the state in appointing Angelo. Moreover, his other accusations of Vincentio's hypocritical lechery equate the ruler with Angelo, his base deputy; he elides Angelo's pursuit of Isabella with his insistence that the duke would "have dark deeds darkly answer'd, he would never bring them to light" (3.2.177–8). When he states that "Lord Angelo dukes it well in his absence; he puts transgression to't," Lucio invokes a double meaning: Angelo has assumed the role of duke well either by getting rid of transgression or by incorporating transgression into the role. Lucio's slanders are precisely what Vincentio fears most at the start of the play. He bemoans the fact that for those of "place and greatness...millions of false eyes / Are stuck upon thee" while "volumes of report / Run with these false, and most contrarious quest / Upon thy doings" (4.1.59–62). He fears being an object of ridicule and slander and hopes that Angelo "may, in th' ambush of my name, strike home, / And yet my nature never in the fight / To do in slander" (1.3.41–43). But even in his supposed absence, Lucio maintains his assault on the duke's character.

Like Thersites in *Troilus and Cressida*, he "coins slanders like a mint, / To match" the ruler "in comparisons with dirt" (1.3.193–4).[58] The fact that the duke himself had commissioned Angelo, as Lucio reminds us, undermines the ruler's ultimate attempt to judge his deputy's actions apart from the stamp of authority he had granted. Although he wants to proclaim Angelo a counterfeit, Lucio's caustic commentary and the audience's recollection of the original deputation expose the underlying debasement. This subversive critique would hit home for an England retaining the memory of Henry VIII's "great debasement." It evokes the hypocrisy of a debasing prince who simultaneously denounces counterfeiters, a hypocrisy Oresme had noted: "it is [the ruler's] duty to condemn false coiners. How can he blush deep enough, if that be found in him which in another he ought to punish by a disgraceful death?" Critics of the debasing medieval king Philip IV or "Philip the Fair" of France even referred to him as "Le Faux Monnayeur" [counterfeiter] to articulate the clear connection between his debasement and the counterfeiting he adamantly condemned.[59] Memories of Philip's debasement and his infamous epithet clearly endured throughout early modern Europe. Sir Robert Cotton mentions the king during his 1626 speech to parliament regarding a proposed weight reduction for the coinage. He cites Bodin in order to contend that a king cannot "alter the price of the moneys to the prejudice of the Subjects, without incurring the reproach of *Faux Monnoyeurs*. And therefore the Stories term *Philip le Bell*, for using it, *Falsificateur de Moneta*." Even by the end of the seventeenth century, John Evelyn declares that "to put a King's Title or Effigies to unweighty Money, and not of authentic Value, is...to render the Prince himself a *Faux Monoyeur*."[60] Such persistent threats of damage to the ruler's reputation resisted the state's attempts to differentiate between "legitimate" and "illegitimate" coinage alteration.

Indeed, the line between "legitimate" and "illegitimate" coiners often became blurred within the mint itself. The most famous such case is that of Eloy Mestrell, who around 1560 was brought from the Paris mint to the Tower to help produce English money. Shortly afterward, in 1561, he was pardoned "for all treasons, felonies and offences committed before 1 March, 1 Eliz., in respect of clipping or counterfeiting coin." Mestrell had quickly slipped from legitimate to illegitimate production of coin, but he was considered so important to the mint that authorities looked the other way until he was no longer of use. In 1569 he was again pardoned after he "procured and abetted" his brother Philip, who had made four counterfeit "Burgundye crownes." Mestrell later sold "a presse and a stampe for dalers ['thalers' or 'dollars']" to a suspected coiner. In 1572 he was commissioned to mechanize the mint using screw presses like those in France. But his experiments bred resentment among moneyers, who feared for their jobs. After examining his experiments' preliminary results, the warden of the mint reported that Mestrell's machines were ten times slower than the manual method, and he was subsequently fired. His experiment a "failure," Mestrell lost favor with the queen and in 1578 a letter to the sheriff of Norfolk states that regarding "one Eloye Minstrell, lately condemned for false coininge, and uppon appellation by him made of other offendours in the like facte was differed, *unles he shalbe able to discover greater matter* the said Sherif is required by their Lordships to see him executed according to justice." No longer of use to the state as moneyer or informer, Mestrell was hanged at Tyburn in that same year.[61]

Mestrell's case points also to the mint's unusual "recruitment" of indicted counterfeiters to produce legitimate money. Indicted counterfeiters could often escape (at least temporarily) from the prescribed punishment for treason as long as they remained useful to the state. In 1577, the privy council spared the life of a condemned counterfeiter called Crompton, since, as it was written in a letter to the lieutenant of the Tower,

> it is thought by reason of his cunninge and experience in working he may do some good service about her Majestys Minte, he shold be imployed in those workes as the Warden of [the] Minte from time to time shall thinke mete to use him, and furder to suffer his wife and frindes to have recourse at convenient times unto him, foreseing that good regard be had that he comitte not any escape.

Ben Jonson seems to have been aware of this practice. In *The Alchemist*, the counterfeiting conman Subtle, speaking to his partner, Face, worries that if the house where they perform their illicit deeds "Should chance to be suspected, all would out, / And [they] be locked up in the Tower for ever, / To make gold there for th' state, never come out." The state thus took a pragmatic approach to counterfeiters' punishment by employing their prodigious skills.[62] But by "hiring" criminals to produce its coinage, the state helped blur the boundary between legitimate and illegitimate coin.

However, the most effective form of resistance to state attempts at differentiating between coining crimes and debasement was to produce metaphors of debasement to accompany, and even mimic, those of coining crimes. For example, the author of *The History of the Life, Reign, and Death of Edward II*, believed by some to be Elizabeth Cary, refers to the king's preferment of and sexual interest in particular courtiers in terms of debasement. Following the banishment of Gaveston, King Edward's "wandring eyes now ravage through the confines of his great Court, made loose by his example. Here he seeks out some Piece, or Copper-metal, whom by his Royal stamp he might make currant," ultimately settling on Spencer.[63] In addition to having sexual implications, "piece" here refers to the blank that is stamped in coinage production, which in this case consists of base copper.[64] Therefore, *The History* exploits sexual connotations of coinage. But rather than constituting an act of illicit procreation, the sexual encounter transforms the body stamped, which receives preferment despite its baseness. A similar version of this metaphor, though in reference to counterfeiting, appears in Webster's *The White Devil*, in which the product of an illicit encounter, perhaps in this case venereal disease, remains in the body of the prostitute who has been "stamped" by her first client. The Cardinal Monticelso asks, "What's a whore? / She's like the guilty counterfeited coin / Which, whosoe'er first stamps it, brings in trouble / All that receive it."[65] *The History* implies that Edward debases nobility itself by stamping a lower-valued metal such as copper, which in turn contaminates the value of the stamp. The king believes his favor confers worth on whomever he chooses, whatever the *mettle* of that individual, just as his royal insignia provides value to whatever *metal* he stamps according to the extrinsic value theory. Resentment among nobility, therefore, induced an association between the arbitrary value assigned to debased coins and the arbitrary advancement, especially because of sexual desirability, of unworthy subjects.

Metaphors of debasement also emerge within the context of treasonous rebellion in works such as Shakespeare's *1 Henry IV*. In his description of the current politico-ethical situation in King Henry IV's England, the rebel Hotspur links the violent overthrow of the state to the passing of damaged or debased currency: "We must have bloody noses and crack'd crowns, / And pass them current too" (2.3.93–4). In numismatic terminology, a "crack'd crown" is a golden coin that has been broken, typically during the minting process (See figure 4.3, www.stephendeng.com). Some of these coins made their way into circulation despite the fact that it was usually illegal to "utter" them, or "pass them current."[66] But the term also intimates the ensuing violence against those loyal to the king, as well as the anticipated result of Hotspur's rebellion: destruction of a symbol of the king's authority. Recall the case of rebellion against Mary that I described in the introduction. Francis and Edmund Verney and Henry Peckham broke one of Mary's coins in two as a sign of agreement to carry out a plot to overthrow the queen. The destruction and defacing of Mary's portrait signaled the symbolic rupture of her authority. The reference to "bloody noses" in a passage from *1 Henry IV* has a similarly violent valence, but it alludes specifically to *debased* coins: the testoons of Henry VIII that, as I discussed in the previous chapter, displayed a prominent and unflattering profile of the king with a large nose and hid a high copper or brass content under a silvered surface.[67] That is, "crack'd crowns" and "bloody noses" were damaged and debased coins produced by the "legitimate" mint itself. Hotspur's poetic violence, therefore, incorporates a strange slippage from raising arms against the state to abuses of authority in coinage offenses *by* the state.

These competing metaphors of debasement indicate resistance to state control over "poetic exchange." Several critics have noted the importance of substitution and exchange in *Measure for Measure*. For example, Kiernan Ryan observes that the play is "riddled with locutions framed to convey symmetry, equivalence, inversion or repetition," and exchange seems to "swarm through the body politic of Vienna like a contagious disease."[68] Noting biblical allusions in the play, especially in its title, Marc Shell analyzes the system of exchange in terms of the "lex talionis" whereby a substitute object, or a figurative equivalent of it, is returned to compensate for the object's loss: "an eye for an eye." If the original object cannot be returned, then some substitute that "can pass for it in some figural or fictional sense" must be found. Shell argues that the second half of the play "enacts the figural or fictional but necessary ground of the lex talionis" by moving through a series of substitutions such that the replacement "to all structural intents and purposes of the plot" becomes the original. This enactment occurs primarily through the proposed substitution and exchange of heads (Barnadine's and Ragozine's) and maidenheads (Isabella's and Mariana's), each of which is made equivalent to Claudio's head. The chief device for this replacement system is disguise, which represents "the visible dramatization of the ultimately fictional or figurative basis of all commensuration" when the replacement object is not the same as the original.[69] Shell argues that the existence of suitable substitutes implies a "moneylike intermediary, or measure" between the original lost object and the object serving to replace it. But he also notes that the system of commensuration implicit in disguise offers a "sympathetic critique of the notion of identity on which exchange often relies."[70] Most substitutions the duke makes occur among things that seem incommensurate if not immeasurable, especially human beings or their various parts.

However, disguise is not the play's only currency. In addition to the exchange of body parts in the second half of the play, we find a prominent system of *poetic* exchange that runs *throughout* the play. In his own analysis, Shell describes the replacement object as equivalent in a "figural or fictional sense," but he emphasizes the theatrical over the poetic. At one point in the play, the theatrical merges with the poetic when figurative associations become literally embodied in the exchange of heads: the head of Ragozine, the thief, stands in for the head of Claudio, the producer of bastards, the latter of which had previously been equated with the head of Barnardine, the murderer. As Shell points out, "Just as Ragozine stole by water, so Barnardine stole a man already made and Claudio stole a man as yet unmade,"[71] an equation that alludes to Angelo's earlier justification for Claudio's severe punishment.

While Shell argues that disguise critiques the notion of identity in exchange, poetic equalities such as the one produced by Angelo bear their own implicit critique of categorical equivalence produced within the system. Alexander Leggatt contends that much of *Measure for Measure*'s

> imaginative and intellectual life depends on this play of likeness and difference, which is also a play on one of the essential conditions of poetry itself, which both examines the likeness of things and asserts their uniqueness: lovers are a pair of compasses, my mistress' eyes are nothing like the sun, a rose is a rose is a rose.

I would argue that the play's coining imagery—especially indications of the coinage's lack, which connotes an inability to establish a stable measure for equivalence between objects—encodes a critique of such metaphoric commensuration. The reason Leggatt finds all the "substitutions that are central to the plot...in various ways, unsatisfying" is that the play's implicit currency, which Shell describes as a "moneylike intermediary" equating objects and their replacements, is somehow deficient.[72] Although the system of equivalence gives the illusion of a stable position against coining crimes (for example, an essential system of value governed by stable terms), the exchangeability of coining for theft, bastardizing, or usurpation of God's authority proved to be based on an arbitrary system employing unstable currency. The very logic of counterfeit, clipped, or debased currency, therefore, offers a powerful trope to undercut any attempt to equate "coining" with other crimes. Coining allusions in *Measure for Measure* are thus both terms to be arbitrarily equated with other crimes as well as indicators that such attempts at establishing pure equivalence are destined to fail.

It is especially the recalcitrant Lucio who refuses to let the duke maintain monopolistic control over the terms of exchange, and by calling him a "very superficial, ignorant, unweighing fellow," he undermines the duke's ability to judge equivalence (3.2.139–40).[73] Lucio mimics Vincentio's various exchanges of people by comparing him to Angelo, and he even equates *himself* with the duke. He claims that the duke, like himself, "had some feeling of the [sexual] sport; he knew the service" of prostitution (3.2.119–20). And in the final scene he turns his own "slanderous" words against the disguised ruler, charging him with having "spoke most villainous speeches of the Duke" (5.1.263–4). Indeed, Angelo and Escalus also charge the unruly friar with slandering the state when, after accusing Angelo of attempted fornication and the duke of injustice, he proceeds to pontificate about the general corruption that he has seen "boil and bubble" as a "looker-on" in Vienna (5.1.317–8). As a slanderer of the state, the duke assumes an identity comparable to Lucio's even though we know he is telling the truth (whether Lucio's accusations about Vincentio are true or not is unknown). M. Lindsay Kaplan claims that the "Duke condemns Lucio not so much for impugning his authority, but for competing with it. Lucio poses a threat to the state precisely because he usurps the Duke's ability to deploy slanders."[74] However, the duke tells the truth in a false guise, which negates the authority of his claims. Although he tries to turn Lucio's accusations back onto him—"You must, sir, change persons with me, ere you make that my report" (5.1.336-7)—his false persona has no power in his current role. Lucio's and the duke's accusations mimic each other without having a stable authority to judge which accusation has substance. Each mirrors the other, and Vincentio even recognizes how he has come to depend on Lucio: "Thou art the first knave that e'er mad'st a duke" (5.1.356).[75] The scene recalls the duke's earlier inability to tell whether it is Angelo or Isabella who is false. The disguised ruler himself had to become the standard of measure in that situation, and the only way he saves himself in this one is by reassuming his right to judge.

Thus, in order to avoid treason charges, the duke must reassume the ability to make arbitrary equivalence between categories.[76] Significantly, as Shell points out, it is his seal ring, the type of ring that historically served as the original stamp for coins, that the duke relies upon to prove his identity to the provost and to prove that Angelo is a counterfeit who has been damaging Vincentio's "character."[77] Without his ruler's stamp, the duke cannot substantiate his right to judge. Moreover, the final judgments destabilize the moral ground of earlier decisions. He countermands his original orders by permitting and even imposing marriages—Claudio to Isabella and Lucio to Kate Keepdown—that his legislation had previously considered illegitimate. And he sends Angelo and Mariana off to get married by Friar Peter even though the marriage has already been consummated according to the duke's plot—that is, his command in the final scene suggests that his earlier advice to Mariana had condoned fornication. The ruler's manipulation was the driving force behind the system of exchange that led up to this moment, and he continues to manipulate terms in order to legitimate what had previously been illegitimate. Like the invisible hand of the market, the duke places himself at the center of a system of mysterious replacements and substitutions whose terms of equivalence are allowed to change over time.

Such arbitrary manipulation, I believe, helps to explain one of the play's many cruxes. Early in the play, before being led to prison, Claudio declares,

> Thus can the demigod, Authority,
> Make us pay down for our offense by weight
> The words of heaven: on whom it will, it will;
> On whom it will not, so; yet still 'tis just. (1.2.120-3)

R. J. C. Watt points out that to "pay down by weight" means to pay based on the weighing of a coin—that is, not relying on the coin's face value—which suggests precise payment. He uses this reading to reinterpret the passage as Claudio's acknowledgment that his punishment is just. But this interpretation requires substantial revision in the first folio's syntax, most importantly a period after "weight" and an apostrophe in "words" ("word's"), so that "words of heaven" is no longer the object of "pay down."[78] Moreover, such a reading does not seem consistent with Claudio's later resentment about his punishment. Rather, in the passage Claudio appears to be condemning the arbitrariness of secular punishment, which is supposed to be based on heavenly decree. The "pay[ing] down...by weight" might be interpreted instead as an ironic equation of the "words of heaven" with a certain quantity of precious metal. The secular authority passes judgment as if the case is a precise commodity transaction. The ironic reading can be further supported if we accept the common explanation of these "words of heaven" as a reference to Romans 9:15: "I will have mercy on him to whom I will show mercy."[79] Mercy is outside of exchange—in fact, it opposes the system of exchange governed by the lex talionis—so it is meaningless to weigh mercy against a quantity of metal.[80] The conclusion—"on whom it will, it will; / On whom it will not, so; yet still 'tis just"—suggests the inscrutability of a legal standard based on the ruler's particular judgment rather than on a set of quantifiable criteria. The duke's ability to legitimate what had previously been considered illegitimate merely proves Claudio's assertion about the arbitrary nature of this system of punishment.

But in addition to providing a rationale for critiquing this system, the arbitrary nature of this equivalence system offered the possibility of appropriation by those wishing to equate such crimes with the state's own actions, especially debasement. The precarious terms of equivalence in the legal standard, therefore, destabilizes the system of poetic exchange comparing various crimes. While coining crimes might be metaphorically equated with bastardy, theft, or usurpation of God's authority, so also might debasement. Moreover, like coining crimes, debasement represented an inability to produce a stable measure of equivalence, so its practice called attention to the failure of a legal currency based on the king's word. For this reason, James I found it better to avoid the practice of debasement entirely rather than risk permanently damaging the king's reputation. Any attempt to debase would permit critics such as Lucio to attack the ruler's reputation, which helped sustain a system of justice as much as of currency. As with structures of deputation, complete control over both economic and poetic exchange remained merely a fantasy of an absolutist state.

However, while the association between coinage and justice constituted a destabilizing factor for the state, other abstract, mystical connotations of coinage, especially that of money as the blood of the body politic, tended to support state prerogatives and was even employed within absolutist discourse. As we will see in the next chapter, the use of a gold coin in a healing ceremony both relied upon and upheld such mystical meanings of money.

Chapter V

"Mysteries of State": The Political Theology of Coinage in *Macbeth*

Following Malcolm's testing of Macduff's loyalty in Act 4, Scene 3 of *Macbeth*, an English doctor informs the two that there is a "crew of wretched souls" suffering from some disease and awaiting the English king Edward the Confessor, at whose "touch, / Such sanctity hath heaven given his hand, / They presently amend" (4.3.143–45). Macduff inquires about this disease, and Malcolm responds with a description of a peculiar ceremony whereby Edward cures patients suffering from scrofula or "the king's evil":

> 'Tis call'd the evil:
> A most miraculous work in this good king,
> Which often, since my here-remain in England,
> I have seen him do. How he solicits heaven,
> Himself best knows; but strangely-visited people,
> All swoll'n and ulcerous, pitiful to the eye,
> The mere despair of surgery, he cures,
> Hanging a golden stamp about their necks,
> Put on with holy prayers, and 'tis spoken,
> To the succeeding royalty he leaves
> The healing benediction. With this strange virtue,
> He hath a heavenly gift of prophecy,
> And sundry blessings hang about his throne
> That speak him full of grace. (4.3.146–59)

Critics have generally concluded that the passage served as a royal compliment to James, who saw an early production of the play, and who continued this ceremony of "touching" for the king's evil. For example, the eighteenth-century actor Francis Gentleman accuses Shakespeare of having "lugged in, by neck and heels, a doctor, for the strange purpose of paying a gross compliment to that royal line, which ridiculously arrogated a power of curing the evil, by a touch," adding that the "scene is properly left out" in performance, which it has often been.[1]

However, the passage, in particular the detail of the king "hanging a golden stamp"—a gold coin called an angel—around the necks of patients, resonates with a general economy of monetary representation in the play. In this chapter I situate *Macbeth* and the healing coin within the context of political theology, especially the charisma of kingship embodied in healing coins and in money in general. The use of this gold coin in the healing ceremony began only with Henry VII, which explains why there is no mention of its employment by Edward the Confessor in Shakespeare's main source, Holinshed's *Chronicles*. With the Tudors, however, the coin became a central component of the ceremony, and subjects were told to continue wearing the coins after the ceremony to maintain the effectiveness of their "cure." In the second section of this chapter, I focus on the significance of the coin, both for popular beliefs about their healing powers and for the political uses of such beliefs. The coin's particular combination of gold, royal and spiritual iconography, and biblical inscription exploited popular mystical beliefs in the healing powers of certain objects. The coin, therefore, became a potent device for promoting personal devotion to monarchs and a more general ideology of mystical kingship. Although both Elizabeth and James considered terminating the ceremony because of its idolatrous implications, they realized its importance for the promotion of English monarchy and continued to hang angels around patients' necks as part of the ritual.

The healing coins, therefore, circulated in both mystical and financial economies, which in *Macbeth* become a source of conflict. Before Duncan's murder, Macbeth experiences tension between the idealistic view of a loyal subject's unequivocal duties to the king and the realization of an unequal relation of material tribute and reward with Duncan. In murdering Duncan, he temporarily suppresses the former while foregrounding the latter. Initially, with the "golden round" staring him in the face, Macbeth becomes intent on claiming what he feels he deserves according to the logic of the balance sheet. Moreover, once he gains the throne, he attempts to depend entirely on the material economy to defend his position. But after the king's murder he recognizes how Duncan's money—the money produced by the legitimate king—bears the mystical power of maintaining a healthy state. He perceives Duncan's body as an emblem of blood-like money coursing through the king's second body, the immortal body politic. Despite the fact that he acquires the "sinews of war" by buying an army and even a system of surveillance for information gathering, he nonetheless intuits some lack in his money's power due to the perceived illegitimacy of his kingship. The lack ultimately attributes to the "gild" that Macbeth and Lady Macbeth have acquired through Duncan's death, the "guilt" that destroys the psyche of Lady Macbeth and extends to the general diseased state of Scotland, which needs to be "purged" by the rightful heir. Futilely trying to attribute the disease to an external source—Malcolm's army—Macbeth eventually locates the source within, his gold that lacks the aura of Duncan's blood flowing through the body politic. This internalization of Macbeth's crime, I contend, is symptomatic of an early modern perception that all money is not equivalent, not alone a sufficient mechanism for legitimacy. Charisma, even in its routinized form, requires a general perception of legitimacy that by itself determines the preservative power of the money flowing throughout the body politic.

THE HEALING COIN AND ITS DISCONTENTS

Geoffrey Bullough believes that Shakespeare interpolated his description of the "royal touch" from Holinshed's brief statement about Edward the Confessor in *The Chronicles of England*:

> As hath beene thought he [the Confessor] was inspired with the gift of prophesy, and also to have had the gift of healing infirmities and diseases. He used to helpe those that were vexed with the disease, commonly called the kings evill, and left that vertue as it were a portion of inheritance unto his successors the kings of this realme.

Critics discussing this passage have focused particularly on the significance of the "inheritance" mentioned by Holinshed and the "healing benediction" left to "succeeding royalty" in the play because one of the inheritors of this gift was James I, who kept this strange ritual alive more than five hundred years after Edward the Confessor.[2]

Yet, despite English belief that the Confessor initiated the "royal touch," it most likely began in France under Robert the Pious (996–1031).[3] The monk Helgald, recording the first known reference to the practice a few years after Robert's death, describes how the king would cure the sick merely by touching their wounds and making the sign of the cross over them: "Such power of bodily healing did the goodness of God bestow on this perfect man, that the touch of his holy hand on the sore places of sick men, together with the imprint of the sign of the Holy Cross, took away from them all the suffering of their sickness."[4] Although Helgald does not specify the disease or diseases cured by Robert, a later reference by Guibert, Abbé de Nogent (1053–1124), which records the specific practice of healing scrofula, suggests that the specialized practice had already become customary by the reigns of Philip I (1061–1108) and Louis VI (1108–37).[5] Evidence from this period indicates that kings did not at first specialize in particular diseases but would heal a number of diseases until it became "clear" which diseases they were most effective at healing. It is quite possible then that Robert had cured scrofula among other diseases and that the success of such healings sparked a tradition that later kings maintained.[6] Marc Bloch summarizes the likely chain of events that led to the origin of healing in France:

> Robert the Pious... was held by his faithful admirers to possess the gift of healing the sick. His successors inherited his power; but as it passed down the generations, this dynastic virtue became gradually modified or rather grew more precise. The idea arose that the royal touch was a sovereign remedy, not for all diseases indiscriminately, but in particular for one extremely widespread disease, scrofula; and by the time of Philip I, Robert's grandson, this transformation had been accomplished.[7]

Although the practice most likely began in France, Edward the Confessor performed a similar rite in England, where he appears to have cured scrofula specifically. According to the anonymous *Vita Aeduardi qui apud Westmonasterium requiescit*, which Raymond Crawfurd dates between 1066 and 1074,[8] Edward cured a scrofulous woman by sprinkling her wounds with water and making the sign of the cross, as did Robert in Helgald's description:

> A vessel of water is brought, and the King dips his hand, and with outstretched fingers besprinkles the woman's face and the parts smitten with the contagion. This act he repeats again and again, signing her the while with the Cross... At the King's anointing the diseased part softens, the scab is loosened, and as he draws back his hand, worms come out from several openings along with much bloody matter.

Although this is the only event described in detail, the *Vita* mentions that Edward had performed similar ceremonies in Normandy. Edward may have witnessed the practice in France and brought it to England. Nevertheless, in England the event seems to be an isolated incident rather than an example of a general practice by Edward. Not until the reign of Henry II (1154–89), when according to Crawfurd "a cult of the Confessor had taken deep root in the English nation," did the belief in healing as a prerogative of monarchy become firmly established in England.[9]

From its inception, the ceremony included, in addition to therapeutic value, economic aid from the king. According to Helgald, Robert the

Pious would visit the houses of the sick and "give them with his own hand a sum of pence" to supplement the healing. The *Vita Aeduardi* records that Edward the Confessor provided alms in kind rather than money: "Thereafter is his royal pleasure that she [the patient] be maintained from day to day at his own cost, until she should be restored to full health." Although subsequent French kings continued to provide money to scrofula sufferers, in England it was not until the reign of Edward I, who kept meticulous household records, that we find the first evidence of monetary alms in England.[10] Since the records note the number of subjects touched on each occasion as well as the aggregate money given, we can calculate that Edward offered each patient one penny, or about a day's wages and sustenance at the time. Household accounts also record one penny payments for the evil during the reigns of Edward II and Edward III, but the records under subsequent kings become silent about the ceremony until the reign of Henry VII.[11] Nevertheless, the earlier king's records, which have fortunately survived, provide a starkly contrasting view of the eventual role of money in the ceremony. In particular, during the Tudor period a gold coin called an angel became a central component of the touching ceremony, contrasting the supplementary alms provided by earlier kings.

The angel was not introduced until the War of the Roses. Edward IV ordered their first minting in 1465, though they do not appear to have been produced until 1470. The angel is a gold coin—initially worth six shillings, eight pence—that on the obverse side depicts the Archangel Michael slaying the dragon and on the reverse, the royal arms and a ship with a cross atop its mast (see figure 5.1, www.stephendeng.com). Numismatists have interpreted particular characteristics of the first coins to suggest that Edward minted the angels primarily for the healing ceremony. For example, the motto inscribed on the coin—*Per Crucem Tua Salva Nos Christe Redemptor* [By this Cross save us Redeemer Christ]—may refer to the ceremonial crossing of patients' sores with the coin. And its representation of the Archangel Michael slaying the dragon has been read as a type for the healer Apollo trampling on the serpent of pestilence.[12] Moreover, the coin's denomination was the typical fee for doctors, pointing to its use in healing. James Maxwell complains that "Phisitions" who cure various diseases "Are wont to reape some Angels one or moe / At the sick hands," whereas James, whom he describes as "*Apollo's* heire, this Ilands *Aesculape*, / ... to his sicke doth golden Angels reeche / Out of his hand."[13]

By the time of Henry VII, the angel had become central to the healing ceremony. Account books of Henry VII contain the first recorded evidence of its use. According to a late seventeenth-century pamphlet, the king's chaplain would repeat a verse from the first chapter of John, who gave "testimony of the Light," which "was the true Light which lightneth every man that cometh into this world," while "the King shall be crossing the Sore of the Sick Person, with an Angel of Gold Noble." After the king crossed the sores, the patient would "have the same Angel hang'd about his Neck, and...wear it until he be full whole." Although this description was published years after his death, Henry's accounts in the British National Archives cite thirteen cases over twenty-one months of angels being given "for heling of...seke folkes."[14] Moreover, many extant angels from his reign have holes bored through them, apparently to attach a ribbon (see figure 5.1, www.stephendeng.com). Finally, while continuing to produce essentially the same angels as did his predecessors, Henry VII issued an alternative coin with the legend "*Jes. Aute-Transiens. Per. Mediu. Illoru*," the same legend as on the noble of Edward III, a coin often employed as a protective amulet in battle. All extant evidence suggests that Henry made the coin part of the ceremony, crossing patients with it and hanging it around their necks rather than handing it to them like the traditional alms. Under Henry the coin assumed a more prominent position in the ceremony rather than being merely a supplement.

Henry's office provided a substantial break from the French version of the ritual, which remained mostly the same until the Tudor period and did not deviate much from this in later years. While the French kings tended to touch in large crowds within open spaces such as a public square, English kings after Henry usually touched in smaller groups within closed and secretive places, such as a church or chapel. In Henry's ceremony, only the king's chaplain and physician were allowed entry. Moreover, the French king walked among kneeling patients while English patients approached and knelt before the king on his throne.[15] F. David Hoeniger attributes the differences to the fact that the English ceremony assumed the form of a liturgical service with the monarch as an officiating priest or minister aided by a chaplain. In the early eighteenth century, William Beckett alleged that Henry had adapted his own form from an exorcism described in *Thesaurus Exorcismorum atque coniurationum Terribilium*.[16] He essentially formalized a monarchical ritual that could be adopted or altered by subsequent rulers. Henry's liturgical form may explain the formal presentation of the angel. While the French king continued to give money only as alms, in England the coin became part of the liturgy itself. Therefore, the form of the service attached to the coin a mystery that had been previously absent.

With this mystery, the coin clearly assumed a significance that transcended economic charity. After all, why would the king ceremoniously hang the coin around patients' necks rather than just hand it to them like alms? The significance of the angel can be inferred from the earliest known contemporary account of the practice, during the reign of Queen Mary. A letter dated May 3, 1556 describes how Mary

> made the sick people come up to her...and taking a gold coin—viz. an angel—she touched the place where the evil showed itself, signed

it with the Cross and passed a ribbon through the hole which had been pierced in it, placing one of them round the neck of each of the patients, and making them promise never to part with that coin, save in case of extreme need.[17]

According to this contemporary account, Mary placed special emphasis on the coin as a memento of the wondrous event, but the qualification "save in case of extreme need" acknowledges that it still bore economic value. Although Mary's initial request encourages an interpretation of the coin as a personally meaningful object outside of commodity exchange cycles, her modification concedes the coin's economic origin—the monetary alms that supplemented the healing touch. The coin's multiple uses after the ceremony suggest potential conflict between gift and market economies.

Such tension between economies may explain the state's later attempt to restrict the coins' commodity potential. By the time of James, the monarchy promoted the view that the coin was an essential component of healing, and *not just* economic aid, so that the cure would be ineffective if subjects parted with it. In 1625 James issued a proclamation warning against patients who "were formerly cured, but then disposed of the gold coins in unlawful ways," presumably selling them or using them as common currency, "and consequently experienced a relapse."[18] This concern may explain why Restoration monarchs replaced the angel with a non-current, though still gold, "touchpiece." Rather than tempt poor subjects with current coin, later Stuarts produced for the occasion an object resembling the former coin but without its primary commodity function. Special production of touchcoins made the tokens even more vital to the ceremony's mystery.

With monarchs hanging this gold coin or touchpiece around patients' necks and telling them not to part with it, it was only a small step to the perception that it was a protective amulet. As a result, subjects began to believe that the object had maintained the healing power of the king and was enough in itself to heal scrofula. Thus, for example, angels and touchpieces were given to other scrofula sufferers who had not gone through the ceremony. In *Adenochoiradelogia* (1684), the royal surgeon John Browne tells an amusing anecdote about a father and son both suffering from the evil. Only the father had been "touched," but he would let his son borrow the gold whenever the son had an outbreak of the disease:

The Father being distempered and ill, keeps the Gold about his neck, which kept him in health, and gave him speedy ease and relief: The Son falling ill, he borrows his Fathers Gold from his neck, and puts it about his own, which likewise gave him ease and relief. The Father after this by leaving his Gold, had his Destemper seized him afresh, and then took the Gold again, and this made it as readily vanish. And thus by the intercourse or change of Gold from Father to Son, and from Son to Father, whoever of them kept the Gold, was defended against any new approach or appearance of his Distemper; and this was kept and maintained by them for many years together.

The story suggests that the curative power had been transferred from the king's touch to the gold itself. The coins/touchpieces even began to circulate as "sacred commodities" separated from their origin in the touching ceremony. According to Browne, touchpieces could be found for sale in goldsmiths' shops.[19] Others were passed down as heirlooms. In 1731 a Luton tinplate worker left as a bequest "two pieces of gold, with the chain which I generally wear by way of prevention of the King's Evil."[20] Bloch discovers that coins of Charles I were passed down from generation to generation for healing scrofula in the Shetland Islands well into the nineteenth century.[21] Even after the healing ceremonies had ceased, the coins or touchpieces used in them continued to circulate as remnants or relics of the mystical event.

However, not all were comfortable with the implications of these angels and touchpieces. In the first systematic treatise on the "evil," *Charisma: Sive Donum Sanationis* (1597), Elizabeth's chaplain William Tooker describes the coin not as an amulet, "but merely [as] a symbol of commencing recovery of health and a token of holy charity."[22] Tooker was apparently responding to common opinion, the belief that the coin constituted a curative talisman. A 1657 account tells how Mary Boyes recovered from the evil after being touched by Charles I at Hampton Court in 1647, but "leaving from about her neck the money given her at the time of her being touched, the disease broke out again and proved irrecoverable."[23] Throughout his book *Adenochoiradelogia*, Browne describes many instances in which the loss of the coin or touchpiece would induce relapses in patients: "for I have seen many upon the loss of their Gold, their Evil has come afresh, and proved troublesome."[24]

Such relics circulating as healing agents could, of course, be considered idolatrous in Protestant England. But the most effective defense against charges of idolatry was to identify the miracle as the work of God, and not that of the monarch, and (like Tooker) to consider the coin as merely a memento of an extraordinary event. Tooker underscores God's role in the ceremony in describing how a flock of country folk approached Elizabeth for healing during one of her progresses through Gloucestershire. Elizabeth told the people that she wished she "could give [them] help and succour," but that only God, who is "the best and greatest physician of all," has the power to relieve their sickness and they must, therefore, pray to Him. Tooker emphasizes the prayer component of the ceremony to prevent the belief that the queen herself performed miracles: "How often have I seen her most Serene Majesty prostrate on her knees, body and soul wrapt in prayer, calling upon God and beseeching the Saviour Christ for such as these."[25] Nevertheless, according to Henry Stubbe, Elizabeth had considered terminating the ceremony because of its idolatrous implications:

> Queen Elizabeth did, for some time, discontinue the Touching for the King's Evil, doubting either the Success, or Lawfulness of that way of Curing. But she soon quitted that Fit of Puritanisme, when the Papists defamed her, as if God had withdrawn from her the gift of Healing in that manner, because she had withdrawn herself from the Roman Church.

The queen at once questioned whether she indeed had the power to cure and whether her performance might constitute idolatry. Stubbe takes a less meticulous view of idolatry, calling her hesitation a "Fit of Puritanisme" to imply that its cessation would constitute an act of zealous iconoclasm. Nevertheless, Elizabeth continued to feel pressure both from Catholics, who thought the queen had no right to perform the mystery, and from Puritans, who thought the practice was idolatrous.[26]

We find in this moment of doubt a conflict between the political need to prove her royal legitimacy against Catholic detractors and an anxiety about whether such proof would affect religious reform. Deborah Willis explains how the ceremony allowed Elizabeth to "tap into the energies of both popular and orthodox religious forms, and put them at the disposal of the secular interests of the Crown"; however, by so doing she made herself "subject to the implications those belief-systems carried with them." While the need to recouch the ritual in Protestant terms pressured the monarch to present herself "in terms of Christian piety and devotion" and appear to be "a Protestant saint," the move to make its source of power more ambiguous diluted "the monarch's sacred mystique, raising questions about the uniqueness of the royal blood and the idea of an inherited sacred power."[27] Elizabeth may have continued the ritual in order to prove her legitimacy against Catholic claims to the contrary, especially after being excommunicated. Tooker describes how Elizabeth healed a Roman Catholic prisoner who testified that the bull of excommunication had not negated her gift. And in a November 16, 1602 sermon, the queen's chaplain John Howson argued from precedent that her persistent healing power legitimated her reign: "when *Vespasian* was seen to perform such a cure the people concluded he should be Emperor, as Tacitus notes."[28] Her healing power was used to justify even giving her ambassadors diplomatic preference over Spanish ambassadors.[29] So despite her initial "Fit of Puritanisme," Elizabeth comprehended the political power inherent in the ritual and continued to provide necessary relief for her subjects.

However, a similar "Fit" in James threatened to terminate the ceremony once and for all. James was concerned about endorsing a ritual ingrained in England's Catholic past, particularly one associated with the iconic Edward the Confessor. Among three requests he made when first coming to England, he asked specifically that he not be required to touch for scrofula, "not wishing to arrogate vainly to himself such virtue and divinity, as to be able to cure diseases by touch alone."[30] In a letter dated June 4, 1603, a Venetian representative reported to the Doge and Senate, "King James says that neither he nor any other King can have any power to heal scrofula, for the age of miracles is past, and God alone can work them."[31] But James' English Council, headed by Cecil, eventually made James understand that discontinuing the ritual would detract from the dignity of the crown. So "inasmuch as it was an ancient usage and for the good of his subjects," as it was recorded in an October 9, 1603 letter, he finally "resolved to give it a trial, but only by way of prayer, in which he begged all present to join him." Still, the anxiety over his actions did not cease with this decision. In the same letter it is recorded that while James was performing the ceremony, "he several times turned his eyes towards the Scotch ministers around him, as though he expected their approval of what he was saying, having first conferred with them."[32] Considering his initial aversion to the ceremony, it is surprising that James eventually helped inspire conviction that the coins had assumed the healing power of the king.

Nevertheless, in order to allay his concerns, James altered the ritual to exclude papist and idolatrous elements, all of which involved the coin. He excluded the practice of crossing the sores of patients with the angel. Also, James removed from the reverse side of his angel a small cross on a ship's mast, and he excluded "*et EST MIRABILE*" from Mary and Elizabeth's motto on their coins: "*A DOMINO FACTUM EST ISTVD et EST MIRABILE in oculis nostris*" ("This was the Lord's doing, and it is marvelous in our eyes"). He wanted to eliminate any suggestion that the "royal touch" involved a miracle performed by the monarch. Still, James continued to perform the ceremony and include the coin. His service calls for the verse from John to be repeated "as often as the King putteth the Angel about their neckes."[33]

The Money Fetish and Routinization of Charisma

Considering all the anxiety that induced James to change the coin and its use, why did he continue to use the coin at all? Why was the coin apparently so important to the healing ritual?[34] Marc Bloch argues that by the

Elizabethan and Jacobean periods the coin had become essential to the rite in the public's eyes: "not to receive it at the hands of the king would have been to miss at least half the miracle." Robert Herrick, who appears to have gone through the ceremony and wrote a poem about it, "To The King, To cure the Evill," is clearly aware of the coin's significance, punning on finding an "angel" along with other biblical sources (the tree of life) and places (Bethesda) of healing during the ceremony:

> To find that Tree of Life, whose Fruits did feed,
> And Leaves did heale, all sick of humane seed:
> To finde *Bethesda*, and an Angel there,
> Stirring the waters, I am come; and here,
> At last, I find, (after my much to doe)
> The Tree, Besthesda, and the Angel too:
> And all in Your Blest Hand, which has the powers
> Of all those suppling-healing herbs and flowers.[35]

While Herrick is careful to specify that it is the king's touch that cures, he employs biblical associations along with the presence of an "angel" to intimate an alternative source for the healing power.

Whether or not it was considered necessary for the healing, the coin figured significantly in the ritual's popularity, both as currency and as personal memento of the monarch. Prior to Henry VII, the gift in all extant records was only a penny. Henry, or possibly one of his immediate predecessors during the War of the Roses, increased the amount to the angel—worth six shillings, eight pence under Henry and about ten shillings by the time of Elizabeth, or around three weeks' wages—providing a stronger incentive for patients to visit the monarch. Bloch finds it significant that this innovation occurred during the War of the Roses, when competing claimants to the throne would want to take advantage of crowds flocking to witness their divine gift.[36] The ability of a rival king to heal could provide testimony to his legitimacy. For example, John Fortescue defended the legitimacy of the Lancastrian Henry VI by denying that the then king, Edward IV, had the healing power.[37] Moreover, the monetary incentive could entice crowds of subjects necessary to prove legitimacy in the public's eyes. So despite concern about patients commodifying their gift, monarchs recognized ulterior motives for both subjects and ruler. The ceremony could, in effect, buy loyalty.

Also, the coin made the ceremony more convincing to others, whether it was interpreted as merely a symbolic token of the event or as a healing amulet. Elizabeth's physician William Clowes describes a seemingly incurable scrofulous individual who, having been wondrously transformed by the queen's touch, showed his "Angell of golde which her Majesty did put about his neck." There was a long tradition of employing coins as amulets, a tradition on which Henry VII likely drew when he incorporated angels into his healing ceremony. Henry Maguire describes the practice in the late Roman period and early Middle Ages, when coins "had value not only in the physical world of human exchange but also in the invisible world of spirits and demons."[38] During the late Middle Ages, soldiers sometimes used coins for protection on the battlefield, worn either around their necks—as English soldiers wore Edward III nobles—or attached to their helmets.[39] Keith Thomas describes how the inscription on Edward III's nobles, "*Jesus autem transiens per medium eorum,*" was believed to prevent the coin from being stolen and to protect its bearer from harm. The practice appears to have continued into the early modern period. Essex, writing to Elizabeth during his 1597 naval expedition against Spain, thanks her for the "five dear tokens" that she had sent him including a watch, a thorn, "and above all the angel which you sent to guard me."[40]

Gold coins such as the angel were especially suitable as amulets. First, gold was thought to have inherent natural properties that could heal certain ailments. The most common medicinal use of gold was the *aurum potabile*, drinkable gold, believed to cure a number of diseases and even to be an elixir of long life.[41] In *2 Henry IV*, Prince Hal addresses his father's crown, comparing the useless, higher-carat gold crown to the useful, lower-carat *aurum potabile*: "Therefore thou best of gold art (worst of) gold. / Other, less fine in carat, (is) more precious, / Preserving life in med'cine potable" (4.5.160–2). Thomas connects the belief to a popular theory that metals were living organisms like plants and so could have medicinal benefits to other living organisms. He relates this to the alchemical quest, especially in Paracelsus, for whom the philosopher's stone served as panacea in addition to having power to transform base metals to gold. "With Paracelsus," Thomas asserts, "alchemy had shifted from a search for gold to a quest for a better pharmacopoeia."[42]

Many believed that gold could cure by being worn *on* the body as well, especially as a ring. For example, monarchs' "cramp rings" allegedly cured epilepsy. Sir John Fortescue describes how English kings would produce these rings during the Good Friday service, and he testifies to their effectiveness according to widespread reports.[43] As with the angels, an elaborate ceremony transformed cramp rings into healing agents. From the time of Edward II through Henry V, the king would place freshly minted gold and silver coins on an altar and then "redeem" these by exchanging them for an equivalent sum in ordinary coin. Finally, he would have these new coins melted down to produce rings from the metal. In the Tudor version, the rings were made ahead of time, and the ordinary coin redeemed the rings themselves from the altar.[44] Thomas locates the practice's source in the belief that offertory coins and communion silver, along with nearly everything else in the Catholic church, were thought to have magical curative powers and to protect one from various dangers. There are even medieval recipes for making magic rings out of church offerings.[45]

In addition to being composed of curative gold, coins typically bore the ruler's image, which from the classical to the Byzantine period was regarded as a protective agent.[46] Some early modern rulers, especially Elizabeth, exploited this tradition. Roy Strong links the English cult of Elizabeth to the Byzantine icon, arguing that the royal portrait filled "the vacuum left by the pre-Reformation image cult." He points out that wearing her portrait came to replace wearing the royal arms as a sign of loyalty. Especially prominent was wearing cameos with the royal image, an act that emulated the antique practice. Moreover, this practice crossed class lines in "an almost universal cult of the royal image in Elizabethan England." While aristocrats wore the elaborate cameos and miniatures, the lower sorts wore medals made of base metals or even coins. Elizabeth's images, the "icons of royal 'power,'" also circulated on official documents from periodically replaced official patterns, like those on seals and coins. Although the Anglicans denounced religious images as popish superstition, royal images, as representations of the state, offered a secularized version of the mystery. Strong finds that subjects would wear Elizabeth's image as a kind of talisman, making her cult "draw to itself mysterious traditions."[47] Indeed, the royal image extended its cult beyond the borders of England and even of Europe. As I discussed in my introduction, Sir Walter Raleigh purportedly gave inhabitants of Guiana freshly minted coins "with her Majestys picture to weare, with promise that they would become her servants thenceforth."[48] Raleigh, in effect, extended the cult of Elizabeth to the "New World" through the aesthetic value of her coins.

But rather than a portrait of the monarch, the angel depicted the archangel Michael, whose image might constitute a remnant of the "pre-Reformation image cult." The figure of Michael slaying the dragon, which has been read as a type for the healer Apollo trampling the serpent of pestilence, is an appropriate representation of mystical healing.[49] Moreover, the circulation of this sacred image on coins could signify the monarch's divine favor. For example, Shakespeare's Richard II employs a common pun on "angels" to affirm his royal prerogative:

> For every man that Bullingbrook hath press'd
> To lift shrewd steel against our golden crown,
> God for his Richard hath in heavenly pay
> A glorious angel; then if angels fight,
> Weak men must fall, for heaven still guards the right. (3.2.58–62)

Richard compares the men Bullingbrook has "press'd" to worthless, steel currency contesting his pure, golden angels. His control over coinage allows Richard to "press" both coins, as in the stamping process, as well as soldiers, who are impressed into his army.[50] Despite the problematic conflation of material and spiritual sources of power in this pun (which might emblematize the play's broader concerns about legitimacy of usurpation), the embattled monarch implicitly transforms the coins he produces into an army of angels sent by God to defend "his Richard." James Maxwell puns on the angels used in James's healing ceremony to describe how the "happy *Britaines*" are "Garded of Angels both by Sea and Land." Angel coins, therefore, embodied the protective power of God's agents, for scrofula sufferers in particular, for the English people in general, and for the monarch bearing the divine gift.[51]

Connections to divinity may also be found in coins' imprinted mottoes, typically taken from scripture. Recall that in Henry VII's ceremony the passage from John accompanied the crossing of patients with the angel, and James initially wanted to cure "only by way of prayer."[52] Although reformists would deny such a connection, prayers might be compared to charms and incantations, which some believed could heal by materially affecting the air, just as ritualistic pronunciation of words in the transubstantiation could transform material objects.[53] Even writing prayers down on paper and wearing them around one's neck served some as spiritual protection. Bishop Joseph Hall describes a belief in the protective power of St. John's Gospel: "printed in a small roundel and sold to the credulous ignorants with this fond warrant, that whosoever carries it about with him shall be free from the dangers of the day's mishaps."[54] The Gowrie plot to murder James, which some critics have related to *Macbeth*, has an interesting version of this phenomenon. When Gowrie was stabbed in the attempt, his body refused to bleed until James removed from his pocket a "little close parchment bag." Once the bag was displaced, "blood gushed out in great abundance" from Gowrie's wounded body. Gowrie's bag was found to be "full of Magicall characters, and words of inchantment, wherin it seemed that hee had put his confidence, thinking himselfe never safe without them."[55] Words on coins were believed to bear similar powers. The legend on Edward III's nobles was a significant factor in the perception that the coins served as protective agents. Similarly, the motto on James's angels, "*A DOMINO FACTUM EST ISTVD*" [This was the Lord's doing...], attested to God's presence during the ceremony, and persistent wearing of this remnant would offer constant protection from scrofula.

Angels, therefore, combined the power of gold, the figure of Michael and royal images, and a prayer or "charm" in the form of the coin's legend. In his ceremonial presentation of the coin in amuletic form, Henry VII channeled, and perhaps exploited, popular beliefs about the magic of coins. Moreover, the ceremony demonstrates the visual power of money, the idea that money's power was not limited to perceptions of its numeric value. As with the earlier passage from Clowes, in which the patient shows the angel he had received from the king, the coin offered both a source of pride for patients and material evidence of the monarch's gift. Many in Shakespeare's audience would likely have seen one of these "golden stamps" and have been reminded of the present king.

Despite its idolatrous implications, the angel proved a potent device for promoting allegiance to the monarch, and it was, therefore, politically expedient for James to adopt its use. To guarantee his position, James would employ the energy of what Thomas calls a "primitive piece of magic" while surrounding it with a religious ceremony to serve as "a protective framework" against charges of idolatry. Although the king's touch was the primary agent in the ceremony, the gold coin, which for James became the mediator between himself and the bodies of ill subjects, assumed an essential role in the perceived efficacy of the ritual. Moreover, from the popular perspective, the coins offered a crucial incentive, whether their value was perceived as primarily mystical, memorial, or monetary. And from the royal perspective, the sight of subjects wearing the king's coins constituted a conspicuous display of allegiance to the monarch and proof of his divinity. The intimate connection between coins and state permitted the monarchs to transform popular superstitions into what James would call the "mystery of State," which I discuss further at the end of this chapter.[56]

The coins, therefore, became an essential component in the circulation of state authority, and their distribution contributed to what Max Weber calls the "routinization of charisma." Weber asserts that in certain forms of government—those based on "charismatic authority" as opposed to the other "pure types of legitimate domination": "rational" (or "legal") and "traditional" authority—the legitimacy of a ruler is based on *charisma*, which he defines as "a certain quality of an individual personality by virtue of which he is considered extraordinary and treated as endowed with supernatural, superhuman, or at least specifically exceptional powers or qualities."[57] The charismatic authority thus stands distinct from the masses and must routinely display this distinction to maintain legitimacy. But beyond the "individual personality," charisma may exist as an "objective, transferable entity" transmitted from one individual to another—especially, for kings, through the ritual of anointing and coronation—thus constituting what Weber terms the *"charisma of office"*: "In this case the belief in legitimacy is no longer directed to the individual, but to the acquired qualities and to the effectiveness of the ritual acts." As Stuart Clark observes, the scrofula ceremony "conforms well to the Weberian ideal-type in its routinized version" since it could be construed as a divine gift "located in the office and not the person of the king."[58] It was indeed the "charisma of office" that James's advisors appealed to when they encouraged him to keep the healing ceremony alive. The public's perception of James's powers, regardless of whether he himself believed he actually possessed them, offered persistent proof of his legitimacy, and the ceremony was, therefore, a potent public display of royal charisma.

Moreover, I would argue that the particular use of the angel in the healing ceremony constitutes an extreme version of routinized charisma found in *all* coinage. Indeed, the ceremony exploited the coin *as* an important form of routinized charisma. Weber himself writes that "the process of routinization of charisma is in very important respects identical with adaptation to the conditions of the economy, since this is the principal continually operating force in everyday life." General usage of coinage signaled the public's acceptance of the king's stamp as guarantor of value, acceptance of the legitimacy of the king's office as producer of money. Historians have noted the presence of charismatic authority in other circulating objects containing royal images. For example, M. T. Clanchy describes how Henry's II's dispersion of writs, especially with their royal seals depicting Henry crowned and seated on his throne, represented an early instance of routinized charisma for the English state because the laws of the realm were accompanied by a visual representation of the monarch's majesty.[59] I would argue that coins such as James's rose ryal, which likewise depicts the monarch seated upon his throne, served in a similar capacity (see cover image and figure 5.2, www.stephendeng.com). Indeed, coins circulated more widely than writs so they could more effectively disseminate royal charisma. Coins could be considered deputies of the state and thus might assume even mystical properties of the ruler, as does the angel in the healing ceremony. Clark, citing Marshall Sahlins, notes that in the deputation process, the "logic of 'descending' authority also ensured the transfer of much of the rhetoric of mystical politics from the prince to his judicial subordinates—'structurally amplifying' the personal effects of charisma...by transmitting them 'along lines of established relationships.'"[60] The sacred nature of the monarch could in this manner "descend" to his coinage as well.

The everyday use of money and the state's monopoly on coinage production represented an early version of routinized charisma ingrained in economic activity. The pinnacle of monetary charisma was reached when the state could produce valuable paper money independent of the state's supply of gold—and, in fact, dependent only on the public's faith in the state. What better sign of the modern state's charisma, its "supernatural" or "superhuman" powers, than its ability to turn an ordinary piece of paper into a valuable commodity? But it would take years for the state to develop such a capability. All legitimate money in early modern England contained precious metals, either gold or silver, and, as we shall see, perceptions of the state's own legitimacy depended on the routinized charisma produced by a healthy flow of metallic money. The health of monetary flow and the state's charismatic power as embodied in coinage ultimately sheds light on the issue of royal legitimacy in *Macbeth*.

Macbeth, Money, and Mystical Kingship

As *Macbeth* begins, we find a conspicuous exchange of courtesies between Macbeth and Duncan, but with an implicit system of accounting for the unequal relation of tribute and reward. Harry Berger notes that the "tone is courtly and effusive, but the language is that of competition, debt and payment."[61] Such coding of courtesy using accounting terms gradually creates tension in the relationship between Macbeth and Duncan. Early on we find suggestions of even exchange when the loyal Macbeth receives the title Thane of Cawdor from the rebel who initially held it: "What [Cawdor] hath lost, noble Macbeth hath won" (1.2.67). Although Angus claims that Rosse and he come not to "pay" Macbeth for his service (1.3.103), Macbeth's prior description of Cawdor as a "prosperous gentleman" (73) suggests that the "addition" (106) he receives from that title is substantial. Along with the material rewards, Macbeth has "bought / Golden opinions from all sorts of people" which he wears "now in their newest gloss" and would "not cast aside so soon" by going against Duncan (1.7.32–35). Such honors come heaping in at the start, as Rosse tells how the posts came to Duncan "as thick as tale" bearing Macbeth's "praises in his kingdom's great defense, / And pour'd them down before him" (1.3.97–100). A note in the *Riverside Shakespeare* explains the phrase "as thick as tale" to mean "as fast as they could be 'told' or counted," as if there is an implicit attempt to enumerate Macbeth's praises within a financial reckoning.[62] Nevertheless, the financial reckoning initially measures social or communal value of individuals based on the "golden opinions" of others, rather than a purely self-interested metric of personal worth to be cashed in for material benefits.

But the dialogue gradually intimates that Macbeth's tribute and service to the king far outweigh the rewards and honors that Duncan has bestowed on him. Macbeth's generosity extends from the courtesies of food and shelter to the provision of military service the king needs to maintain his position. Duncan even uses the metaphor of feeding off of the "commendations" of "so valiant" Macbeth, whose glories provide a veritable "banquet" for him, conflating the luxuries he enjoys from Macbeth's military service and hospitality (1.4.54–56). Moreover, when Rosse describes how "as thick as tale" messengers poured down Macbeth's "praises in his kingdom's great defense," the image connotes tribute given to Duncan rather than to the loyal soldier. The honors that Macbeth receives are immediately bestowed on his king, and Rosse states that when Duncan reads about Macbeth's "personal venture in the rebels' fight, / His wonders and his praises do contend / Which should be" Macbeth's and which Duncan's (1.3.90–93). Duncan is, in fact, profiting from Macbeth's exploits, and we sense conflict even within this outpouring of courtesy. The king explicitly acknowledges, albeit in courteous terms, the imbalance in exchange between Macbeth and himself:

> O worthiest cousin!
> The sin of my ingratitude even now
> Was heavy on me. Thou art so far before,
> That swiftest wing of recompense is slow
> To overtake thee. Would thou hadst less deserv'd,
> That the proportion both of thanks and payment
> Might have been mine! Only I have left to say,
> More is thy due than more than all can pay. (1.4.14–21)

Despite the gracious tone, we sense Duncan's bitterness about having to repay Macbeth for all he has done. He later confesses that "The love that follows us sometime is our trouble, / Which still we thank as love" (1.6.11–12). Duncan feels uncomfortable about all the courtesies and service Macbeth has shown since he can imagine it leading only to resentment.

Outwardly, Macbeth and Lady Macbeth deny any imbalance in the system of reward and tribute. They profess that the honor Duncan has bestowed on them outweighs all they have provided. For example, Lady Macbeth states that their service even "in every point twice done, and then done double, / Were poor and single business" when compared with the "honors deep and broad wherewith" Duncan "loads [their] house" (1.6.15–18). They identify themselves as Duncan's mere "servants," who "have theirs, themselves, and what is theirs, in compt, / To make their audit at [Duncan's] pleasure, / Still to return [his] own" (1.6.25–28). Rather than a quid pro quo economy among strangers, Macbeth describes a hierarchical family unit based on loyalty:

> The service and the loyalty I owe,
> In doing it, pays itself. Your Highness' part
> Is to receive our duties; and our duties
> Are to your throne and state children and servants;
> Which do but what they should, by doing every thing
> Safe toward your love and honor. (1.4.22–27)

Macbeth revises accounting practices so that his glories as well as his debts become Duncan's assets. But although the Macbeths object that their obligation to Duncan transcends the accounting metaphors they use, the very employment of a financial calculus to convey these sentiments calls attention to the scarce and unequal distribution underlying the courtesy. From this perspective, Duncan has unfairly profited from the generosity of the Macbeths and has not come close to redeeming their service.

As Berger points out, Duncan is in a precarious position: "the more his subjects do for him, the more he must do for them; the more he does for them, feeding their ambition and their power, the less secure can he be of his mastery."[63] The tension reaches its breaking point when Duncan names Malcolm as his heir immediately after a speech confessing the imbalance in his accounts with Macbeth, frustrating Macbeth's desires that the prophecy of the witches come true. The investiture of Malcolm as Prince of Cumberland creates an obstacle to obtaining the throne peacefully. Therefore, seeing himself barred from the "golden round / Which fate and metaphysical aid doth seem / To have [him] crown'd withal" (1.5.28–30), Macbeth seems resolved to claim what he feels he deserves according to the logic of the balance sheet. Nonetheless, he requires prodding from Lady Macbeth, who thinks "good to deliver" to her "dearest partner of greatness" the crown as "the dues of rejoicing" that is his (and hence her) "promis'd" greatness (1.5.10–13). She even uses financial terms to spur Macbeth into action. When he at first refuses to carry out the murder, she declares, "From this time / Such I account thy love" (1.7.38–39). Therefore, to balance accounts, Lady Macbeth translates Duncan's being "provided for" from literal courtesies and services due to the king into a problem requiring solution: "He that's coming / Must be provided for" (1.5.66–67).[64] In collecting on Duncan's debt, Lady Macbeth converts provision for Duncan into provision for herself and her husband, thereby inverting the logic of Macbeth's earlier statement that their service to Duncan provided its own reward.

The discourse surrounding the murder of Duncan, especially the assumed motive of the alleged murderers, maintains the early financial language of the play, but it also shifts attention toward recognition of money's mystical implications. In Macbeth's description of Duncan's body, the golden blood of Duncan atop the faces of the grooms suggests a motive of avarice:

> Here lay Duncan,
> His silver skin lac'd with his golden blood,
> And his gash'd stabs look'd like a breach in nature
> For ruin's wasteful entrance; there, the murtherers,
> Steep'd in the colors of their trade, their daggers
> Unmannerly breech'd with gore. (2.3.111–16)

When Macbeth describes the murderers "Steep'd in the colors of their trade," we are reminded of Lady Macbeth's earlier plan to "gild the faces of the grooms" with Duncan's blood, which "must seem their guilt" (2.2.53–54). The first folio's spelling of "guild," which is even closer to the latter "guilt," makes the pun transparent.[65] The references to Duncan's "golden blood" and Lady Macbeth's "gilding" of the suspects' faces indicate a material purpose for the murder—the desire for gold.[66] Donalbain later expresses similar concern that he and Malcolm might be implicated based on a material motive when he quotes to Malcolm what seems like a proverb appropriate for their situation: "the near in blood, / The nearer bloody" (2.3.140–41). The lines are typically interpreted to mean that Donalbain fears that the person who killed Duncan would want to kill them as well. However, the lines also imply that the two might seem to have a motive for murder because they are in line to inherit from the king. They might be considered "nearer bloody" not from being murdered but from gilding themselves with material rewards of the act, the golden blood of Duncan, thereby falsely presenting their guilt. But by fleeing the scene, they merely raise more suspicion, which Macbeth uses for his own ascent. Macbeth, therefore, "lies like truth" by assigning to the false agents the true motive of the crime—the "golden round" and all its ancillary material benefits. The "breach" in Duncan's body lets the Macbeths—and, according to Lady Macbeth's theatrical scheme, the murderers—"breech" themselves in luxury, following the oft-recognized motif of clothing as a sign of position and status throughout the play.[67]

A consummate materialist, Macbeth attempts to use his acquired resources to maintain his position, subscribing to Cicero's popular epithet for money: the "sinews of war."[68] He gathers information from paid spies to discover Macduff's intentions: "There's not a one of them but in his house / I keep a servant fee'd" (3.4.130–1). And when Macduff finally returns to Scotland with an army, he complains that he "cannot strike at wretched kerns, whose arms / Are hir'd to bear their staves" (5.7.17–18), implying that Macbeth has purchased mercenaries for his defense. Michael Hawkins notes the "unquestioned acceptance" in the play, even by the "'saintly'" Duncan, of "fighting essentially for money: it is pinpointed in I.ii.61–4, when Sweno's men are refused burial until he has paid ransom."[69] Although this may be a reference to Mary Queen of Scots, who was said to use foreign mercenaries and place spies in opponents' household (in addition to heeding witches' prophecies), these material resources used to bolster Macbeth's position echo earlier financial tropes. But unlike Duncan, Macbeth will keep his books balanced by paying those who support him according to the value of their service.

Nevertheless, although Macbeth has acquired the "sinews of war" to buy an army and even a system of surveillance for information gathering, his money lacks the mystical aura of the golden blood flowing from Duncan's body. Macbeth's own simile in his description of the murdered Duncan, "like a breach in nature / For ruin's wasteful entrance," depicts an image of unnatural violation. Moreover, this "breach" in Duncan's body resonates with classical and contemporary images of the avaricious plundering of nature. In *Metamorphoses* Ovid explains how during the Iron Age, people "eft...gan to digge, / And in the bowels of the ground unsaciably to rigge, / For Riches couch't and hidden deepe, in places nere to Hell." While gold naturally inheres in the earth's veins, greed drives people to breach the earth in search of riches, which in Ovid are "the spurres and stirrers unto vice, and foes to doing well." And in Book 2 of *The Faerie Queene*, Spenser's knight Guyon describes to Mammon, the figure of avarice, the fall from the "antique world" into the "pride" of "later ages":

> Then gan a cursed hand the quiet wombe
>   Of his great Grandmother with steele to wound,
>   And the hid treasures in her sacred tombe,
>   With Sacriledge to dig. Therein he found
>   Fountaines of gold and siluer to abound,
>   Of which the matter of his huge desire
>   And pompous pride eftsoones he did compound;
>   Then auarice gan through his veines inspire
> His greedy flames, and kindled life-deuouring fire.[70]

Spenser appends to Ovid's vivid violation of nature the sense of "Sacriledge" in looting the "sacred tombe" of the earth. The search for riches, therefore, becomes an affront to both nature and God. The resonance between such images and Duncan's "golden blood" flowing from a "breach in nature" suggests not only the excessive greed motivating Duncan's murderers but also the very sinful violence against nature inherent in the act of stabbing the king's body.

Moreover, according to the theory of the king's two bodies, Duncan's body would simultaneously house the body politic.[71] While the theory was developed primarily for legalistic purposes, ceremonies such as the "royal touch" would offer evidence of this immortal presence. Paul Kléber Monod writes that the healing ceremony "bestowed on monarchs a divine aura that adhered to the royal body itself. It must have seemed to many that the king, like Christ, encompassed a mystical body in his own."[72] However, according to the theory, since the "politic body is immortal, and not subject to death," technically it cannot be endangered, so treason, according to Coke's report on *Calvin's Case* (1608), or "to intend or compass *mortem et destructionem domini Regis*, must needs be understood of his natural body."[73] Therefore, the treasonous act evident in Macbeth's vision of Duncan's bleeding body must first be understood in terms of the violated body natural of the earthly king.

And yet, as Kantorowicz notes, "an attack against the king's natural person was, at the same time, an attack against the body corporate of the realm," that is, an attack against the king's mystical as well as physical body.[74] This explains why Macbeth's metaphoric description of Duncan's body—"silver skin lac'd with his golden blood"—assumes more abstract and symbolic qualities. W. A. Murray interprets Duncan's blood in light of alchemical theories, in particular as an "alchemical tincture, an enormously strong colouring agent made of perfected matter, which has the power of transmuting substances." The image connotes Duncan's sanctity, as his skin "shines with the silver light of heaven" and as his blood "glows and flows in the presence of the murderer. It is golden, for it is already in the hand of God. It is part of the perfection of heaven."[75] The details of Duncan's body transmute the image of earthly violence into an emblem of royal divinity.

However, the violence against Duncan's body also constitutes violence against the realm. The image of divinity simultaneously suggests a more visceral early modern trope: money as the blood of the body politic. For example, Barnabe Barnes writes,

> For even as moneyes are fitly called the sinews of war, so may we likewise properly tearme them the blood of peace: and therefore that state or kingdome, whose treasure is exhausted (though it be most ample, populous, and puissant in other things) may be called bloodlesse and languishing... Riches therefore may bee properly tearmed the blood of peace, that entering the veines or conduits of the liver, which may semblably be likened to the Treasurers office, and reflowing thence, benignely disperseth it selfe into the members of the whole body, resembling analogically the Commonwealth, for the generall sustentation and nurriture thereof.[76]

Or in a passage that resonates with the image of Duncan's body, Gerard Malynes wrote a few years later that "*Bullion* is the very Body and Bloud of Kings, *Money* is but the Medium betweene Subjects and their Kings, *Exchange* the heavenly Mystery that joynes them both together."[77] Duncan's "silver skin" and especially his "golden blood" should be interpreted in light of *both* the circulation of bullion in the form of money—the "Medium betweene Subjects and their Kings"—and the "Mystery that joynes them both together" within the political theology of the king's two bodies. As the source of vitality, money becomes central to this mystical conjunction. In a healthy commonwealth, the mint disburses coinage, which courses through the king's second body, the immortal body politic. In addition to the "sinews of war" whose strength defends the commonwealth's borders, money provides daily nourishment to the body's interior through trade and commerce.

A healthy flow of money keeps the body sound, but if the flow is disturbed, the health of the commonwealth may suffer. Thomas Hobbes calls disruption in monetary flow one of the "Diseases of a Commonwealth," and he specifically compares it to

> an Ague; wherein, the fleshy parts being congealed, or by venomous matter obstructed; the Veins which by their naturall course empty themselves into the Heart, are not (as they ought to be) supplied from the Arteries, whereby there succeedeth at first a cold contraction, and trembling of the limbes; and afterwards a hot, and strong endeavour of the Heart, to force a passage for the Bloud; and before it can do that, contenteth it selfe with the small refreshments of such things as coole for a time, till (if Nature be strong enough) it break at last the contumacy of the parts obstructed, and dissipateth the venome into sweat; or (if Nature be too weak) the Patient dieth.[78]

Following his depiction of Duncan's body, Macbeth describes a similar obstruction of blood flow when he tells Malcolm and Donalbain, "The spring, the head, the fountain of your blood / Is stopp'd, the very source of it is stopp'd" (2.3.98-99). However, Duncan's internal blood flow is disrupted by the *external* wound from Macbeth rather than from an internal ague. Although this fountain of blood does not allude explicitly to a monetary flow, it prefigures the developing sickness in Scotland due to an external obstruction in legitimate inheritance. Therefore, Macbeth's attack on Duncan, which in theory destroys only the body natural, also represents a disturbance in the normal blood flow of the commonwealth. And Duncan's "golden blood" suggests the salutary benefits of money, which keeps the commonwealth vigorous. Spilled golden blood signals renewed awareness in Macbeth that the health of the body politic is inextricably bound with legitimacy, and that only the *legitimate* king can produce the *kind* of money necessary to maintain the country's health.

The introduction of Edward the Confessor and the touching ceremony, which points to the contemporary dissemination of healing coins, dramatizes the stakes of Macbeth's temporary suppression of money's mystical dimension before Duncan's murder. The healing power of the legitimate king's coinage serves as a counterpoint to the various images of disease that proliferate after the murder of Duncan, first in reference to the mental condition of Lady Macbeth, but later in reference to Scotland itself. In her mad ramblings, Lady Macbeth expresses surprise at the excessive blood flowing from Duncan: "Yet who would have thought the old man to have had so much blood in him?" (5.1.39-40). Her madness gives Shakespeare an occasion to introduce a second doctor, whose commentary amplifies the motif of disease. The doctor knows that Lady Macbeth's disease transcends her mental state; he realizes that these "unnatural troubles" are merely signs of "unnatural deeds" (5.1.71–72). Scotland, in fact, suffers from the "king's evil." Moreover, Malcolm and his troops abroad see themselves as the cure, inverting Macbeth's assertion that they are its disease. Cathness describes Malcolm as "the med'cine of the sickly weal, / And with him pour we, in our country's purge, / Each drop of us" (5.2.27–29). Susan Zimmerman ascribes Malcolm's medicinal quality to his father's "generative" blood, which for the Macbeths "is deadly contagion." Only by resuming blood flow from the legitimate line, only by restoring the "due of birth" (3.6.25) to the rightful heir, can Scotland be "purged" of its "king's evil."[79] Therefore, Malcolm significantly "is receiv'd / Of the most pious Edward" (26–27). Of course, as Peter Stallybrass points out, Edward provides Malcolm with the "practical aid of troops" in addition to "metaphysical aid of the 'sundry blessings' which hang about his throne." But it is the metaphysical aid of Edward's "med'cines" rather than the practical aid that is "guaranteed and legitimated by a godly magic which surpasses 'the great essay of art.'" Stuart Clark notes that the attribution of the "royal touch" to anointing of the hands suggested "not only the ability to heal individuals but the power to drive away evil from (and so 'heal') the entire commonwealth."[80] Like Edward curing the king's evil in England, Malcolm hopes to rid Scotland of its own evil.

We find in this connection a site for the production of the ideology of legitimate kingship, the belief that Scotland will be made healthy with the purgation of Macbeth and that the blood of the body politic will flow again. Jonathan Goldberg argues that the ideology of kingship is at first an obstacle for Macbeth, but it also becomes a source of legitimacy for him. By sanctifying Duncan, Macbeth is able to produce a mystical aura around his own reign: "Macbeth succeeds as the king of the image repertoire." Although Macbeth does employ an "image repertoire" surrounding kingship, his perceptions of the golden blood flowing from Duncan, the "stopp'd" blood of Duncan's line, and the diseased state of Scotland suggest that he acknowledges a substantial part of this repertoire. The "blood of the body politic" signifying a healthy state will refuse to flow again until the rightful heir, whom Macbeth *knows* to be Malcolm, is restored to the throne.[81] The difference is that Macbeth's gold is not blessed, not the sacred "blood of the body politic" that sprang from the "now stopp'd" fountain of Duncan. His inability to appropriate the monetary mysticism means that his gild cannot be separated from his guilt. The only way to restart the fountain in Macbeth's eyes is to restore the rightful ruler to the throne. Although externally he can separate the "golden round" from Duncan's head, internally Macbeth cannot generate the golden blood of a legitimate king to keep his country healthy. He thereby learns that all money is not equivalent. Although producing the blood of the social body had become routinized, it still depended on the ability to recreate the charisma of legitimacy.

Mysteries of State

Given the power of this ideology we can understand why James would continue to distribute healing coins to subjects. Indeed, the healing ceremony was in itself an important public spectacle for promoting kingship. Monod notes that even though James publicly acknowledged his ceremony was merely prayer and not the performance of a miracle, many people still "continued to think of it as a claim to personal divinity." Crawfurd believes that the "very performance" of the ceremony "asserted that the King's authority was derived from God. It stamped the King at once as the Lord's Anointed, as king by the grace of God and not by the will of his subjects." And Willis, discussing the ceremony under Queen Elizabeth, argues that the unique combination of strangeness and familiarity as well as divinity and humanity in the ceremony "could work to strengthen the bonds between the monarch and her subjects, arousing in them loyalty, gratitude, and awe."[82] Despite its idolatrous implications, the healing ceremony was too politically powerful to discontinue.

Moreover, the ceremony fit well with the rhetoric of mystical politics James utilized in speeches. In a proclamation of 1610 James complained that various printed works "wade in all the deepest mysteries that belong to the persons or State of Kings or Princes, that are gods upon Earth," and their authors "will freely wade by their writings in the deepest mysteries of Monarchy and politique government." And in a speech to the Star Chamber of 1616, he advised the court not to "Incroach...upon the Prerogative of the Crowne: If there fall out a question that concernes my Prerogative or mystery of State, deale not with it, till you consult with the King or his Councell, or both." Kantorowicz identifies James as a key defender and even creator of the "mysteries of state" [*arcana imperii*], a secular version of the spiritual "mysteries of church" [*arcana ecclesiae*] and a key mystical concept in the new "pontificalism" of early modern states.[83]

Although he did not believe that the king performed a miracle in the healing ceremony, although he believed "the age of miracles is past," James knew that he needed to continue the ceremony, especially the distribution of angels, because he recognized an intimate connection between the gold coin—indeed, coinage in general—and political power. Biblical inscriptions on coins constituted for James an expression of royal prerogative and monarchical connection to divinity. In "A Defence of the Right of Kings," James writes that the "characters of Christs Name" in coin inscriptions "are advertisements and instructions to the people, that in shewing and yeelding obedience unto the King, they are obedient unto the King, they are obedient unto Christ."[84] Coins carried a message of obedience for subjects related to the king's mystical association with God.

James could, therefore, eschew concerns about idolatry because the healing coin connected more strongly to a *symbolic* economy of state—bound up with routinized charisma in coinage circulating within a mystical economy—than to the *miraculous* powers of kingship per se. Macbeth is ultimately unable to appropriate this symbolic economy of state because he perceives a critical difference between his own "sinews of war" and Duncan's "golden blood." Therefore, Macbeth cannot recreate the charisma of legitimacy despite his apparent efficiency in adopting routinized state structures, whereas James was able to discover a potent form of charisma in the healing ceremony despite disbelief in monarchical miracles. Weber describes the "genuine meaning of the divine right of kings" as the monarch's need to persist in demonstrating that he has not been "deserted by his god or his magical or heroic powers" and especially that his leadership continues "to benefit his followers."[85] If James did not believe the ceremony actually cured individual patients, he at least believed it contributed to the political strength of his state, a contribution that would ultimately "benefit his followers." The outflow of coins for the ceremony of the "king's evil" would circulate signs of a healthy state just like the golden blood flowing through the mystical body politic.

Chapter VI

Foreign Coins and Domestic Exclusion in Thomas Dekker's *The Shoemaker's Holiday*

In the previous chapter I discussed the symbolic and mystical import of coins conceived as blood flowing through the body politic. The state's health in this conception depends on a persistent and regular flow to nurture various parts of the realm. But, of course, England was not the only body politic; every sovereign state of Europe produced its own coinage, replete with portraits of rulers and iconography of state. Marx describes how "coined money assumes a *local and political character*, it uses different national languages and wears different national uniforms."[1] In early modern England, several such coins wearing "different national uniforms" circulated among the populace, putting pressure on the English state's claim to monopoly on coin production, as well as on any sense of self-contained national economy. Although there were attempts during the medieval period to prevent foreign coins from entering England, by the sixteenth century economic necessity and the persistence of the intrinsic value theory of money forced the state to recognize publicly given values for certain foreign coins circulating within England, based on the average known quality (gold or silver content) of that denomination.

Nevertheless, an emergent discourse, especially within dramatic texts, critiqued the presence of these foreign coins, in particular those whose quality had deteriorated due to general wear and tear, clipping or other alterations, or debasement by the foreign state. For example, in *Measure for Measure*, Lucio and two gentlemen associate specific continental coins with venereal disease:

> [*1. Gent*]: I have purchas'd as many diseases under her roof as come to—
> *2. Gent*: To what, I pray?
> *Lucio*: Judge.
> *2. Gent*: To three thousand dolors a year.
> *1. Gent*: Ay, and more.
> *Lucio*: A French crown more. (1.2.46–52)

The second gentleman's pun links the "dolors" of disease from frequenting prostitutes to the "dollar" coin—the English name for the German "thaler" as well as for the Spanish "piece of eight" prior to Scottish and later American adoption of the denomination. And Lucio's added "French crown" signifies coins current in England in addition to the bald heads of syphilitic Frenchmen. Although such puns seem to be merely linguistic play, they intimate genuine national concern about dangers from foreign coins circulating within England. The presence of foreign coins complicated the conception of money as blood of the body politic by suggesting that English blood had been "contaminated" by the foreign.

The comparison of coinage to disease may be read in light of Jonathan Gil Harris's *Sick Economies: Drama, Mercantilism and Disease in Shakespeare's England*, which traces connections in early modern England between mercantilist discourse and emergent models of disease spread through "foreign bodies," in opposition to the dominant Galenic model of humoral imbalance. "By provisionally reimagining disease as a foreign body," Harris writes, early modern "people in the sixteenth and seventeenth centuries produced new epistemologies within which objects such as the national economy and the global laws of trade could be preliminarily conceived." He, therefore, argues for the "pathologization of foreign bodies as an enabling discursive condition for the globally connected nation-state."[2] Foreign coins, which played an essential role in global trade while contributing to the emergence of national identity, would seem to function well within this dynamic, and frequent puns on foreign coins as foreign diseases suggest a productive site for the discursive "enabling" of the nation state.

However, I argue that the "pathologization" of foreign coins, made explicit in their association with disease, should also be read in the context of domestic social relations. In Thomas Dekker's *The Shoemaker's Holiday*, English experience with foreign coins depends on socioeconomic status. While merchants and aristocrats in the play employ higher-valued and internationally respected "prestige coins," many of foreign origin, the common laborers use domestic pence or shillings at most. From the perspective of commoners, even a much maligned coin such as the French crown, worth approximately a week's wages for skilled laborers in 1600, would be considered "aristocratic" in contrast to hardworking domestic pennies. Perceptions of the corrupting influence of foreign coins could, therefore, signal class resentment among the lower sorts excluded from the benefits of international trade.

I argue that the final scene of *Shoemaker's*, which most critics have interpreted in terms of inclusive festivity for the apprentice and journeyman shoemakers, instead evokes the laborers' general exclusion from global trade as well as their exploitation in military campaigns. The comic ignorance of Firk concerning foreign coins and the typical magnitude of trade deals, which contrasts with the sophistication shown in the elegant deal crafted by the coalition of the newly made merchant Eyre and his aristocratic partner Lacy, makes clear how separate are the worlds of laborers and bourgeois/aristocrats. Moreover, the body of Ralph, made lame from war with France, exposes a gross irony in the king's nationalistic call for a new troop surge. The only realistic aspiration for laborers to profit from foreign contact is through illicit appropriation while fighting abroad. Upon Ralph's departure for France, Hodge offers him a "blessing": "God send thee to cram thy slops with French crowns." Hodge's common pun on "crowns" as both heads and coins in this context suggests that the only opportunity to acquire foreign wealth for laborers such as Ralph lies in looting bodies after dutifully killing for the state: in order to profit from the foreign, the laborer must become a criminal. Moreover, the coin itself, the appropriated French crown, represents a potent symbol of discontent among laborers. English critique of foreign coins should, therefore, be considered not only as xenophobic expression of English nationalism but also as representative of domestic unrest and a history of economic and political exploitation.

"So Pale, So Lame, So Lean, So Ruinous"

Because of their intrinsic value, early modern coins tended to circulate relatively freely across borders. Indeed, Benjamin Cohen argues that the idea of "One Nation/One Money" is a relatively recent phenomenon.[3] He identifies the foundation of the concept in the 1648 Peace of Westphalia, the treaty that ended the Thirty Years War and, more importantly, created the convention of state sovereignty within geographical boundaries, effectively establishing "territoriality as the sole basis for Europe's political map." Yet, the idea of *monetary* sovereignty took longer to establish. Not until the nineteenth century, when states permitted only their own currency to circulate within their boundaries, did national governments start to secure monopoly control over production and distribution of money, a development Cohen calls the "Westphalian model of monetary geography." Carlo Cipolla notes that through the nineteenth century, adherence to the gold standard prevented states from regulating the movement of currency. However, in the middle of the century, legal prohibition of other currencies from circulating internally facilitated the establishment of monetary sovereignty.[4] Nations began revoking the privilege of foreign coins to serve as legal tender and limited to domestic currency "public receivability," payment of taxes, or other contractual obligations to the state. Cohen sees the modern situation of global competition between forms of money within transactional networks as a reemergence of the past situation, so in addition to being a late development, the Westphalian model of monetary geography did not persist for very long. "Currency spaces now," Cohen writes, "are shaped not by political sovereignty but by the invisible hand of competition— governments interacting together with societal actors in the social spaces created by money's transactional networks." Although governments still attempt formally to preserve their monopoly over monetary production and dissemination, they have limited control over monetary *demand*, which influences how money actually circulates.[5]

Before the nineteenth century, multiple currencies flowed within any given political space: in Cohen's terminology, money was effectively "deterritorialized." B. E. Supple cites a British Museum manuscript claiming that in 1614, 400 different coins circulated within the Low Countries while 82 types of coins circulated in France. In order to manage the numerous denominations, countries tended to translate "real" money, various coins serving as media of exchange, to a standardized system of "imaginary" money, or what Cipolla calls "ghost money," units of account typically related to a pound of pure silver but not usually existing as a particular coin: the "pound sterling" in England, the Latin "libra," or the French "livre."[6] Carolingian monetary reform established a precedent for the relation between pound, shilling, and penny: 240 pennies or 20 shillings were produced from a pound of silver, although for three centuries following the reform, the silver penny was the only coin actually produced—"shilling" and "pound" maintained mere ghostly existences.[7] Not until the end of the twelfth century did states begin to produce coins of higher denominations, whose values were nevertheless convertible to a given number of pennies. Any coin could then be "translated" in England into shillings and pence. For example, in his 1522 proclamation Henry VIII set the Venetian ducat at the value of four shillings and six pence sterling, so that even gold coins could be understood in terms of a certain (though "imaginary") quantity of silver.[8] Accounts were also maintained according to the quantity of pounds, shillings, and pence, denoted as *l.* (or *li.*, for *libra*), *s.* (for *solidus*), and *d.* (for *denarius*, the old Roman coin) respectively, although actual coins used to pay accounts did not necessarily exist in these denominations.

Participants within a domestic economy, then, could translate the value of individual foreign coins into recognizable denominations. According to Cipolla, the foreign coins that tended to circulate internationally were "big, full-bodied coins, the so-called *moneta grossa*," and not the "small fractional coins," often tokens made of a base metal that circulated only around the area of issue. Although many full-bodied coins traversed national borders, certain coins—what Cipolla refers to as "super money" and Rupert Ederer as "prestige-coins," the latter of which I adopt—tended to be more prominent in international circulation because they were in high demand and readily accepted.[9] There was typically only one coin at a given time holding this distinction, but other countries would often imitate them, producing a coin with similar weight, fineness, and even design and inscription. Prestige-coins tended to be relatively valuable, ranging in weight from 3.5 to 4.5 grams of gold; they maintained a stable intrinsic value for a long period after their first issue and the issuing state tended to have a strong economy extensively engaged in international trade.[10]

Versions of prestige-coins date back to ancient Greece, shortly after the Western invention of coinage. Cohen singles out as the "first genuinely international currency" the silver *drachma* of Athens, a coin with the head of Athena on its obverse and an owl on its reverse, which became predominant in the fifth century B.C.E. Athenian *drachmae* could be found as far as India and northern Europe, and they later became the model for the Roman *denarius*, which initially imitated their weight and fineness. However, the *denarius* was less stable than the *drachma*, especially within Indian trade, so Roman authorities continued to mint *drachmae* for trade purposes.[11] From the fifth to seventh centuries, the gold *solidus* of the Byzantine Empire—known as *nomisma* by the Greeks and *bezant* in Western Europe—became the prestige-coin around the Mediterranean.[12] Arabs soon thereafter adopted and adapted the *solidus* into their own *dinar*, even inscribing on them the words of Allah,[13] and the *dinar* eventually replaced the *solidus* as the dominant coin circulating in the Mediterranean.

In 1252, Florence began producing its own gold coin, the *fiorino* (florin), named for the lily—the city-state's emblem—depicted on the coins, and in 1284 Venice first issued the ducat, named after its doges.[14] The florin dominated Mediterranean commerce from the middle of the thirteenth century to the end of the fourteenth, and the ducat rose to prominence in the fifteenth.[15] The ducat became so influential that areas of northern Europe began producing their own ducats, first in Hungary in 1325, and more importantly in the Low Countries in 1586; Dutch ducats soon circulated widely as the Dutch became a dominant player in global trade.[16] After colonization of the Americas the Spanish-Mexican silver *peso*, a "piece of eight" *reals,* later called the Spanish or Mexican "dollar," began to dominate international trade, primarily because most of the world's silver supply came from Mexico and South America after the first Mexican mint was created in 1535. *Pesos* circulated throughout the western hemisphere and much of the Far East via the Philippines and Goa. In the English New World colonies, they were virtually the only coins used, and they became the model for the first American dollar following the Revolutionary War.[17]

Prestige coins circulated relatively freely in England as in most territories. Although the florin was technically illegal in England in the thirteenth century, it became quite common there.[18] By the 1340s, England even issued its own florin, similar to the French version, in an attempt to produce gold coinage suitable for international trade, but it was soon replaced by another gold coin, the noble, whose denomination was more practical for English needs. Issuing its own gold coin was partly an attempt to control currency employed within England. During the Middle Ages, England was more successful than other countries in keeping foreign coins from circulating within its boundaries, primarily because of its relatively strong trade position. In the thirteenth century, Flemish merchants coming to England to buy wool needed to exchange their own coin and bullion for English sterling. Nicholas Mayhew finds in mint records several foreign merchants bringing their silver to the mint, where it was melted down and turned into English coin; the rules seem to have been observed for most transactions.[19]

By the time of the Renaissance, however, the state explicitly authorized many foreign coins, even less prestigious ones. In a 1522 proclamation, Henry VIII permitted florins and unclipped crowns "not soleil" (not French "crowns of the sun" but those from other regions, most often Burgundian or Flemish crowns) to circulate at given values in sterling.[20] A 1525 proclamation also made current the crown-de-soleil; the "carolus," presumably a silver coin of four *reals* struck by Charles V of Spain; "base" florins at a lower exchange than regular florins; "porpynes," most likely *ecus au porcepic*, gold coins struck by Louis XII depicting a porcupine and two ermines or the Dauphin flanked by two porcupines; "and all other crowns being of like fineness, of weight, as the crowns of the sun be."[21] Earlier, in 1469, Edward IV made an agreement with Duke Charles the Rash of Burgundy for English groats and Burgundian double patards to be interchangeable in England and the Low Countries. The Burgundian coins circulated alongside English coins for at least forty-five years after the agreement.[22]

Despite, or perhaps because of, the state's authorization of these foreign coins, English writers frequently alluded to their corrupting influence. In "Elegy XI. The Bracelet" John Donne contrasts his pure English angels, which by the late sixteenth century had become prestigious in northern Europe, to French crowns, which "their natural country's rot...possesseth" and "come here to us / So pale, so lame, so lean, so ruinous" (24–26). The supposedly gold crowns described by

Donne are "pale" from having a high content of a base metal such as tin, and they are "lame" and "lean" from clipping, washing, sweating, or any other means of reducing the precious metal content.[23] Figure 6.1 (www.stephendeng.com) displays a badly clipped French crown. Even though clipping and other forms of alteration were common practices in England, coin alteration, like usury, became associated with foreigners, especially Jews.[24] In the next two lines of "The Bracelet," Donne links circumcision and coin clipping, commenting that "howsoe'er French kings most Christian be, / Their crowns are circumcised most Jewishly" (27–28).[25] Despite their banishment from England, Jews continued to be linked with clipping primarily because of a famous case a few years before Jews were expelled from England in 1290 by Edward I. Holinshed's *Chronicles* records that in 1278, out of 297 people condemned for clipping, "There were but 3. Englishmen among them, all the residue were Jewes."[26]

Although Donne specifies that the poor condition of French crowns is how they "come here to us," much clipping and alteration of foreign coins was performed by the English themselves. There was a longstanding belief that "coining" laws did not pertain to foreign coins. In Shakespeare's *Henry V*, a disguised King Harry speaking with his soldiers attests that "it is no English treason to cut French crowns, and tomorrow the King himself will be a clipper" (4.1.227–9). Shakespeare's legislative knowledge proves deficient to the extent that he is alluding to current coining laws and not to those in effect at the time of Henry V, when the status of altering or forging foreign coins had not been explicitly articulated. Not until 1575 did Elizabeth's parliament issue a statute making clear that any alterations of coins current in England, including French crowns, would be considered treasonous (*18 Eliz.* c. 1).

Other statutes under Mary and Elizabeth attempted to dispel another erroneous belief that *forgery* of foreign coins was permitted. Figure 4.2 (www.stephendeng.com) displays a counterfeit portague whose underlying base metal shows through. In Jonson's *The Alchemist*, the conman Subtle proposes to the Puritan Tribulation a plan to forge foreign coins. He tells Tribulation that he has a "trick" whereby he melts pewter, "and with a tincture make you as good Dutch dollars / As any are in Holland."[27] When Tribulation worries whether "this act of coining, is…lawful" (149), another of the Brethren, Ananias, responds, "We know no magistrate; or, if we did, / This's foreign coin" (150–1). A 1554 statute notes such mistaken beliefs, complaining that "many ill disposed p[er]sons"

> have nowe of late brought into this Realme from the parties of beyonde the Sea greate quantity of forged and counterfeit money like to the said Coine of other foreine Realmes…because the said

ill disposed p[er]sons have perceived and understanded that ther was not nor yet is anye sufficient Lawe or Statute made or provided for the condigne punishement of thoffenders in that behalfn. (1&2 *Phil & Mary* c. 11)

The statute attempts to fill this lack of "sufficient Lawe or Statute" against forgery of foreign coins by clarifying that such offenses are as treasonous as forgery of English coins. Still, uncertainty remained about whether this statute covered foreign coins *not* legally current in England. A 1572 Elizabethan statute protests that subjects who perceived "small or no condigne Punishement" for forging non-current foreign coins were "encouraged and bouldened to counterfaite or forge such kind of Gold and Silver and utter the same in this Realme, in great Deceipte of her Majestys subjectes" (*14 Eliz.* c. 3). Once again, a statute had to close a loophole by stating explicitly that forgery of *any* coins, no matter their legal status as currency in England, would be considered a treasonous offense.

In addition to expressing general concern about the quality of coinage circulating within England, that is, contamination of the "blood of the social body," the state remained apprehensive about the purpose of these foreign coins, especially that they might supply the "sinews of war" for subversive causes. In Chapter IV I mentioned a link between counterfeiting and political subversion in the case against Christopher Marlowe. Enough money would allow any party to gain significant influence in Europe, and if the party could produce its own money, or acquire wealth through alteration of coin, it could threaten the English state. Indeed, Subtle in *The Alchemist* tempts the Brethren with such visions of political influence through money. Tribulation has been assured by "a learnèd elder" from Scotland that "*aurum potabile*" [drinkable gold] is "The only med'cine for the civil magistrate, / T' incline him to a feeling of the Cause; / And must be daily used in the disease" (3.1.40–4). In order to woo Tribulation as a client, Subtle elaborates on examples of how money—in particular, forged foreign coins—might help the cause. If, for example, "some great man in state" should "have the gout," the Brethren can merely "send three drops of [their] elixir" and they will "help him straight." "There," he concludes, "you have made a friend" (3.2.27–29). Subtle concludes in his sales pitch:

> You cannot
> But raise you friends withal, to be of power
> To pay an army in the field, to buy
> The King of France out of his realms, or Spain
> Out of his Indies. What can you not do
> Against lords spiritual or temporal,
> That shall oppone you? (3.2.45–51)

While Subtle's intension is to gull the Brethren, as he does to Sir Epicure Mammon by selling him the philosopher's stone, his proposed plan articulates a common fear of political subversion through illicit production of money.

Subtle suggests he will do for the Puritan cause what other foreign coins have done for the Catholic cause. In the Prologue to Act 2 of *Henry V*, France is described as filling the "hollow bosoms" of the traitors Cambridge, Scroop, and Grey "With treacherous crowns," which induce them to conspire "for the gilt of France," punning as in *Macbeth* on the homophone gilt/guilt that links money with morality (21–22, 26). In scene 2 of this act Harry echoes the Prologue's association of money with morality when he accuses Cambridge of having "for a few light crowns, lightly conspir'd," relating the impurity of the coins to the evil of conspiracy (89). The wordplay recalls Donne's description of French crowns, which "their natural country's rot...possesseth": deterioration in quality of a country's coinage becomes an indicator of that country's moral decay.

Therefore, the moral threat becomes inextricably bound to the political threat of foreign coins. In an account of the 1600 Gowrie conspiracy against James, Gowrie's brother lures the king to the Earl's castle by telling him that a suspicious "base-like fellow" was seen to have "a great wide pot...under his arme, all full of coined golde in great peeces." James suspects that "it had bin some forraine gold brought home by some Jesuites for practicing Papistes (therewith to stirre up some new sedition, as they have oftentimes done before)."[28] Spanish coins in particular were thought to have corrupted and destroyed several states. In "The Bracelet," Donne puns on Spanish coins as military arms when he describes "unfiled pistolets / That (more than cannon shot) avails or lets" (31–32).[29] According to Donne, these deadly coins

> Visit all countries, and have slyly made
> Gorgeous *France*, ruined, ragged, and decayed;
> *Scotland*, which knew no state, proud in one day;
> And mangled seventeen-headed *Belgia*. (39–42)

Spanish coins have led to the ruin of certain potential allies such as France before the conversion of Henri de Navarre and the Protestants in the Low Countries, as well as to the empowering of enemies such as Scotland under Mary Stuart. Importing foreign gold proved much easier than transporting foreign troops, and yet it could pose as immediate a threat to the state.

Forged or altered foreign coins might, therefore, contaminate not only the money supply but also the English Church by allowing "foreign elements," especially Catholicism, to infiltrate the country. While the two were practically linked by the ability of foreign coins to fund political subversion, they also became rhetorically linked with the idea that both involved foreign corruption. Again in "The Bracelet," Donne fears the Catholic influence from foreign coins, the "Spanish stamps, still travelling, / That are become as Catholic as their king" (29–30). Such an association between coins and religion sheds light on Raphael Holinshed's categorization of Elizabeth's restored English coin with her successful defense of the English Church. In his *Chronicles*, Holinshed praises the queen for having achieved "a certeine perfection, purenesse, and soundnesse, as here in hir new stamps and coines of all sorts; so also in Gods religion, setting the materiall churches of hir dominions free from all popish trash."[30] Restoring the purity of English coins by eliminating all base matter is for Holinshed akin to eliminating "all popish trash" in order to purify the Church.

While alluding to Henry VIII's debasement, Holinshed may also be implicitly critiquing Mary I, who appears to have actually produced Spanish coins for a time within England. It was already disturbing for an English people distrustful of the Spanish that Mary included not only the name of her husband, Philip II, on some of her coins but also his effigy next to her own, with the crown, as Helen Farquhar describes it, "which she was unable to bequeath to him,...poised in mid-air between her consort and herself." Now apparently England produced Spanish coins themselves. A commission on August 19, 1557 refers to coinage of the "king's" bullion, and C. E. Challis hypothesizes that the "brief experiment was ended by the accession of Elizabeth, who ensured that the coinage dies and other equipment belonging to Philip II were returned by the mint to their rightful owners," as early entries for Elizabeth's reign in the *Acts of the Privy Council* suggest.[31]

Therefore, Elizabeth's reform of the coin and cessation of Spanish coin production within England implied national purification and restoration. Upholding "Englishness" both materially and symbolically partially required maintaining the purity of English coin while preventing the pernicious influence of foreign coins circulating within England. A xenophobic response to the circulation of foreign coins as "contamination" clearly operated in the early modern period, either from their sheer presence, their corruption of the general quality of coinage circulating in England, or the threats of political subversion they might signal.[32]

However, because most foreign coins tended to enter England primarily through international trade, they were typically higher-valued "full-bodied" coins, usually made of gold, rather than the coins of smaller denomination employed in local commerce. Indeed, while gold French crowns appear often in early modern English drama, references to the silver *denier*, the equivalent of the English penny, are rarer.[33] Moreover, since higher-valued foreign coins tended to circulate only among merchants and aristocrats, discrepancies in value between foreign and domestic coins represented on stage could evoke class division in addition to general connotations of foreignness. Thus, while the circulation of foreign coins could potentially unite all English subjects against the corruption of foreign influence, it could also strain relations between domestic social groups. Although foreign coins might pose danger of conspiracy against the state, they might also arouse feelings of resentment among the lower sorts for a state reliant on obedience through general contentment. In the next section, I argue that allusions to foreign and domestic coins in Thomas Dekker's *Shoemaker's Holiday* reveal such clear socioeconomic divisions, and ultimately class resentment, despite the play's rhetoric of festive inclusiveness.

Domestic Exclusion in *Shoemaker's Holiday*

Carlo Cipolla notes that during the Middle Ages, most of the European populace lacked enough purchasing power to use high-valued prestige coins such as *solidi*, florins, and ducats, so they tended to circulate only among the wealthy; consequently they were generally considered "aristocratic coins." However, in Italy during the sixteenth century, prices and wages increased such that it became more common to see among wage earners gold and large silver coins being used for smaller transactions; the coins started becoming more "democratic."[34] A similar process of democratization for larger denomination coins would eventually occur in England as well. But I would argue that in England around 1600, lower-valued domestic silver coins were still symbolically linked to commoners, while gold and higher-denomination silver coins, especially foreign ones, were associated primarily with nobles and rich merchants.

Given the values of foreign coins commonly circulating in England relative to typical wages, it becomes clear why such coins might be labeled "aristocratic." Consider, for example, the French crown frequently mentioned in early modern drama. The crown was valued at 4–6 shillings during the reign of Elizabeth, most often closer to 6*s*. According to a proclamation of 1587, a skilled carpenter earned around one shilling or 13*d*. per day while an unskilled laborer earned 9*d*. per day without "meat and drink" provided. The wages of shoemakers in the same proclamation are £4 per year with meat and drink, meaning they earned less than 20*d*. per week, plus meals. The difference between a carpenter's wages with and without meat and drink is about 20*d*. per week, so the wage for shoemakers not receiving meals could have been roughly double, or 40*d*. per week.[35] Therefore, the French crown would be worth approximately a week's wages for a skilled carpenter, a week and a half's wages for an unskilled laborer, and almost two weeks' wages for a shoemaker. It is not inconceivable that such individuals would have had experience handling these coins, but they would not have been of much use to them in general: silver pennies and even base tokens would be more effective for daily transactions.

Both *The Jew of Malta* and *The Merchant of Venice* articulate this social hierarchy implicit in the use of gold versus silver coins. In the opening scene of *Jew of Malta*, Barabas refers to the "needy groom that never fingered groat" (a silver coin worth four pence) who "would make a miracle of thus much coin" as the merchant has in his coffers. According to Barabas, the highest coin denominations a "needy groom" would have handled were one or two pence silver coins, petty change for someone like the wealthy merchant. He complains that employment of these "paltry silverlings," which he calls "trash," is not worth the burden of counting them so that a man such as himself would "in his age be loath to labour so, / And for a pound to sweat himself to death."[36] Silver has become burdensome for the wealthy Barabas while the commoner would be astounded at his wealth and quite delighted to count it. Similarly, in *Merchant of Venice*, the "needy" aristocrat Bassanio calls silver "thou pale and common drudge / 'Tween man and man" (3.2.103–4) even as he seeks the financial rewards from marrying the wealthy Portia, after getting his friend Antonio to borrow from Shylock so that Bassanio might "hold a rival place" with the other suitors (1.1.174). Moreover, the haughty Morocco earlier in the play compares Portia's picture, which he hopes lies in the golden casket he has chosen, to an English coin "that bears the figure of an angel / Stamp'd in gold" (2.7.56–7). It is his inability to stoop to choose a metal of lower value than gold that ultimately defeats him. From the perspective of the aristocrats and wealthy merchants, laboring silver or worse should be employed only within common transactions among common people.

From the perspective of the commoner, however, gold, particularly gold *foreign* coins, assumes an air of aristocratic pretension. Though they seem to be minor details needed for a realistic portrayal of London's business culture, allusions to various coin denominations in Thomas Dekker's *The Shoemaker's Holiday* signal an undercurrent of class resentment related to general exclusivity within the cosmopolitan scene of London. While those of the aristocratic and merchant class employ gold—especially foreign gold coins—the laborers of the play rely on and, therefore, become synonymous with domestic, small-denomination silver and other lesser-valued coins. Glyn Davies notes that "silver was mainly the medium of retail and domestic trade, whereas gold became [in the sixteenth century] mainly the medium of wholesale and foreign trade."[37] Therefore, the bimetallic system of coinage in England also served to differentiate people according to socioeconomic status.

This discrepancy between coin use signals the lower sorts' general exclusion from the practices of international commerce and, as I will argue, ultimately from a coalition of state interests at the end of *Shoemaker's Holiday*. Although most critics interpret general inclusivity from its festive environment at the conclusion—with the possible exceptions of "defeated" individuals such as Hammon, Oatley, and Lincoln or of the foreign elements ("Hans," the Dutch skipper) in the play—I read in the final scene clear socioeconomic alignments between aristocrats and merchants (including the newest member of this latter group, Simon Eyre), along with the exclusion and exploitation of common laborers (such as the journeyman shoemakers Firk and Ralph). Although we witness an initial conflict between aristocratic and merchant classes in the antipathy and distrust between Lincoln and Oatley, the play concludes with a coalition of aligned interests between the king, the aristocratic Lacy, and the merchant Simon Eyre. And yet this coalition hinges on hopes of national glory through both trade and war, represented in the respective figures of Eyre (who has reached his status through his impressive trade deal) and Lacy (who is headed to France in order to achieve military glory for England and himself). On the other side of the coin are those excluded from both trade and war: Firk, whose ignorance about magnitudes of trade and differences between foreign coins limits his participation in Eyre's transaction; and Ralph, whose lame body on stage when the king pronounces a new military "surge" serves as a reminder of who pays the costs for England to profit from the foreign. The play, therefore, establishes a clear boundary between beneficiaries and non-beneficiaries, or even victims, of foreign trade and foreign wars, a boundary signaled from the play's start by the discrepancy of coin use within the bimetallic system of currency. The beneficiaries revel in the world of (especially foreign) gold while non-beneficiaries struggle to cope with their hard-working silver.

In the first scene of *Shoemaker's Holiday*, Lord Mayor Sir Roger Oatley promises Roland Lacy twenty pounds as remuneration for serving his country against France.[38] We discover in scene three, however, that Lacy shirks his military duty by posing as Hans the shoemaker in order to remain near his love Rose, Oatley's daughter. As Lincoln subsequently explains to his nephew, "that twenty pound [Oatley] doth bestow / For joy to rid you from his daughter Rose" (1.72–3). Oatley's attempted bribe later resonates with Hammon's offer to pay Ralph for the acquisition of his wife Jane, an offer Ralph quickly refuses though he and Jane obtain the money anyway. Coins in the play become tools for manipulating desire, although in these particular circumstances they prove impotent as love and "true" desire eventually triumph in the end.

But in addition to putatively manipulating desire, coins also serve as signs of social status; the play establishes distinctions between characters based on the particular types of coins they employ. Although Oatley designates the denomination of his gift to Lacy in "pounds," the actual medium of exchange could be in any number of coin types. Yet, Oatley later offers to Dodger "a dozen angels"—initially worth 6s. 8d., but closer to 10s. at the time of the play—in order to be "the means to rid [Lacy] into France" (9.96–97), and another angel to Firk for information on Rose and Lacy's location toward the end of the play (16.93). That is, Oatley, the lord mayor who had become wealthy as a member of the Grocer's Company (wholesale dealers of spices and foreign produce), employs in his bribes high-denomination gold coins, what would be construed as "aristocratic" English coins.

In the same first scene, Sir Hugh Lacy, the earl of Lincoln, gives his nephew Lacy thirty "portagues," Portuguese gold coins also known as *cruzadoes*, which would be considered prestige-coins of the period like the comparable Spanish dollars (see figure 4.2, www.stephendeng.com, that displays a counterfeit version of the portague). The subtle distinction made between Oatley's domestic angels and Lincoln's foreign portagues is symptomatic of class tensions that make the proposed marriage of Lacy and Rose so despicable for both men. Oatley dislikes the pretensions and prodigality of aristocrats such as Lincoln and Lacy while Lincoln believes Rose and Oatley are socially inferior.[39] Oatley's concerns seem well founded since Lacy has learned the shoemaking trade out of necessity: he had squandered all his money while abroad. Such consumption on foreign travel and wares, which harms England's trade balance and, therefore, store of wealth, provides an additional reason for Oatley's contempt. Although the former-grocer-turned-lord-mayor has acquired prestige through social mobility and has gotten rich himself by vending foreign goods, he nevertheless remains partial to prestigious *English* coins such as the angel while eschewing the pretentious cosmopolitanism of the foreign. Doing business with foreigners is fine as long as the English gain at the foreigners' expense, but cosmopolitan tastes for foreign goods and foreign coins threaten the economic health of the English nation.

Therefore, the particular aristocratic coin employed, whether foreign or domestic, initially distinguishes aristocrat from merchant in the play. But the same first scene displays an even starker distinction between social positions through coin use when the shoemakers, seeing their fellow Ralph off to war, mimic Lincoln and Oatley's gifts for military service. Like Oatley, the shoemakers proffer domestic coin, but of much smaller denominations. Simon Eyre offers five sixpences (30d.), Eyre's foreman Hodge offers a shilling (12d.), and the journeyman Firk gives three twopences (6d.). Eyre makes the symbolic association between coins and men explicit a few lines earlier, when he calls his men "you cracked groats, you mustard tokens" (206), referring respectively to damaged four pence coins and base tokens used as currency in local neighborhoods, the "small fractional coins" described by Cipolla. Moreover, the coin denominations and total amounts given to Ralph are far below those extended to Lacy. Eyre's gift is a hundred and sixtieth of the amount Oatley grants Lacy, and assuming that Oatley uses angels to pay Lacy, the silver shilling Hodge gives, the highest-valued coin among the lot, is only 15 percent of the value of the gold angel at its initial value of 6s. 8d. When we recall that Eyre soon thereafter replaces Oatley as lord mayor, we comprehend the extent of Eyre's meteoric rise, even if we allow that Eyre tends not to be very generous with his men despite his rhetoric of magnanimity.[40] The discrepancy between amounts given by Oatley and Lincoln, merchant and aristocrat, and those given by the shoemaker reflects their socioeconomic differences. Paul Seaver argues that the play represents these inequalities in terms of a clash between worlds: while the shoemakers are introduced laboring in their City workshop, Hammon, another citizen who has acquired wealth and status through trade, enters the play engaged in a hunt encoded as a scene of pastoral romance within the suburban setting of Old Ford.[41]

Moreover, the varying amounts granted to Ralph by the shoemakers reflect the hierarchy within the shop: the master bestows five times the amount offered by his journeyman, who gives half the amount of his foreman. Such value relations would seem trivial except for the fact that, as several critics have noted, a clear hierarchy among the shoemakers exists despite a prominent rhetoric of fraternity. Seaver notes that Hodge, Firk, and Ralph are all freemen cordwainers and citizens of London; however, as journeymen to their "master" Simon Eyre, they are also "covenanted servants," contractually bound to labor typically for a year before receiving their contracted wages. He believes this "anomalous position—at once a freeman and citizen but at the same time a servant living in his master's household"—helps to explain "Firk's prickly belligerency, his insistence on his rights and his willingness to walk off the job."[42] Historically, such friction developed within guilds as a whole. David Scott Kastan finds that while the past of the guild structure suggested a "fraternity devoted to the welfare and security of its membership," in the sixteenth and early seventeenth centuries, guilds "became increasingly hierarchical and entrepreneurial, converting work from a system of solidarity to a system of exchange." Kastan points to Dekker's own comments on the changing nature of guilds in *The Seven Deadly Sins of London* (1606), in which he laments the fact that guilds "that were ordained to be communities, had lost their first privilege, and were now turned monopolies."[43] Whether or not the fraternal fantasy ever existed, there was a clear sense of guilds needing to keep out the competition, as well as a sense of competition among members of the guild, and even among workers within a shop.

Competition between workers and the need for maintaining a clear hierarchy may explain a peculiar episode of the play: the workers of

Eyre's shop welcoming the Dutch shoemaker Hans. This event seems to belie general historic disdain for alien labor by English laborers, some of whom were probably present within the play's audience. Both 1593 and 1595, only a few years before the play's composition, witnessed riots incited by anti-foreign worker sentiment and rising rents and food prices, which left around half the population of urban laborers impoverished and destitute.[44] Citing a mayoral precept, Seaver finds that at a time when there were at least 15,000 apprentices and 12,000 journeymen in London, in July 1599,

> less than six months before Dekker's play was staged, the lord mayor complained that divers "riotous and unruly" apprentices in "troops to the number of two or three hundred," armed with "long staves and other weapons," had gathered in the summer evenings "under colour of going to a place called the Old Ford [Oatley's rural retreat in the play] to bathe themselves," in the course of which they had gone about "setting men's corn growing in the fields on fire, breaking down glass windows and signs hanging at men's doors, thrusting down of bricks with their staves from the tops of brick walls, pulling up of gates and stiles, breaking into orchards and...divers other rebellious parts."[45]

At a time when London laborers were literally up in arms over the presence of foreign laborers threatening their jobs, we see in *Shoemaker's Holiday* two journeyman shoemakers willing to walk out on their master if he does not hire a foreigner. Although it is the shop owner Eyre who would benefit from the additional labor pool supplied by foreign workers at the expense of English labor, in the play it is the master who must be persuaded by those same English workers to replace one of their own, Ralph.

Given the context of this general hostility to foreign laborers, how might we account for this reversal? David Bevington reads the scene as an expression of "international brotherhood" among journeyman shoemakers, while Julia Gasper locates the "fraternity" in the Protestant connection with the Dutch in particular. However, Andrew Fleck suggests another possibility: in addition to providing a source of amusement through his funny accent, which would "make [Firk] laugh so" (4.85), the foreigner Hans offers a structural advantage to Firk, who with the departure of Ralph has been left at the bottom of the shop's hierarchy. By establishing his superior position with respect to Hans, Firk thereby "limits the distance between himself and his countrymen," Hodge and Eyre, and thus the apparent hospitality that Firk shows to Hans merely veils his insistence on establishing "his priority over the foreigner."[46] Indeed, while Eyre incidentally places Hans before Firk when calling in his workers, Firk quickly reestablishes his place in the shop hierarchy:

"Soft, yaw, yaw, good Hans. Though my master have no more wit but to call you afore me, I am not so foolish to go behind you, I being the elder journeyman" (4.126–8). By replacing Ralph, Hans restores the relative standing that Firk had previously enjoyed.

But despite Firk's insistence on his superiority to Hans, the aristocrat Lacy beneath the disguise demonstrates his greater financial and cultural capital when he helps elevate the shop's master to a higher social position. In fact, Lacy's worldly knowledge, which contrasts with Firk's parochial ignorance, helps to craft the transaction. In the guise of Hans, Lacy lends Eyre twenty of the very portagues Lincoln had granted him in order to make a down payment on a shipment of Dutch cargo "worth," according to Firk, "the lading of two or three hundred thousand pounds" (7.13–14).[47] As several scholars have noted, the amount Firk mentions is astronomical.[48] While some critics have suggested a textual error,[49] the absurdity of the amount may instead indicate the journeyman's inability to comprehend such large sums or even foreign trade in general. Firk demonstrates similar ignorance about foreign coins when he asks Hodge, "can my fellow Hans lend my master twenty porpentines as an earnestpenny?" (7.22–23). His mistake of "porpentine" for "portague" may be based on a confusion between two foreign coins, French (the *ecu au porcepic* discussed in the previous section) and Portuguese, but the error is more likely linguistic given the comical characterization of the laborer.[50] With his evident ignorance about mercantile matters, the laborer Firk remains merely a spectator for the arrangement between a newly made merchant and a disguised aristocrat. The transaction that introduces Eyre to the mercantile world and enables his rise depends on the aristocratic "shoemaker" Lacy's capital and cosmopolitan knowledge of foreign coins and goods.

Seaver points out that Eyre's assuming the role of a merchant would not be illegal—any freeman of the City, from whichever company, could engage in trade.[51] But this transaction was highly improbable because a shoemaker would not likely have the necessary capital (which in the fiction of play, granted, is provided by an aristocrat), nor the credit to borrow against a small down payment such as twenty portagues, a credit that Lacy, in the guise of Hans, would *not* be able to provide. Moreover, Dekker's London audience would be well aware that, as Seaver observes, "no cordwainer ever rose to be lord mayor, for London had long been a highly stratified society, dominated by a mercantile elite, and its lord mayors all belonged to the liveries of one of the twelve great livery companies," which included the mercers, grocers, drapers, haberdashers, merchant tailors, clothworkers, goldsmiths, skinners, ironmongers, salters, fishmongers, and vintners. Shoemakers instead belonged to the Cordwainers Company, which produced relatively cheap commodities, including shoes, leather pantaloons, jerkins, and gloves. They typically produced in small household shops with a maximum of four apprentices. The historic Simon Eyre had started in the Upholsterers' Company but had eventually become a member of the more prestigious Drapers' Company around fifteen years before becoming sheriff.[52] That is, the historic Eyre represents prestigious merchants rather than humble shoemakers, and in his deal with Lacy within the play, Eyre has already entered the mercantile world.

Therefore, despite an apparent fantasy of social mobility for shoemakers, we witness in the play rather a coalition between mercantile (Eyre) and aristocratic (Lacy) interests, which seems to resolve the earlier conflict between Oatley and Lincoln. The play's true fantasy is the ultimate resolution between merchant and aristocratic classes, not the rise of a humble shoemaker. Indeed, the quid pro quo economy established between Eyre and Lacy suggests possibilities for both to profit from the relationship. Late in the play, after Lacy has revealed himself, Eyre acknowledges the aristocrat's loan as the source of his rise: "Simon Eyre had never walked in a red petticoat, nor wore a chain of gold, but for my fine journeyman's portagues" (17.17–19). And Eyre's appeal to the king on Lacy's behalf appears to be a key reason the aristocrat is ultimately excused for his prior shirking of military responsibilities. In the final scene, the king announces his pardon and tells Rose, "Mistress Lacy, thank my Lord Mayor / For your young bridegroom here" (21.4–5). It is a moment of apparent nationalistic unity as the aristocrat and the newly made merchant cooperate to acquire wealth at the expense of the foreigner, even using foreign coins to do so, while the young aristocrat becomes knighted and attains his love Rose, who is also from the merchant class. Meanwhile, those who had opposed such alignments—Oatley and Lincoln—emerge as defeated killjoys attempting to thwart the festive outcome.

For this reason, despite various problematic elements of the play and the exclusion of the killjoys, critics generally perceive an inclusive festive ending.[53] For example, while acknowledging the problem of Eyre's mercantile exploits bearing "an uncomfortable resemblance to [contemporary and unpopular Lord Mayor John] Spencer's financial dealings," Marta Straznicky indicates the apparent generosity of Eyre toward all shoemakers as a sign that this manner of acquisition ultimately becomes "worthy of celebration," a celebration that "enacts an imaginary appropriation of civic authority and commercial wealth by a group of industrial laborers for whom both privileges were largely a matter of fantasy." Similarly, Kastan concludes that the play's comic form represents "an ideological resolution to the social problems the play engages. Social dislocations are rationalized and contained in a reassuring vision of coherence and community." And for Andrew Fleck, the ending of the play depicts the establishment of national unity at the expense of the Dutch:

In the final fantasy, the foreign presence [Hans] is banished as an *English* man—young Roland in disguise—has enabled Eyre to make his fortune; English apprentices benefit from the generosity of a former London artisan turned Mayor; and England's class lines are temporarily leveled in a feast for prentices and princes. English unity has been asserted and can be turned outward against a foreign foe.[54]

The general tendency of critics is thus to read *"Shoemaker's Holiday"*—the singular possessive form of which would denote Eyre's holiday, either as the holiday's originator or as its solitary celebrant—in the more inclusive sense of "Shoemakers' Holiday," to suggest an unambiguous happy ending for the community of laborers who are at least temporarily unified with their social superiors.

I would argue, however, that the foreigners are not the only ones excluded from a sense of English unity at the play's conclusion—laborers, Firk and Ralph in particular, also remain outside the coalition, which seems more like a coalition of state interests. All of the laborers in Eyre's shop do appear to rise as a result of Eyre's own social elevation: Hodge becomes master, Firk and Ralph become more senior journeymen, and presumably another laborer would eventually be hired to replace Ralph at the bottom of the shop hierarchy.[55] However, the highly unlikely, fortuitous circumstances that cause the rise of Eyre—a disguised aristocrat within his shop when Eyre's ship comes in—imply that Hodge cannot hope for similar social elevation, especially since, as Seaver observes, the historical Eyre's own rise is misrepresented in the play. Although laborers in the audience might celebrate the improbable elevation of one of their own, in all likelihood they cannot imagine a similar fate for Hodge and the other shoemakers, let alone harbor fantasies of their own rise.

In fact, the narrative of the play itself represents the exclusion of laborers from Eyre's peculiar experience. For example, the "feast for prentices and princes" described by Fleck is, in fact, segregated between princes and prentices. As Eyre explains the situation to the king, on a past Shrove Tuesday he had been given his breakfast by "some mad boys," and he consequently promised that "if ever I came to be Lord Mayor of London, I would feast all the prentices." This very day he had feasted them, "and the slaves had an hundred tables five times covered." But he then adds, "They are gone home and vanished. / Yet add more honour to the Gentle Trade: / Taste of Eyre's banquet, Simon's happy made" (21.179–87). The "slaves" have, therefore, dined already, and it is only when they have left that Eyre asks the king to feast with him. Although their "vanishing" may be from pragmatic concerns—the inability to represent a "hundred tables" on the stage—the conspicuous absence of the feted laborers nevertheless subverts any sense of national unity in this final scene. Kastan observes a similar sense of segregated festivity in that "in the presence of the King, Eyre is free to behave as if he *were* among his shoemakers but simultaneously reminded that he is not."[56] Eyre's rise has moved him permanently out of his past social circles. Despite his act of benevolence to the laborers, he is no longer one of them.

Moreover, while key representative laborers, Firk and Ralph, do remain on stage, their very presence calls attention to the exclusion of laborers from a national "brotherhood." I already discussed Firk's exclusion from the trade deal that made Eyre so wealthy. But Ralph offers a conspicuous example of laborers paying the price for English military gains. At the same moment when the king calls for a surge against France, the audience observes its likely outcome for the commoner: the lame body of Ralph standing on the side.[57]

> With the old troop which there we keep in pay
> We will incorporate a new supply.
> Before one summer more pass o'er my head,
> France shall repent England was injurèd.
> What are all those? (21.138–42)

Ralph and the other shoemakers have entered just before this speech, and the king's concluding line—asking "what" rather than "who" they are—emphasizes their baseness and Ralph's lameness. Critics tend to emphasize the king's ideal characterization in this scene rather than the ideological conflict between the king's expression of national pride and Ralph's visual reminder of its effects on the laborer.[58] Kastan, who otherwise reads the class tensions implicit in the play, interprets Ralph's "safe return" as a "welcome fantasy of wish-fulfillment for a nation wearied and worried by war. Even his wound... serves to prove the ability of 'the gentle craft' to protect and provide for its practitioners." He subsequently asserts that Ralph is "still able to function as a shoemaker" and "can make a living and make a life in a community of concern, and when Jane is found and recommits herself to him, her love confirms his place in the comic world and the irrelevance of his wound."[59] However, Ralph can still function as a shoemaker only because he injured his leg and not his hands: "Since I want limbs and lands, / I'll to God, my good friends, and to these my hands" (10.110–11). We sense that if Ralph's injury had prevented him from continuing to practice his craft, he would have been out on the street much like his wife, Jane, who, according to Margery Eyre's enigmatic description about her becoming too "stately" because of marriage, appears to have been forced out of the shop upon Ralph's departure (10.85–86).[60] The fraternity among shoemakers persists only while all members are still able to make shoes.

Although Ralph can still function as a shoemaker, his body on stage, made lame from dutiful soldiering, stands in stark contrast to the unblemished body of Lacy, who is honored despite shirking his patriotic duty. This uneven treatment of soldiers recalls the blatant hypocrisy in the aftermath of the Battle of Agincourt in Shakespeare's *Henry V*. In his reading of *Shoemaker's*, Fleck alludes to the Agincourt speech as indicative of fantasies of social mobility, "of shared responsibilities with wealthier people, of forging a 'band of brothers' in which the basest Englishman who 'sheds his blood' may 'gentle his condition,' and of 'horizontal comradeship' among all Englishmen, essential concepts in the idea of the nation." He takes the term "horizontal comradeship" from Benedict Anderson's concept of "imagined communities" in order to emphasize a conclusion to *Shoemaker's* "with a fantasy of unified classlessness... as king, lords, citizens, and laborers come together in a celebration of England's greatness before taking up the business of fighting a foreign enemy."[61]

However, in invoking Harry's rhetoric of unity in the Agincourt scene from *Henry V*, we should recall the battle's aftermath. The king asks for "the number of our English dead" and subsequently reads the names of "Edward the Duke of York, the Earl of Suffolk, / Sir Richard Ketly, Davy Gam, esquire"; he callously concludes with "None else of name; and of all other men / But five and twenty. O God, thy arm was here" (4.8.102–106). Henry's "band of brothers" has been transformed into a select few of name and the rest into an anonymous statistic. Similarly, in *Shoemaker's*, Dodger reports the outcome of a battle in France: "Twelve thousand of the Frenchmen that day died, / Four thousand English, and no man of name / But Captain Hyam and young Ardington" (8.8–10).[62] The appearance of Ralph Damport's name on Hammon's list of English dead is surprising considering that such commoners are otherwise treated as numbers, so it raises the question of whether Hammon's note is merely a mistake or a deliberate forgery, or even whether Jane cannot, in fact, read despite her protestation that she can (12.83–91).[63]

Regardless, Dodger's letter makes clear that the Lacys of England are treated quite differently than the Ralphs. I believe this discrepancy between experiences must be considered within any argument that the play stages a sense of unity, especially national unity. Many critics ultimately interpret a triumphant ending for Ralph and Jane. For example, Kastan sees their outcome as a sign that love "succeeds in the face of a world that restricts working-class freedom and assails its integrity." Peter Mortenson, however, relates Ralph's experience to that of Lacy, finding in Ralph "Lacy's surrogate or other half in the cruelty of war and in the anguish of lost love." He notes that, just as Ralph finally recovers Jane, Lacy "must march off to war from the arms of his new bride, Rose" and sees this ending as a reemphasis of the "pattern of action in the Eyre plot: one man's gain is another man's [the ship owner's] loss." Julia Gasper does note a possible persistent inequity at the end of the play but ultimately understands it to be a Christian test for Lacy, the outcome of which remains unknown. Lacy could redeem himself by going off to war just as Ralph had done at the beginning of the play. For Gasper, Lacy's silence about his intentions leaves the extent of his redemption an open question.[64] But even if Lacy does go to war, his experience would be quite different from Ralph's. Even in death, Lacy would receive more honor as a person "of name" than would the nameless Ralph.

Despite Lacy's favorable treatment in the end, some critics have read the play as an indictment of the nobility. For example, Bevington sees an alignment between idealized monarchy and bourgeois culture at the expense of scapegoated nobles. And despite interpreting irresolution in the ending, Seaver finds hostility toward landed aristocracy on the part of both artisans and merchants. However, Straznicky interprets antipathy toward the *bourgeoisie* to find in both textual and performance contexts a "mobilization of the power of traditional festivals to conduct controversy in such a way as to reinforce the shared economic and political interests of an industry and court that were slowly being displaced by new capitalist practices."[65] That is, critics have noted the establishment of coalitions in the play, but typically these coalitions described exclude either aristocrats or the new merchant class.

I would argue instead that the ending of the play depicts the formation of a larger coalition between king, aristocracy, and merchants.[66] Although the play begins with tension between the aristocratic and merchant classes (represented by Lincoln and Oatley, respectively), by the end we see reconciliation between aristocracy and merchants, not only in Lacy's camaraderie with the newly made merchant Simon Eyre, but also in the marriage of Lacy and Rose, the daughter of a former grocer. Both classes jointly celebrate with the king while the laborers stand apart. Thus, although the play ostensibly celebrates festive inclusion of all classes, it ultimately enacts a realignment of classes, separating those in the new coalition from those outside of it. Lincoln and Oatley are punished, then, for their antipathy toward the other's class, for their inability to acknowledge a coalition, rather than for being in the class itself. Also, Hammon is punished perhaps for his refusal, in his quick turn of attention from the wealthy Rose to the more humble Jane, to distinguish between the two groups, between the merchant and laboring classes.

Moreover, this coalition depends on the exploitation of territorial boundaries, which relates to differences between gold and silver coins in the bimetallic system. Both merchants and aristocrats are free to traverse national boundaries in order to take advantage of foreign opportunities, either through trade or war. The "aristocratic" gold or prestige coins that they employ and that also tended to circulate freely across national boundaries become emblematic of their status. The monarchy, of course, had an interest in these foreign excursions, in the success of both military exploits of the aristocracy as well as of merchants' trade, since merchants were becoming an increasingly important source of capital. Seaver notes that in December 1598 Elizabeth was hoping to borrow £150,000 from the City, but because of the recent "decay of trade," it was thought she would not be able to obtain the amount.[67] Monarchical dependence on trade and the belief that countries could beggar competing countries in a zero-sum game by accumulating all wealth, effectively conducting economic warfare, explain mercantilist alignments between state and economic interests. However, the excluded laborers are generally bound to the domestic space and limited to the use of silver coins circulating only within local economies. And when they do traverse national boundaries it is typically as infantry in military campaigns, subject to incurring the cost for national gains. Rather than returning home wealthy, Ralph returns with a lame body and loses his wife while Lacy appropriates Ralph's position and woos his future wife, all the while keeping the exorbitant quantity of money, partly foreign, he has been given for his "service."

Therefore, the discrepancy between gold and silver coins in the bimetallic system—the tendency of gold coins to be used in foreign trade and wholesale economies while silver tended to circulate only in local, retail economies—also indicates the different experiences of the socioeconomic groups. Gold, especially gold foreign coins, bound together the coalition of king, aristocracy, and merchants. In *Shoemaker's Holiday*, the camaraderie between Eyre and Lacy appropriately hinges on the lending of portagues for a down payment on the cargo. The camaraderie between the shoemakers instead relies on proffering of silver coins when their brother Ralph heads off to war. And when the shoemakers do acquire gold coins, it is only within morally questionable situations. Firk receives gold angels as bribes for information: the fact that he exploits the situation by providing false information does not negate the intention of the coin's use. Similarly, Ralph ultimately receives twenty pounds "in fair gold" (18.78), as Hammon attests, "in lieu / Of that great wrong I offerèd thy Jane" (18.90–91). The money was initially meant to bribe Ralph into allowing Hammon to marry Jane. Ralph responds to the offer with an expression of virtue among shoemakers: "Sirrah Hammon, Hammon, dost thou think a shoemaker is so base to be a bawd to his own wife for commodity? Take thy gold, choke with it! Were I not lame, I would make thee eat thy words" (18.84–87). But the reference to his baseness and lameness merely calls attention to his relatively powerless position, and he and Jane accept the corrupting gold anyway.

However, the most telling example of a laborer acquiring gold coins via morally dubious means involves gold *foreign* coins. In the opening scene, when the shoemakers see Ralph off, Eyre exhorts Ralph to "Crack me the crowns of the French knaves, a pox on them—crack them" (1.218–9), alluding to damaged French coins and heads in the same breath as the so-called French disease. Hodge extends the joke into a pun on coinage when he offers a "blessing" to Ralph: "God send thee to cram thy slops with French crowns" (1.225). In effect, financial opportunities for the laborers are tied to their duties to state. While killing for England, they may also loot from their victims: collect French crowns for themselves once they have collected French crowns for the state. To profit from the foreign, the laborer must become a killer and a criminal. We are reminded of Pistol at the end of *Henry V*, who, after his frustration in France and news that "Doll" has died from "a malady of France," will return to England a thief and a bawd (5.1.81–89). Pistol's experience of France has criminalized him. But the earlier execution of Bardolph at the express order of the king recalls the dangers of looting, still considered illegal by the state and carrying the same penalties as it does back home. Thus, even limited opportunities for gaining from the foreign while abroad, those for illicit military looting in lieu of legal trade or everyday transactions among aristocrats and merchants, carried risks of corporal punishment by the state.

Gold and Foreign Corruption

Given laborers' limited access to the promise of wealth represented in foreign coins, as well as habitual foreign coin circulation among the elite, we might understand their distrust and resentment of such coins. While foreign gold as the "sinews of war" might signal the possibility of treasonous plots against the state, it might instead connote the exclusion of certain social groups in matters of state interest such as mercantile trade, or even their *exploitation* in other state matters such as military campaigns. Therefore, any expressions of ridicule for foreign coins should be considered in light of their particular context.

Consider another representation of corruption from foreign coins in one of the "clown" scenes from the A-text of *Doctor Faustus*. In a comic parody of an earlier scene in which Faustus seeks to acquire Mephostophilis' service in exchange for his soul, Wagner demands that Robin serve him for seven years, threatening to transform his lice into familiars that would tear him to pieces, a foreshadowing of Faustus's ultimate fate. For the hire Wagner subsequently offers Robin "guilders," a term referring specifically to Dutch coins but often used for any foreign coin, as in *The Comedy of Errors* (1.1.8). Just as Firk mistakes "porpentines" for "portagues" in *Shoemaker's*, Robin mistakes "guilders" for "gridirons," a linguistic pun that also refers to the poor condition of the coins, presumably filled with holes. Wagner clarifies that they are French crowns, which Robin does not seem to recognize but then comments, "Mass, but for the name of French crowns a man were as good have as many English counters," base and, therefore, valueless coins.[68] Because of the "crown's" linguistic association with royalty, Robin assumes they are valuable coins, but the poor quality of this French currency belies the assumption. We might read in this passage a general nationalistic sentiment that supposedly gold French crowns are equivalent in value to base English coins. But the peculiarities of the context suggest that there is more to this exchange. As with *Shoemaker's*, we observe confusion of coin names and misrecognition of coin types by a commoner with limited or no experience of foreign coins. Moreover, we observe clear representation of hierarchy, or at least an attempt at establishing hierarchy, through the use of foreign coins. But most importantly, while attempting at first to return the coins as a refusal of service, Robin ultimately agrees to serve because of Wagner's power to conjure devils. Despite the comic absurdity of the scene, the French crowns become devices for moral corruption, either in their use by the already corrupted Wagner or as a signal of Robin's own corruption in following Wagner.

Many such expressions of corruption were directed outward, at the foreign coins and foreigners, rather than inward at English merchants and aristocrats, a direction that would lead one to interpret a nationalistic impulse in commoners trying to prevent a foreign threat. However, a key exception is the Dutch Church Libel—a poem affixed, during anti-immigrant riots in 1593, to a London church frequented by Dutch immigrants—which explicitly accuses English aristocrats of being already corrupted by foreign gold. One passage of the Libel reads,

> With Spanish gold, you all are infected
> And with [tha]t gould our Nobles wink at feats
> Nobles said I? nay men to be rejected,
> Upstarts [tha]t enjoy the noblest seate*s*
> That wound their Countrys brest, for lucres sake
> And wrong our gracious Queene & Subjects good
> By letting strangers make our harts to ake.[69]

The poem accuses Dutch merchants of importing into England the Spanish gold that flowed freely throughout the Low Countries, that according to Donne "mangled seventeen-headed *Belgia*." But although it is foreigners who are "infected" by this Spanish gold, the Libel suggests that this infection has extended to English nobles, who benefit from foreign gold and, therefore, turn a blind eye to the harm foreigners are doing to the English, including their "gracious" queen. Significantly, the Libel specifies that corruption of English nobles comes from *Spanish* gold, recalling Donne's complaint that Spanish coins have destroyed numerous states. But while Donne's invective might be considered a rallying cry for all English to eschew deadly foreign coins, the Libel complains that English nobles have already been corrupted or "infected" by the gold, and only commoners, who have had little experience with the coins, remain free from their corruptive influence.

The moral high ground assumed in avoiding the infection of foreign gold—like Ralph's pronouncement that shoemakers are too virtuous to be bought by Hammon's gold—represents a rationalized response to the exclusion of the lower sorts from the benefits of foreign trade. Just as English critique of foreign coins appears to constitute an articulation of national unity but, in fact, hides the reality of internal division between elite and commoner, critique of corrupted English aristocrats and expressions of virtue among shoemakers should be interpreted as signs of socioeconomic discontent. The image of English purity threatened by the corruption of foreign influence may be a traditionalist response to the increasing interconnectedness through global commerce, but it also embodies the resentment of certain groups excluded from the global context. As with political concerns about globalization today, we need to consider domestic divisions in early modern England due to divergent experiences with global trade (whether included or excluded, infected or free from infection), especially those experiences with enriching or "ruinous" foreign coins.

Conclusion

The Changing Matter of Money

The complex emotional response of commoners to foreign coins—general English xenophobia combined with particular resentment about economic exploitation by an English elite engaged in global economy—exemplifies the political energies of coinage that I have emphasized throughout *Coinage and State Formation in Early Modern English Literature*. As a circulating embodiment of state authority, whether foreign or domestic, the coin considered strictly in terms of its economic function as medium of exchange or store of value does not sufficiently account for the range of political reactions it instigated: whether frustration with a state producing inferior-quality coinage; a perception of hypocritical injustice in a state that condemns coiners even as it should be condemned itself as a "Faux Monnayeur"; political loyalty inspired by the divine properties of a coinage that is able to maintain a healthy commonwealth; or the sense of collusion with foreign governments prompted by gold foreign coins circulating among English elite. Money in early modern England clearly meant more than just the numerical values assigned to particular coinage denominations. While many critics, following Marx, have emphasized the impersonality of money, which as a measure of value seems to collapse complex characteristics of people and things into a common numerical entity, the diversity of responses exhibits the *personality* of a coinage that constitutes a critical point of contact between state and subject.

Moreover, interrelations between coinage and state in early modern England proved multiple, spreading across at least the five key dimensions of state formation I identified in Chapter I: institutional structures, relations between law and state authority, the state's expansion of law, the political theology of state, and the territorialization of state authority. Within each of these contentious and contingent components of state formation, coinage circulated both materially and symbolically, the latter form especially prominent in complex discursive engagements within literary texts: from the pragmatic use of money as the "root of all evil" to extend state prerogative in More's *Utopia*; to the state's extension of moral and legal codes to encompass coining crimes and the concomitant sense of economic justice implicit in coinage in Shakespeare's *Measure for Measure*; to the mystical and therapeutic, but also perhaps idolatrous and "sacred commodity," properties of coins alluded to in *Macbeth*; to the "aristocratic" associations of certain coins that tended to circulate beyond territorial boundaries in Dekker's *The Shoemaker's Holiday*. Because of the promiscuous nature of these objects bearing images and iconography of state authority, coins became tactical devices whose "uttering" allowed subjects to "utter" their relations to the state.

The personality of coinage inhered in these visual properties as well. Sir Walter Raleigh perceived the potential of Elizabeth's portrait on her newly minted coins to inspire loyalty in New World subjects, but visual elements could sometimes undermine state interest instead. We observe, for example, a notable contrast between the personalities of James's rose ryal (figure 5.2 and the cover image) and Henry VIII's debased shilling/testoon coins (figure 3.1, www.stephendeng.com). While James's gold coin, with the majestic monarch sitting atop his throne, epitomizes the ideal of routinized charisma inspiring loyalty to monarch and state, "old copper nose" Henry, with his unflattering portrait "blush[ing] for shame," conveys the sense of a debilitated state failing in its duty to provide economic justice. Neither is it incidental that one was a high-valued gold coin while the other was a "pale and common drudge / 'Tween man and man." Consideration of early modern money only from contemporary perspectives, such as Alfred Sohn-Rethel's "physical matter" that "has visibly become a mere carrier of its social function," would tend to neglect cases of monetary failure, the dysfunction inherent in Henry's debased coinage, a dysfunction that is merely an extreme version of various coinage problems common throughout the period. Most coins fell somewhere in between James's rose ryal and Henry's testoon, but accounts such as Sohn-Rethel's would lead many to assume that coins tended to be of the "sublime material" described by Slavoj Žižek.

Modern paper money, however, tends to promote idealized representations of state—or perhaps of *nation* to the extent that the two are separable within a joint conception of the "nation-state"—when economic participants willingly employ, as currency, paper differentiated from other paper only by the state's stamp of guarantee. One exceptional case is hyperinflation, when continual devaluation of the currency would fail to inspire loyalty to any image on it. But the typical paper currency whose value depends only on faith in its underwriting state suggests general interpellation of subjects—even foreign "subjects" who rely on the value of a dominant currency such as the dollar—through economic interests. Modern states exploit economic participants' concern only about money's numerical value, which tends to be relatively consistent as long as the state maintains disciplined control over the money supply, debt, and trade. Such discipline is not easy, as contemporary debates over U.S. deficits and debt affecting the value of the dollar and long-term health of the American economy demonstrate, but the very fact that a currency such as the paper dollar has been able to replace gold as the international standard of value exemplifies the power the modern state has acquired. The apparent impersonality of money in this instance assumes the form of an ideological state apparatus veiling an underlying faith in institutional structures of the issuing state.[1]

Early modern coinage, though, was quite different and, therefore, consideration only of its numerical value collapses key components present within its circulation. And yet as I have demonstrated, numerical values, especially those determined by the intrinsic value theory of money, also impacted the meanings of coinage in the period. Much implicit criticism of the state came from this inability to preserve ancient coinage standards that had become customary law despite changing economic circumstances and continual reduction in coinage weights. A purely representational monetary system would offer flexibility to a state constrained by economic circumstances such as bullion supplies and differential prices between gold and silver, just as modern fiat money allows for the immediate "creation" of money whenever the Fed feels that the injection of money into the system would improve economic circumstances. An early modern English economy, subject to public perception that the gold and silver quantity within coinage ultimately determined value, depended on its supply of bullion even as it was required, as guardian of economic justice, to maintain sufficient quality in a coinage circulating beyond its immediate control.

Ironically, it was this obstinate and obsessive upholding of the intrinsic value theory in the 1690s that would lead to the ultimate emptying out of the material—and in England, with the formation of the Bank of England, perhaps of the state as well—from monetary media. I end with this episode because its outcome demonstrates a fundamental shift in monetary thought and a movement toward our contemporary perspective on money. Developments of the period, especially the monetary theories of John Locke, represent an important bridge in the transformation of money between the early modern and modern periods.

During the 1690s England simultaneously experienced many of the coinage-related problems described throughout *Coinage and State Formation*. Various commentators expressed anxiety about the state's ability to maintain enough money for defense in the face of war with France, about the circulation of counterfeit and clipped coins, and about a general flow of specie out of the commonwealth.[2] The state had failed in its office of providing a suitable universal equivalent for transactions, and the economy suffered. As a result, people generally lost faith in the king's stamp as a guarantor of value. Most concluded that a general recoinage—which would help mitigate these problems—was necessary, but how this recoinage would be done became hotly contested, especially among merchants and government officials speaking through a prodigious production of pamphlets and tracts. Among the luminaries who engaged in the public debate were Sir Isaac Newton, later to become master of the mint; the great architect Sir Christopher Wren; Charles Davenant, economist and son of the poet and playwright Sir William Davenant; and the political philosopher John Locke. Two main contenders in the debate emerged: Secretary of the Treasury William Lowndes, who argued that there should be a general enhancement of nominal values for the coinage, and Locke, who argued that the new coins should maintain the previous denominations despite a consequent drop in the overall money supply.

A key point of contention within this public debate was the nature of money, especially the relative merits of intrinsic and extrinsic value theories. While Locke claimed that money was inseparable from its silver content, several others argued that the state's stamp was also essential. Locke upheld what amounts to a natural law of economy, a belief that monetary values have "their Foundation in Nature": money functions in a particular manner according to nature, and no matter what the state does, money will continue to follow its natural course.[3] Any deviation from the "natural" value of money would be fruitless because people tended to trade the silver content of coins rather than their nominal values designated by the stamp. The denominations given to coins (pence, shilling, crown, etc.) are merely convenient markers for making such transactions easier, but in themselves they had no material value. In other words, there was nothing special about these particular coins or about the state mints that had produced them. Locke's establishment of a fixed quantity of silver per denomination of English money demonstrated the persistence of an intrinsic value conception of money in the face of substantial evidence to the contrary, including the predominance of credit and circulating paper instruments tied only to reserves.[4]

Like his early modern forebears, Locke associated money with law, justice, and morality. Nicholas Mayhew notes the peculiarity that even "minds of the caliber of Isaac Newton and John Locke" could be "seduced by the dream of a constant and unchanging currency unit with which to measure personal or public obligations," an influential "moral idea of money...associated in the public mind with concepts of truth and justice and with the belief that a government's word, like an individual's, should be its bond."[5] Money becomes a kind of universal religion for Locke, who was otherwise a proponent of religious diversity.[6] In a

February 14, 1696 letter to John Freke and Edward Clark, he expresses a nostalgic longing—in an almost Dantean vision—for a time when money was treated like royalty in contrast to the contemporary abuses he finds:

> Methinks the silver does wisely not to come into England at this time where it is like to run a perpetuall circle of torment if it stay here. Into the fire it goes at the Exchequer and is noe sooner out but is committd to the tower there to goe into the furnace again to be brought to Standard and then to size and then be pressed in the mill. Assoon as it get free out of the tower it is either lockd up in some Jailors chest from comeing abroad or if it peeps out tis ten to one but the thriveing company of Coiners and clippers put it again into the fire to be joind with bad company. and then to be hammerd and cut and so conveyd to the Exchequer to run the same Gantlet again. If it be not soe pray convince me of my mistake, and ease me of the trouble I am in for a poor Lady which we bookish men find the ancients had such a respect for that they called her *Regina Pecunia*. But this was a great while agon and the world is much alterd since.[7]

Despite the secular pretenses of his tracts, money, especially silver, becomes a sanctified object, "*Regina Pecunia*," in Locke's theory: silver is the unmoved mover that can measure all things but cannot itself be measured in terms of anything else.

But the religion Locke espoused was a religion of his own creation. As Albert Feavearyear notes, his sanctification of mint weights was an entirely new concept that nevertheless seemed like an old one: "Before [Locke's] time few people regarded the weights of the coins as in any way immutable. The king had made them; he had altered them many times; and doubtless if it suited him he would alter them again."[8] That is, Locke insisted on a pure intrinsic value theory of money despite years of coexistence between intrinsic and extrinsic theories. The willingness of subjects to refuse coins that did not have the designated quantity of silver shows that the intrinsic value theory persisted throughout the early modern period. But the recognition that coinage weights had been constantly decreasing over time (as Lowndes pointed out), along with the growing general willingness of people to employ coins of varying quality, demonstrates that the extrinsic theory was operative as well.

Despite a concerted defense of Lowndes' proposal by numerous commentators, Locke's recoinage plan prevailed.[9] The mint was able to produce most of the new silver coins (approximately 90 percent) by the end of 1697. The face value of English silver currency, not including the new plate brought into the mint to serve as bullion, was reduced from approximately £4.7 million to about £2.5 million, and the recoinage cost the state around £2.7 million, not including the loss to those, mostly the poor, who were left holding clipped coins or had to dispense with them at a discounted value.[10] The mint coined almost £7,000,000 worth of silver, but as soon as the new coins were released they disappeared from the market, being either hoarded or melted down. Very little silver was brought to the mint because the market price remained higher than the mint price. The relatively high value of foreign gold coins prompted their importation.[11] The decrease in the currency's face value induced a price deflation and severe economic depression. Moreover, continued deterioration of the coinage led to unpaid rents and unsettled debts, resulting in a near collapse in public credit during the summer of 1696. Government credit was especially hard hit, and William III, who reportedly declared that the recoinage plan was a disastrous mistake, had difficulty continuing to raise funds for his war during the summer of 1696.[12]

Although an immediate economic failure, Locke's plan had profound implications for the relation between money and the state: the state had no power over "true" money or the value of money other than its influence on the supply of silver within England. If there were a "natural" or "intrinsic" quantity of silver for every monetary denomination, then the government's role—other than to protect the currency from clippers, counterfeiters, and other offenders against the coin—would be merely to guarantee a supply of coins produced according to these specifications. His argument and motive bear a striking resemblance to those of Nicole Oresme 350 years earlier; like Oresme, Locke upheld a stringent version of the intrinsic value theory in defending coinage weights as well as purity, despite Lowndes's argument that even when the purity of coinage standards was maintained, the weights of coins had gradually diminished over several centuries of recoinages. If, however, money derived its value from both the content of precious metal *and* the king's stamp, or from the sheer need for some substance to act as a consensus bearer of value between transactions (as defenders of Lowndes had insisted), then the state played a more prominent role in establishing the legal conditions necessary for commerce.[13] For political commentators concerned with curbing the power of the monarch, the ability to establish arbitrary value in money was a key issue. For example, John Briscoe writes,

> as it is a mark of Slavery, so is it the means of Poverty in a State, where the Magistrate assumes a Power to set what Price he pleases on the Publick Coin: It is a sign of Slavery, because the Subject in such Case lives merely at the Mercy of the Prince, is Rich, or Poor, has a Competency, or is a Beggar, is a Free-Man, or in Fetters at his Pleasure.[14]

Locke would concur with such pronouncements while invoking natural law to serve as a basis for economic policy in order to prevent the state from economically enslaving its people.[15]

Meanwhile, another factor emerged that would also curb the state's control over money: the formation of the Bank of England. Initially a private joint-stock operation, the bank assumed authority to issue its own currency based on its gold reserves. Feavearyear emphasizes that from its inception the bank was intended to be a "bank of issue," one that creates a circulating medium, paper notes, backed by reserve deposits.[16] At its founding, the bank issued £480,000 worth of notes called "sealed Bank bills," which began to circulate as money, although primarily in larger transactions and not in everyday commerce, for which coins were still used. Proponents of the bank argued that these bills might ultimately serve the same function as that of coins and even displace coins as the most common measure of commerce. In *England's Glory*, a proposal for the formation of the bank, Humphrey Mackworth writes,

> Money is but a *medium* of Commerce, a Security which we part with, to enjoy the like in Value, and is the Standard of all Commodities, and esteemed so by the World. And such is a Bank-Bill, it will obtain what we want, and satisfy where we are indebted, and may be turned into Money again when the Possessor pleaseth, and will be the Standard of Trade at last.[17]

This new medium, the "Bank-Bill," began to compete with the routinized charismatic authority of the state embodied in coins. Instead of the king's portrait and iconography of state, these bills had the bank's corporate seal and an engraving of the figure of Britannia—that is, iconography of *nation*—seated upon a bank of money.[18] It was not until the Bank of England was nationalized in 1946 that England's paper money finally bore the image of the sovereign.[19]

Locke's glorious failure helped to place the Bank of England in a more prominent financial position as gold became the new national, and ultimately international, standard. Because of the continuation of silver's relative cheapness and gold's relative dearness within England, international markets tended to bring gold into England while draining the country of silver. As a result, many of the silver coins issued by William III had disappeared by the time of Queen Anne's death, while the state began producing more coins out of the gold flowing into England.[20] As a result of Locke's "mistake," gold became the de facto standard within England well before it did so in any other country. During the late seventeenth century, a new gold coin called the "guinea" started becoming more central in commercial transactions and bankers' reserves, primarily because they tended to be in much better shape than silver coins. By the mid-seventeenth century, and not by any conscious decision of the government or the commercial sector, gold had replaced silver as the agreed upon standard, although the acceptance of this new standard was not formalized until 1817.[21] Min-Hsun Li points out the irony that if Lowndes' plan had succeeded and a general devaluation of silver coins had occurred, England would probably not have experienced its great monetary success in the eighteenth and nineteenth centuries.[22] Thanks in part to Locke's error, England became the first nation to adopt the gold standard, an innovation that paved the way for London to become a key financial center in an emerging global economy.

But the Bank of England too was critical to this success. Jack Weatherford argues that it was under the leadership of the bank that "the world operated on a single monetary system based on common adherence to the gold principle."[23] Although a private institution, it became the bearer of reserves for banks all over England, establishing an important precedent for modern central banks. Feavearyear notes that most local country banks, which began spreading throughout England, were "practically compelled to keep an account with a London bank, and the London banks either held Bank of England notes as their reserve or (and this practice was a growing one) kept an account at the Bank," giving the bank an important position of financial control.[24] This practice of maintaining reserves eventually led to its controlling most of the country's gold. Marx describes how the bank began with lending money to the state and issuing a few bank notes to become eventually the "eternal creditor of the nation down to the last farthing advanced" and the "inevitable receptacle of the metallic hoard of the country, and the centre of gravity of all commercial credit."[25] Moreover, it was not long before the bank became a key "centre of gravity" for commercial credit throughout the world. Weatherford points out that in the nineteenth century, the English system of paper money based on gold "spread around the world and became the first completely global money system in the world." The gold standard, the system of reserves, and the development of credit instruments helped establish the bank as the dominant monetary institution within England, far surpassing the royal mint in importance.[26]

Therefore, while nostalgically looking back to a legendary past, Locke's plan, especially its disastrous outcome, had the ironic effect of moving the English monetary system toward a gold standard—which would help place England in a dominant financial position within the world economy—and eventually toward pure fiat money. Moreover, despite his insistence on pure *intrinsic* value, Locke's expression of nostalgia for a time that never was also resembles modern conceptions of money in terms of pure *extrinsic* value. The surest method to get people to treat *Regina Pecunia* properly would be to eliminate the temptation from her materiality. Whereas Sohn-Rethel's fantasy of a coinage that would be immediately replaced when it has been worn with time proved never to be operable as long as coinage contained precious material, with modern paper money, this process of replacement would be easily executed. And with electronic transactions, in which money becomes pure number, even the materiality of paper gets eliminated. Only when money was able to transcend its materiality by becoming purely symbolic, or only when it had come to be composed of a "sublime material," would Locke's fantasy of monetary propriety be realized. But even in this "transcendent" form, money would continue to be abused in other ways, as the inequities of modern financial history prove.

Notes

Introduction   Rough Economies—The Politics and Poetics of Coinage

1. Voltaire, *The Works of Voltaire: A Contemporary Version*, vol. 12, trans. William F. Fleming (Paris: E. R. Dumont, 1901), 13.
2. Books on coinage in literary studies of the period are rare in general. Heather Dubrow expresses the need for more such studies because "it is through this subject that English culture both expressed and repressed concerns about not only gender but also the power of the monarch and the stability of the nation itself." *Echoes of Desire: English Petrarchism and Its Counterdiscourses* (Ithaca: Cornell UP, 1995), 187.
3. All Shakespeare quotes throughout the book are from *The Riverside Shakespeare*. Text references are to act, scene, and line of this edition.
4. Paul Kléber Monod, *The Power of Kings: Monarchy and Religion in Europe, 1589–1715* (New Haven: Yale UP, 1999), 30–31.
5. Nicholas Mayhew describes the history of money in England as "in part the history of kings and bankers, but...also [as] truly popular, since from at least the eleventh century even the lowest peasants used coin and measured their assets and obligations in money terms. When government changed the money, or when it was left untouched, everyone felt the consequences." *Sterling: The History of a Currency* (New York: Wiley, 1999), xiv.
6. Fischer, *Econolingua: A Glossary of Coins and Economic Language in Renaissance Drama* (Newark: U of Delaware P, 1985).
7. Parry and Bloch, "Introduction: Money and the Morality of Exchange," *Money and the Morality of Exchange*, ed. Jonathan Parry and Maurice Bloch (Cambridge: Cambridge UP, 1989), 23.
8. Columbus, *The Diario of Christopher Columbus's First Voyage to America, 1492–1493*, trans. Oliver Dunn and James E. Kelley, Jr. (Norman, OK: U of Oklahoma P, 1989), 244; Richard Hakluyt, *The Principal Navigations Voyages Traffiques & Discoveries of the English Nation*, vol. 7 (London: J. M. Dent, 1926), 336.
9. Louis Althusser, "Ideology and Ideological State Apparatuses (Notes towards an Investigation)," *Lenin and Philosophy and Other Essays*, trans. Ben Brewster (New York: Monthly Review, 1971), 177–83.

According to the *OED*, in the early modern period the word "utter" had the sense of both a verbal utterance and the circulation of coins. *The Oxford English Dictionary*, 2nd ed., s.v. "Utter."

10. Kopytoff, "The Cultural Biography of Things: Commoditization as Process," *The Social Life of Things: Commodities in Cultural Perspective*, ed. Arjun Appadurai (Cambridge: Cambridge UP, 1986), 73. In another example of a coin serving a symbolic function of state, Sir Francis Drake purportedly nailed a sixpence to a post in California, in what Stephen Greenblatt calls "contact...mediated by representations." *Marvelous Possessions: The Wonder of the New World* (Chicago: U of Chicago P, 1991), 119.

11. Purchas, *Purchas His Pilgrimage* (London, 1613), sig. Aaa5v; Purchas, *Purchas His Pilgrimage* (London, 1614), sig. Kkk2v; Maxwell, *The laudable life and deplorable death, of our late peerlesse Prince Henry* (London, 1612), sig. D2v. I discuss this practice further in Chapter V.

12. However, as Ann Rosalind Jones and Peter Stallybrass explain, "the concept of the 'fetish' was...developed literally to demonize the power of 'alien' worn objects (through the association of *feitiço* with witchcraft), while at first preserving the notion of the sacramental object. It was not...mistaken to attribute spiritual powers to an object; rather, it was necessary to distinguish between legitimate and illegitimate objects." *Renaissance Clothing and the Materials of Memory* (Cambridge: Cambridge UP, 2000), 9.

13. Kopytoff, "Cultural Biography," 73; Patrick Geary, "Sacred Commodities: The Circulation of Medieval Relics," *The Social Life of Things*, ed. Arjun Appadurai (Cambridge: Cambridge UP, 1986), 169–91.

14. Marx, *Capital, Volume I*, trans. Ben Foakes (London: Penguin, 1990), 139, 165, 187.

15. Halpern, *The Poetics of Primitive Accumulation* (Ithaca: Cornell UP, 1991), 3, 5; Benjamin, "The Work of Art in the Age of Mechanical Reproduction," *Illuminations*, trans. Harry Zohn (New York: Harcourt, 1968), 218.

16. Kopytoff, "Cultural Biography," 68; Jones and Stallybrass, *Renaissance Clothing*, 8; Parry and Bloch, "Introduction," 21.

17. *TRP*, 1:67.

18. *CPR*, *P&M*, 3:539, 4:81. On *symbola*, see Marc Shell, *The Economy of Literature* (Baltimore: Johns Hopkins UP, 1978), 33 and Jean Christophe Agnew, *Worlds Apart: The Market and the Theater in Anglo-American Thought, 1550–1750* (Cambridge: Cambridge UP, 1986), 25.

19. See Ernst H. Kantorowicz, *The King's Two Bodies: A Study in Mediaeval Political Theology* (Princeton: Princeton UP, 1997), 7–11.

20. Roy Strong, *Portraits of Queen Elizabeth I* (Oxford: Clarendon, 1963), 40. Michael Neill reads the practice of counterfeiting in a

similar light, as a dishonoring of the prince or the public because of beliefs in a magical relation between people and their images: "To assault the image is to inflict damage upon the original." *Putting History to the Question* (New York: Columbia UP, 2000), 153. For an example, relating to *Macbeth*, of the king's image being used for what resembles a voodoo ritual, see Jonathan Goldberg, "Speculations: *Macbeth* and Source," *Shakespeare Reproduced*, ed. Jean E. Howard and Marion F. O'Connor (New York: Methuen, 1987), 249.
21. Michel de Certeau, *The Practice of Everyday Life*, trans. Steven Rendall (Berkeley: U of California P, 1984), xiii.
22. Muldrew, *The Economy of Obligation: The Culture of Credit and Social Relations in Early Modern England* (New York: St. Martin's, 1998).
23. E. Victor Morgan, *A History of Money* (Baltimore: Penguin, 1965), 23.
24. Davies, *A History of Money: From Ancient Times to the Present Day* (Cardiff: U of Wales P, 2002), 65.
25. Also, the designated value of coins must be higher than the value of the metal of which they are composed so that there is no incentive to melt them down.
26. See Malcolm Gaskill, *Crime and Mentalities in Early Modern England* (Cambridge: Cambridge UP, 2000), 123–60.
27. Alfred Sohn-Rethel, *Intellectual and Manual Labour* (London: Macmillan, 1978), 59.
28. Slavoj Žižek, *The Sublime Object of Ideology* (London: Verso, 1997), 18.
29. Karl Marx, *A Contribution to the Critique of Political Economy*, ed. Maurice Dobb (New York: International Publishers, 1970), 108. Hereafter cited in text.
30. Michel Foucault, *The Order of Things: An Archaeology of the Human Sciences* (New York: Vintage, 1994), 169. Hereafter cited in text.
31. Quoted in J. Taylor, "Copernicus on the Evils of Inflation and the Establishment of a Sound Currency," *Journal of the History of Ideas* 16 (1955): 543–44.
32. Thomas J. Sargent and François R. Velde, *The Big Problem of Small Change* (Princeton: Princeton UP, 2002), 17.
33. For more on the recoinage, see Ming-Hsun Li, *The Great Recoinage of 1696 to 1699* (London: Weidenfeld and Nicolson, 1963).
34. Another common connection between money and language in the early modern period is in the idea of rhetoric as a flow of currency. See, for example, Lorna Hutson, *Thomas Nashe in Context* (New York: Oxford UP, 1989), 221.
35. Osteen and Woodmansee, "Taking Account of the New Economic Criticism: an Historical Introduction," *The New Economic Criticism: Studies at the Intersection of Literature and Economics*, ed. Martha Woodmansee and Mark Osteen (London: Routledge, 1999), 21; Jean-Joseph Goux, *Symbolic Economies: After Marx and Freud*,

trans. Jennifer Curtiss Gage (Ithaca: Cornell UP, 1990), 4. Osteen and Woodmansee recognize this limitation in Goux: "Goux's work courts, and perhaps succumbs to, an economism of form and content." "Taking Account," 18.

36. Marc Shell, *Money, Language, and Thought: Literary and Philosophical Economies from the Medieval to the Modern Era* (Berkeley: U of California P, 1982), 3. "Taking Account," 15. Shell writes that "literary works are composed of small tropic exchanges or metaphors, some of which can be analyzed in terms of signified economic content and all of which can be analyzed in terms of economic form." Economic-based literary criticism, therefore, seeks "to understand the relation between such literary exchanges and the exchanges that constitute the political economy." Marc Shell, *The Economy of Literature* (Baltimore: Johns Hopkins UP, 1978), 7.

37. The "new materialism" is Douglas Bruster's term. *Shakespeare and the Question of Culture* (New York: Palgrave Macmillan, 2003). Recent titles in the "new materialism" include Jonathan Gil Harris, *Untimely Matter in the Time of Shakespeare* (Philadelphia: U of Pennsylvania P, 2008); Will Fisher, *Materializing Gender in Early Modern English Literature and Culture* (Cambridge: Cambridge UP, 2006); Natasha Korda, *Shakespeare's Domestic Economies: Gender and Property in Early Modern England* (Philadelphia: U of Pennsylvania P, 2002); Jones and Stallybrass, *Renaissance Clothing*.

38. On the emptying out of the "politics" in the new materialism, see, for example, Bruster, *Shakespeare and the Question of Culture*, 200–04 and David Hawkes, "Materialism and Reification in Renaissance Studies," *Journal of Early Modern Cultural Studies* 4 (2004): 114–29.

39. Guillory, "A New Subject for Criticism," *The Culture of Capital: Properties, Cities, and Knowledge in Early Modern England*, ed. Henry S. Turner (London: Routledge, 2002), 226, 227.

Chapter 1   Dimensions of State Formation

1. See especially Quentin Skinner's comprehensive analysis of the term in his tracing of the evolution of its conceptual framework from that of a particular "condition" to the modern sense of a political entity separate from either the commonwealth or its rulers. "The State," *Political Innovation and Conceptual Change*, ed. Terence Ball, James Farr, and Russell L. Hanson (Cambridge: Cambridge UP, 1989), 90–131.

2. Consideration of Marxist approaches must, of course, begin with Marx, whose clearest statement about the function of state is in *The German Ideology, Karl Marx: Selected Writings*, ed. David McLellan (Oxford: Oxford UP, 1977), 184. For Marx, the state, including its various agents and expressions in the law, is ultimately a product of class relations, the material base of society. Marx's collaborator Engels similarly based the state on class relations in *The Origin of the Family,*

Private Property and the State, trans. Ernest Untermann (Chicago: Charles H. Kerr, 1902), 208. For more recent Marxist analyses of state formation see, for example, Nicos Poulantzas, *State, Power, Socialism*, trans. Patrick Camiller (London: Verso, 2000) and Bob Jessop, *State Power: A Strategic-Relational Approach* (Cambridge, UK: Polity, 2007).
3. Weber, "Politics as a Vocation," *From Max Weber: Essays in Sociology*, ed. H. H. Gerth and C. Wright Mills (New York: Oxford UP, 1946), 78.
4. Tilly, *Coercion, Capital and European States, AD 990–1990* (Oxford: Basil Blackwell, 1990), 1.
5. Braddick, *State Formation in Early Modern England c. 1550–1700* (Cambridge: Cambridge UP, 2000), 18.
6. Poggi, *The State: Its Nature, Development and Prospects* (Stanford: Stanford UP, 1990), 9–10.
7. Braddick, *State Formation*, 17, 15.
8. Jordan, *Shakespeare's Monarchies: Ruler and Subject in the Romances* (Ithaca: Cornell UP, 1997), 20.
9. Braddick, *State Formation*, 18. Braddick later writes, "Defining the state in terms of political power, rather than specific institutional forms or particular functional purposes, leaves open questions about what forms state offices took, what they did and whose interests they served." Ibid., 46.
10. Steve Hindle regrets, "Few historians of early modern England have taken up the implications of this recent sociological thinking, perhaps because sociological definitions imply that political dynamics are fuelled by a routine degree of tension and potential conflict which sits uneasily with revisionist emphases on consensus and stability." *The State and Social Change in Early Modern England, 1550–1640* (Houndmills, Basingstoke: Palgrave Macmillan, 2000), 19.
11. Poggi, *State*, 3, 4, 8–9.
12. Mann, *The Sources of Social Power, Volume I: A History of Power from the Beginning to A. D. 1760* (Cambridge: Cambridge UP, 1986), 26, 22, 24, 25, 27, 37. Braddick draws from Mann his own definition of the state as "a coordinated and territorially bounded network of agencies exercising political power...exclusive of the authority of other political organisations." *State Formation*, 9.
13. Hindle, *State*, 2.
14. The fiscal-military state is an important corollary to the state defined by its monopoly on violence. Tilly claims that the "state structure appeared chiefly as a by-product of rulers' efforts to acquire the means of war." *Coercion*, 14. J. A. Sharpe calls the European state in the early modern period "a vast machine designed essentially to raise money and finance warfare." *Early Modern England: A Social History 1550–1760* (London: Hodder Arnold, 1987), 101. However, Braddick believes that accounts overemphasizing the fiscal-military

dimension of state formation would tend to find a weak early modern state whereas accounts that consider other dimensions, especially social and local histories, paint "a picture of an active and increasingly intrusive state apparatus." *State Formation*, 14.

15. Hindle, *State*, 20–21. Philip Corrigan and Derek Sayer contend that "state formation itself is cultural revolution" because in addition to producing the devices and functions for administration, the state also contributes to the variety of meanings surrounding these devices and functions. *The Great Arch: English State Formation as Cultural Revolution* (Oxford: Basil Blackwell, 1985), 3. See also Braddick, *State Formation*, 21.

16. Hindle, *State*, 23.

17. Black, *Kings, Nobles & Commoners: States & Societies in Early Modern Europe, a Revisionist History* (London: I. B. Tauris, 2004), 2.

18. Hindle, *State*, 16. On blurring distinctions between "public" and "private" in state matters, see ibid., 21–23 and Joseph Strayer, *On the Medieval Origins of the Modern State* (Princeton: Princeton UP, 1970), 7.

19. Political scientists still tend to emphasize state building. See, for example, Thomas Ertman, *Birth of the Leviathan: Building States and Regimes in Medieval and Early Modern Europe* (Cambridge: Cambridge UP, 1997) and Hendrik Spruyt, *The Sovereign State and Its Competitors* (Princeton: Princeton UP, 1994).

20. Braddick, *State Formation*, 7; Hindle, *State*, 9, 19.

21. Black, *Kings*, 2; Hindle, *State*, 23; Corrigan and Sayer, *Great Arch*, 4; Braddick, *State Formation*, 24.

22. For a recent critical reassessment of Elton's argument, see Christopher Coleman, "Introduction: Professor Elton's 'Revolution,'" *Revolution Reassessed: Revisions in the History of Tudor Government and Administration*, ed. Christopher Coleman and David Starkey (Oxford: Clarendon, 1986), 4–11. Although recent scholarship on the state has argued that historians have placed too much emphasis on institutions, especially because of the influence of Elton's three "points of contact"—court, privy council, and parliament—these institutions remain a key component of state formation. For critiques arguing overemphasis on institutions, see Hindle, *State*, 21 and Braddick, *State Formation*, 6.

23. *The Oxford English Dictionary*, 2nd ed., s.v. "State." However, Hindle points out that Starkey uses the word both in terms of a "fully self-conscious reference to a distinct constitutional structure" and in the more traditional sense of "condition." *State*, 17. Perhaps this lexicological vacillation indicates a transitional point from the traditional meaning to the more particular political meaning. Indeed, Hindle accedes that by the middle of the sixteenth century the political usage of the term had become common, especially

among humanists. Ibid., 17. Braddick makes the case that an English state, in the sense of a "network of offices wielding political power derived from a coordinating centre by formal means," existed by 1550, though he does not exclude the possibility of its emergence at an earlier point. Nevertheless, he specifies the use of the term "in a recognisably modern sense" appearing with frequency only within privy council correspondence of the 1590s and royal proclamations of the 1620s, the latter of which suggests familiarity on the part of the general populace by this time. *State Formation*, 20. John Guy also locates the emergence of the state concept in the 1590s, while pointing out that during the reigns of Henry VII and Henry VIII political discourse primarily used terms such as "country," "people," "kingdom," and "realm." *Tudor England* (Oxford: Oxford UP, 1988), 352.

24. Elton, *The Tudor Revolution in Government: Administrative Changes in the Reign of Henry VIII* (Cambridge: Cambridge UP, 1960), 3–4, 8, 415. Elton later argues that any attempt to "dethrone the Reformation" as a key factor in the emergence of the sovereign state is untenable. Ibid., 426.
25. Corrigan and Sayer, *Great Arch*, 21; Marc Bloch, *Feudal Society*, trans. L. A. Manyon (Chicago: U of Chicago P, 1961), 430; Coleman, "Introduction," 7. Mann makes a similar case as Bloch that "by 1150 the English state was probably the most centralized in Europe." *Sources*, 393.
26. Strayer, *Medieval*, 34, 28, 37–38. On the significance of chancery, see ibid., 33.
27. Ibid., 26. Strayer notes that although the Romans did not have an equivalent for "state," "their 'res publica' or 'commonwealth' was fairly close and formed a nucleus around which ideas of the state could crystallize."
28. Quoted in Elton, *Tudor Constitution*, 353.
29. Corrigan and Sayer, *Great Arch*, 17; Elton, *Studies in Tudor and Stuart Politics and Government*, Vol. 3 (Cambridge: Cambridge UP, 1983), 378. On the various strands of critical reaction to Elton, including the *Past and Present* debate, see Coleman, "Introduction," 4–5.
30. Jessop, *State Power*, 9.
31. Corrigan and Sayer, *Great Arch*, 28.
32. Braddick, *State Formation*, 23.
33. Strayer, *Medieval*, 102. Strayer even suggests that such concerns may have stunted the development of centralized institutions for foreign and military affairs, obviously key components of state business during the period. One solution to this problem was to adopt the principle of collegialty so there would be many secretaries, members of councils, boards, and the like. Ibid., 103.
34. Ibid., 94; Braddick, *State Formation*, 26–27.

35. Clanchy, "Does Writing Construct the State?," *Journal of Historical Sociology* 15 (2002): 68.
36. Strayer, *Medieval*, 24, 42.
37. See, for example, Hindle, *State*, 10. Strayer similarly describes the flow of "information, suggestions, propaganda, and directives" moving from the center to local officials in the periphery, while "information, requests, and warnings" moved from the periphery to the council. *Medieval*, 96. Elton himself had acknowledged the need for the study of local government while his own study focused on the center. *Tudor Revolution*, 5.
38. Hindle, *State*, 21; Braddick, *State Formation*, 14, 28. For details on the structure of local government and its relation to the center, see ibid., 28–33 and Hindle, *State*, 4–7. On how parliament became an important institution for coordinating consensus throughout the commonwealth see Corrigan and Sayer, *Great Arch*, 16, 30 and Strayer, *Medieval*, 64–67.
39. Corrigan and Sayer, *Great Arch*, 10.
40. Ertman, *Birth*, 6. I consider "republicanism" in the strict sense of a government with no hereditary monarch and, therefore, not directly pertinent to England's political structure in the period.
41. See Skinner, "The State." Despite the seemingly clear boundaries between these two models of governance, some scholars have observed an operative combination of the two defined by a separation between "absolute" and "ordinary" prerogatives. For example, C. H. McIlwain interprets in Bracton a distinction between *gubernaculum* and *iurisdictio*, the sphere of government according to which the king has "absolute" prerogative, and the sphere of right within which the king had limited power. See Ernst H. Kantorowicz, *The King's Two Bodies: A Study in Mediaeval Political Theology* (Princeton: Princeton UP, 1997), 148. See also Corinne Comstock Weston and Janelle Renfrow Greenberg, *Subjects and Sovereigns: The Grand Controversy over Legal Sovereignty in Stuart England* (Cambridge: Cambridge UP, 1981), 12–32.
42. Robert Eccleshall, *Order and Reason in Politics: Theories of Absolute and Limited Monarchy in Early Modern England* (Oxford: Oxford UP, 1978), 47, 48.
43. Ibid., 58.
44. Ibid., 76; Elyot, *The Boke named the Governour* (London: J. M. Dent, 1907), 8–9.
45. Eccleshall, *Order*, 79. Even in the case of tyranny, absolutists could argue that political matters remained outside the purview of the general populace. Despite the tyrant's abuse of power, they could maintain that God sat in ultimate judgment of the monarch and would remove him if warranted. In *Basilikon Doron*, James writes that "the wickednesse...of the King can never make them that are ordained to be judged by him, to become his Judges." *Political Works of James I*,

ed. Charles H. McIlwain (Cambridge: Harvard UP, 1918), 66. Indeed, as Eccleshall points out, the tyrant could serve as a moral object lesson for the faithful. He could maintain his status as an instrument for punishing evil even while he, as an agent of evil, would test the faith of believers. *Order*, 48.

46. The *Corpus iuris* was divided into four parts: the *Digest* (or *Pandects*), fifty books that included selected works of thirty-nine classical jurists from the second to fourth centuries; the *Institutes*, four books serving as an introductory textbook for students of the law; the twelve books of the *Code* comprised of imperial constitutions, many ordered by Justinian himself; and the supplementary *Novels*, consisting of appended imperial constitutions. Joseph Canning, *A History of Medieval Political Thought, 300–1450* (London: Routledge, 1996), 6.

47. Ibid., 7–8.

48. Kantorowicz, *King's*, 128–29, 132–33, 134. In England, this concept of the monarch as living justice became most pronounced in sixteenth-century representations of Elizabeth as Astraea, the goddess of justice. See ibid., 147 and Stuart Clark, *Thinking with Demons: The Idea of Witchcraft in Early Modern Europe* (Oxford: Clarendon, 1997), 628. Despite their mystical connotations, representations of the ruler as living justice also had a more pragmatic side in the belief that the state, in its goal of maintaining order, should be the main provider of justice. But this duty, of course, had its political advantages. Strayer notes that commoners and lower aristocracy relied on the state's provision of justice to protect them from violence and loss of land while monarchs embraced the loyalty and approval that such provision of justice would offer. Justice thereby became a source of power and authority. *Medieval*, 32. On the significance of the Investiture Conflict in this regards, see ibid., 22–23. Strayer also notes that justice was a source of revenue since most civil cases required monetary payment. Ibid., 29. Hindle similarly identifies "legalism" as one of the defining cultural characteristics of the early modern English state: a "'jurisdictional state' in which the recognition of the monarch as the fountain of all justice was paramount." *State*, 29. Clark notes that "speaking" the law also included bureaucratic duties such as appointing and dismissing judges and magistrates, and offering in higher court judgments appropriate models for the lower courts. *Thinking*, 627.

49. Canning, *History*, 8–9, 11. See also Eccleshall, *Order*, 69.

50. Quoted in Guy, *Tudor England*, 371.

51. Eccleshall, *Order*, 69; Kantorowicz, *King's*, 152. See Henry de Bracton, *On the Laws and Customs of England*, trans. Samuel E. Thorne (Cambridge: Harvard UP, 1968), 2:19.

52. Kantorowicz, *King's*, 150, 151, 155, 159.

53. Starkey, "Which Age of Reform?," *Revolution Reassessed: Revisions in the History of Tudor Government and Administration,*

ed. Christopher Coleman and David Starkey (Oxford: Clarendon, 1986), 21; Fortescue, *A learned commendation of the politique lawes of Englande* (London, 1567), sig. D2v; Eccleshall, *Order*, 102. Jordan notes that Fortescue's text was later appropriated by Jacobean political theorists looking to uphold constitutional rule against absolutist claims, such as were expressed in James I's *Trew Law*. She states that Fortescue's text reads like an "antagonistic pretext" to *The Trew Law*. *Shakespeare's Monarchies*, 23.

54. Eccleshall, *Order*, 45, 36; Bodin, *The Six Bookes of a Commonweale*, trans. Richard Knolles, ed. Kenneth Douglas McRae (Cambridge: Harvard UP, 1962), sig. H6v, sig. I2v.
55. James I, *Political Works*, 63.
56. For example, in "A Speech in the Starre-Chamber, the XX. of Jvne. Anno 1616," James proclaimed that "it is presumption and high contempt in a Subject, to dispute what a King can doe, or say that a King cannot doe this, or that; but rest in that which is the Kings revealed will in his Law." Ibid., 333.
57. Coke, *Le quart part des reportes del Edward Coke Chiualier* (London, 1604), sig. B5r. J. G. A. Pocock notes the apparent contradiction in the idea of customary law, which implies the possibility of change, and the persistent view that laws had always been the same, that they were "immemorial in the precise legal sense of dating from time beyond memory." *The Ancient Constitution and the Feudal Law: A Study of English Historical Thought in the Seventeenth Century* (Cambridge: Cambridge UP, 1987), 36.
58. Canning, *History*, 10.
59. Another case for coinage standards based in natural law would be made by John Locke in the late seventeenth century, an interpretation some economists describe as an early statement of the "quantitative theory of money." See, for example, Walter Eltis, "John Locke, the Quantity Theory of Money and the Establishment of a Sound Currency," *The Quantity Theory of Money: From Locke to Keynes and Friedman* (Hants, England: Edward Elgar, 1995), 4.
60. Perry Anderson points out that Bodin had a "conservative" side in that he promoted the limitation of fiscal and economic rights for rulers, the "reinvigoration of the fief system for military service, and a reaffirmation of the value of Estates." *Lineages of the Absolutist State* (London: Verso, 1979), 50.
61. Ertman, *Birth*, 167–68.
62. Fortescue, *learned*, sig. F1r–F1v.
63. Eccleshall, *Order*, 98–99; Elton, *Tudor Revolution*, 8; Saint German, *Doctor and Student* (London, 1751), sig. M4v.
64. Ertman, *Birth*, 158, 180.
65. Ibid., 178.
66. Eccleshall, *Order*, 115–16. Perhaps this is the reason James ascribed power to make new law solely to the prince in "The Trew Law of Free Monarchies." *Political Works*, 63.

67. Eccleshall, *Order*, 123.
68. Saint German, *Doctor*, sig. K11r; Saint German, *An answere to a letter* (London, 1535?), sig. G6r–G6v. For another example from John Rastell writing around 1513, see Martin Ingram, "Reformation of Manners in Early Modern England," *The Experience of Authority in Early Modern England*, ed. Paul Griffiths, Adam Fox, and Steve Hindle (New York: St. Martin's, 1996), 55.
69. Hindle, *State*, 176; Ingram, "Reformation," 55. Corrigan and Sayer write that "moral regulation is co-extensive with state formation, and state forms are always animated and legitimated by a particular moral ethos." *Great Arch*, 4.
70. Ingram, "Reformation," 65; Hindle, *State*, 177.
71. Stubbes, *Anatomy of Abuses* (London, 1583), sig. ¶5v- ¶6r; Ingram, "Reformation," 67–68.
72. Just as Roman law via Justinian's *Corpus iuris* provided a source of authority for absolutism, it also provided a key source for belief in the monarch's divine authority and the sacred nature of his laws. At the beginning of the *Digest*, Justinian describes himself as "at God's command governing our empire, which has been entrusted to us by heavenly majesty." Canning, *History*, 7.
73. Kantorowicz, *King's*, 16, 9, 206.
74. See Chapter 3 in Kantorowicz, *King's*.
75. Kantorowicz, *King's*, 87; Monod, *The Power of Kings: Monarchy and Religion in Europe, 1589–1715* (New Haven: Yale UP, 1999), 39–40, 37. James's supporters employed the two-body theory in Calvin's Case (1608) to support his attempted unification of England and Scotland. See ibid., 68 and Kantorowicz, *King's*, 14–16, 24.
76. Eccleshall, *Order*, 1; Gardiner, *De Vera Obedientia* (London, 1553), sig. C7v; *An homily against disobedience and wilful rebellion* (London, 1570), sig. A2v; Hindle, *State*, 33.
77. Bodin, *Six Bookes*, sig. O5r; James I, *Political Works*, 307; Crakanthorpe, *A Sermon at the Solemnizing of the Happy Inauguration of... King James* (London, 1609), sig. G3r. Eccleshall suggests that the shift in emphasis toward a spiritual dimension, the mystification of politics, may have been from Arminian supporters of the crown, whose "image of the monarch was that of a being who hallowed the nation by his possession of a mixture of aesthetic and spiritual attributes." *Order*, 77.
78. Strayer, *Medieval*, 107–08. Strayer argues that "both divine right and sovereignty [as articulated by Bodin] were attempts to find theological or legal terms to explain and justify a change that had already taken place in the position of the head of the state. Once these doctrines had been formulated, they reinforced already existing attitudes towards monarchy, but the attitudes existed before the doctrines." Ibid., 91. On a connection in Bodin between the two-body theory and sovereignty, which made the king the "incarnation of a quasi-divine juridical principle," see Monod, *Power*, 74.
79. Strayer, *Medieval*, 9, 45, 56.

80. Ibid., 47, 111.
81. Ibid., 46; Hindle, *State*, 31.
82. Max Weber, *Economy and Society: An Outline of Interpretive Sociology*, ed. Guenther Roth and Claus Wittich (New York: Bedminster, 1968), 1:241, cf. 1:215–16; Clark, *Thinking with Demons: The Idea of Witchcraft in Early Modern Europe* (Oxford: Clarendon, 1997), 606, 585. Hindle notes the theocratic nature of early modern kingship in which the "divine right of kings was a matter of charismatic authority." *State*, 33.
83. Weber, *Economy*, 1:248; Hindle, *State*, 33; Pemberton, *The charge of God and the king, to judges and magistrates, for execution of justice* (London, 1619), sig. A8r–A8v; Monod, *Power*, 10.
84. Weber, *Economy*, 1:263; Clark, *Thinking*, 554, 555. Of course, such beliefs in politico-theological principles would be tested by reformation challenges. See Monod, *Power*, 47–53.
85. Mann calls the state "*territorially centralized* and territorially-bounded" so that it can "attain greater autonomous power when social life generates emergent possibilities for enhanced cooperation and exploitation of a centralized form over a confined territorial area." *Sources*, 27.
86. Strayer, *Medieval*, 5–6, 36.
87. Canning, *History*, 124–25, 168–69.
88. Spruyt, *Sovereign*, 27.
89. James Tully, Introduction to *On the Duty of Man and Citizen* by Samuel Pufendorf, ed. James Tully (Cambridge: Cambridge UP, 1991), xviii.
90. Ertman, *Birth*, 4.
91. Spruyt argues that power structures in the early Middle Ages—like those of feudalism, the Church, and the Holy Roman Empire—were "nonterritorial, and sovereignty was, at best, disputed." *Sovereign*, 35.
92. Ibid., 155, 177, 179, 180.
93. Ibid., 3, 76, 77, 155; Ertman, *Birth*, 3. See also Nicos Poutlantzas's argument about how the emergence of capitalism impacted state formation by transforming conceptions of space. *State, Power, Socialism*, trans. Patrick Camiller (London: Verso, 2000), 101–05.
94. Anderson, *Lineages*, 19, 20, 40, 18.
95. Davies, *A History of Money: From Ancient Times to the Present Day* (Cardiff: U of Wales P, 2002), 26. For more comprehensive histories of the mint, see this work as well as C. E. Challis's *A New History of the Royal Mint* (Cambridge: Cambridge UP, 1992) and *The Tudor Coinage* (New York: Manchester UP, 1978).
96. On the independent development of coinage and paper money in China, see Davies, *History*, 55–58. On Indian coinage, see ibid., 66. In the eastern Mediterranean from around 1100 B. C. E., metal tools

and stamped bars probably served as a form of proto-coinage. Mann, *Sources*, 194.

97. The double-struck coin was made by engraving one pattern on the head of a punch for the obverse of a coin and another on a die for the reverse side. The design for the reverse typically indicated the coin's denomination. E. Victor Morgan, *A History of Money* (Baltimore: Penguin, 1965), 13–14.

98. Davies, *History*, 61–64.

99. Catherine Eagleton and Jonathan Williams, *Money: A History* (Richmond Hill, ON: Firefly, 2007), 24.

100. Arthur R. Burns, *Money and Monetary Policy in Early Times* (London: Keegan Paul, 1927), 75.

101. Glassner, "An Evolutionary Theory of the State Monopoly over Money," *Money and the Nation-State*, ed. Kevin Dowd and Richard H. Timberlake, Jr. (New Brunswick, NJ: Transaction, 1998), 22–24; Ure, *The Origin of Tyranny* (New York: Russell & Russell, 1962), 2; Burns, *Money*, 82–83. Ure also notes, "It may be more than accidental coincidence that the most anti-tyrannical state in Greece [Sparta] was without a real coinage." *Origin*, 24.

102. In the *Politics* Aristotle describes the use of metals "intrinsically useful and easily applicable to the purposes of life." Although at first the value was "measured simply by size and weight,...in process of time they put a stamp upon it, to save the trouble of weighing and to mark the value." *The Politics and Constitution of Athens*, ed. Stephen Everson (Cambridge: Cambridge UP, 1996), 23.

103. Mann, *Sources*, 195.

104. Davies, *History*, 90.

105. Grant, *Roman History from Coins: Some Uses of Imperial Coinage to the Historian* (Cambridge: Cambridge UP, 1958), 69.

106. Davies, *History*, 67, 81, 87. Davies notes that after Alexander, "the power to coin money became more obviously, though not exclusively, a jealously guarded sovereign power, the first to be assumed by any conquering army." Ibid., 87. Images such as those on the Persian coins indicate associations between coinage and military power. Early coins were of high value and so were not likely to have been used for everyday exchange, but instead for compensating mercenaries and receiving taxes and tributes from wealthy subjects. Mann notes that "Military service was the first—and for long the only—form of wage labor." *Sources*, 194. Indeed, the term "soldier" derives from the "solidus" or shilling they received in pay. Davies, *History*, 142.

107. Davies, *History*, 90.

108. Spufford, *Money and Its Use in Medieval Europe* (Cambridge: Cambridge UP, 1988), 9.

Notes

109. Unfortunately, according to the British Museum's latest inventory, there have been no coins found within the recently discovered Staffordshire hoard.
110. Davies, *History*, 120, 124.
111. See ibid., 125–26, on the likely etymology of the term "penny." Because there were no smaller denominations, pennies were often cut in half for a halfpence or into quarters for farthings. The practice probably continued until Edward I introduced halfpence and farthing coins. *The Royal Mint: An Outline History* (London: HM Stationery Office, 1967), 31.
112. Davies, *History*, 125.
113. Nicholas Mayhew, *Sterling: The History of a Currency* (New York: Wiley, 1999), xi, 3. The word "shilling" derives from the Saxon *scilling*, a "piece cut off," referring to fragments of coins or silver. Under the Roman Empire, the term came to be associated with the Roman *solidus*. Morgan, *History*, 18. See also *Royal Mint*, 25.
114. *Royal Mint*, 2.
115. Davies, *History*, 131.
116. *Royal Mint*, 2.
117. Davies, *History*, 130.
118. Mayhew, *Sterling*, 2–3. William Camden dates the establishment of sterling later, during the reign of Richard I, and offers an etymology of the term from the "Easterling" inhabitants of eastern Germany. *Remains Concerning Britain*, ed. R. D. Dunn (Toronto: U of Toronto P, 1984), sig. Aa4v. See Davies, *History*, 143 and Mayhew, *Sterling*, 2–3, for more on the etymology of "sterling."
119. *Royal Mint*, 4; Mayhew, *Sterling*, 10.
120. Davies, *History*, 130.
121. Charles Johnson, "Introduction," *The De Moneta of Nicholas Oresme and English Mint Documents*, trans. Charles Johnson (London: Thomas Nelson, 1956), xix–xx.
122. Davies, *History*, 140.
123. Camden writes that "in King *Stephens* time every Earle and Baron erected his Mynt." *Remains*, sig. Aa4v.
124. Mayhew, *Sterling*, 12.
125. Davies, *History*, 141–42.
126. *Royal Mint*, 4, 6. On the episcopal mints, see Mayhew, *Sterling*, 11.
127. Elton, *Tudor Revolution*, 162; Gould, *The Great Debasement* (Oxford: Clarendon, 1970), 8.
128. Davies, *History*, 191.
129. Ibid., 192.
130. Challis, *Tudor Coinage*, 49, 51.
131. Davies, *History*, 193.
132. Ibid., 193.
133. Brooke, *English Coins* (London: Methuen, 1950), 176–77.
134. Elton, *Tudor Revolution*, 197n2.

Chapter II More's *Utopia* and the Logic of Debasement: Reason, Custom and Natural Laws of Coinage

1. Such a view would persist in the late seventeenth century within John Locke's argument for restoring the coinage to its "natural" state during the great recoinage of the 1690s. See my conclusion.
2. Glyn Davies, *A History of Money: From Ancient Times to the Present Day* (Cardiff: U of Wales P, 2002), 230.
3. Peter Spufford, *Money and Its Use in Medieval Europe* (Cambridge: Cambridge UP, 1988), 301, 302. The French translation is mine.
4. For examples demonstrating the development of this new orthodoxy, see Spufford, *Money*, 301–04. On the significance of Oresme's treatise and its context, see Davies, *History*, 230, and George Sarton, *Introduction to the History of Science*, vol. 2, part 1 (Baltimore: Williams and Wilkins, 1948), 494.
5. Davies, *History*, 230.
6. Spufford, *Money*, 308; Kaye, *Economy and Nature in the Fourteenth Century: Money, Market Exchange, and the Emergence of Scientific Thought* (Cambridge: Cambridge UP, 1998), 156. Following Oresme's death the work circulated in manuscript for 100 years and was eventually printed in Cologne in 1484; around 1511 a sixteen-page small quarto pamphlet was published in Paris. Charles Johnson, "Introduction," *The De Moneta of Nicholas Oresme and English Mint Documents*, trans. Charles Johnson (London: Thomas Nelson, 1956), xii.
7. Spufford, *Money*, 300–01, 316, 310.
8. Oresme, *The De Moneta of Nicholas Oresme and English Mint Documents*, trans. Charles Johnson (London: Thomas Nelson, 1956), 4–5, 9. Hereafter cited in text.
9. Ibid., 8–9. While he suggests that all coins be pure, he acknowledges the necessity of mixing some precious metals with alloys as in so-called black money, or *billon*. However, only less precious metals (e.g., silver) should be mixed, and the proportion of the mixture should be fixed. The prince should never change the money so that it deviates from this fixed proportion. Ibid., 21.
10. In "A Defence of the Right of Kings," James I interprets the passage to mean that "Christ without all ambiguity and circumlocution, by the image and inscription of the money, doeth directly and expressely proove *Caesar* to bee free from subjection, and entirely Soveraigne." *Political Works of James I*, ed. Charles H. McIlwain (Cambridge: Harvard UP, 1918), 226.
11. Oresme cites Uguccio in *Derivationes magnae* on the etymology of "moneta," which comes from the Latin *moneo* (to warn) "because it warns us against fraud in metal or weight." Ibid., 22.
12. He advises every community that uses "black money" to "keep in some public place or places a sample of this proportion or quality

of alloy, to prevent the prince (which God forbid) or the moneyers secretly committing this fraud in the alloy, just as examples of other measures are frequently kept in charge of the community."

13. In such a situation in which the community finds itself reduced to slavery, "it can immediately or otherwise revoke the grant" of coinage. Ibid., 40.

14. Discussing English common law, Glenn Burgess argues that in his attempt to marry reason with custom and maxims, Christopher Saint German believed that "the immemoriality of custom [was] not so much a recognition of long immutable existence as of simple ignorance of origin." *The Politics of the Ancient Constitution: An Introduction to English Political Thought, 1603–1642* (University Park: Pennsylvania State UP, 1993), 7.

15. Eccleshall, *Order and Reason in Politics: Theories of Absolute and Limited Monarchy in Early Modern England* (Oxford: Oxford UP, 1978), 53, 40, 59, 60. On Aquinas's view of monarchy, see *On Politics and Ethics*, trans. Paul E. Sigmund (New York: W. W. Norton, 1988), 18–20. In practice, the community represented in this communal wisdom was typically limited to those with landed interests, even through the early modern period. For example, Steve Hindle argues that Sir Thomas Smith's famous description in 1583 of the English commonwealth as a four-tiered hierarchy quickly dissolves into a two-tiered structure: "'them that bear office, and them that bear none.'" Hindle, therefore, finds in the transformation a "binary model of political participation." *The State and Social Change in Early Modern England, 1550–1640* (Houndmills, Basingstoke: Palgrave Macmillan, 2000), 24–25. On the significance of the juristic conception of the corporation for the development of this political line of thought, see Eccleshall, *Order*, 62–63.

16. Aquinas, *Aquinas Ethicus: or, the Moral Teaching of St. Thomas*, trans. Joseph Rickaby (London, 1896), 1:267–71.

17. Quentin Skinner, *Foundations of Modern Political Thought* (Cambridge: Cambridge UP, 1978), 2:148–49. Eccleshall finds a precedent in John of Salisbury (1159) who "suggested that the pattern of order obtained in political society coincided with the divine design that was reproduced throughout the natural world." *Order*, 51.

18. Oresme, *De Moneta*, 6, 15. Oresme later states that "the community alone has the right to decide if, when, how, and to what extent this ratio is to be altered, and the prince may not in any way usurp it." Ibid., 17.

19. Charles Johnson's translation has "They would have six thousand pence to be a shilling (*solidus*)...," but that equivalency does not make sense. Ibid., 17. The shilling/solidus was never worth that many pence/denarii. I believe the coin names were somehow altered in translation, perhaps by Oresme himself.

20. Ibid., 17.

NOTES 213

21. Ibid., 13. On the relationship between custom and popular sovereignty see J. G. A. Pocock, *The Ancient Constitution and the Feudal Law: A Study of English Historical Thought in the Seventeenth Century* (Cambridge: Cambridge UP, 1987), 20–25.
22. Skinner, *Foundations*, 1:62.
23. Marsilius of Padua, *The Defender of Peace*, trans. Alan Gewirth (New York: Harper & Row, 1967), 45, 46.
24. Ibid., 41, 65.
25. Ibid., 40, 38–39.
26. Oresme, *De Moneta*, 45. Marsilius does, however, paraphrase a passage from the second book of Aristotle's *Metaphysics*, "laws show how great is the power of custom." *Defender*, 35. Oresme's emphasis on custom as law has a clear affinity with later common law politics in the authority of custom within establishment of law. See, for example, Pocock, *Ancient Constitution*, 33. Oresme's belief that "the course and value of money in the realm should be, as it were, a law and a fixed ordinance" employs logic similar to such later defenses for customary law. *De Moneta*, 13. Because monetary conventions were initially devised in a "reasonable" manner and were found to be "good and beneficiall to the people," they had become a custom that with continued practice had eventually obtained the "force of a Law."
27. Ibid., 12, 13.
28. Burgess, *Politics*, 27; Selden, "Notes upon Sir John Fortescue," John Fortescue, *De laudibus legum Angliae* (London, 1616), sig. C1r; Burgess, *Politics*, 39.
29. George C. Brooke, *English Coins* (London: Methuen, 1950), 176.
30. Plutarch. *The Lives of the Noble Grecians and Romans*, trans. John Dryden. (New York: Random House, n.d.), 55–56.
31. More was likely familiar with Plutarch's description, especially since according to Raphael Hythloday the Utopians "are very fond of the works of Plutarch." *The Complete Works of St. Thomas More*, vol. 4, ed. Edward Surtz and J. H. Hexter (New Haven: Yale UP, 1965), 183/1–2. Throughout, I cite both page and line numbers from this edition in text.
32. The motivation for the forgery of the Soderini letter is explained in Frederick Pohl, *Amerigo Vespucci: Pilot Major* (New York: Octagon, 1966), 151–52.
33. *Letter to Piero Soderini, Gonfaloniere, the Year 1504*, trans. George Tyler Northrup (Princeton: Princeton UP, 1916), 44; McCann, *English Discovery of America to 1585* (New York: Octagon, 1969), 85.
34. More's comment in his letter to Peter Giles suggests an attempt to tease the reader as to its location: "we forgot to ask, and he [Raphael] forgot to say, in what part of the new world Utopia lies," and he claims he would be willing to pay a great deal of money for the information (43/1–2).

35. *Letter to Soderini*, 9.
36. Martyr, *De Orbe Novo, the Eight Decades of Peter Martyr D'Anghiera*, trans. Francis Augustus Macnutt (New York: Putnam's, 1912), 1: 221–22, 1: 307. Although Martyr's first part of *De Orbe Novo*, the *Three Decades*, was not published until November 9, 1516, ten days before *Utopia* reached the printers, McCann suggests that More had likely read earlier installments of the work, copies of which circulated prior to publication. *English Discovery*, 89.
37. Levin, *The Myth of the Golden Age in the Renaissance* (Bloomington, IN: Indiana UP, 1969), 61, 59; Martyr, *De Orbe Novo, or the Historie of the West Indies*, trans. R. Eden (London, 1612), sig. H5r; Levin, *Myth*, 60.
38. Ovid, *Metamorphoses*, books 1–8, trans. Frank Justus Miller (Cambridge: Harvard UP, 1992), 11–13. On other classical precedents for communism, see Arthur J. Slavin, "'Tis far off, And rather like a dream': Common Weal, Common Woe and Commonwealth," *Explorations in Renaissance Culture* 14 (1988): 3–6. See also Edward Surtz, "Thomas More and Communism," *PMLA* 64.3 (1949): 550–51, for a discussion of precedents in the Bible, Aquinas, and Duns Scotus and ibid., 555–64 for More's changing attitudes about communism. For a discussion of More's argument that absolute equality is a political necessity, see George M. Logan, "The Argument of *Utopia*," *Interpreting Thomas More's* Utopia, ed. John C. Olin (New York: Fordham UP, 1989), 24.
39. Martyr, *De Orbe Novo*, trans. Macnutt, 2:252; Martyr, *De Orbe Novo*, trans. Eden, sig. K7r. Absence of private property was one characteristic linking the classical Golden Age with the biblical Eden. See Levin, *Myth*, 59. On how Golden Age examples in the New World could lead to social protest and even rebellion in Europe, see Carlo Ginzburg, *No Island is an Island: Four Glances at English Literature in a World Perspective*, trans. John Tedeschi (New York: Columbia UP, 2000), 11–23.
40. See Ovid, *Metamorphoses*, 9–11 and Thomas Andrewe, *The Massacre of Money* (London, 1602), sig. B1v. The persistence of war was a phenomenon that also troubled observers of the New World. See, for example, Martyr, *De Orbe Novo*, trans. Macnutt, 1:79.
41. See Wayne A. Rebhorn, "Thomas More's Enclosed Garden: *Utopia* and Renaissance Humanism," *English Literary Renaissance* 6 (1976): 142. Passages in *Utopia* (125/26–28, 125/34–37, and 127/24–28) suggest that their pursuits are labor-intensive and a far cry from the leisurely Golden Age. See also 131/13–17, on Hythloday's rationale for a redistribution of labor.
42. Ovid, *Metamorphoses*, 9. Andrewe describes how in the Golden Age, "No threatening lawe with sharp spurd punishment, / Gave out edicts to curbe a lawless rowte." *Massacre*, sig. A4v.

43. Fox, *Thomas More: History and Providence* (New Haven: Yale UP, 1982), 69.
44. Marsilius of Padua had assumed "as almost self-evident by induction in all perfect communities" the need for a "standard, which is called a 'statute' or 'custom' and by the common term 'law.'" *Defender*, 34.
45. In Utopia, as in England, all the machinery seems to bear the legitimating stamp of a monarchical will despite its representative government. Its legendary founder Utopus is represented as an enlightened ruler who has "brought the rude and rustic people" in the area "to such a perfection of culture and humanity as makes them now superior to almost all other mortals" (113/5–7).
46. Smith, *De Republica Anglorum* (London, 1583), sig. Q3v; Fox, *Thomas More*, 51; Logan, "Argument," 29; Halpern, *The Poetics of Primitive Accumulation* (Ithaca: Cornell UP, 1991), 142.
47. Ovid, *Metamorphoses*, 13.
48. Martyr, *De Orbe Novo*, trans. Eden, sig. S7v; Ward Barrett, "World Bullion Flows, 1450–1800," *The Rise of Merchant Empires*, ed. James D. Tracy (Cambridge: Cambridge UP, 1990), 28. For an assessment of various theories about the "price revolution," see Davies, *History*, 212–18.
49. Halpern, *Poetics*, 145. On gold's relation to excrement and its contrast to the guilt associated with Luther, see Stephen J. Greenblatt, *Learning to Curse: Essays in Early Modern Culture* (London: Routledge, 1990), 70–73. On Freudian associations between wealth and excrement, see Charles Clay Doyle, "The Utopians' Therapeutic Chamber-Pots," *Moreana* 19.73 (1982): 75. On humanists' conception of evil as either "filth or disease from which the individual must be segregated," see Rebhorn, "Enclosed Garden," 152. Gold's association with excrement may also relate to its origins in the bowels of earth in Ovid's *Metamorphoses*. See also Andrewe, *Massacre*, sig. B2v.
50. See also Katharina Wilson ("An Affront to Gold and Silver: Tertullian's *De Cultu Feminarum* and More's *Utopia*," *Moreana* 19 (1982): 69–74), who finds a source for the Utopians' use of gold in Tertullian's *De Cultu Feminarum*.
51. See, for example, Martial, *Epigrams*, trans. Walter C. A. Ker (London: Heinemann, 1919), 1.53 and J. Duncan Derrett, "The Utopians' Stoic Chamber-Pots," *Moreana* 19.73 (1982): 75–76 on Plutarch's *Moralia*.
52. Ovid, *Metamorphoses*, 9, 11. Robert Shephard comments, "Given the theoretical importance of self-sufficiency and isolation for the success of the Utopian experiment, it comes as a surprise to see how much contact the Utopians have with their neighbors in practice." "Utopia, Utopia's Neighbors, *Utopia* and Europe," *Sixteenth Century Journal* 26 (1995): 845.

53. Another sign of the Utopians' concern about power over trade is that they "think it wiser to carry [exports] out of the country themselves than to let strangers come to fetch them. By this policy they get more information about foreign nations and do not forget by disuse their skill in navigation" (185/11–14).
54. Shephard, "Utopia," 846.
55. Halpern, *Poetics*, 147.
56. Niccolò Machiavelli, *The Discourses*, ed. Bernard Crick (London: Penguin, 1970), 243, 245.
57. The most troubling instance of purchasing lives with money is in their hiring of mercenaries, especially the Zapoletans (146/36; 209/9–15). On the Zapoletans as an allusion to German and Swiss mercenaries of the period and on Eramus's arguments against the hiring of mercenaries, see Edward Surtz, *The Praise of Wisdom: A Commentary on the Religious and Moral Problems and Backgrounds of St. Thomas More's* Utopia (Chicago: Loyola UP, 1957), 294–99. See also Rebhorn, "Enclosed Garden," 147; Shephard, "Utopia," 850; and Logan, "Argument," 10.
58. The inclusion of this latter condition implies the Utopians' willingness to wage war for monetary reasons, which seems to contradict their devaluation of money. As Shephard points out, "the Utopians are willing to sacrifice their resources and maybe their citizens to preserve societies that are corrupt and oppressive by their own standards." "Utopia," 847–48.
59. *A Discourse of the Common Weal of This Realm of England*, ed. Mary Dewar (Charlottesville: UP of Virginia, 1969), 112.
60. Fox, *Thomas More*, 51.

Chapter III The Great Debasement and Its Aftermath

1. Perry Anderson, *Lineages of the Absolutist State* (London: Verso, 1979), 124. Debasement technically refers only to reduction in fineness, but the term is commonly used to describe any reduction in precious metal content of coins (fineness or weight).
2. Nicholas Mayhew, *Sterling: The History of a Currency* (New York: Wiley, 1999), 46. There were other minor incidents when rulers allowed lower-quality coins to pass. See, for example, Henry VII's proclamations ordering subjects to continue using "small, thin, and old pence" as long as "they be silver and whole," as well as cracked coins and clipped coins with at least half the scripture remaining. *TRP*, 1:47, 1:60–61, 1:70–74.
3. There had been an early example of debasement in 1048 under Edward the Confessor; see Glyn Davies, *A History of Money: From Ancient Times to the Present Day* (Cardiff: U of Wales P, 2002), 134. But the effects of the rare earlier English debasements paled in comparison to Henry's debasement.

4. See Carlo M. Cipolla, "Currency Depreciation in Medieval Europe," *Economic History Review*, 2nd series 15.3 (1963): 419. David Glassner declares that the "history of money virtually coincides with a history of the debasement, depreciation, and devaluation of the currency by the state." "An Evolutionary Theory of the State Monopoly over Money," *Money and the Nation-State*, ed. Kevin Dowd and Richard H. Timberlake, Jr. (New Brunswick, NJ: Transaction, 1998), 21.
5. Peter Spufford, *Money and Its Use in Medieval Europe* (Cambridge: Cambridge UP, 1988), 289, 307. For ancient precedents of debasement and depreciation during times of war, see Glassner, "Evolutionary," 26.
6. Spufford, *Money*, 317.
7. Mayhew, *Sterling*, 28–29.
8. Spufford, *Money*, 317–18.
9. Ibid., 318.
10. Mayhew, *Sterling*, 30.
11. George C. Brooke, *English Coins* (London: Methuen, 1950), 175.
12. Mayhew, *Sterling*, 44.
13. *TED*, 2:176–77.
14. *Letters and Papers, Foreign and Domestic, of the Reign of Henry VIII*, vol. 20, part 2 (London: Public Record Office, 1862–1910), 197.
15. Davies, *History*, 199; Mayhew, *Sterling*, 45.
16. Davies, *History*, 198.
17. Mayhew, *Sterling*, 45.
18. Davies, *History*, 200–01.
19. Mayhew, *Sterling*, 45–47. In order to produce all the new coinage, Henry needed to open six additional mints besides the core Tower Mint: a second building in the Tower and mints at Southwark, Durham House in the Strand, Canterbury, York, and Bristol. J. D. Gould, *The Great Debasement* (Oxford: Clarendon, 1970), 3. In fact, the Canterbury and York mints were the same ecclesiastical mints that Henry had previously closed; these proved especially useful for coining metal that had come from the dissolution of the monasteries. Davies, *History*, 200.
20. Davies, *History*, 202.
21. Mayhew, *Sterling*, 47; *A Speech Made by Sir Rob. Cotton...His Opinion Touching the Alteration of Coin, Select Tracts and Documents Illustrative of English Monetary History 1626–1730*, ed. William. A. Shaw (London, 1896), 24; Davies, *History*, 207.
22. Machyn, *The Diary of Henry Machyn*, ed. John Gough Nichols (London, 1848), 122.
23. Quoted in John Craig, *The Mint* (Cambridge: Cambridge UP, 1953), 110.
24. See Mary Dewar, "Introduction," *A Discourse of the Common Weal of This Realm of England*, ed. Mary Dewar (Charlottesville: UP of Virginia, 1969), xx.
25. *Discourse*, 98–100.

26. Mayhew, *Sterling*, 51.
27. Cotton, *Speech*, 29; *TED*, 2:182–83; Mayhew, *Sterling*, 46. There were some benefits from debasement, especially on the balance of trade, but even this caused further economic problems. Moreover, the extent of the trade benefit has been disputed. See Davies, *History*, 201–02. Because the pound's value decreased, English exports, especially English cloth, were now relatively cheap and, therefore, demand for them quickly increased. However, this increased demand for English wool led to an increased usage of land for sheep farming and a consequent decrease in production of other agricultural products. Mayhew, *Sterling*, 51–52.
28. *Discourse*, 100, 101, 108. In addition to noting the dearth of commodities, the participants in the *Discourse* recognize the debasement's effects on prices. See *Discourse*, 101, J. D. Gould sees the debasement as one cause of the "price revolution" in England. *Great Debasement*, 2.
29. Heywood, *John Heywoodes Woorkes* (London, 1562), sig. Z1v, sig. AA3r.
30. *The Royal Mint: An Outline History* (London: HM Stationery Office, 1967), 25.
31. Davies, *History*, 200. See Sandra Fischer's entry for "nose" in *Econolingua: A Glossary of Coins and Economic Language in Renaissance Drama* (Newark: U of Delaware P, 1985), 99.
32. Camden, *Remains Concerning Britain*, ed. R. D. Dunn (Toronto: U of Toronto P, 1984), sig. Bb3v.
33. Cotton, *Speech*, 24; Mayhew, *Sterling*, 55. On Edward's apparent attempts at reform, see Gould, *Great Debasement*, 42. See *TRP*, 1:519, for a subtle justification by Edward of devaluing his father's base money without offending his father's memory. On Mary's preliminary discussions on recoinage, see Davies, *History*, 204.
34. Challis, *The Tudor Coinage* (New York: Manchester UP, 1978), 120; *TED*, 2:196.
35. Davies, *History*, 205–06.
36. *Discourse*, 102; Cotton, *Speech*, 24.
37. Gould, *Great Debasement*, 42–43, 58–59.
38. Quoted in Norman L. Jones, "William Cecil and the Making of Economic Policy in the 1560s and Early 1570s," *Political Thought and the Tudor Commonwealth: Deep Structure, Discourse and Disguise*, ed. Paul A. Fideler and T. F. Mayer (London: Routledge, 1992), 170.
39. Clinton W. Potter, Jr., "Images of Majesty: Money as Propaganda in Elizabethan England," *Money: Lure, Lore, and Literature*, ed. John-Louis DiGaetani (Westport, CT: Greenwood, 1994), 72.
40. Mayhew, *Sterling*, 56; Camden, *Remains*, sig. Bb3v. Despite coinage reform, inflation persisted. Mayhew attributes it to a general flight from distrusted money to goods, but he also points out that the

"restored" coinage under Elizabeth still had an intrinsic value equal only to the base 1547 issues. *Sterling*, 50. See *Discourse*, 143–45, for a section included in the 1581 printing (and not present in the 1549 manuscript) that offers reasons for the continued inflation under Elizabeth.
41. Davies, *History*, 207.
42. Cotton, *Speech*, 25; Joan Thirsk and J. P. Cooper, eds., *Seventeenth-Century Economic Documents* (Oxford: Clarendon, 1972), 599; Mayhew, *Sterling*, 56. For more on Elizabeth's restoration of the coin, see *TRP*, 2:8, 2:51–52, and 2:67–68.
43. Cotton, *Speech*, 29; *Discourse*, 69–70. However, Copernicus, who argued for an extrinsic value theory, also saw the ill effects of debasement, primarily because debasement would prompt an excess production of coinage that would in turn impact prices. Davies, *History*, 231.
44. Smith, *De Republica Anglorum* (London, 1583), sig. G3r.
45. Cotton, *Speech*, 24.
46. Jack Weatherford, *The History of Money* (New York: Three Rivers, 1997), 53.
47. Davies, *History*, 112. For a detailed account of the Roman debasement, inflationary effects, and various attempts at coinage reform, see ibid., 95–108.
48. James I, *Political Works*, 26; Cotton, *Speech*, 24.
49. Sargent and Velde, *The Big Problem of Small Change* (Princeton: Princeton UP, 2002); Brooke, *English Coins*, 218.
50. On the initial investigation of these brass tokens, see *APC*, 10:92.
51. Davies, *History*, 208.
52. Ibid., 209–10. James's copper farthings, like Henry's debased coinage, induced widespread counterfeiting of tokens. See Malcolm Gaskill, *Crime and Mentalities in Early Modern England* (Cambridge: Cambridge UP, 2000), 126, 163.
53. Evelyn, *Numismata: a Discourse of Medals Antient and Modern* (London, 1697), sig. C4v; Davies, *Money*, 210.
54. Brooke, *English Coins*, 195.
55. Mayhew, *Sterling*, 65. See ibid., 66, for a further explanation of problems resulting from subsequent monarchs learning "the lesson of Tudor debasement... too well."
56. Gould, *Great Debasement*, 1.
57. Cotton, *Speech*, 23.
58. Mayhew, *Sterling*, 74–75.
59. Cotton, *Speech*, 26.
60. James I, *Political Works*, 307–08.
61. H. R. Trevor-Roper, "George Buchanan and the Ancient Constitution," *The English Historical Review*, supplement 3 (1966): 14.
62. Buchanan, *A History of Scotland*, trans. James Aikman (Glasgow, 1827), 2:602–03.

Chapter IV Coining Crimes and Moral Regulation in *Measure for Measure*

1. James I, *Basilikon Doron* (London, 1603), sig. D8r; Henry Peacham, *Minerva Britanna, or a Garden of Historical Devices* (London, 1612), sig. H4r; Bredbeck, *Sodomy and Interpretation* (Ithaca: Cornell UP, 1991), 5. See also Bruce R. Smith, *Homosexual Desire in Shakespeare's England* (Chicago: U of Chicago P, 1991), 14. An exception to the neglect of "false coin" is an article by Will Fisher, who traces the discursive history of the particular connection between sodomy and counterfeiting as in James's list. "Queer Money," *ELH* 66 (1999): 6–7.
2. Gaskill, *Crime and Mentalities in Early Modern England* (Cambridge: Cambridge UP, 2000), 139. Another monetary crime, *usury*, might be more appropriately included in this list since its critics often appealed to biblical (as well as classical) sources to argue for its immorality.
3. For a survey of early critical comparisons between *Measure for Measure* and *Basilikon Doron*, see Josephine Walter Bennett, *Measure for Measure as Royal Entertainment* (New York: Columbia UP, 1966), 82–104. Critics find James reflected in the duke, especially in his distaste for crowds and concerns about administration of the law. See, for example, Ernest Schanzer, *The Problem Plays of Shakespeare* (London: Routledge, 1963), 120–25 and Alvin Kernan, *Shakespeare, the King's Playwright: Theater in the Stuart Court, 1603–1613* (New Haven: Yale UP, 1995), 63–65.
4. George Chapman, Ben Jonson, and John Marston, *Eastward Ho!, The Roaring Girl and Other City Comedies*, ed. James Knowles (Oxford: Oxford UP, 2001), 4.1.192–94, 4.1.198–204. The particular act of blanching is often mentioned in court records. See, for example, *CPR, P&M*, 3:277–78. Michael Neill points out that the name assumed by Vindice in *The Revenger's Tragedy*, "Piato," means plated or "blanched" coin, and Gratiana and Castiza are liable to be "changed / Into white money" by Vindice's labors. *Putting History to the Question* (New York: Columbia UP, 2000), 156.
5. *CPR, P&M*, 4:451; Jonson, *The Alchemist, Three Comedies*, ed. Michael Jamieson (London: Penguin, 1985), 3.2.142–45. See also *CPR, P&M*, 4:379–80. In John Donne's elegy "The Bracelet," he describes pistolets,

    Which negligently left unrounded, look
    Like many-angled figures in the book
    Of some great conjurer that would enforce
    Nature, as these do justice, from her course.

    John Donne's Poetry, 2nd ed., ed. Arthur L. Clements (New York: W. W. Norton, 1992), ll. 33–36.

6. The first such statute was *Hen. V* s. 2. c. 6. See also *5 Eliz.* c. 11 and *18 Eliz.* c. 1.
7. Fulbecke, *A parallele or conference of the civill law, the canon law, and the common law of this realme of England* (London, 1601), sig. L6r.
8. *APC*, 9:115.
9. Chapman, Jonson, and Marston, *Eastward Ho!*, 4.1.206–08, 4.1.210–12. See the entries for "clip" and "wash" in Sandra K. Fischer, *Econolingua: A Glossary of Coins and Economic Language in Renaissance Drama* (Newark: U of Delaware P, 1985), 55–56, 136.
10. Quoted in Gaskill, *Crime*, 136. On filing, see, for example, *CPR, P&M*, 3:453; and for a pun on monetary "shaving," see Jonson, *Alchemist*, 4.4.131–32.
11. *CPR, P&M* 4:379–80; *Kent*, no. 3032; Machyn, *The Diary of Henry Machyn*, ed. John Gough Nichols (London, 1848), 69, 91. See also the cases of Thomas Smythe hanged for coining (*Kent*, no. 1622) and of Stephen Daye and John Allen (*Kent*, no. 2008). Pardons for coiners were frequent, however. Often pardons were granted for informing on other coiners. See, for example, *APC*, 5:100, 9:391–92; *CSP, Dom.*, 8:278. And coiners sometimes provided other services to the state, such as military service, in exchange for pardons. See, for example, *CPR, Eliz.*, 8:186.
12. Baines's "A Note Containing the Opinion of One Christopher Marly Concerning His Damnable Judgement of Religion" is at the British Library, Harley MS 6848 ff. 185–86, and a copy is in Harley MS 6853 ff 307–08, 1593. The full text of Baines's note can be found in Millar Maclure, ed., *Marlowe: The Critical Heritage, 1588–1896* (London: Routledge, 1979), 36–38. All citations from Baines in this volume are from this text.
13. The letter, which is in the State Papers (Holland) at the British National Archives, is transcribed in Charles Nicholl, *The Reckoning* (Chicago: U of Chicago P, 1992), 237–39.
14. The coiner Quicksilver similarly claims to have learned his illegal trade from associating with those in the gold trade. Chapman, Jonson, and Marston, *Eastward Ho!*, 4.1.187–88.
15. For an example of foreign fears of English counterfeiters, see Thomas Nashe, *The Unfortunate Traveler, The Unfortunate Traveler and Other Works* (London: Penguin, 1972), 303–04. Jack Wilton is duped by a prostitute, who gives him counterfeit coins, and her accomplice, who informs on him. He and Surrey end up before the master of the mint, who "thought [Wilton and Surrey] had a mint in [their] heads of mischievous conspiracies against their state."
16. Nicholl, *Reckoning*, 241–42.
17. Ibid., 244–46.
18. George C. Brooke, *English Coins* (London: Methuen, 1950), 177.

19. Gaskill, *Crime*, 160, 150–51, 139. Coining was not just a crime of the lower orders. Stephen Martin-Leake writes that "as it had been a fashionable Vice, we find Persons above the vulgar Sort concerned in this Practice." *An Historical Account of English Money* (London, 1745), 212. For examples of nobles, clergy, and others in important positions involved in coining, see ibid., 212; *Surrey*, no. 2375; *Kent*, no. 1681; *APC*, 15:330, 385; *APC*, 5:85; *Surrey*, no. 2919.
20. See *TRP*, 2: 179–80 and Challis, *Currency* 26–27. Some counterfeiters were even considered highly respectable craftsmen. For example, Samuel Pepys describes a "cheat" in the mint who produced counterfeits "as good, nay better, then those that commonly go; which was the only thing that they could find out to doubt them by." *The Diary of Samuel Pepys*, ed. Robert Latham and William Matthews (Berkeley: U of California P, 1970–83), 4:143–44.
21. *Salisbury*, 4:537; *CPR, P&M*, 4:451; *APC*, 10:84; *CSP, Dom.* 2:391; *Salisbury*, 17:309; *APC*, 16:155–56.
22. Quoted in Gaskill, *Crime*, 133.
23. Sharpe, *Crime in Early Modern England 1550–1750* (London: Longman, 1984), 12.
24. Valenze, *The Social Life of Money in the English Past* (Cambridge: Cambridge UP, 2006), 19; Gaskill, *Crime*, 127. Gaskill does briefly note the attempts to associate coining with other crimes. Ibid., 128–29.
25. Seaver, *Wallington's World* (Stanford: Stanford UP, 1985), 141 (emphasis mine).
26. Ibid., 141–42.
27. *TRP*, 1:67.
28. Ibid., 2:267.
29. See, for example, *18 Eliz.* c. 1, *5 Eliz.* c. 11 and *1&2 Phil. & Mar.* c. 11. On deceit see *14 Eliz.* c. 3.
30. In fact, there is a fourth term in the murder metaphor: that of "stealing" a life.
31. Martin Ingram, "Reformation of Manners in Early Modern England," *The Experience of Authority in Early Modern England*, ed. Paul Griffiths, Adam Fox, and Steve Hindle (New York: St. Martin's, 1996), 67.
32. Steve Hindle, *The State and Social Change in Early Modern England, 1550–1640* (Houndmills, Basingstoke: Palgrave Macmillan, 2000), 185.
33. Ingram, "Reformation," 66.
34. Aristotle, *Generation of Animals*, trans. A. L. Peck (Cambridge: Harvard UP, 1953), 185.
35. *Oxford English Dictionary*, 2nd. ed., s.v. "Character."
36. John Donne was particularly fascinated by the body/soul implications of the minting process. See John Carey, "Donne and Coins," *English Renaissance Studies Presented to Dame Helen Gardner in Honour of*

Her Seventieth Birthday, ed. John Carey and Helen Peters. (Oxford: Clarendon, 1980), 151–63. On this stamping metaphor's extension to other media such as writing and printing, see Margreta De Grazia, "Imprints: Shakespeare, Gutenberg and Descartes," *Alternative Shakespeares Vol. 2*, ed. Terence Hawkes (London: Routledge, 1996), 74–94.

37. Lampe, *The Seal of the Spirit: A Study in the Doctrine of Baptism and Confirmation in the New Testament and the Fathers* (London: Longman, 1951), 254. For Lampe, the illegitimate coin represents the soul of the unbeliever, who "does not bear the image of the Spirit" and thus "cannot be put into the royal treasuries of the Kingdom of Heaven...."

38. Quoted in Winfried Schleiner, *The Imagery of John Donne's Sermons* (Providence: Brown UP, 1970), 113.

39. Donne, *The Sermons of John Donne*, ed. Evelyn M. Simpson and George R. Potter (Berkeley: U of California P, 1953–62), 4:288.

40. Pemberton, *The charge of God and the king, to judges and magistrates, for execution of justice* (London, 1619), sig. A3r; Finch, *Law, or, a discourse thereof in foure books* (London, 1627), sig. G1r; Rawlinson, *Vivat Rex* (Oxford, 1619), sig. B4r; Valentine, *God save the King* (London, 1639), sig. B3r.

41. Clark, *Thinking with Demons: The Idea of Witchcraft in Early Modern Europe* (Oxford: Clarendon, 1997), 627; Cotton, *A Speech Made by Sir Rob. Cotton... His Opinion Touching the Alteration of Coin, Select Tracts and Documents Illustrative of English Monetary History 1626–1730*, ed. William. A. Shaw (London, 1896), 25.

42. Aristotle, *The Nicomachean Ethics*, trans. David Ross (Oxford: Oxford UP, 1980), 124–25; Thomas Aquinas, *Aquinas Ethicus: or, The Moral Teaching of St. Thomas*, trans. Joseph Rickaby (London, 1896), 2:22; Camden, *Remains Concerning Britain*, ed. R. D. Dunn (Toronto: U of Toronto P, 1984), sig. Aa1r–Aa1v.

43. Kaye, *Economy and Nature in the Fourteenth Century: Money, Market Exchange, and the Emergence of Scientific Thought* (Cambridge: Cambridge UP, 1998), 127, 133, 221; Camden, *Remains*, sig. Aa1v; Oresme, *The De Moneta of Nicholas Oresme and English Mint Documents*, trans. Charles Johnson (London: Thomas Nelson, 1956), 20.

44. This association between Angelo and angels has been noted by a number of critics. See, for example, Allan Shickman, "Shakespeare's 'Figure of an Angel': An Iconographic Study," *Colby Library Quarterly* 17 (1981): 7; Arthur C. Kirsch, "The Integrity of *Measure for Measure*," *Shakespeare Survey* 28 (1975): 99–100; and William Shakespeare, Measure for Measure: *An Old-Spelling and Old-Meaning Edition*, ed. Ernst Leisi (New York: Hafner, 1964), 43–47. The pun recurs later when, upon finding out about Angelo's plan, the duke wonders, "what may man within him hide, / Though angel on the

outward side," suggesting pure surprise that his issue has proven base (3.2.271–72).

45. Glyn Davies, *A History of Money: From Ancient Times to the Present Day* (Cardiff: U of Wales P, 2002), 146.
46. Shell, *The Economy of Literature* (Baltimore: Johns Hopkins UP, 1978), 32–33. See also Jean Christophe Agnew, *Worlds Apart: The Market and the Theater in Anglo-American Thought, 1550–1750* (Cambridge: Cambridge UP, 1986), 25. Indentures, legal documents of which each party received half in order to verify an agreement, were a later extension of this principle.
47. Goldberg, *James I and the Politics of Literature* (Stanford: Stanford UP, 1983) 235. Clark describes the king's gaze as "the ocular equivalent of the principle of *lex loquens* [speaking law], and its most usual metaphorical application was to the vigilant, personal administration of royal justice." *Thinking*, 626.
48. Clark, *Thinking*, 631; Crompton, *A short declaration of the ende of traitors, and false conspirators against the state, and of the duety of subjectes to their soveraigne governour* (London, 1587), sig. F1v–F2r. Similarly, David Starkey points out that a human representative of the king "could be both royal agent and royal symbol, with the former role being given unique strength and resonance by the latter." "Representation Through Intimacy: A Study in the Symbolism of Monarchy and Court Office in Early Modern England," *Symbols and Sentiments: Cross-Cultural Studies in Symbolism*, ed. Ioan Lewis (London: Academic, 1977), 192.
49. De La Perriere, *Mirrour of policy* (London, 1598), sig. Gg1v; Barnes, *Foure bookes of offices enabling privat persons for the speciall service of all good princes and policies* (London, 1606), sig. T2r.
50. Sohn-Rethel, *Intellectual and Manual Labour* (London: Macmillan, 1978), 59; Žižek, *The Sublime Object of Ideology* (London: Verso, 1997), 19. J. W. Lever cites the *OED* to show that this terminology relates to the testing of fine gold coins before passing them into circulation. William Shakespeare, *Measure for Measure*, ed. J. W. Lever (London: Methuen, 1965), 6. Theresa Nugent reads the passage as an allusion to the parable of the talents, with the duke in the role of the master leaving his talents (gold coins) with his servants in order to test their powers of investment. "Usury and Counterfeiting in Wilson's *The Three Ladies of London* and *The Three Lords and Three Ladies of London*, and in Shakespeare's *Measure for Measure*," *Money and the Age of Shakespeare*, ed. Linda Woodbridge (New York: Palgrave Macmillan, 2003), 209.
51. Sohn-Rethel, *Intellectual*, 59.
52. Lever, Introduction to *Measure for Measure* by William Shakespeare, ed. J. W. Lever (London: Methuen, 1965), xxxiv.
53. Alexander Leggatt argues that while each substitution in the play "fails in its overt intent," it nevertheless "tests the character of the

substitute." "Substitution in *Measure for Measure*," *Shakespeare Quarterly* 39 (1988): 349.

54. Since the duke's justification for switching Isabella with Mariana is that Angelo and Mariana are already in effect married, Angelo's seduction of Isabella is tantamount to *adultery*. Michael Neill has shown a relation between adultery and adulteration of coin, especially the linguistic association in the Latin *adulter* and its connection to bastardy. *Putting*, 151–53. The association was so strong that Elizabeth felt the need to clarify that for nobles who counterfeit, the "Heire or Heires of any suche Offendour" or the wife should not be judged to have "Corrupcion of Bloud" (*18 Eliz*. c.1).

55. Shakespeare, *Measure for Measure*, ed. Lever, 94; Watt, "Three Cruces in *Measure for Measure*," *Review of English Studies* 38 (1987): 233. Leggatt even sees the duke's deputation as an exploitation of Angelo: "In being the Duke's substitute, Angelo is also his victim." "Substitution," 346.

56. This point has been made by Nevill Coghill, who reads the duke's speech as a polite warning to Angelo. "Comic Form in Measure for Measure," *Shakespeare Survey* 8 (1955): 19. See also Cynthia Lewis, "'Dark Deeds Darkly Answered': Duke Vincentio and Judgment in *Measure for Measure*," *Shakespeare Quarterly* 34 (1983): 274.

57. Crane, "Male Pregnancy and Cognitive Permeability in *Measure for Measure*," *Shakespeare Quarterly* 49 (1998): 282.

58. Schanzer notes that James was particularly sensitive about slander, passing a Scottish Act of Parliament in 1585 that classified slander as treason, punishable by death. *Problem Plays*, 125.

59. Oresme, *De Moneta*, 30; Dante Alighieri alludes to the notorious king in Canto XIX of *Paradiso*. *The Divine Comedy of Dante Alighieri: Paradiso*, trans. John D. Sinclair. (New York: Oxford UP, 1961), 277.

60. Cotton, *Speech*, 25; Evelyn, *Numismata: a Discourse of Medals Antient and Modern* (London, 1697), sig. Gg2v.

61. *APC*, 7:153; *CPR*, 5:no. 1945; *APC*, 10:229, 209 (emphasis added).

62. *APC*, 9:326–27; Jonson, *The Alchemist, Three Comedies*, ed. Michael Jamieson (London: Penguin, 1985), 4.4.80–82. Even when counterfeiters did not work for the state, debasement provided extra incentive to practice their craft. See, for example, Oresme, *De Moneta*, 34–35 and *TRP*, 1:518.

63. *The History of the Life, Reign, and Death of Edward II* (London, 1680), 47–48. Historically, Edward II's reign did, in fact, experience anxiety about debasement. See Peter Spufford, *Money and Its Use in Medieval Europe* (Cambridge: Cambridge UP, 1988), 303–04.

64. On a peculiar connection between copper and sexuality, see Fisher, "Queer Money," 3–5.

65. John Webster, *The White Devil. The Duchess of Malfi and Other Plays*, ed. René Weis (Oxford: Oxford UP, 1996), 3.2.98–101.

66. See Fischer's entry for "crack" in *Econolingua*, 61. Another prominent reference to cracked coins is in *Hamlet*, when the prince advises one of the players, "Pray God your voice, like a piece of uncurrent gold, be not crack'd within the ring" (2.2.427–28).
67. "Bloody noses" appear in *1 Henry IV* when Falstaff attempts to "coin" Bardolph's ruddy nose as well as his cheeks, which were also prominent in Henry's coins, in order to pay his debt to Mistress Quickly (3.3.77–79). See also Falstaff's admission that he has "misus'd the King's press damnably," suggesting both impressing men and pressing coins (4.2.12–13).
68. Ryan, "*Measure for Measure*: Marxism before Marx," *Marxist Shakespeares*, ed. Jean E. Howard and Scott Cutler Shershow (London: Routledge, 2001), 242. Leggatt calls the proposed substitution of Isabella's maidenhead for Claudio's head, "virtually a chain reaction, that runs through the play." "Substitution," 342.
69. Shell, *The End of Kinship: Measure for Measure, Incest, and the Idea of Universal Siblinghood* (Stanford: Stanford UP, 1988), 120, 122, 121.
70. Ibid., 120, 122.
71. Ibid., 131.
72. Leggatt, "Substitution," 355, 344. Valerie Forman argues that this quality of counterfeiting is already implicit in money: "Money is like counterfeiting; it is already a force that disrupts the relation between sign and referent. Counterfeiting, then, mimics and reproduces a discrepancy that money itself generates." "Marked Angels: Counterfeits, Commodities, and *The Roaring Girl*," *Renaissance Quarterly* 54 (2001): 1539.
73. Whether consciously or not, Lucio also calls attention to one of the most problematic actions of the duke: he listens to confessions while disguised as a friar. See Coghill, "Comic Form," 23–24, Leggatt, "Substitution," 344, and Shell, *End*, 130.
74. Kaplan, *The Culture of Slander in Early Modern England* (Cambridge: Cambridge UP, 1997), 93.
75. Leggatt notes the play's prominent "series of mirroring effects, of likenesses that are striking but not quite exact" in which "characters, ideas, and actions are explored for their similarities and differences." "Substitution," 350. And Kaplan points out that Lucio's "very name suggests his ability to reflect what surrounds him; *luce* means 'light,' as well as 'looking glass,' and it can also signify the capacity of discernment, artistic perfection, and fame." *Culture*, 96.
76. Goldberg argues that it is this sovereign power, both "real and stamped" that "sustains the exchange system of society, the endless refiguration of the king in representative acts of substitution." *James I*, 234.
77. Shell, *End*, 129–30.
78. Watt, "Three Cruces," 227–28. See Watt's proposed emendation. Ibid., 229.

79. See, for example, the footnote to this line in *The Riverside Shakespeare*.
80. Compare the absurdity of measuring mercy with Arthegall's refutation of the Giant's ability to measure all things with his scale in Edmund Spenser, *The Faerie Queene*, ed. Thomas P. Roche, Jr. (London: Penguin, 1978), 5.2.42.

Chapter V "Mysteries of State": The Political Theology of Coinage in *Macbeth*

1. Shakespeare, *Bell's Edition of Shakespeare's Plays as They are Now Performed at the Theatres Royal in London* (London, 1773–74), 1:55. See also Arthur Clark, who calls the passage "an excrescence from a dramatic point of view." *Murder under Trust or the Topical Macbeth* (Edinburgh: Scottish Academic, 1981), 23. And see Gary Wills on its connection to Malcolm, who becomes a capable physician in contrast to Macbeth's failure in Scotland. *Witches and Jesuits: Shakespeare's Macbeth* (Oxford: Oxford UP, 1995), 122. Henry Paul has a more elaborate theory that impetus for the passage's inclusion came from James's plotting council, including Master of the Revels Sir George Buck, who wanted James to incorporate the angel into his ceremony of touching. *The Royal Play of Macbeth* (New York: Macmillan, 1950), 379–86. Even recent interpretations that find discontinuity between *Macbeth* and James's absolutist vision still interpret the passage as a royal compliment. For example, Alan Sinfield reads the scene as epitomizing James's strategy of differentiating the usurping tyrant from the legitimate king. "*Macbeth*: History, Ideology and Intellectuals," *Materialist Shakespeare*, ed. Ivo Kamps (London: Verso, 1995), 97.
2. Bullough, *Narrative and Dramatic Sources of Shakespeare* (London: Routledge, 1957–75), 7:508. See Wills, *Witches*, 122, for an interpretation of this "gift of prophesie" in relation to James's discovery and dissolution of the Gunpowder Plot in 1605. The general critical tendency has been to use this passage as an example of how earlier readings distinguished the good and legitimate rule of Edward the Confessor from the evil, illegitimate rule of Macbeth. See, for example, Sinfield, "History," 97, and Jonathan Goldberg, "Speculations: *Macbeth* and Source," *Shakespeare Reproduced*, ed. Jean E. Howard and Marion F. O'Connor (New York: Methuen, 1987), 251. For more on the topical connection to the Gunpowder Plot, see Steven Mullaney, *The Place of the Stage* (Ann Arbor: U of Michigan P, 1995), 122–23. The healing ritual continued until the reign of Queen Anne in the early eighteenth century.

3. Prior to Robert, there was a long history of healing by rulers. The spiritual tradition goes back to Christ as healer. See Raymond Crawfurd, *The King's Evil* (Oxford: Clarendon, 1911), 10.
4. Trans. in Crawfurd, *King's Evil.* 12. See also ibid., 15–17, on legends about Clovis I and St. Marcoulf performing similar healings, and ibid., 69 for English legends about King Lucius and Joseph of Arimathaea. Bloch, however, argues that Lucius existed only in the "imagination of scholars." *The Royal Touch*, trans. J. E. Anderson (New York: Dorset, 1989), 23.
5. See Crawfurd, *King's Evil*, 14, and Bloch, *Royal Touch*, 12–14, on Philip appearing to have lost the gift for falling "under some reproach or other."
6. See Crawfurd, *King's Evil*, 12, and Bloch, *Royal Touch*, 20. Reasons for specializing in scrofula can be explained by the nature of the disease. Scrofula, or "struma" in Latin, is a tubercular gland condition that affects the lymphatic system. The *OED* defines it as "a constitutional disease characterized mainly by chronic enlargement and degeneration of the lymphatic glands." *The Oxford English Dictionary*, 2nd ed., s.v. "Scrofula." But F. David Hoeniger points out that "scrofula" was a general name given for a number of ailments that had similar symptoms as in the description from *Macbeth*: "All swollen and ulcerous, pitiful to the eye" (4.3.276). Physicians typically examined patients before they were taken to the king to make sure they were indeed suffering from scrofula. Since scrofula is a chronic condition, its symptoms often disappear for long periods, so it is not surprising that many testified to a miraculous healing effected by the king. Its epithet as "the king's evil" likely derived from the apparent success of the kings' healing. *Medicine and Shakespeare in the English Renaissance* (Newark: U of Delaware P, 1992), 276–77. Keith Thomas suggests that Bloch and others underestimate the deadliness of the disease. *Religion and the Decline of Magic* (New York: Charles Scribner's, 1971), 192.
7. Bloch, *Royal Touch*, 21.
8. Bloch, however, is skeptical about this dating, questioning the motive of these records describing Edward's practice of healing scrofula as political propaganda under Henry I. According to him, Henry II is the first English king, just as Philip I is the first French king, who could be said with certainty to have cured scrofula specifically and whose followers claimed to have inherited the gift. Ibid., 27.
9. Crawfurd, *King's Evil*, 19, 20, 26.
10. Ibid., 12, 19. The "Computus Hospitii" of Edward I records a number of instances of "pence given to sick persons blessed by the King." Ibid., 34.
11. There are entries for cramp rings under Richard II and Henry IV, but none for the king's evil. Fear of infection may have prompted this absence. See Ibid., 41–42.

12. See Helen Farquhar, "Royal Charities, Part I—Angels as Healing-pieces for the King's Evil," *British Numismatic Journal* 12 (1916): 69–70 and Noël Woolf, "The Sovereign Remedy: Touch Pieces and the King's Evil," *British Numismatic Journal* 49 (1979): 101.
13. *The laudable life and deplorable death, of our late peerlesse Prince Henry. briefly represented* (London, 1612), sig. D3r. See also Crawfurd, *King's Evil*, 50.
14. *The Ceremonies for the Healing of Them that be Diseased with the Kings Evil As they were Practiced in the Time of King Henry VII* (London, 1686), 11–13; Crawfurd, *King's Evil*, 50. Deborah Willis believes that the passage from John links the monarch "to John the Baptist, bearing witness to the light, while the gold coin represents the 'true light' itself." "The Monarch and the Sacred: Shakespeare and the Ceremony for the Healing of the King's Evil," *True Rites and Maimed Rites: Ritual and Anti-Ritual in Shakespeare and His Age*, ed. Linda Woodbridge and Edward Berry (Urbana and Chicago: U of Illinois P, 1992), 154. This part of the office seems to have remained mostly the same through Elizabeth. Although there is no direct record of Henry VIII's office, it most likely resembles that of Mary found in her manual that is currently in the Roman Catholic Cathedral of Westminster and was published in *The Journal of the Archaeological Association* in 1871. Mary's manual also contains three miniatures, including one depicting Mary touching a patient and one depicting her cramp ring ceremony. Elizabeth's office is recorded in her chaplain William Tooker's treatise, *Charisma: Sive Donum Sanationis* (1597), the relevant part of which is translated in Crawfurd, *King's Evil*, 72–75.
15. See Farquhar, "Royal Charities," 43.
16. Hoeniger, *Medicine*, 278; Beckett, *A Free and Impartial Enquiry into the Antiquity and Efficacy of Touching for the Cure of the King's Evil* (London, 1722), 52. John Donne describes the "royal touch" of the kings of England and France in the same breath as exorcism by the king of Spain, as both healing involving touching or "charms." *Biathanatos* (London, 1648), sig. Ee2r.
17. M. A. Faitta to Ippolito Chezzuola, London, 3 May 1556, Archives of Venice, trans. in Crawfurd, *King's Evil*, 67.
18. Quoted in Bloch, *Royal Touch*, 183.
19. Browne, *Adenochoiradelogia* (London, 1684), sig. Nn1v, sig. Kk3r. On coins as "sacred commodities," see my introduction.
20. Quoted in Thomas, *Religion*, 196n5.
21. Bloch, *Royal Touch*, 223.
22. Crawfurd, *King's Evil*, 76.
23. Quoted in Thomas, *Religion*, 196.
24. Browne, *Adenochoiradelogia*, sig. Mm6r. For other examples, see ibid., sig. Pp4r, sig. Pp7r, sig. Ppv, sig. Qq1v.
25. Translated in Crawfurd, *King's Evil*, 75, 74.

26. Stubbe, *The Miraculous Conformist* (Oxford, 1666), sig. B4r. Stuart Clark points to another concern in the relation between royal and folk healing, which was often associated with the devil. *Thinking with Demons: The Idea of Witchcraft in Early Modern Europe* (Oxford: Clarendon, 1997), 663. Moreover, healing coins strikingly resemble the emergent notion of fetishism. See William Pietz, "The Problem of the Fetish I," *Res* 9 (1985): 5, 10.
27. Willis, "Monarch," 156–57.
28. Quoted in Hoeniger, *Medicine*, 281.
29. H. M. C., Hatfield, x, pp. 166–67, quoted in Thomas, *Religion*, 195.
30. Roman transcripts, General Series, 88.8.11, trans. in Crawfurd, *King's Evil*, 84.
31. *CSP, Ven.*, 10:44. In addition to believing that the ceremony was ineffective and superstitious, James was unusually repugnant to disease. See Crawfurd, *King's Evil*, 70–71, 87.
32. Extracted from letters from London of October 9, 1603, Vatican Archives, Public Records Office, Roman transcripts, General Series, vol. 87, trans. in Crawfurd, *King's Evil*, 82–83. Early in his reign James appears to have used his status as "King of France" to distance himself from the ceremony. The June 4, 1603 letter states that James "will have the full ceremony so as not to lose this prerogative which belongs to the Kings of England as Kings of France." See also *CSP, Ven.*, 11:465 and William Brenchley Rye, *England as Seen by Foreigners* (London, 1865), 151–52. On James's skepticism about the ceremony, see Paul, *Royal Play*, 384 and Arthur Wilson, *The history of Great Britain, being the life and reign of King James the First...* (London, 1653), 289.
33. The service is found in a broadside of 1618, "Hum. Dyson. tempore Jacobi Regis," and was included in the Book of Common Prayer of 1634.
34. See Paul's theory that James's council plotted to persuade James to use the angel in his ceremony. *Royal Play*, 379–86. Paul's theory is based on thin circumstantial evidence and relies on a *post hoc* fallacy: because James appears to have adopted the coin after seeing it represented in *Macbeth*, the play must have prompted it.
35. Bloch, *Royal Touch*, 56; Herrick, "To The King, To cure the Evill," *Hesperides* (London, 1648), sig. F2r.
36. Bloch, *Royal Touch*, 66–67.
37. Ibid., 65.
38. Clowes, *A right frutefull and approoued treatise, for the artificial cure of that malady called in Latin Struma* (London, 1602), sig. H1v; Maguire, "Money and Magic in the Early Middle Ages," *Speculum* 72 (1997): 1039. Maguire cites archaeological evidence from late antiquity and the Byzantine period suggesting that people wore coins as mystical pendants. Ibid., 1040–45.

39. Farquhar has found several such coins whose reverse sides had been worn down from friction. "Royal Charities," 49–50. William Camden also mentions the practice. *Remains Concerning Britain*, ed. R. D. Dunn (Toronto: U of Toronto P, 1984), sig. Bb2r.
40. Thomas, *Religion*, 232; quoted in Julian Stafford Corbett, *The Successors of Drake* (London: Longman, 1900), 168.
41. A humorous anecdote from the late seventeenth century describes how Richard Baxter swallowed a gold bullet to cure his chronic illness but was unable to remove it until his congregation helped facilitate its passage through prayer. *The Certainty of the World of Spirits* (London, 1834), 70.
42. Thomas, *Religion*, 228.
43. Fortescue, *Defensio Juris Domus Lancastriae* (1462), trans. in Crawfurd, *King's Evil*, 45.
44. See Bloch, *Royal Touch*, 92–107. Queen Mary's manual in the Roman Catholic Cathedral of Westminster includes a description of her cramp ring ceremonies as well as a miniature depicting them.
45. Thomas, *Religion*, 33. A market for cramp rings eventually developed, driven by a high demand for these curative tokens. Bloch, *Royal Touch*, 184–85.
46. See Maguire, "Money," 1039–40, on the putative power of the emperor's portrait during the classical period and the early Middle Ages, which included subjects wearing them to show the emperor's sovereignty and protection.
47. Strong, *Portraits of Queen Elizabeth I* (Oxford: Clarendon, 1963), 39, 29, 32, 31.
48. Richard Hakluyt, *The Principal Navigations Voyages Traffiques & Discoveries of the English Nation*, vol. 7 (London: J. M. Dent, 1926), 336.
49. See Farquhar, "Royal Charities," 69–70 and Woolf, "Sovereign Remedy," 101.
50. In *1Henry IV*, Falstaff employs a similar conflation of the two meanings of "pressing" when he has "misus'd the King's press damnably" by turning "a hundred and fifty soldiers" into "three hundred and odd pounds" (4.2.12–14).
51. Maxwell, *laudable life*, sig. D3v–D4r. The *angel*'s reverse side depicted the royal coat of arms, which could stand in for the monarch. Thomas Bilson writes that respect for the coats of arms or other royal images "is accepted as rendred to their owne persons, when they can not otherwise be present in the place to receive it." *The True Difference between Christian Subjection and Unchristian Rebellion* (Oxford, 1585), sig. Pp1r.
52. The ritual's complexity permitted numerous identifications of the cure's source. Reginald Scot states that in identifying the source, "some refer to the propriety of [the monarchs'] persons, some to

the peculiar gift of God, and some to the efficacy of words." *The Discovery of Witchcraft* (London, 1665), sig. Q2r. *Macbeth* also represents this uncertainty. The first mention of it by an English doctor attributes the cure to the king's touch (4.3.144–46). But Malcolm's subsequent description adds the detail of the "golden stamp...put on with holy prayers," suggesting either the coin or prayer as curative source (4.3.151–55).

53. See Thomas, *Religion*, 33, 227.
54. Hall, *The Works of the Right Reverend Father in God Joseph Hall*, vol. 7, ed. P. Wynter (Oxford, 1863), 329. Thomas points out that the people who wore the prayers around their necks were often illiterate, so "the very impenetrability of the formula helped to give it its power." *Religion*, 182. For other examples of written prayers worn on the body, see ibid., 179, 183.
55. *The Earle of Gowries Conspiracie against the Kings Majesty of Scotland* (London, 1600), sig. C2r. On the association between the Gowrie plot and the play, see Mullaney, *Place*, 116 and Clark, *Murder*, 109–26. There is also an interesting connection between the healing ceremony and the Gunpowder Plot: in 1611 James healed for scrofula on the plot's anniversary. Rye, *England*, 144–45.
56. Thomas, *Religion*, 197; James I, *Political Works of James I*, ed. Charles H. McIlwain (Cambridge: Harvard UP, 1918), 332.
57. Weber, *Economy and Society: An Outline of Interpretive Sociology*, ed. Guenther Roth and Claus Wittich (New York: Bedminster, 1968), 1:241. See also ibid., 1:215–16.
58. Ibid., 1:248. Clark, *Thinking*, 655.
59. Weber, *Economy*, 1:254; Clanchy, *England and Its Rulers 1066–1272* (Totowa, NJ: Barnes and Noble, 1983), 156. On writs as routinized charisma, see also Braddick, *State Formation in Early Modern England c. 1550–1700* (Cambridge: Cambridge UP, 2000), 22.
60. Clark, *Thinking*, 628–29.
61. Berger, "The Early Scenes of *Macbeth*: Preface to a New Interpretation," *ELH* 47 (1980): 20.
62. See definitions 2.8 and 2.9 in *The Oxford English Dictionary*, 2nd ed., s.v. "Tale."
63. Berger, "Early," 24–25.
64. "Provide" in this passage also has an important etymological connection to the technical term "purveyance," which, according to the *OED*, denotes "the requisition and collection of provisions, etc., as a right or prerogative; *esp.* the right formerly appertaining to the crown of buying whatever was needed for the royal household at a price fixed by the PURVEYOR, and of exacting the use of horses and vehicles for the king's journeys." *The Oxford English Dictionary*, 2nd ed., s.v. "Purveyance."
65. For a discussion of Shakespeare's various puns on "gild," "gilt," and "gelt," see Gabriel Egan, "Gilding Loam and Painting Lilies:

Shakespeare's Scruple of Gold," *Connotations* 11.2–3 (2001/2002): 166–72.
66. The image of "golden blood" partially relies on an early modern perception of gold as "red" in color. Sandra Fischer lists "ruddock" or "ridduck" as a slang term for a gold coin because of its reddish color. *Econolingua: A Glossary of Coins and Economic Language in Renaissance Drama* (Newark: U of Delaware P, 1985), 117. Fischer also cites the phrase "Kissing the ruddie lips of angels," in *Old Fortunatus.* Ibid., 41. See also Egan, "Gilding," 169–71.
67. On the clothing imagery in *Macbeth*, see Caroline F. E. Spurgeon, *Shakespeare's Imagery and What It Tells Us* (Cambridge: Cambridge UP, 1935), 324–27 and Cleanth Brooks, *The Well Wrought Urn: Studies in the Structure of Poetry* (New York: Harcourt, 1947), 38–39.
68. Cicero's term is "*nervos belli, pecuniam infinitam.*" *Philippics*, trans. Walter C. A. Ker (Cambridge, MA: Harvard UP, 1926), 5.2.5. The translated term "sinews of war" became a common epithet for money in early modern England. See, for example, *A Discourse of the Common Weal of This Realm of England*, ed. Mary Dewar (Charlottesville: UP of Virginia, 1969), 86.
69. Hawkins, "History, Politics and *Macbeth*," *Focus on Macbeth*, ed. John Russell Brown (London: Routledge, 1982), 167.
70. Ovid, *Ovid's Metamorphoses*, trans. Arthur Golding, ed. John Frederick Nims (Philadelphia: Paul Dry, 2000), 1:154–57, 158; Edmund Spenser, *The Faerie Queene*, ed. Thomas P. Roche, Jr. (London: Penguin, 1978), 2.7.16, 17.
71. See my section on "Political Theology" in Chapter I.
72. Monod, *The Power of Kings: Monarchy and Religion in Europe, 1589–1715* (New Haven: Yale UP, 1999), 40.
73. Quoted in Ernst H. Kantorowicz, *The King's Two Bodies: A Study in Mediaeval Political Theology* (Princeton: Princeton UP, 1997), 15.
74. Ibid., 15. In legal discourse on the theory, the terms "body politic" and "mystical body" seem to be used without great discrimination. For example, Coke, when discussing the body politic of the king, added the following in parenthesis: "and in 21 E.4 [1482] it is called a mystical body." Quoted in ibid., 15.
75. Murray, "Why Was Duncan's Blood Golden?," *Shakespeare Survey* 19 (1966): 41, 42. For another example of Duncan's "golden blood" read as a sign of his sanctity, see Paul A. Jorgensen, *Our Naked Frailties: Sensational Art and Meaning in* Macbeth (Berkeley: U of California P, 1971), 87–88.
76. Barnes, *Foure bookes of offices enabling privat persons for the speciall service of all good princes and policies* (London, 1606), sig. B1v. See also *Usury Arraigned and Condemned* (London, 1625), 1–2. For an earlier (14th c) example, see Nicholas Oresme, *The De Moneta of Nicholas Oresme and English Mint Documents*, trans. Charles Johnson (London: Thomas Nelson, 1956), 43–44.

234 NOTES

77. Malynes, *The center of The circle of commerce* (London, 1623), 139.
78. Hobbes, *Leviathan*, ed. C. B. Macpherson (London: Penguin, 1985), 373–74.
79. Zimmerman, "Duncan's Corpse," *A Feminist Companion to Shakespeare*, ed. Dympna Callaghan (Chicester, West Sussex: Wiley-Blackwell, 2001), 329. Scrofula was believed by some to have been called the "king's evil" because it was caused, not healed, by the king. See Clark, *Thinking*, 666.
80. Stallybrass, "*Macbeth* and Witchcraft," *Focus on* Macbeth, ed. John Russell Brown (London: Routledge, 1982), 201; Clark, *Thinking*, 661.
81. Goldberg, "Speculations," 250. Willis notes that Edward's sacred healing power "contrasts with the magic the witches seduce Macbeth into believing he has—a magic of equivocation that comments ironically on Macbeth's lack of a true king's power." "Monarch," 158.
82. Monod, *Power*, 68; Crawfurd, *King's Evil*, 105; Willis, "Monarch," 156.
83. James I, *Political Works*, 332; Kantorowicz, "Mysteries of State: An Absolutist Concept and its Late Mediaeval Origins," *Selected Studies* (Locust Valley, NY: J. J. Augustin, 1965), 382.
84. James I, *Political Works*, 226.
85. Weber, *Economy*, 1:242.

Chapter VI Foreign Coins and Domestic Exclusion in Thomas Dekker's *The Shoemaker's Holiday*

1. Karl Marx, *A Contribution to the Critique of Political Economy*, ed. Maurice Dobb (New York: International Publishers, 1970), 107.
2. Harris, *Sick Economies: Drama, Mercantilism and Disease in Shakespeare's England* (Philadelphia, PA: U of Pennsylvania P, 2004), 21, 2.
3. From the inception of coinage in the ancient world, the state's local monopoly on coin production felt pressure from the mints of competing states. See David Glassner, "An Evolutionary Theory of the State Monopoly over Money," *Money and the Nation-State*, ed. Kevin Dowd and Richard H. Timberlake, Jr. (New Brunswick, NJ: Transaction, 1998), 24–25.
4. Cohen, *The Geography of Money* (Ithaca: Cornell UP, 1998), 14, 4; Cipolla, *Money, Prices, and Civilization in the Mediterranean World: Fifth to Seventeenth Century* (New York: Gordian, 1967), 14.
5. Cohen, *Geography*, 34, 6, 5, 17.
6. Ibid., 6; Supple, "Currency and Commerce in the Early Seventeenth Century," *The Economic History Review* 10, series 2 (1957–58): 240n1. See ibid., 239, Cipolla, *Money*, 38–51 and Cohen, *Geography*, 32. The pound sterling was initially based on the Roman pound of

12 ounces. The current symbol for the pound (£) derives from the Latin term "libra."
7. See Cipolla, *Money*, 39–40. According to Cipolla, the shilling or *solidus* was "an old name and unit introduced into the reform to link the new money with the immediate past and to facilitate its insertion into the system of already established debts." Ibid., 40. Even when pennies were debased, a "pound" or "pound-tale" was equated to 240 pennies, so eventually it did not necessarily equal a "pound-weight" of silver. Ibid., 42.
8. Rogers Ruding, *Annals of the Coinage of Great Britain and Its Dependencies*, 3rd. ed., Vol. 1 (London, 1840), 302. Because of fluctuating price ratios between gold and silver and problems of debasement, the value in "imaginary money" was not stable. See Cipolla, *Money*, 43–49.
9. Cipolla, *Money*, 14; Ederer, *The Evolution of Money* (Washington, DC: Public Affairs, 1964), 85. Cipolla notes that fractional coins constituted only a small percentage of total circulation value. *Money*, 14–15.
10. Ibid., 15, 23–24.
11. Cohen, *Geography*, 29; Elgin Grosclose, *Money and Man: A Survey of Monetary Experience*, 4th ed. (Norman: U of Oklahoma P, 1976), 20–21.
12. See Cipolla, *Money* 15. Lopez calls the *solidus/bezant* the "dollar of the Middle Ages."
13. In addition to *dinars*, Arabs adopted Persian "*dirhems*." Cipolla, *Money*, 16. See ibid., 18–19 for an amazing story related to the inscription on *dinars*.
14. Cohen, *Geography*, 30.
15. Cipolla, *Money*, 20–21.
16. Shepard Pond, "The Ducat: Once an Important Coin in European Business," *Bulletin of the Business Historical Society* 14.2 (April 1940): 18–19.
17. See Cohen, *Geography*, 30–31; Shepard Pond, "The Spanish Dollar: The World's Most Famous Silver Coin," *Bulletin of the Business Historical Society* 15.1 (Feb., 1941): 12–15. The *real* ("royal") was a denomination instituted in 1442 and later confirmed, in 1497, by Ferdinand and Isabella. Ibid., 12.
18. Nicholas Mayhew, *Sterling: The History of a Currency* (New York: Wiley, 1999), 31.
19. Ibid., 25.
20. Ruding, *Annals*, 302.
21. Ibid., 303. The two "porpynes" mentioned are the *ecu au porcepic de Bretagne* and the *ecu au porcepic du Dauphin*, respectively.
22. Mayhew, *Sterling*, 33–34.

23. All citations of Donne's "The Bracelet," which are hereafter in text, are from *John Donne's Poetry*, 2nd ed., ed. Arthur L. Clements (New York: W. W. Norton, 1992).
24. See Harris' chapter, "Taint and Usury: Gerard Malynes, the Dutch Church Libel, *The Merchant of Venice*," in *Sick Economies*, 52–82.
25. For more on the relation between coin clipping and circumcision, see Marc Shell, *Art and Money* (Chicago: U of Chicago P, 1995), 35–36.
26. Raphael Holinshed, *Chronicles of England, Scotland and Ireland* (London, 1586), sig. Dd6r.
27. Ben Jonson, *The Alchemist, Three Comedies*, ed. Michael Jamieson (London: Penguin, 1985), 3.2.142–45. Hereafter cited in text.
28. *The Earle of Gowries Conspiracie against the Kings Majesty of Scotland* (London, 1600), sig. A2r, sig. A3v.
29. C. E. Challis calls these coins "the ubiquitous pistolets" during the early 1560s. Between 1576 and 1582 they accounted for approximately 35 percent of all bullion bought and stored in the Exchequer. *The Tudor Coinage* (New York: Manchester UP, 1978), 193–95.
30. Holinshed, *Chronicles*, sig. Aaaaaa2r.
31. Farquhar, "Portraiture of Our Tudor Monarchs on Their Coins and Medals," *British Numismatic Journal* 4 (1908): 122; Challis, *Tudor Coinage*, 117–18.
32. In her reading of John Collop's coin imagery within the "ugly beauty" tradition, Heather Dubrow suggests a connection between concerns about contamination in "the foreignness of women with black and golden skins" and the manner in which "foreignness functioned in monetary exchanges." *Echoes of Desire: English Petrarchism and Its Counterdiscourses* (Ithaca: Cornell UP, 1995), 189.
33. Of course, this may be because the denier does not offer as many possibilities for linguistic play. An exception to the relative dearth of references to small denomination foreign coins is the doit, a copper penny of the Low Countries.
34. Cipolla, *Money*, 26, 37.
35. *TRP*, 2:536–39.
36. Christopher Marlowe, *The Jew of Malta, The Complete Plays*, ed. Frank Romany and Robert Lindsey (London: Penguin, 2003), 1.1.12–13, 6–7, 17–18.
37. Davies, *A History of Money: From Ancient Times to the Present Day* (Cardiff: U of Wales P, 2002), 201.
38. Thomas Dekker, *The Shoemaker's Holiday*, ed. Anthony Parr (London: A & C Black, 1990), 1.64–68. Hereafter cited as scene and lines in text.
39. Paul Seaver notes that Oatley as well as Eyre, who are "producers of wealth," express contempt for "a class of social parasites" represented by Lincoln and Lacy. "Thomas Dekker's *The Shoemaker's Holiday*: The Artisanal World," *The Theatrical City: Culture, Theatre and*

Politics in London, 1576–1649, ed. David L. Smith, Richard Strier, and David Bevington (Cambridge: Cambridge UP, 1995), 100.
40. See, for example, 7.71–77.
41. Seaver, "Artisanal," 96–97.
42. Ibid., 96. David Bevington points out that Eyre "resists his workers demands as long as he can until, faced with labour unrest beyond his control, he does his best to take credit for having a progressive attitude." "Theatre as Holiday," *The Theatrical City: Culture, Theatre, and Politics in London, 1576–1649*, ed. David L. Smith, Richard Strier and David Bevington (Cambridge: Cambridge UP, 1995), 110.
43. Kastan, "Workshop and/as Playhouse: *The Shoemaker's Holiday* (1599)," *Staging the Renaissance: Reinterpretations of Elizabethan and Jacobean Drama*, ed. David Scott Kastan and Peter Stallybrass (New York: Routledge, 1991), 153.
44. Ibid., 152. Seaver attributes the price increases to bad harvests. He points out that prices of meat and flour rose by 30 percent and beer by 48 percent while wages of skilled workmen such as Ralph, Hodge and Firk rose only by 10 percent, so real income decreased. "Artisanal," 88.
45. Seaver, "Artisanal," 91.
46. Bevington, "Theatre," 110; Gasper, *The Dragon and the Dove: The Plays of Thomas Dekker* (Oxford: Clarendon, 1990), 19; Fleck, "Marking Difference and National Identity in Dekker's *The Shoemaker's Holiday*," *Studies in English Literature, 1500–1900* 46.2 (Spring 2006): 358. Fleck sees the apparent incorporation of the foreigner as ultimate exclusion for a "sense of national purpose." Ibid., 365.
47. Gasper explains Eyre's newfound wealth as "a reward for their act of hospitality" in accommodating a stranger, a "Christian" and especially "Protestant" act. *Dragon*, 20.
48. Seaver, for example, suggests that the amount, closer to the entire crown debt than to any feasible value for a ship's cargo, is a "clue that the audience was being presented with a happy piece of wish fulfillment rather than any kind of mercantile reality." "Artisanal," 93–94.
49. See, for example, the note to this line in Parr's edition of *Shoemaker's*.
50. While the reading English public had access to works such as those of Andrew Boorde (*The fyrst boke of the Introduction of knowledge* [London, 1555]), which provided information on the "maner of coines of money, the which is currant in every region," and of Richard Verstegan's (*The Post For divers partes of the world* [London, 1576]), which offered English readers a useful account of the "value of the coine used in sundry Regions" by listing relative values of coins produced in various European mints, an average shoemaker such as Firk would not likely have knowledge of relatively obscure coins such as

the *ecu au porcepic*. I would like to thank Matthew Dimmock for referring me to these sources.
51. Several critics have noted, however, that the method of Eyre's rise seems morally questionable. Hodge mentions that the owner of the ship whose cargo Eyre buys "dares not show his head, and therefore this skipper, that deals for him, for the love he bears to Hans offers my master Eyre a bargain in the commodities" (16–19). A note in Parr's edition suggests that the merchant "dares not show his head" because in 1597, Hanseatic merchants were expelled from England, so the merchant may have been forced to sell his goods quickly at a loss. Seaver observes that as an alien merchant, the Dutch captain would need to find a citizen broker in order to sell his goods on the London market. "Artisanal," 93.
52. Seaver, "Artisanal," 92–93. Seaver notes that even Dick Whittington, who had risen to the mayoralty, had been apprenticed to a merchant, and the mythic component of his rise was that he had done so without the necessary capital, only his cat. Ibid., 92. He concludes that although "great wealth did not automatically lead to high office,... London's ruling elite was drawn from among the wealthiest of the mercantile inhabitants." Ibid., 95.
53. On various problematic aspects of the play, see Kathleen E. McLuskie, *Dekker and Heywood: Professional Dramatists* (New York: St. Martin's, 1994), 71; Kastan, "Workshop," 151; and Peter Mortenson, "The Economics of Joy in *The Shoemaker's Holiday*," *Studies in English Literature, 1500–1900* 16.2 (Spring 1976): 248.
54. Straznicky, "The End(s) of Discord in *The Shoemaker's Holiday*," *Studies in English Literature, 1500–1900* 36.2 (Spring 1996): 367–68; Kastan, "Workshop," 152; Fleck, "Marking," 365.
55. See Seaver, "Artisanal," 96 on Hodge's rise in particular.
56. Kastan, "Workshop," 158.
57. Seaver notes that Ralph's experience of being drafted into the army would have been a common sight at the time since in the spring of 1598 the earl of Essex brought 12,000 men to Ireland and the privy council was considering sending another 4,000. "Artisanal," 87–88. McLuskie, *Dekker and Heywood*, 71 and Kastan, "Workshop," 151 both indicate Ralph's wounding as among the darker elements of the play, but they both still follow the common interpretation of ultimate harmony rather than discord. See also Gasper, *Dragon*, 16.
58. See, for example, Bevington, "Theatre," 115; Seaver, "Artisanal," 89; and Kastan, "Workshop," 159.
59. Kastan, "Workshop," 155, 156.
60. Mortenson also notes how "Margery's glee in Eyre's social elevation as Sheriff coincides with Rafe's return lame from the French war. She crudely and condescendingly relishes the glories of her new station in the face of Rafe's grim return...." "Economics," 248.
61. Fleck, "Marking," 351–52, 365.

62. Kastan does note this discrepancy in treatment of the war dead. "Workshop," 155.
63. McLuskie argues, "There is no evidence to suggest that the false information about Rafe's death is given in anything but good faith for consistency of character is always subordinated to the demands of a particular scene." *Dekker and Heywood*, 70. But Gasper raises the possibility of forgery. *Dragon*, 34.
64. Kastan, "Workshop," 157; Mortenson, "Economics," 249, 251; Gasper, *Dragon*, 28.
65. Bevington, "Theatre," 116; Seaver, "Artisanal," 100; Straznicky, "End(s)," 368.
66. Though I do not interpret the play as a representation of absolutism, I am following here Perry Anderson's argument about how the absolutist state ultimately served to align the interests of the aristocracy and bourgeois at the expense of "peasant masses." *Lineages*, 18. Bevington does note that while the play seems to invite sympathy for the "dispossessed," we realize that the protagonists—Hans, who is actually an aristocrat, and Eyre, an emergent merchant—"are not as different from autocratic authority figures as a romantic view might suppose." "Theatre," 104–05.
67. Seaver, "Artisanal," 88.
68. Christopher Marlowe, *Doctor Faustus, The Complete Plays*, ed. Frank Romany and Robert Lindsey (London: Penguin, 2003), 4.26–28, 31–36.
69. Quoted in Harris, *Sick Economies*, 62–63, based on Arthur Freeman's transcription in his essay "Marlowe, Kyd, and the Dutch Church Libel," *English Literary Renaissance* 3 (1973): 44–52.

Conclusion   The Changing Matter of Money

1. Electronic money, which tends to empty money of its materiality completely, is a more complex case. To the extent that the national denomination remains a critical determinant of value, state institutional structures retain their importance. But to the extent that any number is readily convertible to another number of a different denomination, the institutions of any given nation become less important. Territorial boundaries for paper money, for example, do not necessarily hold for electronic money.
2. In the middle of this decade, King William III desperately needed monetary aid in his war against France, a financial need that became a key factor in the founding of the Bank of England in 1694.
3. Locke, *Further Considerations Concerning Raising the Value of Money, Locke on Money*, vol. 2, ed. Patrick Hyde Kelly (Oxford: Clarendon, 1991), 403.
4. Locke's ideas on the recoinage can be found in *Some Considerations of the Consequences of the Lowering of Interest and Raising the Value*

of Money, Locke on Money, vol. 1, ed. Patrick Hyde Kelly (Oxford: Clarendon, 1991) and Locke, *Further Considerations.*

5. Mayhew, *Sterling: The History of a Currency* (New York: John Wiley, 1999), xi.
6. Constantine George Caffentzis writes that "Locke, who is so tolerant of religious deviation, is almost religiously devoted to the quantitative and substantial 'integrity' of silver and gold; so much so that the violators of the body of money become the real 'robbers of the faith' in his demonology." *Clipped Coins, Abused Words, and Civil Government: John Locke's Philosophy of Money* (Brooklyn, NY: Autonomedia, 1989), 46.
7. Locke, *The Correspondence of John Locke,* vol. 5, ed. E. S. De Beer (Oxford: Clarendon, 1979), 540.
8. Feavearyear, *The Pound Sterling: A History of English Money,* 2nd ed. (Oxford: Clarendon, 1963), 148.
9. Joyce Appleby argues that it did so "because of the harmony between his ideas and the interests of the parliamentary magnates." *Economic Thought and Ideology in Seventeenth-Century England* (Princeton: Princeton UP, 1978), 230. For a detailed description of steps in the recoinage and problems that emerged from it, see Ming-Hsun Li, *The Great Recoinage of 1696 to 1699* (London: Weidenfeld and Nicolson, 1963), 111–38.
10. Feavearyear, *Pound Sterling,* 141–42. Not all parties lost out, however. Although the poor and those paying the cost of recoinage suffered, landlords and creditors gained from the recoinage, and there was a small public outcry about this inequity. Appleby, *Economic Thought,* 235–40.
11. Li, *Great Recoinage,* 143.
12. Patrick Hyde Kelly, "General Introduction: Locke on Money," *Locke on Money,* vol. 1, ed. Patrick Hyde Kelly (Oxford: Clarendon, 1991), 64, 65.
13. See Appleby, *Economic Thought,* 217.
14. Briscoe, *Historical and Political Essays or Discourses on Several Subjects* (London, 1698), sig. C1r–C1v.
15. Appleby concludes that "Locke's definition of money made way for the nineteenth-century belief in natural economic laws beyond the reach of political authority." *Economic Thought,* 239.
16. Feavearyear, *Pound Sterling,* 126.
17. Mackworth, *England's Glory, or, the Great Improvement of Trade in General, by a Royal Bank, or Office of Credit, to Be Erected in London* (London, 1694), sig. B3r.
18. See Feavearyear, *Pound Sterling,* 127. Compare this displacement of the monarch for a figurative representation of the country to Richard Helgerson's discussion of the iconographic shift from Christopher Saxton's atlas to Drayton's *Poly-Olbion. Forms of Nationhood: The*

Elizabethan Writing of England (Chicago: U of Chicago P, 1992), 112–20. Money seems to have evolved more slowly than maps, but a similar historical progression may be noted in the movement from coinage to paper money. Moreover, the bank's bills take the progression a step further. In addition to replacing the monarch on the sealed bank bills with the figure of Britannia, the bank even replaced the throne with a "bank of money," which came to be the true source of England's greatness. Financial rather than dynastic power would become the dominant source for English pride. As Feavearyear notes, much of the commercial realm in England had faith in the bank and its bills while the king's money, and even credit, remained suspect. *Pound Sterling*, 127.

19. Elizabeth II was the first monarch depicted on paper notes. Jack Weatherford, *The History of Money* (New York: Three Rivers, 1997), 166.
20. Interestingly, an argument was made that if silver was to disappear from England, it would be better if it were in coin form, since, as Li puts it, "if the country's coins could circulate in a foreign land, it would also enhance the prestige of the country abroad." *Great Recoinage*, 145. This argument reflects the continued importance of coin's visual and propagandistic properties.
21. See Feavearyear, *Pound Sterling*, 154–58 and John F. Chown, *A History of Money: From AD 800* (London: Routledge, 1994), 66.
22. Li, *Great Recoinage*, 179.
23. Weatherford, *History of Money*, 159.
24. Feavearyear, *Pound Sterling*, 166. Feavearyear argues that the intention of an Act of 1708 was "to give the Bank of England a monopoly of joint-stock banking." Ibid., 168.
25. Karl Marx, *Capital, Volume I*, trans. Ben Foakes (London: Penguin, 1990), 920. However, Weatherford points out that "the gold standard acted as a huge restraint on governments so long as the country could not print paper money greater than the supply of gold backing it." *History of Money*, 160.
26. Weatherford, *History of Money*, 156. See ibid., 159. Ironically, national and international faith in the bank reached its zenith even as the power of the bank had begun to diminish. See ibid., 164–66 and Chown, *History of Money*, 266–70.

WORKS CITED

Acts of the Privy Council of England. 32 vols. Edited by J. R. Dasent. London: Her Majesty's Stationery Office, 1890–1907.
Agnew, Jean Christophe. *Worlds Apart: The Market and the Theater in Anglo-American Thought, 1550–1750.* Cambridge: Cambridge UP, 1986.
Alighieri, Dante. *The Divine Comedy of Dante Alighieri: Paradiso.* Translated by John D. Sinclair. New York: Oxford UP, 1961.
Althusser, Louis. "Ideology and Ideological State Apparatuses (Notes towards an Investigation)." In *Lenin and Philosophy and Other Essays*, 127–86. Translated by Ben Brewster. New York: Monthly Review, 1971.
Anderson, Perry. *Lineages of the Absolutist State.* London: Verso, 1979.
Andrewe, Thomas. *The Massacre of Money.* London, 1602.
Appleby, Joyce Oldham. *Economic Thought and Ideology in Seventeenth-Century England.* Princeton: Princeton UP, 1978.
Aquinas, Thomas. *Aquinas Ethicus: or, The Moral Teaching of St. Thomas.* Translated by Joseph Rickaby. 2 vols. London: Burns and Oates, 1896.
——— . *On Politics and Ethics.* Translated by Paul E. Sigmund. New York: W. W. Norton, 1988.
Aristotle. *Generation of Animals.* Translated by A. L. Peck. Cambridge: Harvard UP, 1953.
——— . *The Nicomachean Ethics.* Translated by David Ross. Oxford: Oxford UP, 1980.
——— . *The Politics and Constitution of Athens.* Edited by Stephen Everson. Cambridge: Cambridge UP, 1996.
Barnes, Barnabe. *Foure bookes of offices enabling privat persons for the speciall service of all good princes and policies.* London, 1606.
Barrett, Ward. "World Bullion Flows, 1450–1800." In *The Rise of Merchant Empires*, edited by James D. Tracy. Cambridge: Cambridge UP, 1990.
Baxter, Richard. *The Certainty of the World of Spirits.* 1691. London, 1834.
Beckett, William. *A Free and Impartial Enquiry into the Antiquity and Efficacy of Touching for the Cure of the King's Evil.* London, 1722.
Benjamin, Walter. "The Work of Art in the Age of Mechanical Reproduction." In *Illuminations*, 217–51. Translated by Harry Zohn. New York: Harcourt, 1968.
Bennett, Josephine Walter. *Measure for Measure as Royal Entertainment.* New York: Columbia UP, 1966.
Berger, Harry. "The Early Scenes of *Macbeth*: Preface to a New Interpretation." *ELH* 47 (1980): 1–31.

Bevington, David. "Theatre as Holiday." In *The Theatrical City: Culture, Theatre, and Politics in London, 1576–1649*, edited by David L. Smith, Richard Strier and David Bevington, 101–16. Cambridge: Cambridge UP, 1995.

Bilson, Thomas. *The True Difference between Christian Subjection and Unchristian Rebellion*. Oxford, 1585.

Black, Jeremy. *Kings, Nobles & Commoners: States & Societies in Early Modern Europe, a Revisionist History*. London: I. B. Tauris, 2004.

Bloch, Marc. *Feudal Society*. Translated by L. A. Manyon. Chicago: U of Chicago P, 1961.

———. *The Royal Touch*. Translated by J. E. Anderson. New York: Dorset, 1989.

Bodin, Jean. *The Six Bookes of a Commonweale*. Translated by Richard Knolles. Edited by Kenneth Douglas McRae. Cambridge: Harvard UP, 1962.

Boorde, Andrew. *The fyrst boke of the Introduction of knowledge*. London, 1555.

Bracton, Henry de. *On the Laws and Customs of England*. 2 vols. Translated by Samuel E. Thorne. Cambridge: Harvard UP, 1968.

Braddick, Michael. *State Formation in Early Modern England c. 1550–1700*. Cambridge: Cambridge UP, 2000.

Brathwait, Richard. *The English Gentleman: Containing Sundry Excellent Rules, or Exquisite Observations*. London, 1630.

Bredbeck, Gregory W. *Sodomy and Interpretation*. Ithaca: Cornell UP, 1991.

Briscoe, John. *Historical and Political Essays or Discourses on Several Subjects*. London, 1698.

Brooke, George C. *English Coins*. London: Methuen, 1950.

Brooks, Cleanth. *The Well Wrought Urn: Studies in the Structure of Poetry*. New York: Harcourt, 1947.

Browne, John. *Adenochoiradelogia*. London, 1684.

Bruster, Douglas. *Shakespeare and the Question of Culture*. New York: Palgrave Macmillan, 2003.

Buchanan, George. *A History of Scotland*. Translated by James Aikman. 4 vols. Glasgow, 1827.

Bullough, Geoffrey. *Narrative and Dramatic Sources of Shakespeare*. London: Routledge, 1957–75.

Burgess, Glenn. *The Politics of the Ancient Constitution: An Introduction to English Political Thought, 1603–1642*. University Park: The Pennsylvania State UP, 1993.

Burns, Arthur R. *Money and Monetary Policy in Early Times*. London: Keegan Paul, 1927.

Caffentzis, Constantine George. *Clipped Coins, Abused Words, and Civil Government: John Locke's Philosophy of Money*. Brooklyn, NY: Autonomedia, 1989.

Calendar of Assize Records: Kent Indictments, Elizabeth I. Edited by J. S. Cockburn. London: HM Stationery Office, 1979.
Calendar of Assize Records: Surrey Indictments, Elizabeth I. Edited by J. S. Cockburn. London: HM Stationery Office, 1980
Calendar of State Papers, Domestic Series, of the Reigns of Edward VI, Mary, Elizabeth (and James I) 1547–1625. Edited by Robert Lemon. Nendeln, Liechtenstein: Kraus, 1967.
Calendar of State Papers, Foreign Series, of the Reign of Mary, 1553–1558. Edited by William B. Turnbull. London, 1861.
Calendar of State Papers—Venetian. 37 vols. London, 1864–.
Calendar of the Manuscripts of the Most Hon. The Marquess of Salisbury. 24 vols. Edited by Richard Arthur Roberts and Giuseppe Montague Spencer. London: HM Stationery Office, 1883–1976.
Calendar of the Patent Rolls, Elizabeth I. 8 vols. London: HM Stationery Office, 1939–86.
Calendar of the Patent Rolls, Philip and Mary. 4 vols. London: HM Stationery Office, 1936–9.
Camden, William. *Remains Concerning Britain.* Edited by R. D. Dunn. Toronto: U of Toronto P, 1984.
Canning, Joseph. *A History of Medieval Political Thought, 300–1450.* London: Routledge, 1996.
Carey, John. "Donne and Coins." In *English Renaissance Studies Presented to Dame Helen Gardner in Honour of Her Seventieth Birthday*, edited by John Carey and Helen Peters. Oxford: Clarendon, 1980.
The Ceremonies for the Healing of Them That Be Diseased with the Kings Evil as They Were Practiced in the Time of King Henry VII. London, 1686.
Challis, C. E. *Currency and the Economy in Tudor and Early Stuart England.* London: Historical Association, 1989.
———. *A New History of the Royal Mint.* Cambridge: Cambridge UP, 1992.
———. *The Tudor Coinage.* New York: Manchester UP, 1978.
Chapman, George, Ben Jonson and John Marston. *Eastward Ho!* In *The Roaring Girl and Other City Comedies*, edited by James Knowles. Oxford: Oxford UP, 2001.
Chown, John F. *A History of Money: From AD 800.* London: Routledge, 1994.
Cicero, Marcus Tullius. *Philippics.* Translated by Walter C. A. Ker. Cambridge, MA: Harvard UP, 1926.
Cipolla, Carlo M. "Currency Depreciation in Medieval Europe." *Economic History Review*, 2nd series 15.3 (1963): 413–22.
———. *Money, Prices, and Civilization in the Mediterranean World: Fifth to Seventeenth Century.* New York: Gordian, 1967.
Clanchy, Michael T. "Does Writing Construct the State?" *Journal of Historical Sociology* 15 (2002): 68–70.
———. *England and Its Rulers 1066–1272.* Totowa, NJ: Barnes and Noble, 1983.

Clark, Arthur Melville. *Murder Under Trust or The Topical* Macbeth. Edinburgh: Scottish Academic, 1981.

Clark, Stuart. *Thinking with Demons: The Idea of Witchcraft in Early Modern Europe*. Oxford: Clarendon, 1997.

Clowes, William. *A right frutefull and approoued treatise, for the artificial cure of that malady called in Latin Struma*. London, 1602.

Coghill, Nevill. "Comic Form in Measure for Measure." *Shakespeare Survey* 8 (1955): 14–27.

Cohen, Benjamin. *The Geography of Money*. Ithaca: Cornell UP, 1998.

Coke, Edward. *Le quart part des reportes del Edward Coke Chiualier*. London, 1604.

Coleman, Christopher. "Introduction: Professor Elton's 'Revolution.'" In *Revolution Reassessed: Revisions in the History of Tudor Government and Administration*, edited by Christopher Coleman and David Starkey. Oxford: Clarendon, 1986.

Columbus, Christopher. *The Diario of Christopher Columbus's First Voyage to America, 1492–1493*. Translated by Oliver Dunn and James E. Kelley, Jr. Norman, OK: U of Oklahoma P, 1989.

Corbett, Julian Stafford. *The Successors of Drake*. London: Longmans', 1900.

Corrigan, Philip and Derek Sayer. *The Great Arch: English State Formation as Cultural Revolution*. Oxford: Basil Blackwell, 1985.

Cotton, Robert. *A Speech Made by Sir Rob. Cotton...his Opinion touching the Alteration of Coin*. 1651. In *Select Tracts and Documents Illustrative of English Monetary History 1626–1730*, edited by William. A. Shaw. London, 1896.

Craig, John. *The Mint*. Cambridge: Cambridge UP, 1953.

Crakanthorpe, Richard. *A Sermon at the Solemnizing of the Happy Inauguration of...King James*. London, 1609.

Crane, Mary Thomas. "Male Pregnancy and Cognitive Permeability in *Measure for Measure*." *Shakespeare Quarterly* 49 (1998): 269–92.

Crawfurd, Raymond. *The King's Evil*. Oxford: Clarendon, 1911.

Crompton, Richard. *A short declaration of the ende of traitors, and false conspirators against the state, and of the duety of subjectes to their soveraigne governour*. London, 1587.

Davies, Glyn. *A History of Money: From Ancient Times to the Present Day*. Cardiff: U of Wales P, 2002.

De Certeau, Michel. *The Practice of Everyday Life*. Translated by Steven Rendall. Berkeley: U of California P, 1984.

De Grazia, Margreta. "Imprints: Shakespeare, Gutenberg and Descartes." *Alternative Shakespeares Vol. 2*. Edited by Terence Hawkes. London: Routledge, 1996.

Dekker, Thomas. *Northward Ho. The Dramatic Works*. Vol. 2. Edited by Fredson Bowers. Cambridge: Cambridge UP, 1955.

———. *The Shoemaker's Holiday*. Edited by Anthony Parr. London: A & C Black, 1990.

De La Perriere, Guillaume. *Mirrour of policy*. London, 1598.

Deng, Stephen. "Global Œconomy: Ben Jonson's *The Staple of News* and the Ethics of Mercantilism." In *Global Traffic: Discourses and Practices of Trade in English Literature and Culture, 1550–1700*, edited by Barbara Sebek and Stephen Deng. New York: Palgrave Macmillan, 2008.

Derrett, J. Duncan M. "The Utopians' Stoic Chamber-Pots." *Moreana* 19.73 (1982): 75–6.

Dewar, Mary. Introduction to *A Discourse of the Common Weal of This Realm of England*, edited by Mary Dewar. Charlottesville: UP of Virginia, 1969.

A Discourse of the Common Weal of This Realm of England. Edited by Mary Dewar. Charlottesville: UP of Virginia, 1969.

Donne, John. *Biathanatos: a declaration of that paradoxe, or thesis, that self-homicide is not so naturally sin, that I may never be otherwise*. London, 1648.

———. *John Donne's Poetry*. 2nd ed. Edited by Arthur L. Clements. New York: W. W. Norton, 1992.

———. *The Sermons of John Donne*. Edited by Evelyn M. Simpson and George R. Potter. Berkeley: U of California P, 1953–62.

Doyle, Charles Clay. "The Utopians' Therapeutic Chamber-Pots." *Moreana* 19.73 (1982): 75.

Dubrow, Heather. *Echoes of Desire: English Petrarchism and Its Counterdiscourses*. Ithaca: Cornell UP, 1995.

Eagleton, Catherine and Jonathan Williams. *Money: A History*. Richmond Hill, ON: Firefly, 2007.

The Earle of Gowries Conspiracie against the Kings Majesty of Scotland. London, 1600.

Eccleshall, Robert. *Order and Reason in Politics: Theories of Absolute and Limited Monarchy in Early Modern England*. Oxford: Oxford UP, 1978.

Ederer, Rupert J. *The Evolution of Money*. Washington, DC: Public Affairs, 1964.

Egan, Gabriel. "Gilding Loam and Painting Lilies: Shakespeare's Scruple of Gold." *Connotations* 11.2–3 (2001/2002): 165–79.

Eltis, Walter. "John Locke, the Quantity Theory of Money and the Establishment of a Sound Currency." In *The Quantity Theory of Money: From Locke to Keynes and Friedman*. Hants, England: Edward Elgar, 1995.

Elton, G. R. *Studies in Tudor and Stuart Politics and Government*. Vol. 3. Cambridge: Cambridge UP, 1983.

———, ed. *The Tudor Constitution: Documents and Commentary*. 2nd ed. Cambridge: Cambridge UP, 1960.

———. *The Tudor Revolution in Government: Administrative Changes in the Reign of Henry VIII*. Cambridge: Cambridge UP, 1960.

Elyot, Thomas. *The Boke named the Governour*. London: J. M. Dent, 1907.

Engels, Frederick. *The Origin of the Family Private Property and the State*. Translated by Ernest Untermann. Chicago: Charles H. Kerr, 1902.

Ertman, Thomas. *Birth of the Leviathan: Building States and Regimes in Medieval and Early Modern Europe*. Cambridge: Cambridge UP, 1997.
Evelyn, John. *Numismata: a Discourse of Medals Antient and Modern*. London, 1697.
Farquhar, Helen. "Royal Charities, Part I—Angels as Healing-pieces for the King's Evil." *British Numismatic Journal* 12 (1916): 39–135.
———. "Portraiture of Our Tudor Monarchs on Their Coins and Medals." *British Numismatic Journal* 4 (1908): 79–143.
Feavearyear, Albert. *The Pound Sterling: A History of English Money*. 2nd ed. Oxford: Clarendon, 1963.
Finch, Henry. *Law, or, a discourse thereof in foure bookes*. London, 1627.
Fischer, Sandra K. *Econolingua: A Glossary of Coins and Economic Language in Renaissance Drama*. Newark: U of Delaware P, 1985.
Fisher, Will. *Materializing Gender in Early Modern English Literature and Culture*. Cambridge: Cambridge UP, 2006.
———. "Queer Money." *ELH* 66 (1999): 1–23.
Fleck, Andrew. "Marking Difference and National Identity in Dekker's *The Shoemaker's Holiday*." *Studies in English Literature, 1500–1900* 46.2 (Spring 2006): 349–70.
Forman, Valerie. "Marked Angels: Counterfeits, Commodities, and *The Roaring Girl*." *Renaissance Quarterly* 54 (2001): 1531–60.
Fortescue, John. *A learned commendation of the politique lawes of Englande*. London, 1567.
Foucault, Michel. *The Order of Things: An Archaeology of the Human Sciences*. New York: Vintage, 1994.
Fox, Alistair. *Thomas More: History and Providence*. New Haven: Yale UP, 1982.
Fulbecke, William. *A parallele or conference of the civill law, the canon law, and the common law of this realme of England*. London, 1601.
Gardiner, Stephen. *De Vera Obedientia*. London, 1553.
Gaskill, Malcolm. *Crime and Mentalities in Early Modern England*. Cambridge: Cambridge UP, 2000.
Gasper, Julia. *The Dragon and the Dove: The Plays of Thomas Dekker*. Oxford: Clarendon, 1990.
Geary, Patrick. "Sacred Commodities: The Circulation of Medieval Relics." In *The Social Life of Things*, edited by Arjun Appadurai, 169–91. Cambridge: Cambridge UP, 1986.
Ginzburg, Carlo. *No Island Is an Island: Four Glances at English Literature in a World Perspective*. Translated by John Tedeschi. New York: Columbia UP, 2000.
Glassner, David. "An Evolutionary Theory of the State Monopoly over Money." In *Money and the Nation-State*, edited by Kevin Dowd and Richard H. Timberlake, Jr. New Brunswick, NJ: Transaction, 1998.
Goldberg, Jonathan. *James I and the Politics of Literature*. Stanford: Stanford UP, 1983.

———. "Speculations: *Macbeth* and Source." In *Shakespeare Reproduced*, edited by Jean E. Howard and Marion F. O'Connor. New York: Methuen, 1987.
Gould, J. D. *The Great Debasement*. Oxford: Clarendon, 1970.
Goux, Jean-Joseph. *Symbolic Economies: After Marx and Freud*. Translated by Jennifer Curtiss Gage. Ithaca: Cornell UP, 1990.
Grant, Michael. *Roman History from Coins: Some Uses of Imperial Coinage to the Historian*. Cambridge: Cambridge UP, 1958.
Greenblatt, Stephen J. *Learning to Curse: Essays in Early Modern Culture*. London: Routledge, 1990.
———. *Marvelous Possessions: The Wonder of the New World*. Chicago: U of Chicago P, 1991.
Grosclose, Elgin. *Money and Man: A Survey of Monetary Experience*. 4th ed. Norman: U of Oklahoma P, 1976.
Guillory, John. "A New Subject for Criticism." In *The Culture of Capital: Properties, Cities, and Knowledge in Early Modern England*, edited by Henry S. Turner. London: Routledge, 2002.
Guy, John. *Tudor England*. Oxford and New York: Oxford UP, 1988.
Hakluyt, Richard. *The Principal Navigations Voyages Traffiques & Discoveries of the English Nation*. Vol. 7. London: J. M. Dent, 1926.
Hall, Joseph. *The Works of the Right Reverend Father in God Joseph Hall*. Vol. 7. Edited by P. Wynter. Oxford, 1863.
Halpern, Richard. *The Poetics of Primitive Accumulation*. Ithaca: Cornell UP, 1991.
Harris, Jonathan Gil. "Shakespeare's Hair." *Shakespeare Quarterly* 52 (2001): 479–91.
———. *Sick Economies: Drama, Mercantilism and Disease in Shakespeare's England*. Philadelphia, PA: U of Pennsylvania P, 2004.
———. *Untimely Matter in the Time of Shakespeare*. Philadelphia: U of Pennsylvania P, 2008.
Hawkes, David. "Materialism and Reification in Renaissance Studies." *Journal of Early Modern Cultural Studies* 4.2 (2004): 114–29.
Hawkins, Michael. "History, Politics and *Macbeth*." In *Focus on Macbeth*, edited by John Russell Brown. London: Routledge, 1982.
Helgerson, Richard. *Forms of Nationhood: The Elizabethan Writing of England*. Chicago: U of Chicago P, 1992.
Herrick, Robert. "To The King, To cure the Evill." In *Hesperides*. London, 1648.
Heywood, John. *John Heywoodes Woorkes*. London, 1562.
Hindle, Steve. *The State and Social Change in Early Modern England, 1550–1640*. Houndmills, Basingstoke: Palgrave Macmillan, 2000.
The History of the Life, Reign, and Death of Edward II. London, 1680.
Hobbes, Thomas. *Leviathan*. Edited by C. B. Macpherson. London: Penguin, 1985.

Hoeniger, F. David. *Medicine and Shakespeare in the English Renaissance.* Newark: U of Delaware P, 1992.
Holinshed, Raphael. *Chronicles of England, Scotland and Ireland.* 6 vols. London, 1586.
An Homily against Disobedience and Wilful Rebellion. London, 1570.
Hutson, Lorna. *Thomas Nashe in Context.* New York: Oxford UP, 1989.
Ingram, Martin. "Reformation of Manners in Early Modern England." In *The Experience of Authority in Early Modern England,* edited by Paul Griffiths, Adam Fox and Steve Hindle. New York: St. Martin's, 1996.
James I. *Basilikon Doron.* London, 1603.
———. "By the King. This later age and times of the world wherein we are fallen, is so much given to verball profession, aswell of religion ..." London, 1610.
———. *Political Works of James I.* Edited by Charles H. McIlwain. Cambridge: Harvard UP, 1918.
Jessop, Bob. *State Power: A Strategic-Relational Approach.* Cambridge, UK: Polity, 2007.
Johnson, Charles. Introduction to *The De Moneta of Nicholas Oresme and English Mint Documents.* Translated by Charles Johnson. London: Thomas Nelson, 1956.
Jones, Ann Rosalind and Peter Stallybrass. *Renaissance Clothing and the Materials of Memory.* Cambridge: Cambridge UP, 2000.
Jones, Norman L. "William Cecil and the Making of Economic Policy in the 1560s and early 1570s." In *Political Thought and the Tudor Commonwealth: Deep Structure, Discourse and Disguise,* edited by Paul A. Fideler and T. F. Mayer. New York: Routledge, 1992.
Jonson, Ben. *The Alchemist.* In *Three Comedies,* edited by Michael Jamieson. London: Penguin, 1985.
Jordan, Constance. *Shakespeare's Monarchies: Ruler and Subject in the Romances.* Ithaca: Cornell UP, 1997.
Jorgensen, Paul A. *Our Naked Frailties: Sensational Art and Meaning in Macbeth.* Berkeley: U of California P, 1971.
Kantorowicz, Ernst H. *The King's Two Bodies: A Study in Mediaeval Political Theology.* 1957. Princeton: Princeton UP, 1997.
———. "Mysteries of State: An Absolutist Concept and Its Late Mediaeval Origins." In *Selected Studies.* Locust Valley, NY: J. J. Augustin, 1965.
Kaplan, M. Lindsay. *The Culture of Slander in Early Modern England.* Cambridge: Cambridge UP, 1997.
Kastan, David Scott. "Workshop and/as Playhouse: *The Shoemaker's Holiday* (1599)." In *Staging the Renaissance: Reinterpretations of Elizabethan and Jacobean Drama,* edited by David Scott Kastan and Peter Stallybrass, 151–63. New York: Routledge, 1991.
Kaye, Joel. *Economy and Nature in the Fourteenth Century: Money, Market Exchange, and the Emergence of Scientific Thought.* Cambridge: Cambridge UP, 1998.

Kelly, Patrick Hyde. "General Introduction: Locke on Money." *Locke on Money*. Vol. 1. Ed. Patrick Hyde Kelly. Oxford: Clarendon, 1991.

Kernan, Alvin. *Shakespeare, the King's Playwright: Theater in the Stuart Court, 1603–1613*. New Haven: Yale UP, 1995.

Kirsch, Arthur C. "The Integrity of *Measure for Measure*." *Shakespeare Survey* 28 (1975): 89–105.

Kopytoff, Igor. "The Cultural Biography of Things: Commoditization as Process." In *The Social Life of Things: Commodities in Cultural Perspective*, edited by Arjun Appadurai, 64–91. Cambridge: Cambridge UP, 1986.

Korda, Natasha. *Shakespeare's Domestic Economies: Gender and Property in Early Modern England*. Philadelphia: U of Pennsylvania P, 2002.

Lampe, G. W. H. *The Seal of the Spirit: A Study in the Doctrine of Baptism and Confirmation in the New Testament and the Fathers*. London: Longman, 1951.

Layton, Henry. *Observations Concerning Money and Coin, and Especially Those of England*. London, 1697.

Leggatt, Alexander. "Substitution in *Measure for Measure*." *Shakespeare Quarterly* 39 (1988): 342–59.

Letter to Piero Soderini, Gonfaloniere, the Year 1504. Translated by George Tyler Northrup. Princeton: Princeton UP, 1916.

Letters and Papers, Foreign and Domestic, of the Reign of Henry VIII. Vol. 20. Part 2. London: Public Record Office, 1862–1910.

Lever, J. W. Introduction to *Measure for Measure* by William Shakespeare. Edited by J. W. Lever. London: Methuen, 1965.

Levin, Harry. *The Myth of the Golden Age in the Renaissance*. Bloomington, IN: Indiana UP, 1969.

Lewis, Cynthia. "'Dark Deeds Darkly Answered': Duke Vincentio and Judgment in *Measure for Measure*." *Shakespeare Quarterly* 34 (1983): 271–89.

Li, Ming-Hsun. *The Great Recoinage of 1696 to 1699*. London: Weidenfeld and Nicolson, 1963.

Locke, John. *The Correspondence of John Locke*. Vol. 5. Edited by E. S. De Beer. Oxford: Clarendon, 1979.

———. *Further Considerations Concerning Raising the Value of Money*. In *Locke on Money*. Vol. 2. Edited by Patrick Hyde Kelly. Oxford: Clarendon, 1991.

———. *Some Considerations of the Consequences of the Lowering of Interest and Raising the Value of Money*. In *Locke on Money*. Vol. 1. Edited by Patrick Hyde Kelly. Oxford: Clarendon, 1991.

Logan, George M. "The Argument of *Utopia*." In *Interpreting Thomas More's Utopia*, edited by John C. Olin. New York: Fordham UP, 1989.

Lopez, Robert S. "The Dollar of the Middle Ages." *Journal of Economic History* 11.3 (Summer, 1951): 209–34.

Machiavelli, Niccolò. *The Discourses*. Edited by Bernard Crick. London: Penguin, 1970.

Machyn, Henry. *The Diary of Henry Machyn*. Edited by John Gough Nichols. London, 1848.
Mackworth, Humphrey. *England's Glory, or, the Great Improvement of Trade in General, by a Royal Bank, or Office of Credit, to be Erected in London*. London, 1694.
Maclure, Millar, ed. *Marlowe: The Critical Heritage, 1588–1896*. London: Routledge, 1979.
Maguire, Henry. "Money and Magic in the Early Middle Ages." *Speculum* 72 (1997): 1037–54.
Malynes, Gerard. *The Center of the Circle of Commerce*. London, 1623.
Mann, Michael. *The Sources of Social Power, Volume I: A History of Power from the Beginning to A.D. 1760*. Cambridge: Cambridge UP, 1986.
Marlowe, Christopher. *The Complete Plays*. Edited by Frank Romany and Robert Lindsey. London: Penguin, 2003.
Marsilius of Padua. *The Defender of Peace*. Translated by Alan Gewirth. New York: Harper & Row, 1967.
Martial. *Epigrams*. Book 1. Translated by Walter C. A. Ker. London: William Heinemann, 1919.
Martin-Leake, Stephen. *An Historical Account of English Money*. London, 1745.
Martyr, Peter. *De Orbe Novo, or the Historie of the West Indies*. Translated by R. Eden. London, 1612.
———. *De Orbe Novo, the Eight Decades of Peter Martyr D'Anghiera*. 2 vols. Translated by Francis Augustus Macnutt. New York: G. P. Putnam's, 1912.
Marx, Karl. *Capital, Volume I*. Translated by Ben Foakes. London: Penguin, 1990.
———. *A Contribution to the Critique of Political Economy*. Edited by Maurice Dobb. New York: International Publishers, 1970.
———. *The German Ideology. Karl Marx: Selected Writings*. Edited by David McLellan. Oxford: Oxford UP, 1977.
Maxwell, James. *The laudable life and deplorable death, of our late peerlesse Prince Henry. briefly represented*. London, 1612.
Mayhew, Nicholas. *Sterling: The History of a Currency*. New York: Wiley, 1999.
McCann, Franklin T. *English Discovery of America to 1585*. New York: Octagon, 1951, reprint 1969.
McLuskie, Kathleen E. *Dekker and Heywood: Professional Dramatists*. New York: St. Martin's, 1994.
Monod, Paul Kléber. *The Power of Kings: Monarchy and Religion in Europe, 1589–1715*. New Haven: Yale UP, 1999.
More, Thomas. *The Complete Works of St. Thomas More*. Vol. 4. Edited by Edward Surtz and J. H. Hexter. New Haven: Yale UP, 1965.
———. *The works of Sir Thomas More Knight, sometime Lorde Chauncellor of England, written by him in the English tonge*. London, 1557.
Morgan, E. Victor. *A History of Money*. Baltimore: Penguin, 1965.

Mortenson, Peter. "The Economics of Joy in *The Shoemaker's Holiday.*" *Studies in English Literature, 1500–1900* 16.2 (Spring 1976): 241–52.
Muldrew, Craig. *The Economy of Obligation: The Culture of Credit and Social Relations in Early Modern England.* New York: St. Martin's, 1998.
Mullaney, Steven. *The Place of the Stage.* Ann Arbor: U of Michigan P, 1995.
Murray, W. A. "Why Was Duncan's Blood Golden?" *Shakespeare Survey* 19 (1966): 34–44.
Nashe, Thomas. *The Unfortunate Traveler.* In *The Unfortunate Traveler and Other Works.* London: Penguin, 1972.
Neill, Michael. *Putting History to the Question.* New York: Columbia UP, 2000.
Nicholl, Charles. *The Reckoning.* Chicago: U of Chicago P, 1992.
Nugent, Theresa Lanpher. "Usury and Counterfeiting in Wilson's *The Three Ladies of London* and *The Three Lords and Three Ladies of London*, and in Shakespeare's *Measure for Measure.*" In *Money and the Age of Shakespeare*, edited by Linda Woodbridge, 201–17. New York: Palgrave Macmillan, 2003.
Oresme, Nicholas. *The De Moneta of Nicholas Oresme and English Mint Documents.* Translated by Charles Johnson. London: Thomas Nelson, 1956.
Osteen, Mark and Martha Woodmansee. "Taking Account of the New Economic Criticism: an Historical Introduction." In *The New Economic Criticism: Studies at the Intersection of Literature and Economics*, edited by Martha Woodmansee and Mark Osteen. London: Routledge, 1999.
Ovid. *Metamorphoses.* Books 1–8. Translated by Frank Justus Miller. Revised by G. P. Goold. Cambridge: Harvard UP, 1992.
———. *Ovid's Metamorphoses.* Translated by Arthur Golding. Edited by John Frederick Nims. Philadelphia: Paul Dry, 2000.
Parry, Jonathan and Maurice Bloch. Introduction to *Money and the Morality of Exchange*, edited by Jonathan Parry and Maurice Bloch. Cambridge: Cambridge UP, 1989.
Paul, Henry. *The Royal Play of Macbeth.* New York: Macmillan, 1950.
Peacham, Henry. *Minerva Britanna, or a Garden of Historical Devices.* London, 1612.
Pemberton, William. *The charge of God and the king, to judges and magistrates, for execution of justice.* London, 1619.
Pepys, Samuel. *The Diary of Samuel Pepys.* 11 vols. Edited by Robert Latham and William Matthews. Berkeley: U of California P, 1970–83.
Pietz, William. "The Problem of the Fetish I." *Res* 9 (1985): 5–17.
Plutarch. *The Lives of the Noble Grecians and Romans.* Translated by John Dryden. Revised by Arthur Hugh Clough. New York: Random House, n.d.
Pocock, J. G. A. *The Ancient Constitution and the Feudal Law: A Study of English Historical Thought in the Seventeenth Century.* Cambridge: Cambridge UP, 1987.

Poggi, Gianfranco. *The State: Its Nature, Development and Prospects.* Stanford: Stanford UP, 1990.
Pohl, Frederick. *Amerigo Vespucci: Pilot Major.* New York: Octagon, 1966.
Pond, Shepard. "The Ducat: Once an Important Coin in European Business." *Bulletin of the Business Historical Society* 14.2 (April, 1940): 17–19.
———. "The Spanish Dollar: The World's Most Famous Silver Coin." *Bulletin of the Business Historical Society* 15.1 (Feb., 1941): 12–16.
Potter, Clinton W., Jr. "Images of Majesty: Money as Propaganda in Elizabethan England." In *Money: Lure, Lore, and Literature*, edited by John-Louis DiGaetani, 69–76. Westport, CT: Greenwood, 1994.
Poulantzas, Nicos. *State, Power, Socialism.* Translated by Patrick Camiller. London: Verso, 2000.
Purchas, Samuel. *Purchas his pilgrimage. Or Relations of the world and the religions observed in all ages and places discovered, from the Creation unto this present.* London, 1613.
———. *Purchas his pilgrimage. Or Relations of the world and the religions observed in all ages and places discovered, from the Creation unto this present.* London, 1614.
Rawlinson, John. *Vivat Rex.* Oxford, 1619.
Rebhorn, Wayne A. "Thomas More's Enclosed Garden: *Utopia* and Renaissance Humanism." *English Literary Renaissance* 6 (1976): 140–55.
The Royal Mint: An Outline History. London: HM Stationery Office, 1967.
Ruding, Rogers. *Annals of the Coinage of Great Britain and Its Dependencies.* 3rd. ed. Vol. 1. London, 1840.
Ryan, Kiernan. "*Measure for Measure*: Marxism before Marx." In *Marxist Shakespeares*, edited by Jean E. Howard and Scott Cutler Shershow. London: Routledge, 2001.
Rye, William Brenchley. *England as Seen by Foreigners.* London, 1865.
Saint German, Christopher. *An answere to a letter.* London, 1535?.
———. *Doctor and Student.* London, 1751.
Sargent, Thomas J. and François R. Velde. *The Big Problem of Small Change.* Princeton: Princeton UP, 2002.
Schanzer, Ernest. *The Problem Plays of Shakespeare.* London: Routledge, 1963.
Schleiner, Winfried. *The Imagery of John Donne's Sermons.* Providence: Brown UP, 1970.
Scot, Reginald. *The Discovery of Witchcraft.* London, 1665.
Seaver, Paul S. *Wallington's World.* Stanford: Stanford UP, 1985.
———. "Thomas Dekker's *The Shoemaker's Holiday*: The Artisanal World." In *The Theatrical City: Culture, Theatre and Politics in London, 1576–1649*, edited by David L. Smith, Richard Strier and David Bevington, 87–100. Cambridge: Cambridge UP, 1995.
Selden, John. "Notes upon Sir John Fortescue." In *De laudibus legum Angliae* by John Fortescue. London, 1616.

Shakespeare, William. *Bell's Edition of Shakespeare's Plays as They Are Now Performed at the Theatres Royal in London.* London, 1773–4.

———. *Measure for Measure.* Edited by J. W. Lever. London: Methuen, 1965

———. Measure for Measure: *An Old-Spelling and Old-Meaning Edition.* Edited by Ernst Leisi. New York: Hafner, 1964.

———. *The Riverside Shakespeare.* 2nd ed. Edited by G. Blakemore Evans and J. J. M. Tobin. Boston: Houghton Mifflin, 1997.

Sharpe, J. A. *Crime in Early Modern England 1550–1750.* London: Longman, 1984.

———. *Early Modern England: A Social History 1550–1760.* London: Hodder Arnold, 1987.

Shell, Marc. *Art and Money.* Chicago: U of Chicago P, 1995.

———. *The Economy of Literature.* Baltimore: Johns Hopkins UP, 1978.

———. *The End of Kinship: Measure for Measure, Incest, and the Idea of Universal Siblinghood.* Stanford: Stanford UP, 1988.

———. *Money, Language, and Thought: Literary and Philosophical Economies from the Medieval to the Modern Era.* Berkeley: U of California P, 1982.

Shephard, Robert. "Utopia, Utopia's Neighbors, *Utopia* and Europe." *Sixteenth Century Journal* 26 (1995): 843–56.

Shickman, Allan. "Shakespeare's 'Figure of an Angel': An Iconographic Study." *Colby Library Quarterly* 17 (1981): 6–25.

Sinfield, Alan. "*Macbeth*: History, Ideology and Intellectuals." In *Materialist Shakespeare*, edited by Ivo Kamps, 93–107. London: Verso, 1995.

Skinner, Quentin. *Foundations of Modern Political Thought.* 2 vols. Cambridge: Cambridge UP, 1978.

———. "The State." In Political Innovation and Conceptual Change, edited by Terence Ball, James Farr, and Russell L. Hanson, 90–131. Cambridge: Cambridge UP, 1989.

Slavin, Arthur J. "'Tis far off, And rather like a dream': Common Weal, Common Woe and Commonwealth." *Explorations in Renaissance Culture* 14 (1988): 1–27.

Smith, Bruce R. *Homosexual Desire in Shakespeare's England.* Chicago: U of Chicago P, 1991.

Smith, Thomas. *De Republica Anglorum.* London, 1583.

Sohn-Rethel, Alfred. *Intellectual and Manual Labour.* London: Macmillan, 1978.

Spenser, Edmund. *The Faerie Queene.* Edited by Thomas P. Roche, Jr. London: Penguin, 1978.

Spruyt, Hendrik. *The Sovereign State and Its Competitors.* Princeton: Princeton UP, 1994.

Spufford, Peter. *Money and Its Use in Medieval Europe.* Cambridge: Cambridge UP, 1988.

Spurgeon, Caroline F. E. *Shakespeare's Imagery and What It Tells Us.* Cambridge: Cambridge UP, 1935.

Stallybrass, Peter. "*Macbeth* and Witchcraft." In *Focus on* Macbeth, edited by John Russell Brown, 189–209. London: Routledge, 1982.

Starkey, David. "Representation Through Intimacy: A Study in the Symbolism of Monarchy and Court Office in Early Modern England." In *Symbols and Sentiments: Cross-Cultural Studies in Symbolism*, edited by Ioan Lewis, 187–224. London: Academic, 1977.

———. "Which Age of Reform?" In *Revolution Reassessed: Revisions in the History of Tudor Government and Administration*, edited by Christopher Coleman and David Starkey. Oxford: Clarendon, 1986.

Statutes of the Realm. 4 vols. London, 1810–28. Reprint, 1963.

Strayer, Joseph R. *On the Medieval Origins of the Modern State.* Princeton: Princeton UP, 1970.

Straznicky, Marta. "The End(s) of Discord in *The Shoemaker's Holiday*." *Studies in English Literature, 1500–1900* 36.2 (Spring 1996): 357–72.

Strong, Roy. *Portraits of Queen Elizabeth I.* Oxford: Clarendon, 1963.

Stubbe, Henry. *The Miraculous Conformist.* Oxford, 1666.

Stubbes, Phillip. *Anatomy of Abuses.* London, 1583.

Supple, B. E. "Currency and Commerce in the Early Seventeenth Century." *The Economic History Review* 10, series 2 (1957–8): 239–55.

Surtz, Edward. *The Praise of Wisdom: A Commentary on the Religious and Moral Problems and Backgrounds of St. Thomas More's* Utopia. Chicago: Loyola UP, 1957.

———. "Thomas More and Communism." *PMLA* 64.3 (1949): 549–64.

Taylor, J. "Copernicus on the Evils of Inflation and the Establishment of a Sound Currency." *Journal of the History of Ideas* 16.4 (Oct. 1955): 540–47.

Thirsk, Joan and J. P. Cooper, eds. *Seventeenth-Century Economic Documents.* Oxford: Clarendon, 1972.

Thomas, Keith. *Religion and the Decline of Magic.* New York: Charles Scribner's, 1971.

Tilly, Charles. *Coercion, Capital and European States, AD 990–1990.* Oxford: Basil Blackwell, 1990.

Trevor-Roper, H. R. "George Buchanan and the Ancient Constitution." *The English Historical Review* supplement 3 (1966): 1–53.

Tudor Economic Documents. 3 vols. Edited by R. H. Tawney and Eileen Power. London: Longmans, 1924.

Tudor Royal Proclamations. 3 vols. Edited by Paul L. Hughes and James F. Larkin. New Haven: Yale UP, 1964–69.

Tully, James. Introduction to *On the Duty of Man and Citizen* by Samuel Pufendorf. Edited by James Tully. Cambridge: Cambridge UP, 1991.

Ure, P. N. *The Origin of Tyranny.* New York: Russell & Russell, 1962.

Usury Arraigned and Condemned. London, 1625.

Valentine, Henry. *God Save the King.* London, 1639.

Valenze, Deborah. *The Social Life of Money in the English Past.* Cambridge: Cambridge UP, 2006.

Verstegan, Richard. *The Post For divers partes of the world.* London, 1576.

Voltaire. *A Philosophical Dictionary.* In *The Works of Voltaire.* Vol. 12. Translated by William F. Fleming. Paris: E. R. Dumont, 1901.

Watt, R. J. C. "Three Cruces in *Measure for Measure*." *Review of English Studies* 38 (1987): 227–33.
Weatherford, Jack. *The History of Money*. New York: Three Rivers, 1997.
Weber, Max. *Economy and Society: An Outline of Interpretive Sociology*. Edited by Guenther Roth and Claus Wittich. New York: Bedminster, 1968.
———. "Politics as a Vocation." *From Max Weber: Essays in Sociology*. Edited by H. H. Gerth and C. Wright Mills. New York: Oxford UP, 1946.
Webster, John. *The White Devil*. In *The Duchess of Malfi and Other Plays*. Edited by René Weis. Oxford: Oxford UP, 1996.
Weston, Corinne Comstock and Janelle Renfrow Greenberg. *Subjects and Sovereigns: The Grand Controversy over Legal Sovereignty in Stuart England*. Cambridge: Cambridge UP, 1981.
Willis, Deborah. "The Monarch and the Sacred: Shakespeare and the Ceremony for the Healing of the King's Evil." In *True Rites and Maimed Rites: Ritual and Anti-Ritual in Shakespeare and His Age*, edited by Linda Woodbridge and Edward Berry, 147–68. Urbana and Chicago: U of Illinois P, 1992.
Wills, Gary. *Witches and Jesuits: Shakespeare's Macbeth*. Oxford: Oxford UP, 1995.
Wilson, Arthur. *The History of Great Britain, Being the Life and Reign of King James the First*.... London, 1653.
Wilson, Katharina. "An Affront to Gold and Silver: Tertullian's *De Cultu Feminarum* and More's *Utopia*." *Moreana* 19 (1982): 69–74.
Woolf, Noël. "The Sovereign Remedy: Touch Pieces and the King's Evil." *British Numismatic Journal* 49 (1979): 99–115.
Zimmerman, Susan. "Duncan's Corpse." In *A Feminist Companion to Shakespeare*, edited by Dympna Callaghan. Chicester, West Sussex: Wiley-Blackwell, 2001.
Žižek, Slavoj. *The Sublime Object of Ideology*. London: Verso, 1997.

INDEX

absolutism, 18, 33–39, 44, 45, 49–50, 60, 68, 70, 88, 98, 101, 102, 118, 121–22, 123, 132–33
accounting, 151–53
Act of Appeals (1533), 31
adultery, 114–15
Aegidius Romanus, 35
alchemy, 67, 105–6, 146, 156
Alexander of Bruchsal, 56
Alexander the Great, 53
Althusser, Louis, 25
  see also interpellation
ancient constitution, 38
Anderson, Benedict, 181
Anderson, Perry, 49, 206 n60, 239 n66
Andrewe, Thomas, 214 n42
Appleby, Joyce, 240 n9, 240 n15
Aquinas, Thomas, 34, 37, 67, 68, 119, 212 n15
Archangel Michael, 139, 147–48
Aristotle, 18, 34, 35, 59, 60, 63, 64, 66–67, 69, 70, 111
  De Generatione Animalium, 104, 115
  Nicomachean Ethics, 65, 119
  Politics, 63, 65, 69, 70, 209 n102
  Rhetoric, 69
artificial and natural riches, 60, 62, 63
artificial reason, 38
assaying coins, 10, 15, 91, 105, 121, 123–24
Assize of Winchester, 55
Athelred II, 54

Athelstan, 54
Augustine, 34, 117
aurum potabile, 146

Baines, Richard, 108–9
Balboa, Vasco, 74
Bank of England, 189, 193–94
bank-notes, 9, 193
banking, reserve, 9, 194
Barnes, Barnabe, 122, 156
Barrett, Ward, 77–78
Bartolus of Sassoferrato, 48, 68
bastardy, 18, 43, 104, 113–17, 130, 132
Baxter, Richard, 231 n41
Beckett, William, 140
Benjamin, Walter, 6
Berger, Harry, 151, 153
Bevington, David, 176, 182, 237 n42, 239 n66
biblical scripture, 53, 63–64, 117, 139–40, 144, 148, 159–60
bills of credit, 13
Bilson, Thomas, 231 n51
bimetallic ratio, 67–68, 91, 100
Black, Jeremy, 27, 28
"blanch," 90, 105
blanks, 121, 127–28
Bloch, Marc, 30, 138, 142, 144–45, 228 n4, 228 n8
"bloody noses," 94, 121, 128
Bodin, Jean, 33, 34, 37–38, 39, 45, 126, 206 n60, 207 n78
body politic, 65, 123, 133, 155–56, 160, 161
Boorde, Andrew, 237–38 n50

Bracton, Henry of, 35–36, 38
Braddick, Michael, 25, 27, 28, 31–32, 201 n9, 201 n12, 201–2 n14, 202–3 n23
Bredbeck, Gregory, 103
Briscoe, John, 192
Brooke, George, 57
Browne, John, 141–42
Brutus, 52
Buchanan, George, 101
Bullough, Geoffrey, 137
Burgess, Glen, 70–71, 212 n14
Burns, Arthur, 52
Byzantine period, 147

Caesar, Julius, 52, 53
Caffentzis, Constantine George, 240 n6
Camden, William, 15–16, 94, 96, 119–20, 210 n118, 210 n123
Canning, Joseph, 39
Cappadocia, 51
Cary, Elizabeth, 127
Cassiodorus, 65, 68, 120
Catholicism, militant, 108–9, 169–70
Cecil, William, Lord Burleigh, 93, 94, 95, 96, 108, 109
Celtics, 53
Challis, C. E., 50, 56, 94, 170, 236 n29
Chapman, George, Ben Jonson and John Marston
Eastward Ho!, 105, 106
"character," 116, 120, 123, 124–25
charisma
of kingship, 5, 19, 45–46, 117, 136–37, 149–50
of office, 46, 149
routinized, 19, 46, 52–53, 55, 58, 137, 149–51, 159, 160, 188, 193
Charlemagne, 44, 54
Charles I, 99–101, 142
Charles IV, king of France, 61
Charles V, king of France, 61, 62

Cicero, 63, 154
Cipolla, Carlo, 163–65, 171, 174, 235 n7, 235 n9
city-league, 48
city-state, 48–49, 51–52
Clanchy, Michael, 32, 150
Clark, Arthur, 227 n1
Clark, Stuart, 46, 47, 118, 122, 149–50, 158, 205 n48, 224 n47, 230 n26
class tension, 19–20, 49–50, 162–63, 171–86
Claudius, 53
clipping of coins, 3, 10, 18, 20, 43, 88, 89, 106, 111, 130, 161, 167, 189, 191, 192
Clowes, William, 145
Coghill, Nevill, 225 n56
Cohen, Benjamin, 163, 164, 165
coin hoards
Crondall, 53
Sutton Hoo, 53
coinage
as amulets and healing agents, 5, 6, 7, 19, 45, 118, 133, 136, 141–51, 157, 188
as "blood of the social body," 46, 133, 136–37, 156–60, 161, 162, 168
charges, 56, 88
cracked, 128
depreciation/devaluation, 10, 81, 85, 88, 92–93, 95–96, 97–98, 192
enhancement, 17, 59, 81
foreign, 19–20, 161–86
French, 55, 61, 89
"full-bodied," 165, 170
gold vs. silver, 13, 20, 50, 51, 90, 100, 105, 170–75, 182–86
iconography, 2, 58, 65, 101–2, 109, 136, 139, 161, 188, 193
insignia, 51–52, 56–57
invention in Lydia, 2, 16, 51–52
Irish, 90
as measure of wealth, 14–15

Index

as memento, 7, 141, 142
monarchical prerogative, 16, 33, 39, 53–54, 57, 59–60, 87–88, 96, 97, 121
monopoly of production by state, 1, 2, 51–52, 57, 85, 150, 161
mottoes/legends, 2, 58, 65, 101, 113, 136, 139, 140, 144, 146, 148, 159–60
portraiture, 2, 4, 19, 52–53, 56–57, 58, 147, 161, 193
"prestige coins," 19–20, 162, 165, 171, 182–83
propaganda, 6, 52, 56–57, 101–2
Roman, 53, 60, 88, 98
Scottish, 101–2
small denomination, 12, 99–100, 110
Spanish, 162, 165–66, 169–70, 185–86
standards, 12, 16–17, 33, 39, 55, 64, 65, 87–88, 95, 99, 100, 101, 118, 191
standards as law, 65, 70, 71, 96–97, 189
as "sublime" or "ideal" material, 11–13, 122–23, 188, 195
as symbol, 13
as tokens, 1, 4, 5, 13, 97, 142
wear and tear, 10, 12, 13, 56, 88, 161
weights and weighing, 10, 11, 15, 30, 51, 52, 55, 63, 64, 88, 89–90, 96, 97–98, 100–1, 105, 106, 122–23, 126, 131–32, 165, 189, 191, 192
see also assaying coins; blanks; clipping of coins; "coining;" counterfeiting; debasement; dies (coinage); filing (coins); hoarding of coins; mint masters; mints; moneyers; recoinage; seignorage; shaving of coins; stamp (of coins); sweating (coins); touchpieces; units of account (pounds, shillings, pence); washing (coins)
"coining," 18, 43, 103–33, 167–68, 191
coins, English
angel, 5, 7, 93, 106, 120, 136, 139–51, 159, 174, 175, 183
crown, 93, 105, 128
groat, 106, 109, 166, 174
guinea, 193–94
half crown, 106, 112
half sovereign, 8, 105
noble, 121, 140, 146, 166
penny, 54, 55, 88, 139, 145, 164, 172
rose ryal, 150, 188
shilling/testoon, 56, 91–92, 94, 96, 107, 109, 111–12, 121, 128, 174, 175, 188
sixpence/half shilling, 107, 112, 174
sovereign, 56
three-farthing, 99
three-halfpenny, 99
twopence, 174
unite, 52, 100
coins, foreign
archer, 53
"carolus," 166
crown (Burgundy), 126, 166
crown (Flemish), 166
crown (French), 20, 109, 162–63, 166–67, 169, 170, 171–72, 183–84, 185
denarius, 54, 165
denier, 54, 170
dinar, 165
dollar (*peso*), 126, 162, 165–66, 174
double patard, 166
drachma, 165
ducat, 165
ecu au porcepic, 166, 177
excelente, 3, 5, 7
florin, 165, 166
guilder, 184–85

Index

coins, foreign—*Continued*
  harp, 90
  pistolet, 109, 169
  portague (*cruzado*), 105, 167, 174, 177, 183
  shilling (Dutch), 108
  solidus (*nomisma/bezant*), 165
  sword-dollars, 101
  talent, 68
  thaler, 162
Coke, Sir Edward, 38, 110, 155
Columbus, Christopher, 3, 6, 74
"commonwealth," 36
communism, 75
consecration of kings, 44, 46
consiliarism, 36
Constantine, 44
constitutionalism, 33–37, 41, 60, 70, 102
Copernicus, 15
corpus mysticum, 43–44
  corpus ecclesiae mysticum, 44
  corpus reipublicae mysticum, 44
Corrigan, Philip and Derek Sayer, 28, 30, 31, 33, 202 n15, 207 n69
Cotton, Sir Robert, 91, 94, 95, 96, 98, 99, 100, 101, 118–19, 124, 126
Council of Greatley, 54
counterfeiting, 3, 7–8, 12, 18, 20, 43, 56, 58, 63, 64, 65–66, 95, 102, 103, 104, 105–11, 112–17, 124, 125, 126–27, 128, 130, 131, 167–68, 189, 192
Crakanthorpe, Richard, 45
cramp rings, 146–47
Crane, Mary Thomas, 125
Crassus, 74, 82–83
Crawfurd, Raymond, 138, 159
credit, 9, 71, 79–80, 190, 192, 194
Crompton, Richard, 122
Cromwell, Thomas, 29, 31, 57
customs, 89

Davies, Glyn, 9, 50–51, 56, 90, 91, 98, 172, 209 n106
de Certeau, Michel, 9
de La Perriere, Guillaume, 122
debasement, 3, 10, 12, 16–18, 20, 39, 59–62, 64–66, 69, 71, 72, 85, 86, 87–102, 103, 104, 115, 125, 126–28, 130, 132, 161, 188
  Roman, 88, 98
  see also "great debasement"
Dekker, Thomas
  Northward Ho, 111
  The Shoemaker's Holiday, 19–20, 50, 162–63, 171–86, 188
dies (coinage), 54, 64
Discourse of the Common Weal of this Realm of England, 59, 84, 92–94, 95, 97
disease, 161–62
divine right of kings, 44–46
Donne, John, 117–18, 229 n16
  "Elegy XI. The Bracelet," 19, 166–67, 169–70, 185, 220 n5
Drake, Sir Francis, 198 n10
Dubrow, Heather, 197 n2, 236 n32
"dumps" (coinage), 51
Dutch Church Libel, 185–86

Eccleshall, Robert, 33, 34, 35–36, 37, 40, 44, 66–67, 207 n77, 212 n17
Eden, Richard, 75, 77
Ederer, Rupert, 165
Edgar, 54
Edward I, 39, 55–56, 139
Edward II, 127–28
Edward III, 17, 89, 105, 108, 140, 146, 148
Edward IV, 95, 139, 145, 166
Edward VI, 87, 93
Edward the Confessor, 5, 135–36, 137–39, 144, 157
electrum, 51

Elizabeth I, 10, 94–96, 99, 106–7, 113, 142–43, 146, 147, 159, 167, 170
Elton, G. R., 29–30, 31, 40, 56, 203 n24, 204 n37
Elyot, Sir Thomas, 34
Engels, Friedrich, 200–1 n2
Ephesus, 51
equator, 73–74
Ertman, Thomas, 40, 41, 48
Essex, Robert Devereux, 2nd Earl of, 146
Evelyn, John, 100, 126
exchequer, 30, 32, 50

factors (financial agents), 71, 84
Farquhar, Helen, 170, 231 n39
"Faux Monnayeur" [counterfeiter], 18, 61, 104, 126, 187
Feavearyear, Albert, 191, 193, 194, 240–41 n18, 241 n24
fetishes, 5–6, 7
filing (coins), 106
Finch, Henry, 118
Fischer, Sandra K., 2, 233 n66
Fisher, Will, 220 n1
Fleck, Andrew, 176, 178–79, 181, 237 n46
Forman, Valerie, 226 n72
fornication, 114–15
Fortescue, Sir John, 34, 36–37, 40, 145, 146
Foucault, Michel, 14–16
Fox, Alistair, 76–77, 85
Fulbecke, William, 106

Ganymede, 103
Gardiner, Stephen, 44
Gaskill, Malcolm, 103, 105, 109–10, 111
Gasper, Julia, 176, 182, 237 n47
Gentleman, Francis, 136
Glassner, David, 52, 217 n4
gold standard, 13–14, 163–64, 193–94

Goldberg, Jonathan, 121, 158, 226 n76
Golden Age, 17, 60, 71, 73, 74–77
goldsmiths, 9
Gould, J. D., 56
Goux, Jean-Joseph, 20–21
Gowrie plot, 148, 169
Grammont, Scipion de, 14–15
Grant, Michael, 52
"great debasement," 10, 14, 17–18, 51, 56, 57, 88, 90–94, 126, 170
greenbacks, 13
Greenblatt, Stephen, 198 n10
Gresham, Thomas
"Gresham's Law," 10
Guibert, Abbé de Nogent, 137–38
guilds, 175
Guillory, John, 21
Guy, John, 202–3 n23
Gyges, 52

Hall, Joseph, 148
Halpern, Richard, 6, 77, 78, 81
Hanseatic League, *see* city-league
Harris, Jonathan Gil, 162
Hawkins, Michael, 154
Heaberth of Kent, 54
Helgald, 137
Helgerson, Richard, 240–41 n18
Henry I, 55
Henry II, 30, 55, 138, 150
Henry IV, 89, 128
Henry V, 106
Henry VI, 145
Henry VII, 56–57, 94, 113, 136, 139–40, 145–46, 148–49
Henry VIII, 10, 17, 29, 31, 32, 41, 51, 56, 57, 76–77, 81, 85, 86, 87, 89–94, 96, 97, 99, 101, 121, 126, 128, 170
Herrick, Robert, 145
Herrup, C. B., 28
Heywood, John, 94, 125

Hindle, Steve, 26, 27–28, 32, 42, 45, 46, 201 n10, 202–3 n23, 205 n48, 208 n82, 212 n15
History of the Life, Reign, and Death of Edward II, 127–28
hoarding of coins, 10, 51, 53, 80–81, 192
Hobbes, Thomas, 157
Hoeniger, F. David, 140, 228 n6
Holinshed, Raphael, 136, 167, 170
Holy Roman Empire, 44
Howson, John, 143
Hundred Years War, 41, 61–62

ideological state apparatus, *see* interpellation
idolatry, 136, 142–44, 149, 159–60
incest, 103, 114–15
indentures, 8, 32
inflation, 78, 92, 95–96, 97–98
Ingram, Martin, 42–43, 115
Innocent III, 48
interpellation, 4, 7, 9, 188–89
intrinsic and extrinsic value theories of money, 1, 3, 10, 13–16, 17–18, 57, 60, 85, 87–88, 92, 97–98, 99, 100, 128, 161, 189, 190, 191, 192, 194–95
Ionia, 51
Isabella and Ferdinand of Spain, 3

James VI and I, 5, 18, 19, 33, 38, 39, 45, 52, 88, 98–102, 132, 135–36, 137, 141, 144, 148, 149, 150, 159–60, 169, 188, 204–5 n45, 206 n56, 211 n10
Basilikon Doron, 98, 103, 113
Jessop, Bob, 31
Jews, 167
John II, king of France, 61–62
John of Salisbury, 44, 212 n17
Johnson, Charles, 212 n19
Jones, Ann Rosalind and Peter Stallybrass, 7, 198 n12
Jonson, Ben

The Alchemist, 127, 167–69
Jordan, Constance, 25, 205–6 n53
justice, 18–19, 35, 46, 64–67, 69, 104, 118–21, 130–33, 188, 190–91
commutative justice, 119
Justinian
Corpus iuris civilis, 34–36, 38–39, 205 n46, 207 n72

Kantorowicz, Ernst, 35, 36, 37, 43, 156, 159
Kaplan, M. Lindsay, 130–31, 226 n75
Kastan, David Scott, 175, 178, 179–80, 181, 238 n57, 239 n62
Kaye, Joel, 61, 119, 121
king-in-parliament, 29, 39, 40, 42
king's evil and "touching" ceremony, 5, 7, 19, 45, 135–60
king's two bodies, 8, 43–44, 155–56, 207 n75
Knolles, Richard, 37
Kopytoff, Igor, 5, 7

labor, 75–76, 162–63, 171–73, 175–77, 179–80
Lampe, G. W. H., 117, 223 n37
Lane, William, 93
law
  absence of, 75–76
  common law (English), 37, 38, 39, 40, 41, 45, 50, 70, 71, 76
  customary, 16–17, 23, 33, 38–39, 41, 59–60, 63, 65, 69–70
  divine, 23, 33, 37–38, 65, 67
  eternal law, 67
  ius non scriptum [unwritten law], 38–39
  lex [written law], 38–39
  lex animata [living law], 34–35, 43
  lex regia [royal law], 35–38
  lex talionis, 129

natural, 16–17, 23, 33, 37–38, 59–60, 62, 65, 67–68, 70–71
positive, 23, 33, 67, 68, 69, 70
Roman, 34–39
statute, 29, 38, 39–43, 105, 106–7, 113, 114–15, 167–68
Leggatt, Alexander, 130, 224–25 n53, 225 n55, 226 n68, 226 n75
Lever, J. W., 123, 124, 224 n50
Levin, Harry, 74–75
Li, Ming-Hsun, 194, 241 n20
limited monarchy, *see* constitutionalism
livery companies, 177–78
Livy, 101
Locke, John, 16, 189, 190–95, 206 n59, 211 n1
Logan, George, 77
Lowndes, William, 190, 191, 192, 194
Lycurgus, 72–73
Lydia, *see* coinage, invention in Lydia

Machiavelli, Niccolò, 82
Machyn, Henry, 91
Mackworth, Humphrey, 193
Magna Carta, 36, 39
magnum consilium, 39, 40
Maguire, Henry, 146, 230 n38, 231 n46
Malynes, Gerard, 156
Mann, Michael, 25, 52, 208 n85, 209 n106
Marcel, Etienne, 62
Marlowe, Christopher, 3, 108–9, 110, 168
Doctor Faustus, 184–85
Jew of Malta, 172
Marsilius of Padua, 68–70, 213 n26, 215 n44
Martin-Leake, Stephen, 222 n19
Martyr, Peter, 74, 75, 77
Marx, Karl, 194, 200–1 n2
A Contribution to the Critique of Political Economy, 12–13, 161
on "mystery of money" (*Capital*), 6
Marxian perspectives on money, 2, 11, 187
Mary, Queen of Scots, 154, 169
Mary I, 2, 3, 7–8, 91–92, 107, 128, 140–41, 170
Maxwell, James, 5, 139, 148
Mayhew, Nicholas, 50, 55, 89, 90, 93, 100, 166, 190, 192 n5, 218–19 n40
McCann, Franklin, 73, 214 n36
McIlwain, C. H., 204 n41
McLuskie, Kathleen, 238 n57, 239 n63
mercantilism, 14–15
mercenaries, 19, 71, 83
Mercia, 53–54
Mestrell, Eloy, 126–27
mettle/metal, 121, 123–25, 128
mint masters, 55, 56
mint rate/mint price, 56, 89, 90–91, 95
mints, 54, 55, 56, 217 n19
ecclesiastical, 53, 54, 56, 57, 109
see also royal mint; Tower of London
mixed monarchy, 36–37
monasteries, dissolution by Henry VIII, 87, 91
moneta, 119
money
demand, 17–18, 57, 58, 85, 164
electronic, 195, 239 n1
fiat, 13, 21, 194
"imaginary" or "ghost," 164
and language, 20–21
paper, 5, 13–14, 150, 188–89, 193, 195
as "root of all evil," 80, 82, 188
as "universal equivalent," 6, 20–21
visible quality, 2, 6

money-changing, 64
moneyers, 55, 120, 126–27
Monod, Paul Kléber, 44, 46–47, 155, 159
More, Thomas, 71
   Utopia, 16–18, 59, 60, 71–86, 188
Mortenson, Peter, 181–82, 238 n60
Mulcaster, Richard, 36–37
Muldrew, Craig, 9
Murray, W. A., 156
"mystery of state," 19, 149, 159–60

Nashe, Thomas
   The Unfortunate Traveler, 221 n15
nationalism, 19, 161–63, 170–71, 174, 178–79, 181–82, 185
Neill, Michael, 198–99 n20, 220 n4, 225 n54
neoplatonism, 34
new economic criticism, 20–21
new materialism, 21
"New World," 3–5, 9, 17, 60, 71–75, 85, 147, 165–66
Nicholl, Charles, 108
Nixon, Richard, 13
Northern Rebellion, 44–45
Northumbria, 53
Nugent, Theresa Lanpher, 224 n50

Offa, 54
Oresme, Nicole, 17, 39, 59–71, 85, 120, 126, 192
   publication of *De moneta*, 61–62, 211 n6
Osteen, Mark and Martha Woodmansee, 20–21, 199–200 n35
Ovid, 17, 60, 74–75, 76, 77, 155

Paget, James, 90
Paracelsus, 146
parliament, 39–42, 89, 100, 101

Parry, Jonathan and Maurice Bloch, 2–3, 7
Paul, Henry, 227 n1, 230 n34
Peacham, Henry, 103
Peckham, Henry, 8, 128
Pemberton, William, 46, 118
Pepin the Short, 54
Pepys, Samuel, 220 n20
Persia, 53
Philip II, king of Spain, 170
Philip IV, king of France, 18, 61, 126
Philip VI, king of France, 61–62
Philip of Macedon, 53
Plowden's Reports, 43
Plutarch, 72–73, 118
Pocock, J. G. A., 206 n57
Poggi, Gianfranco, 25–26
political theology, 19, 23–24, 43, 136, 156
Poulantzas, Nicos, 208 n93
"price revolution," 78
Purchas, Samuel, 5

Raleigh, Sir Walter, 3
   "The Discovery of Guiana," 4, 6, 147, 188
Rawlinson, John, 118
recoinage, 10, 12, 14, 16, 54, 55, 88–89, 91, 95–96, 190–92
records (written), 32
"reformation of manners," 42–43, 114–15
republicanism, 35, 67, 68
Richard III, 56
riots, 176, 185–86
Robert the Pious, 137–39
Rokkan, Stein, 48
royal mint, 16, 24, 30, 32, 50–51, 55–58, 96, 100, 126–27
Ryan, Kiernan, 129

"sacred commodities," 5, 7, 188
Sahlins, Marshall, 150

Index

Saint-German, Christopher, 40–41, 42, 212 n41
Sargent, Thomas and François Velde, 99
Schanzer, Ernest, 225 n58
Schmitt, Carl, 43
Scot, Reginald, 231–32 n52
scrofula, *see* king's evil and "touching" ceremony
Seaver, Paul, 112, 175, 176, 177, 179, 182, 183, 236–37 n39, 237 n44, 237 n48, 238 n51, 238 n52, 238 n57
seignorage, 52, 56
Selden, John, 70
Shakespeare, William
　Cymbeline, 116–17
　Edward III, 116
　Hamlet, 226 n66
　1 Henry IV, 128, 226 n67, 231 n50
　2 Henry IV, 146
　Henry V, 167, 169, 181, 184
　King John, 99
　Macbeth, 19, 135–37, 151–60, 188
　Measure for Measure, 18–19, 43, 46, 104–5, 111, 113–16, 120–26, 129–33, 161–62, 188
　The Merchant of Venice, 172
　Richard II, 147–48
　Timon of Athens, 2, 6
　Troilus and Cressida, 126
Sharpe, J. A., 105, 111, 201–2 n14
shaving of coins, 10, 43
Shell, Marc, 20–21, 121, 129–30, 131, 200 n36
Shephard, Robert, 80, 215 n52, 216 n58
Sidney, Robert, 108
"sinews of war," 19, 136–37, 154, 156–57, 160, 168, 184
Sinfield, Alan, 227 n1
Skinner, Quentin, 33, 200 n1
slander, 130–31
slavery, 76, 78, 81
Smith, Sir Thomas, 37, 76, 92, 94, 95, 97–98, 212 n15
　see also *Discourse of the Common Weal of this Realm of England*
"social power," 16, 24–26
Soderini letter, 73–74
sodomy, 103
Sohn-Rethel, Alfred, 11, 122–23, 188, 195
sovereignty, 24, 29, 38, 39, 40–41, 45, 47–49, 50, 67, 68–69, 163
　monetary, 163–64
Spenser, Edmund
　The Faerie Queene, 155, 227 n80
Spruyt, Hendrik, 48, 208 n91
Spufford, Peter, 53, 61, 62
Stallybrass, Peter, 158
stamp (of coins), 10, 13, 18, 19, 63, 64, 92, 97, 120–21, 124, 125, 126, 127–28, 147–48
　children as men's stamp in material of women, 18, 104, 114, 115–17, 120
　God's stamp in humans, 18, 104, 115, 116–19, 120
Stanley, Sir William, 108, 109
Starkey, David, 30, 36, 37, 224 n48
Starkey, Thomas, 29, 41
state
　affective qualities, 23–24, 47
　as authority, 2, 27
　bureaucracy, 31–32
　center and periphery, 32
　and economy, 1–2, 11, 24
　iconography, 2
　institutions, 16, 23, 29–32, 50
　loyalty to, 4, 19, 23–24, 45–46
　offices, 25
　and society, 24, 27, 32
　territorialization of authority, 24, 25
　violence and threat of violence, 24, 25, 33, 55, 92

state formation
  dimensions of, 1, 16, 23–24, 28–50
  versus state building, 27–28
Statute of Purveyors, 17, 89, 90
Stephen and Matilda, 55
sterling, 54–55, 88, 96
Strayer, Joseph, 30, 31, 32, 45, 47, 50, 203 n27, 203 n33, 204 n37, 205 n48, 207 n78
Straznicky, Marta, 178, 182
Strong, Roy, 8, 147
Stubbe, Henry, 143
Stubbes, Phillip, 42
Supple, B. E., 164
sweating (coins), 106, 167
sword-blade currencies, 53
symbola, 8, 121

taxes, 26, 41, 48, 52, 61, 64, 82, 85, 88, 89, 90, 91
Thirty Years War, 163
Thomas, Keith, 146–47, 149, 232 n54
Tilly, Charles, 24–25, 48, 201–2 n14
tokens (base), 99–100, 110, 165, 172, 174
Tooker, William, 142–43, 229 n14
torrid zone, 73
Tortuga, 3
touchpieces, 141–42
Tower of London, 55–56, 126, 127
treason, 3, 8, 10, 43, 105–11, 114–15, 128, 131
Trial of the Pyx, 121
tyranny, 36, 52, 65, 70

units of account (pounds, shillings, pence), 54, 68, 88, 164

Ure, P. N., 52, 209 n101
usury, 18, 64
"uttering" of coins, 4, 8, 128, 188

Valentine, Henry, 118
Valenze, Deborah, 111
Vaughan, Stephen, 57, 93
Verney, Francis and Edmund, 8, 128
Verstegan, Richard, 237–38 n50
Vespucci, Amerigo, 73
Voltaire, 1

wages, 20, 139, 145, 162–63, 171–72
Wallington, Nehemiah, 111–13
War of the Roses, 30, 56, 139, 145
war reparations, 71, 83–84
washing (coins), 106, 167
Watt, R. J. C., 124, 132
Weatherford, Jack, 194, 241 n25
Weber, Max, 19, 24–25, 33, 45–47, 49, 149–50, 160
Webster, John
  The White Devil, 128
Westminster Abbey, 96
Westphalia, Treaty of, 48, 163
William I, 54
William III, 192, 193, 239 n2
William de Tunemire, 56
Willis, Deborah, 143, 159, 229 n14, 234 n81
Wills, Gary, 227 n1, 227 n2
Wolsey, Thomas, 57, 89, 109
Wriothesley, Thomas, 90

Zimmerman, Susan, 158
Žižek, Slavoj, 11–12, 123, 188